THE BEST LAND

THE BEST LAND

FOUR HUNDRED YEARS OF LOVE AND BETRAYAL ON ONEIDA TERRITORY

SUSAN A. BREWER

THREE HILLS
AN IMPRINT OF
CORNELL UNIVERSITY PRESS
Ithaca and London

First published 2024 by Cornell University Press

Printed in the United States of America

Library of Congress Cataloging-in-Publication Data

Names: Brewer, Susan A. (Susan Ann), 1958- author.
Title: The best land : four hundred years of love and betrayal on Oneida territory / Susan A. Brewer.
Description: Ithaca, NY : Cornell University Press, [2024] | Includes bibliographical references and index.
Identifiers: LCCN 2023059500 (print) | LCCN 2023059501 (ebook) | ISBN 9780801452598 (hardcover) | ISBN 9781501777240 (pdf) | ISBN 9781501777257 (epub)
Subjects: LCSH: Oneida Indians—Land tenure—New York (State)—Madison County—History. | Oneida Indians—New York (State)—Madison County—Claims—History. | Oneida Indians—New York (State)—Madison County—History. | Indians, Treatment of—New York (State)—Madison County—History. | White people—New York (State)—Madison County—Relations with Indians—History. | Settler colonialism—New York (State)—Madison County—History. | Madison County (N.Y.)—History.
Classification: LCC F127.M2 B74 2024 (print) | LCC F127.M2 (ebook) | DDC 974.7/64004975543—dc23/eng/20240220
LC record available at https://lccn.loc.gov/2023059500
LC ebook record available at https://lccn.loc.gov/2023059501

To everyone who has called Oneida home

Contents

Preface *ix*

Note to Readers *xv*

My Family *xix*

Family of Polly Denny and Jacob Doxtator *xxiii*

1. The People of the Standing Stone and the Axe Makers 1
2. Of One and Many People in the Mohawk Valley 24
3. For King or Country 48
4. As Long as the Grass Shall Grow 71
5. "We Shall All Be Americans": The Story of Polly and Angel 96
6. Making Way for the Erie Canal 122
7. Squatters, Tenants, Owners 149
8. Realms of Orchards 176
9. Fire and Water 203
10. Ancestral Claims 227

Acknowledgments *251*

List of Abbreviations *257*

Notes *259*

Bibliographic Essay *319*

Index *335*

Preface

"The best land in Madison County," said Grandpa as we looked at the cornfield. I was about eight years old, but I knew a rare pronouncement when I heard it from a man who wasn't much of a talker. DeVerne Franklin Brewer, who was born on the best land in 1899, had lived on his farm in Oneida, New York, for almost seventy years. I lived there, too, with my parents, brothers, and sister.

From our front yard, we waved at the engineer as the trains on the New York Central line rolled by. If we followed the creek called Cowaselon to the south, we reached the Indian trail that had become the Great Genesee Road, also known as the Seneca Turnpike, or today as Route 5. If we followed the creek north, we crossed the old Erie Canal, which cut through our back fields. I couldn't wait to go off to see the world. I believed I always would be able to come home.

The story of the best land I knew as a child was a simple one. My great-grandparents Frank and Jennie Clement Brewer had purchased the farm from the grandchildren of a Frenchman named Angel Deferrier and his Indian wife, Polly Denny. Before that, the land belonged to the Oneida Indians whose territory once stretched from Canada to Pennsylvania. Like all children in New York State, I was taught in seventh grade social studies that the Mohawks, Oneidas, Onondagas, Cayugas, and Senecas made up the mighty confederacy called the Five Nations. They lived in longhouses and vanished from our history books after the American Revolution.

While I was learning that Indigenous people belonged in the past, the Oneida Indians claimed rightful ownership of their ancestral lands in central New York. Out of their original six million acres, they still held a thirty-two-acre reservation over on West Road, about four and a half miles southeast of the best land, where the people lived in secondhand trailers provided by the US government.

The Oneidas stunned everyone with a victory in the courts in the 1970s. The judge ruled that 180 years earlier, the State of New York had acquired Oneida lands in violation of federal law. The land claims

FIGURE 1. Aerial photograph of Brewer Farm, Oneida, NY, in the 1960s. The New York Central Railroad ran in front of the farm, and the Erie Canal is hidden by the trees at the north end of the property. Brewer Collection.

cases unsettled what most people, including my family, believed had been settled long ago. The story of the best land, it turned out, was not simple at all.

Confusion accompanied the assertion of sovereignty by the Oneidas. A faction called the Warrior Society refused to allow the Oneida City Police Department to enter their territory on West Road. When the fire department declared that it would not go to the territory without the police, my father, Herbert DeVerne Brewer, the part-time mayor of the city of Oneida, ordered that city police and firefighters would not serve the reservation.

Some months later, I answered the phone. "There's a fire!" someone from the reservation shouted. "Send help. People are dying. Do something." I don't recall what I did then, but I never forgot the plea. The fire department, as ordered, did not respond. A man and a woman died in a burning trailer. Grief, outrage, defiance, and more confusion followed.

I left Oneida in 1976 for a summer job and then college. After that, I came home for holidays, weddings, and funerals. I worked on Capitol

Hill in Washington, studied international history at the London School of Economics, and earned a doctorate at Cornell University, where I specialized in the history of US foreign relations. I moved to Wisconsin, where I taught history at the University of Wisconsin–Stevens Point.

Like many girls who grew up on farms, I was "raised to leave." That suited me fine. I was useless around machinery and preferred reading any day. On my travels, I carried with me memories of the landscape I had loved first and where I was first loved. I knew the feelings of belonging and alienation that tie a person to a place and take her away. From a distance I followed the dispute over land claims. I heard that local residents waved American flags when they protested at Oneida Indian–owned businesses.[1]

How could the people of Oneida live side by side and be so divided from each other? From the first, I had no difficulty believing the claim of the Oneida Indians that they had lost their lands as a result of dishonesty and corruption. I listened to people I had known all my life admit that wrongs probably had been done long ago and declare that they should not be held responsible for them. At the same time, they defended their right to their property because it had been in their family for generations.

What about my own family? I knew about Frank and Jennie but not much about where they came from or who they were. I knew Polly and Angel were buried in a small cemetery up the road but not how they had become owners of Oneida land. I wanted to find out what happened to the best land. Why, I wondered, was the history I had learned so at odds with the history told by the Oneidas? Why had I, as a child of Oneida, not even known that Oneidas still lived there?

This book tells the story of the best land and the two families, Polly Denny's and mine, who lived on it over the past three centuries. Learning why these people called the same place home, I believe, is essential to understanding the controversy over it. It is my way, after all these years, of answering the plea to "do something" made over the phone at the time of the fire.

To follow the paths the two families took to get to the best land, I go back to the 1600s. Polly's family and my ancestors were part of Mohawk, Oneida, Dutch, French, German, and English-speaking communities of kinfolk, trading partners, and rivals for land. For generations, they were the type of people who could communicate across cultures and serve as go-betweens. They should not be considered representative of their nations. They lived intertwined yet distinctive lives.[2]

FIGURE 2a and 2b. *Top*: Portrait of Polly Denny Deferrier (1775–1853), ca. 1850. Frederick Spencer, artist. From the Collection of the Madison County History Society, Oneida, NY. *Bottom*: Photograph of Jennie Clement Brewer (1866–1926), late 1800s, Brewer Collection.

With a few exceptions, Polly's family and mine were not the sort of people who typically are featured in history books. They lived their ordinary lives in extraordinary times in colonial New York, where the story of dispossession begins. In the chaotic aftermath of the American Revolution, Polly's extended family of Mohawks and Oneidas moved from the Schoharie and Mohawk Valleys to Oneida Territory. My forefathers and foremothers followed. Polly's people had the land my people wanted. Later my people had the land Polly's people wanted back.

The Oneidas and Mohawks trace their lineage through the mother and the Europeans through the father. For this book, I traced the people of the best land through both mothers and fathers. Mohawks, Oneidas, European immigrants, pioneers, and farmers depended on networks of kinfolk for just about everything. I had intended to focus only on my grandfather DeVerne Brewer's ancestors, but my grandmother Mabelle Greene, as in life, refused to be left out. I kept running into her forebears as squatters on Oneida land or as neighbors of Polly's relatives along Oneida Creek in the Stockbridge Valley. It's only right that Mabelle demanded attention in this story, which addresses the role of women as keepers of the land. In Polly's family, and sometimes in mine, the women were the Mistresses of the Soil.[3]

My grandfather prized the best land for its long, flat fields, fertile soil, and excellent drainage. Others valued it because the way west ran through our farm, a feature that I took for granted and never thought much about until I investigated the history of the best land. For centuries, the Oneidas and the Mohawks lived along the only relatively flat passage through the Appalachian Mountain range, which extends 1,500 miles from Alabama to Newfoundland. Most important for travel by water was the Oneida Carrying Place, named for the portage between the Mohawk River and Wood Creek located at present-day Rome, fifteen miles northeast of the best land. From the Oneida Carrying Place, a person could canoe east down the Mohawk to the Hudson River or west to Oneida Lake and on to Lake Ontario. Whoever controlled this passageway controlled the continent. The Five Nations knew its worth, as did the Dutch, French, and English colonizers who desired it. General George Washington considered it to be vital. The founders of the Empire State could not wait to get their hands on it.

In the late twentieth century, the land claims controversy launched a battle over the past. My hometown was torn apart over whose story got to be heard and recognized. Some people paid no attention, while others stopped speaking to their neighbors. The debate carried echoes

FIGURE 3. The Appalachian Mountains. From the Atlantic Ocean up the Hudson River to the Mohawk River through the Oneida Carrying Place was the one route west by water. Detail, North America, NASA/JPL.

of old disputes about who was civilized and who was not, who was a real American and who was not, and who belonged on the land and who did not.[4]

Mother Earth was alive with spirits, said the Oneidas, who believed the land was a sacred place to be protected for the children to come through seven generations. European colonizers decreed that divine providence ordained their dominion over the land. The Americans who took it over had a vision of small landholders cultivating the soil on which they would build a nation of democracy and freedom. "Everything in U.S. history is about the land," writes the scholar Roxanne Dunbar-Ortiz. "To learn and know this history is both a necessity and a responsibility to the ancestors and descendants of all parties."[5]

"This is a very strange place," confided a historian of Oneida. "Yes," I agreed. *Strange* means unknown, unfamiliar, unusual. In Medieval English, Old French, and Latin, it meant to be of or belonging to another country, originating or situated outside one's own land, foreign, alien, not native, belonging to others or some other place. The word now means peculiar, extraordinary, unaccountable. It means surprising in a way that is unsettling or hard to understand. Strange is a good description of a place of two peoples who belong and do not belong, depending on who you ask. This story is about a place I thought I knew well and didn't know at all. This book is dedicated to everyone who has called Oneida home.

Note to Readers

This book is the story of two families who lived on what I call the best land in central New York, the ancestral home of the Oneidas. The family of Polly Denny, the daughter of a Mohawk woman and a French Oneida man, and my own family did not leave much of a written record. Many of these Oneidas, Mohawks, and European immigrants did not read or write, and, if they did, little was preserved. Church, court, military, and land records provide bits and pieces of information. The records, such as they are, can be vague and contradictory.[6]

The political and religious leaders who kept the records sometimes portrayed Polly's people and mine as troublemakers. They may have been right. This story has its share of rogues and con artists. Then again, these same authorities believed that they should be in charge of the land and those who inhabited it, which was a belief that Polly's family and mine did not share. I found myself talking back to these sources. I questioned their characterization of individuals and interpretation of events. I noticed what they left unsaid and speculated about what may have happened. I was reluctant to allow their written record, valuable as it is, to tell the whole story.

The Oneidas have an oral tradition of remembering the past through stories of land and family. For generations, Oneida children grew up hearing that the land of their ancestors rightfully belonged to them, although by the twentieth century some assumed it was just another legend. The memories of treaties passed down by the elders said one thing. The history books, until recent years, said another. Not all oral history is true or complete. Names and dates get confused, painful incidents may be buried or an account slanted to favor one faction over another. Oral history can conflict with written accounts that Europeans and Americans long have considered superior and taken more seriously. That said, the oral tradition of the Oneidas conveyed truths about the land, while many of the meticulously recorded treaties, patents, and deeds were based on broken laws and lies.[7]

Old local histories also relied on oral tradition as well as written records. They recounted stories of families who came to live on the hills or in the hollows as well as remembrances of the Native inhabitants. They told tales of pioneers bringing civilization to the wilderness, the sacrifices of patriots during the American Revolution and the Civil War, and the building of schools, transportation networks, and industry. As much as I cherish these nineteenth-century tomes, I recognize that their epics of progress trample over troubling issues of injustice. Indians appear as romantic figures, often violent, sometimes comic, rarely as real people. Most residents wanted their history books to praise the place where they made a living, not raise uncomfortable questions about it.[8]

Sometimes it is possible to sort out fact from fiction in local history, oral tradition, and official papers, and sometimes it is not. Part of the problem is missing documents and lost oral testimony. Another problem is the sometimes deliberate, sometimes careless, erasure or silencing of Indigenous voices, which took place alongside campaigns for Indian removal and assimilation. That practice did not stop the Oneidas from speaking out in council, with petitions, at hearings, and to newspaper reporters. Those voices preserved in Native and non-Native accounts show us that the best land is a place of many stories. One of them is how history can be twisted to serve a purpose.[9]

In an era of random spelling in a place of many languages, colonial officials rarely recorded a Mohawk or Oneida name the same way twice. European recordkeepers, almost always male, typically disregarded Native women and seldom noted their names. Some of the Oneidas used both European and Indian names. I refer to the war chief Honyery Tehawenkaragwen Doxtator as Honyery, a version of his German name Johan George, by which he is known in Oneida history today. A Dutch person in the seventeenth century could have five or six names. They might be known by their province or hometown, their occupation as a baker or brewer, or their father's first name or patronymic. Women, who took the last name of their husbands, might have three or four surnames over their lifetimes. To be consistent, I chose one name and spelling; in the endnotes, however, I used the spelling as it appeared on the document in question. In Polly's family and mine, it was common to name children after their grandparents, parents, aunts, and uncles, which meant that there might be more than one person with the same name living in the same place at the same time. Sometimes I can distinguish among them and sometimes I cannot.[10]

I try as much as possible to identify people as they identified themselves. Oneidas identified who they were by clan, by place or village, and by faction, as in the Christian or Pagan Party. Over time, they have referred to themselves as the people, Indians, or Natives. Europeans referred to themselves as "white," "Christian," "English," or "Dutch." The people of the United States called themselves Americans. I quote people using the terms they used. Some of these terms were meant to be demeaning and offensive in their day; others now are viewed that way. Such terms tell us something about the worldview of the people who used them, as, for example, when Europeans referred to Natives as "savages."

The Mohawks (Kanien'kehá:ka), Oneidas (Onyota'a:ká:), Onondagas (Onoñda'gegá'), Cayugas (Gayogohó:nǫ'), and Senecas (Onöndowá'ga':) called themselves the Haudenosaunee, or the People of the Longhouse. The French called them the Iroquois. The English called them the Five Nations and later the Six Nations after the Tuscarora (Skarù • ręʔ) joined the confederacy. The Americans called them by all these names. I use these terms interchangeably. As an example of how complicated identities could be, my ancestor Christian Harp, a man of Dutch and German heritage who lived next door to Oneida Indians in the nineteenth century, called himself a Native American when he joined a political party that opposed immigration.

To tell the story of the best land and its people, I have pored over old treaties, maps, and deeds, talked to many generous souls, wandered around overgrown cemeteries, and searched for roads that no longer exist. In this book, I have located settlements, streams, and crossroads so that the people of Oneida will recognize them. To orient yourself on a map of New York State, place the little finger of your right hand over Canandaigua Lake and the rest of your fingers on top of Seneca, Cayuga, and Skaneateles Lakes. Set your thumb on Oneida Lake in the center of the state. The best land is to the south of the tip of your thumb.

My Family

Harmen Myndertsz Van den Bogaert (1612–1648), my ninth great-grandfather

Jellesje Claesen Swits (1616–d), my ninth great-grandmother

Frans Van den Bogaert (1640–1690), my eighth great-grandfather; son of Harmen and Jellesje

Claes Van den Bogaert, my seventh great-grandfather; son of Frans

Marie du Trieux (1617–d), my eighth great-grandmother; daughter of Philip du Trieux (1586–ca. 1653)

Arnout Viele (1640–d), son of Marie du Trieux and Cornelis Volkertsen Viele

Jan Peake (ca. 1615–ca. 1660), my eighth great-grandfather; husband of Marie du Trieux

Jacobus Peake (1656–1731), my seventh great-grandfather; son of Marie and Jan

Anna Peake (1688–d), my sixth great-grandmother; daughter of Jacobus Peake; wife of Joseph Clement

Joseph Clement, my sixth great-grandfather; husband of Anna Peake

Johan Friederich Bellinger (1691–ca. 1768), my seventh great-grandfather

Jacob Timmerman (ca. 1690–1739), my sixth great-grandfather; husband of Margaret Schütz

Margaret Schütz (ca. 1693–d), my sixth great-grandmother; wife of Jacob Timmerman

Henry Timmerman (1737–1807), my fifth great-grandfather; son of Jacob and Margaret; husband of Margaret Bellinger

Margaret Bellinger (1752–1815), my fifth great-grandmother; granddaughter of Johan Friederich Bellinger; wife of Henry Timmerman

Anna Rosina Timmerman (1776–1865), my fourth great-grandmother; daughter of Henry and Margaret; wife of my fourth great-grandfather Johannes Vedder, the great-grandson of Claes Van den Bogaert

Johannes Clement (1723–d), my fifth great-grandfather; son of Joseph and Anna

Jacobus Clement (1718–ca. 1766), son of Joseph and Anna

Elizabeth Clement (1721–d), daughter of Joseph and Anna; wife of William Powell

Lewis Cobes Clement (1725–1781), son of Joseph and Anna

Lieutenant Joseph Clement (1750–d), son of Lewis Clement; cousin of my fourth great-grandfather Lambert

Lambert Clement (1757–1842), my fourth great-grandfather; son of Johannes Clement and Rachel Radcliffe (1728–1812)

John Myers (1752–1823), my fourth great-grandfather

Mary Hetzel, my fourth great-grandmother; daughter of Michael Hetzel, wife of John Myers

Johannes Moet/John Moot (1734–1814), my sixth great-grandfather

Conrad Moot (1760–1843), my fifth great-grandfather; son of John Moot

John Conrad Moot (1785–1839), my fourth great-grandfather; son of Conrad Moot and Catharina Taylor

George Harp (ca. 1760–1815), my fifth great-grandfather

Christian Harp (1804–1886), my fourth great-grandfather; son of George Harp and Cornelia Van Sile

Caroline Harp (1826–1892), my third great-grandmother; daughter of Christian Harp and Hannah Ratnour; wife of Charles Green Sr. (1827–1872), the son of Jeduthan Green and Sally Gregg

John Gregg (1764–1846), my fifth great-grandfather; father of Sally Gregg Green

Lewis Clement (1803–1877), my third great-grandfather; son of Lambert Clement and Maria Vedder; husband of Dorothy Vedder

Dorothy Vedder (1803–1884), my third great-grandmother; daughter of Anna Rosina Timmerman and Johannes Vedder; wife of Lewis Clement

John Moot (1810–1892), my third great-grandfather; son of John Conrad Moot and Sabrina Lovejoy

William Moot (1833–1897), son of John Moot and Lucy Bortle

Catharine Myers (ca. 1792–d), my third great-grandmother; daughter of John Myers and Mary Hetzel; wife of Abraham Brewer

Abraham Brewer (1783–ca. 1837), my third great-grandfather; son of Peter Brewer and Catrina Crisler

James Brewer (1816–1853), my third great-uncle; son of Abraham Brewer and Catharine Myers; husband of Maria Frances Avery

Abraham Brewer (ca. 1819–1903), my great-great-grandfather; son of Abraham Brewer and Catharine Myers

William Clement (1827–1874), my great-great-grandfather; son of Lewis Clement and Dorothy Vedder; husband of Elizabeth Moot

Elizabeth (Lizzie) Moot (1836–1916), my great-great-grandmother; daughter of John Moot and Lucy Bortle; wife of William Clement

Lucy Clement (1861–1895), my great-great-aunt; daughter of William Clement and Elizabeth Moot; wife of Frank Brewer

Jennie Clement (1866–1926), my great-grandmother; daughter of William Clement and Elizabeth Moot; wife of Frank Brewer

Frank Brewer (1861–1940), my great-grandfather; son of Abraham Brewer and Louisa Snyder

Hazel Brewer Taylor (1900–1996), my great-aunt

Reta Brewer (1907–1994), my great-aunt

DeVerne Franklin Brewer (1899–1978), my grandfather; son of Frank Brewer and Jennie Clement

Mabelle Greene (1903–1984), my grandmother; daughter of Ella Taylor and Charles E. Greene (1877–1964), the grandson of Charles Green Sr. and Caroline Harp

Robert "Bob" Brewer, my uncle; son of DeVerne and Mabelle

Virginia "Ginny" Brewer, my aunt; daughter of DeVerne and Mabelle

Richard "Dick" Brewer, my uncle; husband of Joanne Fedder; son of DeVerne and Mabelle

Herbert "Herb" Brewer (1930–2016), my father; son of DeVerne and Mabelle

Mary Lou Sipperley, my mother

Russell "Russ" Brewer, my brother

Thomas "Tom" Brewer, my brother

Elizabeth "Beth" Brewer, my sister

Holly Brewer Rogers, my niece

Casey Brewer, my niece

Nathan Brewer, my nephew

Joshua Brewer, my nephew

Family of Polly Denny and Jacob Doxtator*

Catharine, Oneida Wolf Clan, grandmother of Jacob

Honyery Tehawenkaragwen (b.–1794), father of Jacob

Honyost Thaosagwat (b.–1779), uncle of Jacob

Plattcop Tonyentagoyon/Henry Schuyler (b.–ca. 1826), uncle of Jacob

Honyery's sister, wife of Shagoyontha/Henry Cornelius; aunt of Jacob

Sarah Martin Tyonajanegan (b.–1833), wife of Honyery; mother of Jacob

Cornelius Doxtator (ca. 1754–1814), son of Honyery and Sarah; husband of Jenny Skenandoah; brother of Jacob

Dolly Doxtator (ca. 1758–1833), daughter of Honyery and Sarah; wife of John Denny; sister of Jacob; sister-in-law of Polly

Peter Doxtator (bp. 1787–d), son of Honyery and Dolly Cobus; brother of Jacob

Louis Denny, Oneida Bear Clan, father of Polly

Maria Denny, Mohawk Turtle Clan, mother of Polly

John Denny (1763–1807), son of Louis and Maria; husband of Dolly Doxtator; brother of Polly; brother-in-law of Jacob

Louis Denny Jr. (1772–1842), son of Louis and Maria; brother of Polly

Martinus Denny (1777–1839), son of Louis and Maria; brother of Polly

* The Mohawk/Oneida family of the best land here is traced through the connected families of Polly Denny (1775–1853) and Jacob Doxtator (ca. 1756–1832)

Louis Denny (1785–d), son of John Denny and Dolly Doxtator, husband of Jenny Skenandoah Doxtator; nephew of Polly; nephew of Jacob

Abraham Denny (1790–ca. 1846), son of John Denny and Dolly Doxtator; husband of Catharine Nellis; nephew of Polly; nephew of Jacob

John "Dr. Sundown" Denny (1791–1882), son of John Denny and Dolly Doxtator; nephew of Polly; nephew of Jacob

Sarah (Sally) Denny (1787–d), daughter of John Denny and Dolly Doxtator; wife of John Garlock; niece of Polly; niece of Jacob

Martin Denny, son of John Denny and Dolly Doxtator; nephew of Polly; nephew of Jacob

Angel Deferrier (1769–1832), son of Charles César d'Algret d'Olède, Seigneur de Ferriere and Marie Angelique Breard; husband of Polly

Nancy Deferrier (1800–1852), daughter of Polly and Angel Deferrier; wife of John Hadcock (1795–1883)

Sophia Deferrier (1803–1864), daughter of Polly and Angel Deferrier; wife of Thomas T. Loomis (1797–1871)

Charles Deferrier (1804–1890), son of Polly and Angel Deferrier; husband of Theresa Bedlow

Lucy Deferrier (1816–1855), daughter of Polly and Angel Deferrier; wife of George Pine

Mary Deferrier (1817–1894), daughter of Polly and Angel Deferrier; wife of Nelson Cobb (1816–1896)

Lewis S. Denny (1824–ca. 1892), son of John "Dr. Sundown" Denny; great-nephew of Polly; great-nephew of Jacob

Moses Schuyler (ca. 1775–1871), son of Plattcop/Henry Schuyler; cousin of Jacob

Jacob L. W. Doxtator (1808–1883), son of George Doxtator and Polly Mytop; husband of Mary Catharine Denny; grandson of Jacob

Mary Catharine "Catharine" Denny (1812–1894), daughter of Abraham Denny and Catharine Nellis; wife of Jacob L. W. Doxtator; great-niece of Polly; great-niece of Jacob

Sophia Denny (ca. 1815–1902), daughter of Louis Denny and Jenny Skenandoah Doxtator; wife of Henry Jordan; great-niece of Polly; great-niece of Jacob

William Doxtator (ca. 1820–1894), son of Jacob Doxtator and Polly Antone; stepson of Turtle Clan chief Christian Beechtree (although William is identified here as the son of Jacob Doxtator [ca. 1756–1832], it is possible that he was the son of Jacob's son, also named Jacob Doxtator, born in 1803)

Louis Doxtator (1855–1894), son of William Doxtator and Dolly John (1821–1904); grandson of Jacob

Lydia Doxtator (1859–1926), daughter of William Doxtator and Mary Chrisjohn; granddaughter of Jacob

Charles Cobb (1850–1928), son of Nelson Cobb and Mary Deferrier; grandson of Polly

Irene Cobb (1844–1904), daughter of Nelson Cobb and Mary Deferrier; granddaughter of Polly

Angel Deferrier Loomis (1829–1909), son of Thomas Loomis and Sophia Deferrier; grandson of Polly

Dewitt C. Hadcock (1831–1924), son of John Hadcock and Nancy Deferrier; grandson of Polly

John Denny (1864–1942), son of John "Dr. Sundown" Denny and Jane George (ca. 1825–1883); husband of Sophia Powless (1877–1921); great-nephew of Polly; great-nephew of Jacob

Stella Doxtator (1884–1945), daughter of Louis Doxtator and Nancy George (1869–1899); wife of Jacob Miller; great-granddaughter of Jacob

Irma Miller (b. 1924), niece and adopted daughter of Stella Doxtator; great-great-granddaughter of Jacob

Anna Doxtator (1885–1966), Turtle Clan mother, daughter of Louis Doxtator and Nancy George; wife of Josiah Johnson (1879–1926); wife of Nelson Skenandoah (1876–1956); great-granddaughter of Jacob

Emily Doxtator (1888–1984), daughter of Louis Doxtator and Nancy George; wife of Nelson Johnson (1885–1965); great-granddaughter of Jacob

Electa Doxtator (1889–1937), daughter of Louis Doxtator and Nancy George; wife of Lyman John (1889–1972); great-granddaughter of Jacob

Lyman K. "Jake" John (1928–1983), son of Electa Doxtator and Lyman John; great-grandson of Jacob

Marion John Miles (1923–1998), daughter of Electa Doxtator and Lyman John; great-great-granddaughter of Jacob

Martin John (1917–1993), son of Electa Doxtator and Lyman John; husband of Ella Mae Staudt; great-great-grandson of Jacob

Rebecca "Becki" John, daughter of Martin John and Ella Mae Staudt; wife of Terry Karst; great-great-great-granddaughter of Jacob

F. Dewitt Cobb (1890–1982), son of Charles Cobb; great-grandson of Polly

THE BEST LAND

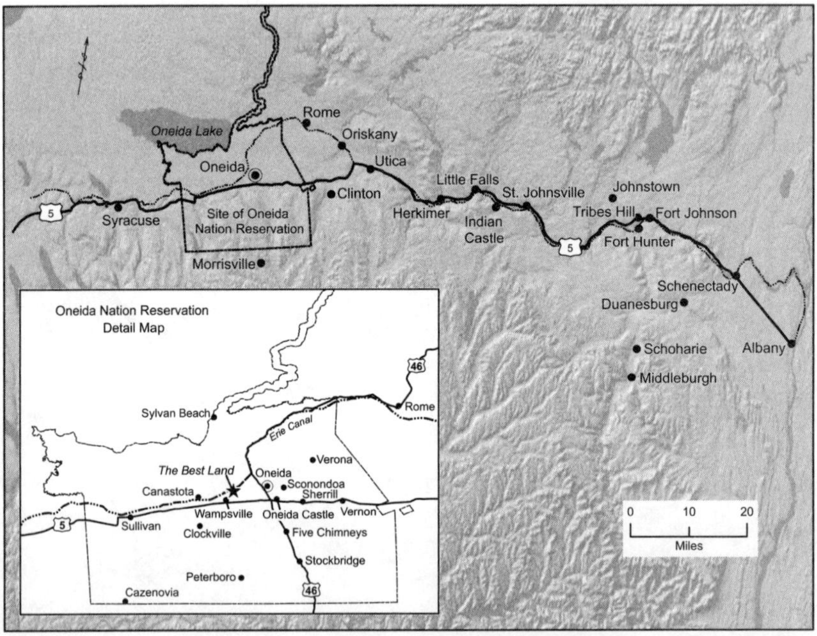

MAP 1. Oneida and the Mohawk Valley with the historic Erie Canal. Map by Gordie Thompson. Polly Denny was born near what is now Middleburgh and lived at Canaseraga, now Sullivan, before settling on the best land. As a girl, she would have known Indian Castle as Canajoharie, the upper castle of the Mohawks. Five Chimneys is the old name for the intersection of Route 46, or West Road, with Peterboro Road.

CHAPTER 1

The People of the Standing Stone and the Axe Makers

The Oneidas and Mohawks, I was astonished to discover, met a forefather of mine four hundred years ago. In December 1634, three Dutchmen traveled to the Oneida town then located on a hill a few miles south of the present-day city of Oneida. One of them, Harmen Myndertsz Van den Bogaert, was my ninth great-grandfather. As he was about to enter the village, Harmen recorded, he looked to the north. Far off, he saw "extremely high ground which seemed to lie in the clouds." To the northwest, he said, he saw a very large body of water, which was Oneida Lake. From that description I knew that Harmen had gazed on the best land.[1]

During the 1600s, few Europeans saw the best land located deep in the territory of the Oneidas. Who were Harmen and my other ancestors, I wondered, and why did they come to this continent? As a child I was told about the friendly first Thanksgiving in New England and the Dutch purchase of Manhattan for beads. Later I learned that these celebrated stories left out the violence and exploitation. I hoped that if I could figure out where my forebears lived, I might be able to uncover what sort of interactions, if any, they had with Indigenous people. I was unable to trace Polly's family back to the 1600s, so I looked at Oneidas and Mohawks in general. What was their life like in Iroquoia? How did they respond to the arrival of people they called the axe makers?

Harmen and his fellow Dutchmen were from a watery country with few natural resources of its own. At the time, the people of the Netherlands were nearing the end of a long and gory revolt against their Spanish rulers. By the early 1600s, the Dutch Republic had become home to Europe's foremost trading fleet and banking system. Eager to cash in on the spice trade, merchants hired the English explorer Henry Hudson to find a northeastern route to Asia. After failing twice, Hudson disobeyed his instructions and crossed the Atlantic. He had heard a rumor that north of Virginia there was a route west to the great water, which he hoped meant the Pacific Ocean.[2]

In 1609, Hudson sailed into the best natural harbor on the Atlantic coast, at present-day New York City. He went up the river that would be named after him until it turned too shallow to go any farther, around present-day Albany. The route west, it turned out, did exist for people who traveled by canoe to the Oneida Carrying Place and on to the Great Lakes, but not for Europeans in ships on the way to Asia. Hudson met hospitable people who gave gifts of furs. He noted that the land was "the finest for cultivation that I ever in my life set foot upon." His backers were not interested in land, but they thought the beaver furs might turn a profit.[3]

The republic in 1621 chartered the Dutch West India Company to make money out of furs, tobacco, and sugar from the Americas. It established the colony of New Netherland, which included parts of present-day New York, New Jersey, Delaware, and Connecticut. A trading post was constructed at Fort Orange (present-day Albany) where the Dutch soon learned that their most important relationship was with the Mohawks. Do not offend them, the company instructed its traders, and then it did just that when it put in charge of Fort Orange a Dutchman who had killed a Mohawk leader. Nine hundred warriors surrounded the fort, burned a ship, and killed livestock.[4]

The West India Company wanted good relations restored, or else the Mohawks might ignore their traders in favor of the French to the north or New Englanders to the east. It sent twenty-two-year-old Harmen Myndertsz Van den Bogaert and two others to Mohawk and Oneida territory to acquire as much business as possible for Fort Orange. Four years earlier, Harmen had arrived in New Netherland as the barber-surgeon aboard the company ship *Eendracht*. Boys typically were apprenticed for four years to learn the skills required of barber-surgeons, including how to shave, pull teeth, do bloodletting, set broken bones, treat diseases, and dissect a corpse.[5]

Educated and trained to observe, Harmen recorded what he saw and heard and did on his mission in the earliest known written account of the Oneidas by a European. In his journal, Harmen presents himself as the dauntless chronicler, Jeronimus de la Croix as the timid bumbler whose pants fell in the fire while they were visiting the Oneidas, and Willem Thomassen as the quick-tempered sailor who repaired the pants using cloth provided by the chief's mother. The journal reveals how much the Dutch did not know. They referred to the Haudenosaunee as either Mohawks or Sinnekens (Senecas). Not until Harmen arrived at Oneida did he learn there were Five Nations.[6]

The Mohawks, Oneidas, Onondagas, Cayugas, and Senecas were united under the Great Law of Peace taught to them by the prophet known as the Peacemaker and his helper, the warrior Haywentha, sometimes called Hiawatha. The Haudenosaunee formed a Great Council where leaders from each nation reached consensus on matters of importance. They used strings or belts of beads made of shells called wampum to record and recall significant events. By the time of Harmen's visit, Dutch traders had learned that Natives prized wampum, but they did not understand its historical and sacred value. Instead they used it as money.[7]

With Mohawk guides, Harmen, Jeronimus, and Willem traveled west from Fort Orange along the Mohawk River. They stopped at towns where Harmen, collecting Native vocabulary, learned that the Mohawks referred to Europeans as "axe makers." For raccoon, an animal he did not recognize, Harmen wrote down "cat." He saw longhouses full of grain and beans as well as hundreds of beaver pelts. He ate a lot of good food, including venison, turkey, hare cooked with chestnuts, and corn

FIGURE 4. Replica of the Hiawatha Belt. The ancient national wampum belt of the Haudenosaunee records the decision of the Mohawks, Oneidas, Onondagas, Cayugas, and Senecas to bury their weapons and live in unity and peace. National Museum of the American Indian, Smithsonian Institution (26/9056). Photo by NMAI Photo Services.

bread baked with sunflower seeds and dried berries. In addition to signs of plenty, Harmen saw evidence of mass fatalities, the result of the 1633 smallpox epidemic, one of many that wiped out Native populations following contact with Europeans. "I could see nothing else but graves," he wrote about a Mohawk town.[8]

On the day after Christmas, the Dutchmen and their guides set out for Oneida territory. They saw otters and beavers and tracks of bear and elk in forests of oak, beech, and birch. Harmen found it tough going through two and a half feet of snow. Near the top of one high hill, he fell so hard that he broke the handle of his sword. As the men approached the Oneida town, they met a woman who gave them baked pumpkin to eat. Harmen did not mention whether he learned that pumpkin or squash, along with corn and beans, grown together and called the Three Sisters, were revered by the Haudenosaunee. Developed over generations, this exemplary agricultural practice and nutritional system was managed by the women.[9]

At the time of Harmen's visit, the land had been home to the Oneidas for centuries. Oneida means people of the standing stone, after the boulder that served as their national symbol. The standing stone, the Oneidas believed, followed them when they moved their town every twenty-five years or so when the firewood supply ran low. In the 1500s and 1600s, the Oneidas built many of their towns on what are now called West Hill and East Hill overlooking the Stockbridge Valley. The Europeans thought the towns, surrounded by simple walls or palisades, looked like castles. The town visited by Harmen is believed to have been on West Hill north of where Oneida Creek dropped a hundred feet in a series of cascades now known as Stockbridge Falls.[10]

When Harmen and his companions reached the Oneida town, the Oneidas asked the Dutchmen to shoot their guns, which they did. After reloading, the visitors walked into the castle between two rows of people. The entrance was topped by three large carved images of men. Next to the images were three scalps waving in the breeze. The locks of hair, reported Harmen, had been "cut from the heads of slain Indians as a token of truth, that is to say, victory." To the Oneidas, an enemy's scalp meant much more than a trophy. It could be taken to avenge a death and allow a loved one to find peace in the next world, or it could be symbolically adopted to revive the spiritual power of those still living.[11]

"We were cold, wet, and tired," Harmen wrote. "We received food immediately, and they built a good fire." After the Dutchmen had rested, an Oneida man asked what they were doing in his country and what had they brought for gifts. Harmen replied that they had come for a visit and brought nothing. They were worth nothing, responded the Oneida, because they had brought no presents. He said that earlier that year, French traders had given good gifts such as axes, shirts, razors, and wampum. The Oneida man had opened negotiations by praising the competition and teaching the visitors fundamental protocols. To the Five Nations, presents not only conveyed friendship and generosity. They made true the promises of the giver, who was understood to represent the consensus of those who had prepared the gifts.[12]

Harmen was not being honest when he said they were there just to visit. He was collecting information and pursuing trade. The castle, he noted, was surrounded by two rows of palisades. Inside were sixty-six houses, "built much better and higher than all the others" he had seen thus far. Harmen asked where all the Oneida castles were. The Oneidas showed him by placing kernels of corn and stones, from which Jeronimus drew a map. The Oneidas pointed to the high country to the north and said there were many beavers there, but there were also Natives who were allies of the French and people with horns. Perhaps Harmen misunderstood about the horns, or the Oneidas, too, were being less than completely honest. In any event, the Oneidas were making the point that they, not the Dutch, knew the territory, its inhabitants, and its resources.[13]

When an Oneida called the Dutchmen scoundrels again, Willem became angry. When asked why, Harmen replied that it was the Oneida who was the scoundrel. This retort pleased the Oneidas, who did not respect submissive behavior. The Oneida man laughed and said, "You must not be angry. We are happy that you have come here." Harmen had concluded that if the Oneidas meant to hurt the three of them, they could do so with very little trouble. They had not, which led Harmen to adopt a bold attitude, or so he said. He and his companions, it should be noted, had reloaded their guns. The Dutchmen demonstrated that they had learned the lesson of gift giving when Jeronimus gave the chief some knives, scissors, and needles.[14]

The Oneidas told the visitors not to be afraid as they opened trade talks. An old man came over and placed his hand on Harmen's heart. He reported back that Harmen was not scared. The Oneidas wanted assurance that if they traveled to Fort Orange loaded with furs, they would be able to obtain axes, kettles, cloth, and wampum. They did not want to make a long trip for nothing. Harmen said he had no authority to accept the deal, but he would inform his commander and return with a reply. "You must not lie," said the Oneidas. "[C]ome in the spring to us and bring us all an answer." The Oneidas gave Harmen five beavers and sang a confirmation of the agreement.[15]

The Dutchmen fired three shots to celebrate the new year and honor "our Lord and Redeemer Jesu Cristo," wrote Harmen. This display pleased the Oneidas and was also part of the typical Dutch New Year celebration, which involved drinking alcohol and shooting off firearms into the air. A group of Onondaga men and women came to exchange gifts and invite the visitors to their country in the summer. Two Oneidas asked Harmen to come and see how they drove the devil out of a sick man. Harmen said he had seen that before, but they insisted. An old woman with a turtle-shell rattle sang while twelve men with red painted faces stomped on the floor, sucked on the sick man's neck, and spit on an otter. When they started to eat fire and throw around hot embers, Harmen ran out of the house.[16]

Harmen garnered little understanding of Oneida healing practices. For the Oneidas, maintaining the health of both mind and body was important. They feared witches who could spread sickness and mental disorder. They believed that dreams revealed the desires of the soul. If those desires were denied or ignored, the soul might rebel against the body, cause illness, and create distress. The people interpreted the meanings of their dreams and addressed the revealed desires accordingly. The mental and physical health of one affected the health of all in a communal society where everyone depended on each other.[17]

After the Dutchmen had been at Oneida for over a week, a Haudenosaunee man delivered a letter from Fort Orange. "Our people were very troubled because we did not return, thinking that we had been killed," wrote Harmen, who appeared to be in no hurry to leave Oneida. Five days later the visitors departed with twenty-eight beavers worth about seven months' wages. Harmen assumed that the Oneidas who accompanied them would carry the Dutchmen's baggage, but the Oneidas said they had enough of their own to carry. "However, after much grumbling and nice words, they went with us in company, carrying our goods," Harmen wrote. The people asked them to shoot again, and the Dutchmen fired three shots. Nine days later they arrived in Fort Orange, thanks to help from the Indians, Harmen wrote, who "knew the paths better than we."[18]

Harmen and the Dutch, like the Spanish, French, and English, saw themselves as spreading a superior civilization. In claiming the Americas, Europeans cited the doctrine of discovery. Any land not inhabited by Christians could be claimed by Christian rulers, the pope had decreed back in the late 1400s. With their Jesu Cristo and their guns, Harmen and his companions may have expected to leave the Mohawks and the Oneidas awestruck, but his account shows they did not. Instead the Dutchmen neglected to bring presents, dropped pants into the fire, needed help to carry their belongings, and did not know the way.[19]

With the Dutch traders, the Oneidas had practiced the Haudenosaunee traditions of hospitality and diplomacy. They liked the guns, tools, and cloth the Europeans could provide and offered reciprocity among equals. They had given their visitors an indication of the extensive range and communications network of the Five Nations. Harmen, for some unknown reason, did not keep his promise to return with an answer to the Oneida trade proposal. His journal shows us a glimpse of what the People of the Standing Stone and the axe makers had in common and what they did not. It tells me that four centuries ago, an Oneida man placed his hand over the heart of my ancestor to learn how he was feeling.[20]

One People

For the Mohawks and Oneidas, trade with the Dutch was not their most serious problem. The immediate crisis was that they were dying. Harmen had seen an empty village and graves, but he did not understand that the Haudenosaunee had little immunity to smallpox, measles, and other diseases communicated by Europeans. By the early 1640s, the population of the Five Nations had been cut in half. The Mohawks, hit the hardest, lost an estimated 75 percent of their people. The population of the Oneidas was down from about 4,000 to 1,500–1,800. The pain and grief of Polly's ancestors must have been beyond immense.[21]

The Mohawks and Oneidas relied on tradition and adaptation to respond to the arrival of the axe makers and the devastation of death they brought with them. The Haudenosaunee believed that everything and everyone was related. Earth was the mother, the moon the grandmother, and the sun the elder brother. They gave thanks to the Creator and all beings on earth and in the sky at the ceremonies of Mid-Winter, Maple (March), Thunder (April), Planting (May), Strawberry (June), Green Bean (July), Green Corn (August), and Harvest (October). At these celebrations, they expressed their gratitude for the land they called the Turtle's Back or Turtle Island.[22]

Each person belonged to the clan of his or her mother. The Oneida clans of Turtle, Bear, and Wolf were led by women called the clan mothers. When a sachem, or hereditary chief, died, the clan mothers chose a man to take on the name and the responsibility of leadership. To mourn the death of a sachem and recognize his successor, delegates from the Five Nations held a Condolence Ceremony. Grief, the Haudenosaunee knew, caused eyes to be filled with tears, ears to stop hearing, and throats to become choked by sobs. At the ceremony, the condolers sang, prayed, and recounted the epic of the Peacemaker and Haywentha. In this way, they helped to clear the eyes, ears, and throats of the bereaved so that peace and reason could be restored and so they again could see clearly the path they walked on the earth.[23]

When he had brought the Five Nations together under the Great Law of Peace, the Peacemaker instructed the people to envision their homeland of Iroquoia as a longhouse inhabited by kinfolk. The Mohawks guarded its eastern door, the Senecas guarded the western door, and the Onondagas kept the council fire at the center. The Five Nations placed important towns near the main trail that ran east–west through their territory. News was delivered by the fastest runners, who formed a relay system capable of covering eighty miles a day or more. They had no police force, no jails, and no permanent army. If individuals opposed the consensus decision, they might outwardly accept it for the time being or split off from the whole. Both diversity and unity were honored in Iroquoia, where children were raised to think for themselves and take care of each other.[24]

Confronted with epidemic fatalities in the mid-seventeenth century, the Five Nations attempted to rebuild their population by conducting what were called "mourning wars." Grieving clan mothers demanded that warriors go to war to take prisoners from other nations. The clan mother then decided whether a captive would be adopted to take the place of a deceased loved one, as happened in Polly Denny's family. If not, the prisoner might be subjected to ritual humiliation, torture, death, and cannibalism. With the help of guns and powder sold by the Dutch, the Five Nations seized captives and furs in conflicts with the Algonquins, the Wyandots (Huron), the Odawas (Ottawa), the Shawnees, and the Susquehannocks.[25]

The Five Nations also invited some of the Europeans to assimilate or, as they put it, become "one people." Baffled by the celibacy practiced by French Jesuits who wanted to be called Father, an Oneida asked a priest "to become a real father." The Haudenosaunee told the missionaries,

"If you love, as you say you do, our souls, love our bodies also, and let us be henceforth but one nation." The Dutch authorities in 1638 outlawed sexual relations with "heathens," which by their definition included Natives and Africans. Many colonists out of the predominantly male population broke this law. A Dutchman reported that several of his countrymen had become infatuated with Indigenous women, who, he said, "have an attractive grace about them."[26]

There were advantages to these attachments. For the woman, marriage meant that she remained in charge of the home and the land. The children typically stayed with her to be raised by her mother and brothers. She and her family acquired European kettles and cloth at a time when many makers of pots and scrapers of hides had died. From the women, the men gained access to trade and land. To acknowledge the political power of a Haudenosaunee woman as well as raise his own status in front of Europeans, a man might claim that his wife had royal rank. For example, the Mohawk woman Otstok was known as the "princess" who married the colonist Cornelis Antonissen Van Slyck, called Broer or Brother Cornelis because he was accepted as an equal by the Mohawks.[27]

While aspects of the "one people" idea appealed to some Europeans and Haudenosaunee, most preferred their own ways. In 1642, three colonists made their way to Mohawk territory to promote a peaceful trading relationship. They probably followed the same trail used by Harmen a decade earlier, but they knew enough to bring presents. They were from Rensselaerswyck, the patroonship, or estate, of one million acres near Fort Orange on the Hudson granted by the West India Company to the Amsterdam merchant Killian Van Rensselaer. The trio, which included a French carpenter named Jean Labatie, conducted a treaty of friendship between the people of New Netherland and Iroquoia.[28]

At the time, Harmen was promoted to be commissary of stores in New Amsterdam, the trading post on the island the Natives called Manhattan. The new job put him in the top category of company employees, with a salary of sixty guilders a month, more than double the pay of a ship's surgeon. In 1638 he had engaged in what the Dutch considered to be the patriotic harassment of Spain by privateering in the West Indies. Before he sailed, Harmen made a will that left his property to Jellesje Claesen Swits, maiden, from Zierikzee, southwest of Rotterdam. Jellesje probably was the daughter of Claes Cornelissen Swits, a wheelwright whose house at Turtle Bay (around present-day Forty-Seventh Street and Second Avenue) was a stopping place popular with Natives, traders, and company officials. When he returned from the Caribbean, Harmen married Jellesje, my ninth great-grandmother.[29]

For Harmen and Jellesje, the murder in 1641 of Claes Cornelissen Swits by a young Native was a personal loss. For company director William Kieft, it was justification for slaughter. Some of the residents of New Amsterdam believed that the killer may have slain Swits to avenge the murder of his uncle by a colonist. They objected to the brutal retaliation known as Kieft's War, in which, in a surprise attack, soldiers and settlers hacked to death entire Native families. The Algonquian people from the region united to respond with deadly raids against colonists. By the time peace was negotiated in 1645, some New Netherlanders feared they might be as cruel as Spain. Others fretted that conflict with Natives was bad for business.[30]

Harmen, meanwhile, was given the prestige appointment of commissary at Fort Orange, which was a more peaceful place thanks to good relations with the Five Nations. He commanded the garrison, managed the stores, and inspected the merchandise on ships that came up the river and anchored in front of the fort where the goods were unloaded. Then the ships would be packed with furs and maybe wheat, lumber, or tobacco and would return to New Amsterdam. Harmen traveled back and forth to Manhattan, where he and Jellesje had three children. He acquired a handsome property on the Common Highway, later Stone Street. With Broer Cornelis as his partner, Harmen invested in the ship *La Garce*, captained by a well-known pirate.[31]

Harmen's career came to a shocking end in 1647. He was charged with "a certain infamous and scandalous crime" committed with a company servant, an enslaved youth named Tobias. Considered too awful for colonial officials to name, the act of sodomy was severely punished. In the Dutch Republic, the authorities justified the execution of homosexuals as necessary to protect society from corruption and God's punishment. In New Amsterdam, a man convicted of sodomy by force had been sentenced to be strangled and burned to ashes. His victim, a ten-year-old enslaved boy, was ordered to watch the execution while being tied to a post with wood piled around him and then beaten with rods. I don't know how old Tobias was or what happened to him. Even though he had no power to consent, he, too, would have been considered guilty of a crime. As for Harmen, this accusation raises a lot of questions about who he was that remain unanswered.[32]

To evade punishment, Harmen lit out to seek sanctuary at one of the Mohawk towns he had visited thirteen years earlier. There he reportedly lived "as an Indian." This move was unusual. Rarely did Dutch colonists, even those who had children with Native women, leave behind colonial society. When the posse sent to retrieve Harmen cornered him in a longhouse, he tried to escape by torching the building. The fire destroyed the town's winter provisions, furs, and wampum. The posse captured Harmen and returned him to Fort Orange. He broke out of prison again and this time headed east. As Harmen crossed the frozen Hudson River, the ice broke underneath him and he drowned.[33]

There was talk of suicide. A "sad and miserable death," concluded the colonial council in New Amsterdam. The council and Peter Stuyvesant, Kieft's successor as company director, decided to sell Harmen's garden lot in Manhattan and use the proceeds to compensate the Mohawks who had sent a complaint detailing their losses. Such an action, the council resolved, was "in the best interest and advantage of this country." It is significant that when Harmen sought and was given shelter by the Mohawks, he repaid their generosity by destroying the bounty of the year's hunt and harvest. His other legacies included the abuse of an enslaved youth, an invaluable account of his journey to Oneida, and his descendants.[34]

It was important to me to learn what had happened to Jellesje. As was typical of widows with young children, she soon remarried. For her second husband, she chose the Frenchman Jean Labatie, also known for his ventures into Iroquoia. Jean and Jellesje sold Harmen's house in Manhattan, and the family moved to the trading post next to Fort Orange called Beverwyck (Beaver District) at present-day Albany. Although he had made several trips to the Five Nations and would make more, Jean refused to undertake a mission in 1650. He would not go for anything in the world, he said around the time Jellesje gave birth to their daughter. When I read that Jean sold a property for beavers and enough scarlet cloth to make his wife a fashionable waistcoat, I hoped it meant Jellesje's second marriage was a happy one.[35]

The Banishment of Marie

I found out that, like Jellesje, my eighth great-grandmother Marie du Trieux lived a life marked by scandal and connection to the Five Nations. Marie was born in 1617 in Leiden, the Dutch Republic's vibrant second city, home to the young Rembrandt and exiled English Puritans who soon would leave for Massachusetts. Her family were Protestants called Walloons, from the French-speaking part of the Spanish Netherlands (now Belgium and northern France). They had sought refuge in the republic because it permitted freedom of conscience at a time when Europe was torn apart by warring Protestant and Roman Catholic Christians.[36]

The West India Company needed people in its colony to provide for the traders, but it could not convince Dutch families to leave home in an era known as the Dutch Golden Age. The company recruited refugees like the Walloons. Thirty families agreed to serve without pay for six years in return for free passage, a two-year supply of food, and the promise of land. At the end of their indenture, the colonists would be free to keep or sell their farms. It took six weeks for the company ship *New Netherlander*, crammed with livestock, tools, and 110 people, to reach New Amsterdam in 1624. For seven-year-old Marie, setting foot on land meant freedom. For the rest of her life, she would defy restrictions.[37]

At first, Marie and her fellow settlers lived in cellars dug in the ground. Many died or grew discouraged and returned to Europe once they had served out their time. Not many remained to be joined by new arrivals, as the du Trieux family did. "A motley collection" was how company officials described the few hundred inhabitants, who included Walloon and Fleming Protestants, French Huguenots, Germans from the Rhine

FIGURE 5. New Amsterdam, the childhood home of Marie du Trieux (1617–ca. 1680). Hartgers View of Manhattan from *Beschrijvinghe Van Virginia Nieuw Nederland*, 1626–28. Joost Hartgersz, 29.100.792, Museum of the City of New York.

Valley, Scandinavians, Englishmen, and enslaved Africans brought from the Caribbean to build the fort. The company hired clerks, carpenters, a midwife, and a slave master. Marie's father, Philip du Trieux, became the court messenger, which made him a minor official like the dogcatcher and the town crier. The company eventually granted Philip a lot on the beach along the East River.[38]

The officials of the West India Company handed out land they believed they had acquired from the Indigenous people by buying it. The Dutch did not understand that the Natives of Manhattan, the Lenape, had no concept for selling land. For the Lenape, the "purchase" was instead a ceremony validated by an exchange of goods that committed the Dutch to taking care of the land and the people on it. In the Dutch tradition, the legal transfer of ownership was documented before local magistrates and recorded in a public register. Once completed, the owner had land rights—the right to possess it, use it, sell it, and leave it to heirs and assignees.[39]

Marie, like other New Netherlanders, viewed land as a private commodity and a place to raise her children. At age twenty, she had a daughter fathered by a prominent New Amsterdam colonist. Then she had a son named Arnout whose father, Cornelis Volkertsen Viele, an explorer and shipowner, she married. With Cornelis, who owned a tavern along the Indian path the colonists widened and called the Groote Heere Weg (Broadway), Marie had three more children. After Cornelis died, Marie had four children with her next husband, the fur trader Jan Peake, my eighth great-grandfather.[40]

Jan Peake traded furs on the Hudson River at a stream that would be named Peek's Kill after him. The company appointed him a trade broker because he spoke both Dutch and English. In the 1650s, Jan applied for the rights of a small burgher. With these rights, he could keep a shop or exercise a trade. Required to do guard duty, each small burgher was assigned to the Orange or Blue Company, after the colors in the flag of the republic. Every man had to bring his own weapon, show up sober and on time for night patrols, and refrain from shooting up weathervanes. To improve their defenses when commercial rivalry with the English triggered the First Anglo-Dutch War, the colonists built a palisade at what would become Wall Street. It was around this time that Marie's father and brother were killed by Indians, according to family history.[41]

The colonial records show that Jan and Marie achieved notoriety by operating a tavern out of their home on the East River at Maiden Lane and Pearl Street. To the disgust of Director Stuyvesant, one-fourth of

New Amsterdam had been turned into taverns. Taverns attracted sailors in port, soldiers off duty, and burghers practicing the custom of confirming a deal by sharing "a drink on the bargain." After signing, sealing, and recording a land sale, the buyer, seller, witnesses, clerks, and officials headed to the tavern. Drunks, according to Dutch law, were not competent to bind themselves to a contract. They could cancel within twenty-four hours or take their case to court. In one case, the witnesses for the buyer testified that, yes, the buyer had been drunk, but so was the seller, and for that matter no one present had been "very sober."[42]

With little popular support, Stuyvesant cracked down on tavern keepers, known as tappers. Jan was arrested for repeated nights of drunkenness at his home. For his "disorderly housekeeping and evil life, tippling, dancing, gaming and other irregularities, together with tapping at night and on Sunday during preaching," Jan's license was annulled. He shall not tap anymore, ruled the court, until he vindicates himself. Jan testified that he was a longtime resident burdened "with a housefull of children and more besides." The court allowed Jan to continue his business as long as he comported himself properly. A month later, Jan again appeared in court for tapping at night, a charge he denied.[43]

The tavern business had its brutal side. When Marie went to the fort to ask the provost marshal to pay his tavern bill, he kicked her out and threatened to throw her in the hole or dungeon if she did not go away. "Then I can't pay either!" said Marie. "Have your husband come," retorted the provost marshal. "I'll pay him the same way." Marie was accused of prostitution. It is not clear from the records whether she herself was being charged with prostitution or with allowing prostitution in her tavern. She got off with the warning that she must change her ways or face banishment. Two years later, Stuyvesant ordered Jan to be arrested for beating and wounding a company soldier. Jan defended his actions by saying that he was protecting Marie from the soldier, who threatened to run her through with his sword.[44]

Jan and Marie, who spoke Native languages, conducted illegal trade with Indians. Colonial authorities had forbidden the sale of alcohol to Indians, a prohibition that was violated frequently. Punishments included high fines, flogging, and banishment, but they were rarely imposed. Typically, the transgressor could get off by showing remorse and promising to behave. The authorities wanted to appease Native leaders who complained about the devastating impact of alcohol on their people, but they also knew that the sale of alcohol integrated Indigenous people into trade. Natives wanted only so many kettles or guns, but they used alcohol as a medicine or anesthetic, as an offering in hospitality rituals and at diplomatic councils, and to drink. Besides, they resented being denied alcohol at taverns where Europeans were served. Taverns, the authorities worried, were places where inebriated Natives could be cheated, insulted, or attacked, which could lead to conflict.[45]

Marie's downfall came when she sold brandy to Indians during the New Year's holiday at the end of 1663. Following the death of Jan a few years earlier, Marie had asked the court for help supporting her children. She tried and failed to collect debts owed to her as well as pay her own. For selling alcohol to Natives, Marie was fined and banished from Manhattan. She petitioned for a revision of the sentence by pointing out that she was "one of the oldest inhabitants of the city of New Amsterdam." At age forty-seven, she may have meant that as a resident for four decades, she had lived there longer than almost any other European. She asked to be allowed to resettle in Beverwyck. The authorities agreed to set aside her fine for the time being and granted her permission to remove to Long Island. Marie did as she wanted and went north to Beverwyck.[46]

Marie chose to live near the Five Nations, where she and her family could put their skills to work during the trading season. Hundreds of Natives came to Beverwyck to trade with Europeans from New Netherland, New England, and New France. Colonists neglected their jobs and mortgaged their property to trade. Such risky behavior, along with the possibility that a farmhand, for instance, could make several years' wages by selling furs, led to high-pressure tactics. The Haudenosaunee complained that in the woods before they even reached town, they were subjected to bribes and assault by colonists after furs. When the authorities cracked down on such behavior, the colonists, including my ancestors, claimed they were in the woods only to look for blueberries or lost hogs.[47]

The Europeans of Beverwyck learned to conduct Haudenosaunee rituals and give gifts, not because they valued these ceremonies but because it was part of doing business. The Mohawks and Oneidas participated in trade not for profit but to practice reciprocity and acquire needed goods and services. They asked the colonists for help in repairing their castles or ransoming a loved one held by the French. The Natives did not understand that a gunsmith insisted on being paid because he needed to make a living. They did understand that Beverwyck traders lacked sincerity. "The Dutch say we are brothers and that we are joined together with chains," concluded a Mohawk delegation, "but that lasts only as long as we have beavers."[48]

From Beverwyck, the families of Marie and Jellesje moved closer to Iroquoia by settling in the new frontier town of Schenectady. "Beyond the pines" was where the Mohawks chose to place settlers and where the settlers wanted to be. The Mohawks, who had taken the territory from the Mahicans in the 1620s, found it convenient to have a trading post halfway between the Hudson and the easternmost Mohawk castle. The settlers believed they could score an advantage in the fur trade if they lived at the spot where the Natives left the Mohawk River to carry their packs down the trail to Beverwyck.[49]

This first recorded acquisition of land from the Five Nations was negotiated by the Mohawks and the Dutch in mutual misunderstanding. From the Dutch perspective, the two parties, with the help of interpreters, bargained over a price, which the Dutch paid with cloth, axes, gunpowder, and wampum. To them, a deed signed by Mohawk leaders meant that the land had become private property. No one could own land, believed the Haudenosaunee. It only could be distributed temporarily to someone to use. In accordance with the idea of "one people," the Mohawks agreed to share the land with kinfolk. The deed, for example, was witnessed by Jacques Cornelissen Van Slyck, the son of Broer Cornelis who had grown up in Canajoharie, the Mohawk town of his mother, Otstok.[50]

Director Stuyvesant approved the creation of Schenectady in the hope that it would help the Dutch fend off European rivals. "The best and safest plan," Stuyvesant proposed to the company, "would be to forestall the English by peopling and settling the lands with some good and clever farmers." The idea that farmers might be helpful was a change of tune for Stuyvesant, who in the past had derided the Boers or farmers as slow-witted primitives with uncontrolled sexual appetites who spread out into distant and lonely places and failed to develop the civic virtue of the burgher. Stuyvesant's vision of useful farmers was at odds with the plans of the Mohawks and the founders of Schenectady, who ignored the director's ban on the fur trade there.[51]

Stuyvesant's effort to impose control over Schenectady came to an end when the English seized New Netherland in 1664. Mismanagement, a lack of settlers, Indian wars, and clashes with Europeans had made the colony vulnerable. The colonists did not put up a fight when the English offered mild terms of capitulation. Charles II and his brother the Duke of York, later James II, wanted their new colony to carry on making money. The great landowners like the Van Rensselaers maintained their holdings. New rules brought order to trading and enhanced the wealth of Dutch merchants, who became more anglicized as they cooperated with the conquerors. Settlers, meanwhile, continued Dutch customs, which meant that Saint Nicholas, or Sinterklass, still brought sweets for good children. The colony and the town of New Amsterdam became New York, and Beverwyck became Albany, while Schenectady remained Schenectady.[52]

Now perched on the outskirts of an English colony, Schenectady was a Dutch town that conducted friendly relations with the Mohawks and the French. In her last years, Marie was surrounded by her extended family, who knew the fur trade, the tavern business, and how to speak Dutch, English, French, and Native languages. For instance, her daughter Anna Peake, who married John Alexander Glen, the son of a Scottish trader and settled on a farm called Scotia north of the river, was remembered as "a great humanitarian" for her hospitality to the Mohawks and aid to escaped French captives.[53]

The inhabitants of Schenectady developed their own blended trade language, called Mohawk Dutch. Marie's sons, Arnout and Cornelis Viele, served as interpreters. Cornelis, who may have married a Mohawk woman, ran a popular tavern, as did his fellow interpreter Jacques Van Slyck. As the children of Otstok, Jacques and his sister Hilletie, also an interpreter, had no trouble finding spouses in Schenectady. Marriage to the Van Slycks meant kinship with the Mohawks and access to land, trade, and protection. Hilletie's life among the Europeans came with heartache, however. Her devotion to Christianity led to a rift with her mother and unpleasantness with some of the townspeople, who, when she rebuked them for their drunkenness and foul language, called her a "converted sow." Her brother, who was described as not as good as she was, appears to have fit in more easily. With their blended language, kinship ties to the Haudenosaunee, and location along the Mohawk River, the families of Schenectady, including those of Jacques, Hilletie, Marie, and Jellesje, became known as the Mohawk Dutch.[54]

Small and Grand Settlements

The Five Nations, along with their Mohawk Dutch neighbors, lived in the middle of what the French and English viewed as a theater of war for empire. In search of furs to sell after depleting their own beaver population, the Haudenosaunee forced Native trading rivals out of the way as they ranged from Virginia to the Ohio Valley to Canada. Down to a population of 8,600 following more outbreaks of disease, they conducted mourning wars. The Iroquois must be subdued, decided Louis XIV, who was determined to make New France a profitable colony. In 1666, French troops and their Native allies destroyed Mohawk crops and villages.[55]

As a peacemaking gesture, the Oneidas and Mohawks invited French missionaries to their lands. A Jesuit priest recorded what he saw as wrong with the People of the Standing Stone. There was drunkenness, which he blamed on the Dutch. There was too much sexual freedom, observed the priest, who disapproved of the ease with which a man or woman could end an unhappy marriage and then marry someone else. The belief in dreams as expressions of hidden desires that must be understood and fulfilled, he felt, was evil. The Oneidas might be the least populous of the Five Nations, noted the Jesuits, but they were "the proudest and most insolent of all." Some of the Haudenosaunee who converted to Roman Catholic or Protestant faiths relocated to Christian communities. These moves not only strained family relations, as in Hilletie's case; they also tested the cohesion of the people of the longhouse.[56]

The English of New York proceeded to claim Iroquoia with the rituals of discovery that included planting flags, raising crosses, and posting royal crests. They sent Jean Labatie and Broer Cornelis to "take possession of ye Sinnekes Countrey." Thirty years earlier, the West India Company had sent Jean to Seneca territory to put the company's mark on three great black oak trees as a legal signal to other Europeans that the Dutch were the first discoverers and therefore possessors of this land. Now the English relied on the husbands of Jellesje and Otstok to replace the company's mark with the king's coat of arms. Whether this ritual impressed the Senecas, Jean did not say.[57]

The Five Nations and the English affirmed that they were linked together by the Covenant Chain, their name for a relationship of friendship and trade that had begun with the Dutch and that would be renewed and redefined at councils and treaties over the years. This commitment did not prevent the governor of New York, who wanted to strengthen the bond with the Five Nations, from sending Arnout Viele to Onondaga with a message that had the opposite effect. He told Arnout to instruct the Great Council not to negotiate with the French. The sachems and warriors listened in outrage as Arnout delivered the governor's assertion that he was "complete master of their country" and that the Five Nations "belonged to the King of England and the Duke of York." The Creator had granted them their country, the sachems replied, and they were subject to no one. They sent Arnout back with the message that they would settle matters with the French.[58]

The English built up their military strength. They garrisoned soldiers at Albany and ordered every male in Albany, Rensselaerswyck, and Schenectady over fifteen and under sixty, including my forefathers Jacobus Peake and Frans Van den Bogaert, to have a gun, ammunition, and militia training. The governor supplied Oneida and Mohawk warriors with firearms and ammunition. War parties heading north departed from Schenectady. That had to stop, concluded the French, who planned an expedition against New York that would make Louis XIV the "absolute master of all the Iroquois."[59]

One hundred and thirty Frenchmen and their eighty Native allies attacked Schenectady at midnight on 8 February 1690. They silently entered the stockade through an open gate and went from house to house under orders, according to a French attacker, "to murder and DeStroy all People they mett." Surprise and lack of preparation made it a one-sided fight. The attackers, who lost one Frenchman and one warrior, killed 60 out of a population of 250. The raiders spared the family of Anna Peake Glen for their past kindness to French captives.[60]

Among the slain were Frans Van den Bogaert and Arnout Viele's daughter Marie and her children. Adam Vrooman, reputed to be a giant

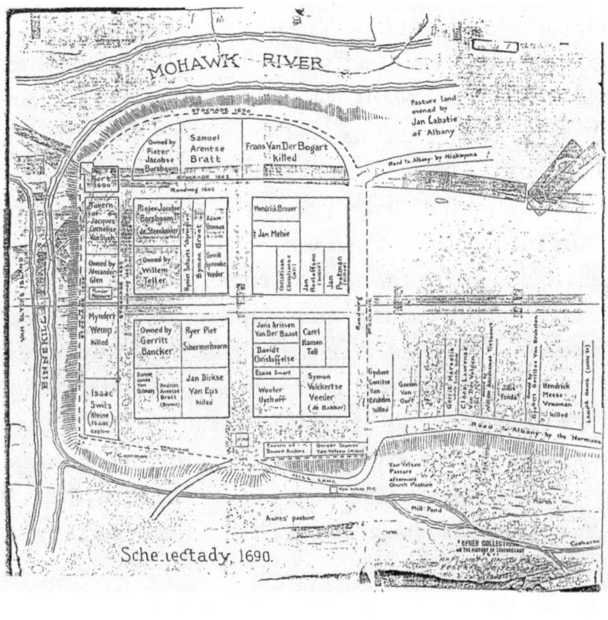

FIGURE 6. Schenectady 1690. Among those killed in the attack was Frans Van den Bogaert. Across the road, the house of Adam Vrooman was the former home of Marie du Trieux. Courtesy of the Efner History Center, Schenectady, NY.

of a man, impressed the French with his defense of his house, but he could not save his wife and baby or prevent the capture of his sons. The raiders set the town on fire and left with twenty-seven prisoners, forty of the best horses, and the head of the village minister. They took as captives young men and boys who could travel fast in heavy snows. They left behind women (who would be slowed down by their long skirts), the elderly, and small children. The captives included a son of Frans, my seventh great-grandfather Claes Van den Bogaert.[61]

Mohawks and Mahicans set off to track the raiders. A force of Europeans and Indians followed, after they had buried the dead. Asked by the Albany government "to come & live & Plant at Shinnectady lately Destroyed," the Mohawks helped to round up livestock scattered in the woods, provide food, and protect the village. "We do esteem this evil as if done to ourselves," the Mohawks said in condolence interpreted by Arnout and Hilletie. The grateful colonial government sent presents to the Mohawks. The homeless took shelter in Albany, where troops, warriors, and refugees, including Jacques Van Slyck, succumbed to a smallpox outbreak.[62]

People who lost spouses remarried. Several widows married English soldiers even though these unions may have caused the women a loss of status. The Dutch were known to refer to the soldiers as "English dogs," and the English thought the Dutch were odd. I wonder whether my foremother, the widow of Frans Van den Bogaert, felt safer remarried to a professional soldier. Over time, eighteen of the captives escaped or were rescued by Europeans, Mohawks, and Oneidas. Seven years after the attack, Adam Vrooman went north to the province of New France, called Canada, to negotiate the release of his sons. Claes Van den Bogaert returned and married my seventh great-grandmother Barbara Heemstraat in 1699. Perhaps Claes was the unidentified captive brought home by an Oneida warrior, who received rum and cloth in gratitude.[63]

Although the majority of European captives returned, those between the ages of seven and fifteen were the most likely to want to stay with their Native families to enjoy the affection, independence, and unselfishness of a way of life not dedicated to personal gain. Other captives who did not return were enslaved Africans. Nothing is known about what happened to five enslaved men taken captive at the time of the massacre, but in the past enslaved people from Schenectady had fled to Canada to seek their freedom.[64]

Europeans and Natives were led by Peter Schuyler, a wealthy merchant of Albany and its first mayor, in an unsuccessful punitive expedition against Canada. When the French burned three Mohawk towns, the colonists provided food and shelter to homeless Mohawks, while the militia joined warriors in pursuit of the raiders. After the French torched their town, the Oneidas took refuge in Mohawk villages and at Albany, where they were provided for by order of the colonial government. As a result of war, dislocation, and disease, the Oneidas and Mohawks lost dozens of warriors, while the European population of Albany County declined.[65]

Attacked by the French and lorded over by the English, the Five Nations also were subjected to a land grab by the leading men of Albany, including Peter Schuyler, who served the colony as commissioners of Indian affairs. The commissioners persuaded Mohawk leaders to sign a deed giving them two hundred square miles of land on both sides of the Mohawk River from Schenectady to present-day Herkimer. The Mohawks mistakenly thought that this deed put the land in trust to protect it from the French and anyone else. When they learned otherwise, they complained to the new governor, who pushed to overturn the grant and assured the Mohawks that the territory was theirs again. He meant that they had the right of occupancy. The land, he believed, belonged to the English Crown.[66]

To preserve their autonomy, the Five Nations turned to diplomacy. They sought to gain access to western hunting grounds, as well as European goods, while holding together their pro-English and pro-French factions. In 1701, they negotiated a policy of neutrality with France and England called the Grand Settlement. The Five Nations would not interfere in conflicts between England and France, but they would hold the balance of power. If one side displeased them, they could threaten to go to the other. The Europeans praised Iroquois treaty making, oratory, and oral memory. The Dutch observer Jasper Danckearts noted that, using wampum, the children were taught to remember what was said, "so that they may not become treaty-breakers, which is an abomination to them."[67]

Danckearts did not think the colonists were a good influence on the Natives. They had, he thought, introduced greed to a people who lived like nobles—hunting, fishing, going to war. He observed that Indians did not have to labor like Europeans and that their children inherited nothing, because there was "nothing but the ground" to inherit, which was free for all of them. The phrase "nothing but the ground" illustrated a world of difference between Natives and Europeans. The Mohawks and Oneidas believed the land they shared with multitudes of plant and animal brothers and sisters was the foundation of their strength and unity. To European colonizers seeking waterways and riches, the land, which they saw as practically vacant and teeming with resources to be exploited, was a base for empire.[68]

On this contested ground lived Polly's ancestors joined by mine. My forebears, I learned, were a "motley collection" of refugees, indentured servants, and West India Company employees. They traded, raised families, committed crimes. Some suffered violent deaths, and one was banished. They were desperate for land, which, claimed by kings, companies, and colonists with their papal decrees, charters, and deeds signed in misunderstanding, belonged to the Indigenous people.

By the end of the 1600s, the families of Marie and Jellesje, chasing after opportunity and security, had located themselves at the eastern door of the Haudenosaunee. They became useful to the Five Nations as go-betweens. In gratitude for his trouble in "going back and forth among them," the Mohawks gave Arnout land on the Mohawk River next to his half brother Jacobus Peake. The Peake family enjoyed kinship ties to the Mohawks thanks to the marriage of a son to a granddaughter of Broer Cornelis and Otstok. For my Mohawk Dutch ancestors, life on the edge of Iroquoia meant practicing aspects of the "one people" notion of family on shared ground, while dreaming of a place of their own.[69]

The home of Jacobus Peake was on the Mohawk River, five miles above Schenectady at a small settlement called the Bush or the Wilderness. Although their fellow colonists considered Jacobus and his family to be beyond civilization, the Peakes were in a position to be well informed, because they hosted Natives and Europeans on their way to and from the land of the longhouse. My sixth great-grandmother Anna Peake was twelve when a delegation from Albany stayed the night in 1700. Two Indian commissioners accompanied Colonel Wolfgang Romer, a royal engineer tasked with conducting a strategic reconnaissance of the all-important Oneida Carrying Place as well as a site for an English fort on Lake Ontario.[70]

From Anna's home, the delegation made their way to Oneida, where they were greeted with friendliness. The visitors called the sachems together to ask them if the Oneidas could make a canoe and leave it at the Carrying Place for Colonel Romer. The Oneida leaders made several excuses about why they could not do so. The travelers went on to Onondaga, where Romer asked to see the place where the river from Oneida Lake ran into Lake Ontario at present-day Oswego. The Onondagas took him nowhere near there on a canoe tour of Onondaga and Oneida Lakes.[71]

The travelers returned to Oneida, where they asked again to go to the Oneida Carrying Place. Someone eventually took them by a "most miserable path," reported Romer. Sixty-five years after Harmen Myndertsz Van den Bogaert had visited their town, the Oneidas remained welcoming but wary, while the delegation from Albany was frustrated. The Europeans were determined to extend their reach into the American continent, but without the Oneidas to guide them, the newcomers were bewildered by the great forests of Turtle Island.[72]

Chapter 2

Of One and Many People in the Mohawk Valley

In the early 1700s, the best land remained sheltered on the western side of Oneida territory, while my ancestors moved closer to the Five Nations. Anna Peake and her husband, Joseph Clement, my sixth great-grandparents, chose an excellent site between Schenectady and Tiononderogue, the lower Mohawk castle. With a population of three to four hundred people, Tiononderogue was situated where Schoharie Creek flowed into the Mohawk River. It was there in 1712 that Governor Robert Hunter of New York ordered carpenters from Schenectady to build Fort Hunter and a chapel named for Queen Anne. To the south in the Schoharie Valley lived Polly Denny's Mohawk grandparents.[1]

I did not know that my family and Polly's came from the Mohawk and Schoharie Valleys, and I wanted to find out what my ancestors did to obtain a place to live in Mohawk territory. I wondered how Polly's extended family of Mohawks and Oneidas responded to the newcomers. How did the Mohawks and Oneidas try to preserve their territory from Europeans hell-bent on acquiring it? What happened to all of them in the tumultuous contest for empire between the British and the French?

In the eyes of sachems and colonial officials, the Clements, a Mohawk Dutch family with kinship ties to the Haudenosaunee, were troublemakers as well as handy go-betweens. As had Anna's grandmother Marie du Trieux, the Clements ran a tavern, an important meeting place on the frontier where trade was conducted, news exchanged, and refreshment taken. Although Indians, contrary to repute, did not drink as much as colonists, the availability of alcohol caused disturbances in Tiononderogue. Joseph Clement and others, complained a Mohawk sachem to the Indian commissioners in 1720, "sold Rum so plentifully as it ware water out of a fountain and if that Cannot be Privinted they Cannot Live Peaceably in their Castle."[2]

An even more fraught issue was property. Following an era of corrupt deals, the colony of New York instituted reforms to make the purchase of land from Indian nations appear proper and legitimate. The prospective buyer first had to petition the governor for permission to purchase land from the Indians and receive a license to purchase. Second, the buyer had to conduct the purchase of the land and obtain a deed signed by the Native owners. Third, a survey of the land had to be completed and certified. Finally, the attorney general of New York, on behalf of the governor on behalf of the Crown, issued a patent or grant for the property.[3]

This process made the legal acquisition of land too expensive for most colonists. It cost a lot to pay fees and bribes; hire surveyors, clerks, and interpreters; and buy presents for the Natives. Even then, the purchase might fall through without help from friends in high places. Colonial officials, who typically also were speculators hoping to profit by buying and selling land, tended to enforce the regulations only against rivals. For decades, the key post of secretary for Indian affairs was held by the family of Robert Livingston, the Scottish clerk who married Alida Schuyler Van Rensselaer. While serving as Indian commissioners, members of the influential Schuyler-Van Rensselaer-Livingston clan invested in land, including tracts declared by the Mohawks and Oneidas to be stolen.[4]

When Governor Hunter tried to acquire the beautiful Schoharie Valley for himself, he was scolded by the Mohawks for failing to follow the rules he was responsible for enforcing. They were willing to sell a part of the valley, said the Mohawks, but not the fertile plain near the distinctive cliff called Onistagrawa, or Corn Mountain, where the Schoharie Mohawks planted their crops. Polly's grandmother, a Turtle Clan woman, lived in this mixed community of Mohawks, Mohicans, Lenapes, Tuscaroras, and Oneidas, which also included a few Africans who had freed themselves from slavery by running away.[5]

The Mohawks initially welcomed Adam Vrooman of Schenectady to Schoharie. After Adam's first wife was killed in the 1690 massacre, he married her sister, who was the widow of Jacques Van Slyck. Such a marriage did not make him kin to Mohawks but rather their "loving acquaintance," as they stated in their deed of 260 acres to Adam in 1711. Adam, who settled in Schoharie with his third wife, my eighth great-aunt Grietje Heemstraat, later had his property resurveyed with the result that it doubled in size. Onistagrawa later became known as Vrooman's Nose.[6]

Natives and newcomers brought their babies to be baptized at Queen Anne's Chapel, where the parents of Native infants were not required to convert. According to church records, the Clements often stood as sponsors or godparents at the side of new parents, including Mohawks, Oneidas, enslaved Africans, and English and Irish soldiers without family or Christian relatives at hand. The only European woman to do so, Anna joined prominent sachems as sponsors of Mohawk infants. As godparents, Joseph and Anna probably followed the Dutch tradition of giving gifts to the newborn. While it is unlikely that they presented each baby with the customary silver spoon, they would have known well the Mohawk children who grew up with their own.[7]

Refugees called Palatines, including ancestors of mine, came to live in the Schoharie and Mohawk Valleys. The German speakers had fled the Rhine River Valley on the war-torn border between France and the Holy Roman Empire. Fifteen thousand people, mostly Protestant, journeyed to London in 1709 because they believed a rumor that Queen Anne would transport them across the Atlantic so they could settle on free land in America. While they camped outside the city, the British Board of Trade, which supervised colonial affairs, discussed what to do with them.[8]

The board thought the Palatines might be useful as a barrier between the British and the French in what it viewed as the New York backcountry. It hoped the refugees would contribute to peacekeeping by intermarrying with their Native neighbors "as the French do." And in such a dangerous place, the board concluded, the Palatines would be "expendable in case of attack." Queen Anne approved the plan to transport the refugees to New York, where they would be given forty acres to farm in return for several years of labor to cover the costs of their travel and settlement. The families who agreed to go indentured themselves to pay off this debt. Ten ships carrying three thousand people sailed in 1710. About a third of the refugees died from disease and shipwreck.[9]

Soon after they arrived, three hundred Palatine men marched north with the colonial militia in a failed attempt to seize Canada from the

French during Queen Anne's War. In Europe, the war was fought over the succession to the Spanish throne, while in England's American colonies the conflict was considered a battle over control of North America. The Palatine volunteers included Johan Friedreich Bellinger, a carpenter's son born near Frankfurt who was my eighth great-grandfather. Border conflicts over empire were not new to these men, but serving alongside Mohawk and Oneida warriors was.[10]

Governor Hunter settled Palatine families on Livingston Manor, the 160,000-acre estate south of Albany that belonged to Robert Livingston, who was known as the 1st lord. He put them to work producing naval stores, including tar and pitch, needed by the Royal Navy. For months, the men labored in the forests and the women farmed, while their families were provided with inadequate tents for winter housing. The refugees had come to America "to secure lands for our children," they said, not to starve and freeze to death. In defiance, they became "idle and backwards," according to the governor, who posted troops to keep the men at work before he gave up on the unsuccessful naval stores project. The Palatines were "liars and imposters," said Livingston, "worse than northern savages."[11]

In search of good land, Palatine families made their way to Schoharie. They had permission from the Mohawks to settle there, but they did not follow the procedures for land purchase. Deemed squatters, they were not welcomed by the speculators who claimed to own the valley or by Adam Vrooman, who complained that Palatines trashed his property. The sheriff, sent to investigate, was met by Palatine women armed with kitchen knives and broomsticks. My guess is that by this time, the women had had enough of being moved around by officials. They covered the sheriff with manure and chicken feathers and dumped him on the road to Albany. The governor ordered out the militia after the women, who hid in the hills to evade arrest. My Palatine foremothers probably knew Polly's, because they survived their first winter in Schoharie thanks to help from the Mohawks.[12]

Some of the Palatines decided to move to the Mohawk Valley. Governor Hunter's successor liked the idea of the German speakers as a buffer on the frontier. They were "headstrong and ignorant," he thought, but a "laborious and honest" people. Around 1725, my sixth great-grandparents Jacob and Margaret (Anna Margaretha Schütz) Timmerman settled on the north side of the Mohawk River at the site of present-day St. Johnsville. Along with the Klock and Bellinger families, the Timmermans acquired land purchased from the Mohawks by a speculator for seven hundred beaver skins. On streams running down the hill, the Timmermans and Klocks built mills where Palatines, Mohawks, and Oneidas could have their corn ground and catch up on the gossip after they got to know each other.[13]

The Timmermans settled close to Canajoharie. This town, the upper castle of the Mohawks, had grown in significance. It was located below Little Falls, the spot where the Mohawk River cut through the Appalachian Range and became the gateway to the west. The Six Nations, as they were known after the Tuscaroras joined them, had accepted the British presence in Iroquoia. Choosing peace and access to trade on which they now depended, they renewed the Covenant Chain. The British built a fort at the Oneida Carrying Place and another in Onondaga territory at Oswego on Lake Ontario. As the fur trade shifted its base from Albany to Oswego, furs and goods flowed through the longhouse of the Haudensaunee. Shipments of merchandise and provisions for the forts came upriver, where boats had to stop and be unloaded and the cargo carried around Little Falls.[14]

Canajoharie attracted the interest of speculators. Philip Livingston, the 2nd lord of Livingston Manor, claimed that he and his partners had bought part of the upper castle. The Mohawks denounced the so-called Canajoharie Patent. "Our land is our life," they said. Following the loss of so many to disease and conflict, they rebuilt their population with adopted captives. In addition, they had welcomed a few Mohawk Dutch settlers, including David Schuyler of Albany, who acquired 1,500 acres. An investor in the disputed Canajoharie Patent, Schuyler had kinship ties to the upper castle.[15]

To Margaret Timmerman, the Mohawks granted a valuable tract on the river across from Canajoharie. The 1734 deed, signed by Hendrick of the Bear Clan, Seth of the Wolf Clan, and Margaret of the Turtle Clan and witnessed by David Schuyler, said, "Out of pure love and affection with the consent of the entire Castle of Kannajoharie, both Indian men and women, we give and make over, in the name and on behalf of his Majesty King George of Great Britain, to our friend Anna Marragrieta Timmerman of Tyenindoke, spinner in the county of Albany, for her and her heirs, executors, administrators and assigns, forever, a parcel of flat land." Margaret's grant mixed the European vocabulary of property ownership with Haudenosaunee associations of the land with women, gifts, and affection. Although the Canajoharie Mohawks claimed to act on behalf of George II, this deed, written in Dutch for Mohawk and German speakers, did not conform to English colonial law.[16]

I don't know why the Mohawks granted land to Margaret Timmerman. An accomplished weaver, Margaret may have provided them with homespun cloth. She and other Palatine women, like Mohawk women, tended the crops. They told stories from German folklore about witches who flew on broomsticks and turned into animals, believed in omens, and used charms to ensure a safe birth. Margaret of the Turtle Clan may have consoled Margaret Timmerman over the loss of her babies born after she moved to Canajoharie or taught her how to use plants as medicines. Even if Margaret of the Turtle Clan shared her knowledge of Haudenosaunee birth control practices, it seems unlikely that Margaret Timmerman adopted them. Her fifteenth and last child, my fifth great-grandfather Henry, was born in 1737.[17]

Some marriages and less formal relationships took place between the Palatines and the Haudenosaunee. Most important to the best land were the children born to the Oneida Wolf Clan woman named Catharine. She probably was from the easternmost Oneida town of Oriske, or the Place of Nettles, located where Oriskany Creek flows into the Mohawk River. Catharine had two boys, it is believed, with a son of Johan George and Anna Elizabeth Doxtator who lived downriver in German Flatts (present-day Herkimer), the westernmost Palatine settlement.[18]

Catharine's sons, who would become esteemed warriors, chiefs, and councilors of the Oneida Nation, had both Oneida and German names. The eldest, Tehawenkaragwen (He Who Takes Up the Snowshoe) also was called Johan George or Johan Jury, in accordance with the German custom in which the firstborn son was named for the father's father. Usually known as Honyery, a version of his German name, he probably was born in the 1720s. His brother Thaosagwat (His Lip Follows Him) was known as Honyost for his German name, Johan Joseph. Catharine also had children with a man named Schuyler. She had a daughter whose name is not known, and a son named Tonyentagoyon (Old Legs). He was called Plattcop or Flathead and in later life was known as Henry Schuyler.[19]

As boys, Honyery and his brothers learned how to hunt, the most important skill for Haudenosaunee men, who were expected to provide for their families. They became expert at stalking game, communicating with each other through bird and animal calls, and marksmanship. When at home, Oneida and Mohawk men and boys kept fit with lacrosse games, footraces, and tomahawk throwing, while Palatine boys like the Timmerman brothers were raised to be farmers and millers. It's not hard to guess which way of life a boy may have preferred. Native families taught the Europeans how to make maple sugar, while the settlers mended tools for the Oneidas and Mohawks. Although tensions among the neighbors were inevitable, they helped each other out at cornhusking bees and barn raisings. "We intend to live our lifetime together as brothers," said the Mohawks about the Palatines.[20]

William Johnson Does Much Business

Downriver from Canajoharie, the prime location of the Clements attracted twenty-three-year-old William Johnson, who would become one of the most famous men in colonial North America. Admired in his day for his successful diplomacy with the Six Nations on behalf of the British Empire, the charismatic Johnson left behind volumes of documents that have been relied on by historians ever since. In these, the families of the best land make minor appearances as assets and obstacles.

William Johnson came from Ireland to manage the Mohawk Valley estate of his rich uncle. Exceeding his instructions, he purchased land on the north side of the river in 1739. It was the "properest place" for a store, Johnson explained to his uncle. All the Germans passed by, and so did "all the upper Nations of Indians, whose trade is pritty Valluable." He added, "The chief thing is a fine creek to build a saw mill on." A glitch in Johnson's plans was that the other half of the creek belonged to Joseph Clement, or so claimed Joseph. "I desired a copy of Clements writings which he told me I should freely have, but he thought better of it, and now tells me the key of his trunk is lost," wrote Johnson, who called that excuse "a sham." It was possible that Joseph had no writings, meaning no deed or patent. Johnson proceeded to construct a dam to divert water from the creek to run his mill.[21]

The Fort Hunter church records reveal a gentler side to the relationship between the Irishman and his Mohawk Dutch neighbors. William Johnson joined Joseph and Anna as a sponsor at the baptism of their first grandchild, born in 1740 to their daughter Elizabeth and her spouse, an Indian trader named William Powell. Johnson, however, did not appear in the record of the christening of his own baby a month later. With Catharine Weisenberg, the German-speaking runaway indentured servant who became his housekeeper, Johnson had fathered the first of their three children. Anna Clement did what she had done for other unwed mothers when she served as godmother at the baptism of Catharine's daughter, Ann. Three years later, Elizabeth Clement Powell and her husband stood as sponsors at the baptism of Catharine's son, John Johnson.[22]

Over the next decade, William Johnson also had children with Mohawk women. He learned the Mohawk language and handed out presents of food, clothing, guns, ammunition, hatchets, rum, and beer. The Mohawks called him Warraghiyagey, which has been translated as "doer of great things" or "one who does much business." Johnson shipped furs and flour to New York, London, and the West Indies. He built a bigger trading enterprise than that of the Schuylers in Albany.[23]

William Johnson established himself as a leader of the Mohawks during King George's War from 1744 to 1748. In Europe, this conflict was known as the War of the Austrian Succession, while in the American colonies it was viewed as another French and Indian War. Painted like a war chief, Johnson rode into Albany at the head of Mohawk warriors. The colonial government replaced the Albany Indian commissioners with Johnson as the Indian agent of the colony and made him a colonel of the militia. From his fortified house known as Mount Johnson, Britain's Indian agent provisioned the war parties he sent out to harass the French and their Native allies. He paid warriors an extra reward for every scalp taken.[24]

Johnson complained to New York governor George Clinton that as soon as he paid the Indians their money, they went to Clement's tavern and spent it all, which "leaves them poor as ratts." This "vile practice" of selling alcohol to Indians cost the government a great deal of money, wrote Johnson, because delays of drunkenness increased the length of time he had to house, feed, and clothe the Indians when they came to councils. "The worst of all," reported Johnson, was "Joseph Clement who sells liquor within 20 yards of my house." Johnson had forbidden Clement several times but in vain. He asked Governor Clinton to decree that no liquor be sold to Indians.[25]

In His Majesty's name, Governor Clinton commanded that Joseph Clement was in no way to sell, give, or exchange "any Ale, Beer, Sider, Rum, Brandy or any other spirituous liquors whatsoever, to any Indian, or Soldier . . . on his Peril." Drunkenness among the Indians and soldiers, the governor said, made them unfit for action. Joseph thought the ban was unfair because his neighbor routinely provided alcohol to Indians. "You had promised me that no drink would be sold in your fort," Joseph wrote in Dutch to Colonel Wyllem Jansen. "If you cannot keep your word," he concluded, "it is no wonder that I do not keep my promise."[26]

Johnson resolved the difficulty by buying out the Clements in 1749. "Glad you've Got Rid of so bad a Neighbor & hope You'll take a little pains to drive all of his sort out of that place and Plant Christians in their places," wrote a business associate of Johnson's from New York City. Vilified by Johnson as a nuisance to himself and the empire, Joseph may well have been a bad neighbor even though his wife and daughter were the godmothers of Johnson's children. With his and Anna's long-standing connections, good and bad, to the Mohawks, Joseph also may have somehow undermined or rivaled Johnson's influence. The Clements left their home of over thirty years to settle on a large farm at Tribe's Hill across the river from Tiononderogue. The Clements, I notice, followed the example of Anna's grandmother Marie, who also had been deemed a disturbance. They moved deeper into Iroquoia.[27]

In an attempt at retaliation, Joseph and Anna's sons tried to discredit Johnson's reputation as a leader of Mohawks. Jacobus and Johannes, my fifth great-grandfather, declared before Edward Collins, justice of the peace, that Johnson's Indian regiment was a fictitious organization and that an expedition undertaken in 1747 was without sincere purpose. Collins may have been the correct recipient of this testimony, but as Johnson's attorney not a congenial one. The Clement brothers' accusation came to the attention of Governor Clinton, who was unsympathetic.[28]

The governor counted on William Johnson to be what he claimed to be. In the 1740s, Clinton had enough problems with New Yorkers who carried on the Dutch practice of trading with anyone, including the French. The colonists, he observed with exasperation, pursued their own interests with the Six Nations rather than Britain's as he assumed they should. New Yorkers, Clinton complained to London, were "an ignorant, illiterate people, of republican principles who had no knowledge of the English Constitution or love of their Country." With Johnson, the governor had a talented man who advanced his personal ambitions while also serving the Crown. Clinton praised Johnson for his "good management and most Extraordinary interest with the Indians" and told him, "These Stubborn Dutchmen wont do you the justice they ought."[29]

William Johnson solidified his prominence around the lower Mohawk Castle by building a two-story stone house and trading post called Fort Johnson. Then he looked to expand his influence upriver at Canajoharie. There he identified the Palatine trader George Klock as an even bigger troublemaker than Joseph Clement. Klock was a fluent Mohawk speaker who helped the Canajoharies manage the rents paid in corn or wheat by their German tenants. He provided a home for twenty Mohawks and Oneidas, including Honyery and Plattcop, who may have played a part in his fur-trading business. In no way was the Palatine trader deferential to His Majesty's Indian agent. When Johnson ordered Klock to stop selling liquor to the Indians, Klock told Johnson to go hang himself.[30]

George Klock's closest neighbors, the Timmermans, decided to secure proper title to the land the Mohawks had granted their mother, Margaret. In partnership with the Snell family, the Timmermans followed the rules by obtaining a license to purchase a four-thousand-acre tract along the west bank of East Canada Creek. They gave gifts, including tea and coffee, to the Mohawks as symbols of good faith and acquired a deed signed by Hendrick, who had put his Bear Clan mark on Margaret's grant. Cadwallader Colden, the colonial surveyor general, did the survey for the Snell-Timmerman Patent granted in 1755. The Timmermans settled along the Mohawk River on their section, which included only about a third of Margaret's grant.[31]

The Mohawks viewed both William Johnson and George Klock as useful friends, but they sympathized with their Palatine brothers over land. It was Johnson and the rich people who had writings, noted Hendrick. "The Germans are poor and have no Writings." As the Snell-Timmerman Patent was in the process of being approved, Hendrick asked the colonial government to "give the Germans Writings for these Lands." What troubled the Bear Clan sachem was the Canajoharie Patent. He complained that land speculators from Albany "have Cheated Us out of Our Land, Bribed our Chiefs to sign Deeds for them, and treat Us as Slaves."[32]

Hendrick led a delegation to New York City in 1753 to protest to Governor Clinton. The Mohawks warned of French aggression, complained about the rising prices of goods, and said they wanted no harm to come to George Klock. They decried the Canajoharie Patent. They charged David Schuyler and others with taking more land than they had been given. Clinton replied that the patents were in order. He referred the Mohawks to the Indian commissioners he reinstated in 1752 after William Johnson had resigned because the New York Assembly had refused to reimburse his liberal spending on presents. The Mohawks said they did not trust the commissioners.[33]

"You have always desired us to keep the Roads amongst our Nations open & clear," said Hendrick. "If you dont endeavor to redress our Grievances the rest of our Brethren the Five Nations shall know of it and all Paths will be stopped." To the governor's unsatisfactory response regarding encroachments on their land, the Bear Clan sachem replied, "Brother, All what we have desired to be done for our Good is not

FIGURE 7. Hendrick Theyanoguin (d. 1755). This portrait of the Bear Clan sachem of Canajoharie, who was known to have a sunburst tattoo near his ear, was done by an unknown artist. To Haudenosaunee leaders, dressing in the style worn by prominent Europeans signaled prestige, diplomatic respect, and kinship. This image, titled "The brave old Hendrick the great Sachem or Chief of the Mohawk Indians, one of the Six Nations now in Alliance with & Subject to the King of Great Britain," was published in London. Courtesy of the John Carter Brown Library.

granted which makes our hearts ache very much." Hendrick declared the Covenant Chain broken. The delegation left without making the usual courtesies. The Mohawks had not threatened violence. They had shut the door of the longhouse of the Haudenosaunee.[34]

When the news reached London, the Board of Trade ordered the colonial governors to mend relations at once. As the threat of war with France loomed in 1754, seven American colonies sent representatives to Albany to convene for the first time. At the Albany Congress, the British reaffirmed the Covenant Chain. The Mohawks' request that William Johnson be reinstated as superintendent was granted. Their objection to the Canajoharie Patent paid off when the heirs of Philip Livingston said they would give up their rights to it. The Keepers of the Eastern

Door had demonstrated their strength. By this time, however, the few hundred Mohawks who remained in the valley were outnumbered by over four thousand Europeans. The unity of the Six Nations was tested by divisions over whether to support the British or the French or remain neutral.[35]

At Albany, the idea of unity was on the mind of Benjamin Franklin, delegate from Pennsylvania. Franklin advocated western expansion and a government capable of overseeing it. He proposed the creation of a Grand Council made up of representatives from each colony. "It would be a very strange Thing, if six Nations of ignorant Savages should be capable of forming a Scheme for such an union and be able to execute it in such Manner as that it has subsisted Ages and appears indissoluble," he wrote, "and yet that a like Union should be impracticable for ten or a Dozen English Colonies." The Albany Congress adopted Franklin's Plan of Union, but no colonial assembly approved it. Franklin, who envisioned a North American society without Indians, enslaved Africans, or "Palatine Boors," did not give up on his dream of unity.[36]

Some sort of unity was needed, because twenty-two-year-old George Washington of the Virginia militia had clashed with French forces over the Ohio Valley. The confrontation triggered the cataclysmic Seven Years War, a contest between France and Britain for global primacy that spread over five continents. In the American colonies, it was known as the French and Indian War, the fourth since the 1690s. The longhouse of the Six Nations stretched over the most important east-west military route in North America. Although many Mohawks and Oneidas, along with their Palatine and Mohawk Dutch neighbors, wanted to stay out of the conflict, their homes were about to be fought over in the name of kings.

To Dazzle and Scorch

In time of war, the Clement family became useful to William Johnson, who was made major general of the militia with the expectation that he would rally the support of the Six Nations. The Clements hosted a "frolic," or dance, for the Canajoharie Mohawks, attended by Johnson's Indian officers, who brought two sheep, two hogs, and beer to the party and joined the Mohawks in the war dance all night long. My forefather Johannes Clement served in the militia. His younger brother Lewis Clement, who worked for Johnson's trading enterprise, accompanied war parties. At the Oneida Carrying Place, Lewis saw why William

Johnson's task was challenging. A captain from New England cheated and offended the Oneidas to the dismay of the New Yorkers present, who knew how much they depended on the chiefs and scouts. The captain ordered Lewis to beat up the colonist who witnessed the mistreatment of the Oneidas and spoke out against it. I imagine that Lewis followed orders.[37]

General Johnson depended on local interpreters, including my sixth great-uncle Jacobus Clement, who just a few years earlier had challenged Johnson's reputation. On behalf of Johnson and the British Empire, Jacobus traveled hundreds of miles to deliver messages, wampum belts, and presents of knives, jewelry, lace-trimmed hats, and gallons of rum to the Six Nations. He urged the sachems to accept British troops marching through their country and called them to councils with General Johnson. He witnessed Johnson's prickly exchanges with the Oneidas.[38]

At council with the Six Nations, Johnson spoke about rekindling the fire to "dazzle and scorch" the French. He extolled the Covenant Chain. "You know that we became as one body, one blood and one people," said the father of Mohawk children. Johnson threw down the war belt and ordered a large tub of punch so all could drink to the king's health. The Oneidas made their priority clear. Kanagweas, the young man newly raised up as a Wolf Clan sachem, declared, "We desire that you take care that we may keep our lands for ourselves."[39]

General Johnson, who had hoped to recruit a thousand Haudenosaunee warriors, persuaded three hundred to help him stop the French from moving south through Lake Champlain to the Hudson River. He failed to take Crown Point as ordered, but his force of militia and warriors achieved a costly victory at Lake George. Johnson came back with a musket ball in his hip that would pain him for the rest of his life. For his service, he was made superintendent of Indian affairs of the northern colonies and awarded a baronetcy, which elevated Johnson, now known as Sir William, into the lesser nobility. The Mohawks lost many warriors, including the aged Hendrick. The Oneidas and Tuscaroras came to Canajoharie to conduct condolence for the Bear Clan sachem.[40]

The French burned the British forts at the Oneida Carrying Place and took Oswego. Johnson asked Oneida warriors to accompany British troops to the Carrying Place, "now our Barrier to all this country." Kanagweas explained that little could be done to secure the vulnerable portage. Displeased, Johnson said he suspected the fidelity of the People of the Standing Stone. The Oneidas were right about the Carrying Place, concluded British military officers, who ordered their troops to return to German Flatts. There they transformed the storehouse of the Herkimers, a Palatine family of traders, into Fort Herkimer, which became the main defensive position of the British on the New York frontier.[41]

Soldiers were "infesting my house" and taking what they wanted, complained Honyost Herkimer, whose son Nicholas was a captain in the militia. The Herkimers became so unhelpful that the British forced them off their property. Nor did the troops endear themselves to the Mohawks and the Oneidas, who charged the "Red Coats," as they called them, with spreading disease and stealing. A soldier assaulted a sachem's wife, who was chopping wood and able to defend herself with an axe. Rape, a white man's crime, was incomprehensible to the Haudenosaunee. The Mohawks asked that the forts be garrisoned by the militia, "as they are People we are acquainted with & can agree better together," like the officer Peter D. Schuyler, David's son, who was married to Honyost Herkimer's daughter Elizabeth.[42]

Many Oneidas and Palatines preferred neutrality. The Oneidas sent wampum belts to the French, asking them not to attack German Flatts because they depended on provisions from there. The Oneidas passed on a message from the Palatines, who declared that they were determined to live and die by the Six Nations and begged the protection of the French. They were not white people anymore but Oneidas, wrote the Palatine leaders. "Their Blood was mixed." When the French demanded that the Palatines join them, the Palatines refused. In 1757, French soldiers and their Native allies burned German Flatts, killed forty, and carried away grain, livestock, and captives. Margaret Timmerman's granddaughter was left scalped and alive, but her husband and baby were killed. This attack, I suspect, changed some minds about neutrality. Kanagweas and the Oneidas came to condole with "our Brethren the Germans."[43]

The British turned the war around in 1758. General Johnson defeated the French at Niagara, and Major General James Wolfe captured Quebec. On the way to Montreal in 1760, General Jeffrey Amherst, the commander in chief, marched his force of four thousand regulars and six thousand colonials from Schenectady to the Carrying Place and on to Oswego and down the St. Lawrence. General Amherst relied on Mohawk Dutch men like Captain Jelles Fonda to mediate between the British troops and the six hundred warriors, including the Oneida brothers Honyery and Honyost, who joined him.[44]

At Montreal, the overwhelmed French command of 2,400 surrendered to the British. The French "sent a fladg of Truse to Genral amhost that theay would Capetelate and give op all the Contry to ous," wrote

Captain Fonda. When Fonda stopped at the Timmermans' on the way home, he no doubt regaled the family with an account of the momentous end to the contest for empire. I wonder what "all the Contry" meant to Fonda and the Timmermans. Who did they think of as "ous"? Did the Mohawk Dutch and the Palatines see themselves as fighting to defend the land of King George or the Six Nations, or their own? The Oneidas, for their part, expected Sir William to keep his word about preventing settlement in their country. They presented him with a six-row wampum belt that affirmed their truth: "This land which was given us by the Divine Being, we love as our lives."[45]

Befitting his new status, Sir William built a mansion called Johnson Hall and a town (present-day Johnstown) eight miles west of Fort Johnson. On his seven-hundred-acre estate, he set up a mill, a blacksmith shop, and a store stocked with Indian shirts sewed by local women like Elizabeth Clement Powell. The largest slave owner in the colony, Johnson hired an overseer to manage his white indentured servants and his thirty Black enslaved farmhands. In colonial New York, wealthy landlords owned several enslaved people, and many Dutch and English families had enslaved household servants or farmhands, as did the Palatine trader Nicholas Herkimer.[46]

The head of Sir William's establishment was Molly Brant, or Gonwatsijayenni (Someone Lends Her a Flower), a Wolf Clan woman from Canajoharie. Sir William's children with Catharine Weisenberg were

FIGURE 8. *Johnson Hall (Sir William Presenting Medals to the Indian Chiefs of the Six Nations at Johnstown, NY, 1772).* Edward Lamson Henry (1841–1919), artist. 1903. Albany Institute of History & Art purchase, 1993.44.

in their teens when Molly joined him in 1759, the year of Catharine's death. His eight children with Molly were raised at Johnson Hall, where Molly hosted Native leaders and colonial officials who might stay for weeks. To entertain his guests and the locals no matter what languages they spoke, Sir William held sports day events that included horse races in which the contestants rode seated backward and competitions to see who could sing the worst song or make the funniest face.[47]

Johnson had taken Molly's younger brother, Joseph Brant, or Thayendanegea (Two Sticks of Wood Bound Together), on the Lake George campaign. Then he sent Joseph to the Reverend Eleazar Wheelock's school in Connecticut, where Native and European pupils studied Latin, Greek, agriculture, and Christian theology. Johnson disapproved of the way religious instructors tried to make Native students give up their "Morality for a Sett of Gloomy Ideas" and engage in psalm singing rather than managing their worldly affairs. What he wanted was educated Mohawks who could contribute to the colony and its purpose of enriching the empire. The accomplished Joseph Brant had his own agenda, which included the preservation of Mohawk homes at Canajoharie.[48]

Following the victory over the French, Joseph Brant, Honyery, and the Timmermans saw the scramble for land at the upper castle turn ugly. George Klock and his German neighbors had "got all that may be called Good land," observed a colonial administrator to Sir William, who promised tracts to him and other officials who helped block patents on properties that Klock had properly purchased. Klock revived the controversial Canajoharie Patent by acquiring from the Livingstons the quitclaim deed, which transferred their interest in the property to him. The Mohawks protested to Sir William, who wrote that he would make it appear that Klock not only was villainous but had also threatened to cause "a great deal of trouble" and "hurt his Majesty's Indian interest."[49]

As he collected testimony against Klock's character and the legitimacy of the Canajoharie Patent, Sir William put local people on the spot by asking them to take sides. Conrad Timmerman, Margaret's son, and Jacob Klock, George's brother, agreed that the Mohawks never would have sold that land. Jacob complained about boisterous gatherings hosted by George at the Indian settlement at his house. A tavern owner testified that the signers of Klock's deed were not the sachems of Canajoharie but Mohawks from Tiononderogue and an Oneida, who confessed that he had been made drunk by George. Asked to support Klock, David Schuyler refused because he feared retaliation by the Mohawks.[50]

From Sir William's papers, I learned that Honyery backed his friend George Klock in this dispute. The sachems of Canajoharie sent a letter complaining that Klock and his people, "the Indians . . . who are in love with him for some rum" or something else illegible, might commit murder. The sachems reported that "one onyde Han Juery" threatened to kill old Brant's wife and old Brant. Some Oneidas stepped in to prevent any violence. The Mohawks, who blamed the Canajoharie Patent for causing unrest among them, said that George Klock should take his supporters back to his place. Unfortunately, there is no account of Honyery's side of this story that pits Honyery and George Klock against the Brants and Johnson.[51]

In hope that Sir William would preserve Canajoharie, the Mohawks agreed to give him the huge tract of land he wanted. George III validated this transaction by presenting Johnson with the Royal Grant of some one hundred thousand acres. Johnson knew that certain prominent New Yorkers opposed his acquisition of so much property. "I can't see the least reason why they, or any others should envy me, as my motive is the Settling the Country," he wrote, "which I have been promoting all the War at a very considerable expense, and risk." Contrary to the wishes of the Mohawks, Sir William recruited Europeans to settle on the Royal Grant. He urged the prosecution of Klock, but in the case *The King v. George Klock*, the jury acquitted George.[52]

Henry Timmerman had no reason to applaud Sir William's Royal Grant, which bordered his family's property and appears to have included a significant portion of the land the Mohawks had granted to his mother. At age thirty-one, Henry, a widower with three children, married my fifth great-grandmother Margaret Bellinger. With a Bellinger father and a Walrath mother, Margaret was connected to Palatine families throughout Canajoharie and German Flatts. One of Margaret's aunts was married to Jacob Klock, who was Henry's militia captain during the war. Another aunt and her husband, George Klock, had served as sponsors at Margaret's baptism. Margaret's uncle George, according to Sir William, was "one of the greatest Villains on this Continent."[53]

Local historians agree that George Klock may have been a scoundrel, but they suspect that he was trying to block William Johnson from achieving control over Little Falls and by extension the entire valley. The Royal Grant made Johnson the preeminent landowner around Canajoharie, where settlers like the Timmermans and Klocks deployed proper and improper methods to secure title to properties. As for the Mohawks, the more land they lost to their longtime neighbors as well as to newcomers and speculators, the more they relied on His Majesty's Indian superintendent to protect what they had left.[54]

The neighbors, splintered over land as they were, came together to build an Anglican church for the Canajoharie Mohawks. Sir William paid for it, and Joseph Brant donated the land. George Klock and his son-in-law Ebenezer Cox supplied the lumber. The Timmermans and Herkimers helped to construct it. The Indian Castle Church, which still stands, was presented to Joseph Brant, who accepted the gift on behalf of the Mohawks. To the Europeans, the presence of a church made the ground sacred. To the Haudenosaunee, it already was.[55]

Dividing Lines

After the French and Indian War, Honyery and his wife, an adopted Shawnee captive named Sarah Martin, also called Tyonajanegan (Two Kettles Together), lived at Oriske. Honyery had a successful farm, where, as the hunting declined, he took up the European practice of keeping domestic livestock. The Oneidas also earned income by operating a portage service at the Carrying Place. Oriske, like Canajoharie, was endangered. For decades, the Oneidas had protested the Oriskany Patent of thirty thousand acres, acquired by wealthy colonial officials back in 1705. From London, the Board of Trade had recommended a legal obliteration of the fraudulent patent, but nothing happened. Sir William, who had plans to build a canal at the Carrying Place, speculated on the Oriskany Patent.[56]

The Oneidas spread out around their territory in towns no longer surrounded with palisades. Many of them lived in cabins furnished with European goods, including teapots and candlesticks. A new town (present-day Oneida Castle) on Oneida Creek was called Kanonwalohale, or "where there is a skull impaled." Christian converts lived there along with Samuel Kirkland, their Presbyterian missionary. Kanagweas, who felt the old beliefs were best, lived six miles east at Old Oneida, located between present-day Vernon Center and Sherrill.[57]

Polly's father, Louis Denny, lived in the Schoharie Valley with his wife's family. Born a Frenchman on the Illinois River, Louis was eighteen when he fought against the Six Nations. He and his brother Martin were taken prisoner. They were separated at Niagara Falls, and Louis never saw his brother again. Louis, who was about five feet eight inches tall with light blue eyes and a deep, powerful voice, was adopted by the Oneidas into the Bear Clan. He married Maria, a Mohawk of the Turtle Clan, who was described as a large, noble-looking woman. Prominent Schoharie Mohawks and white landowners sponsored the baptisms of the Denny children, who grew up speaking Mohawk, Oneida, and French at home and Dutch, German, and English with the neighbors.[58]

Although Louis Denny remained friendly with the Vroomans of Schoharie, he witnessed the loss of Mohawk land to that family. The Schoharie Mohawks sent a petition asking that the sale of their lands by a few Indians without their consent be disregarded. Sir William thought the Vroomans should refrain from pressuring the Schoharie Mohawks to sell if they did not want to, but he did not stop the sale. In Schoharie at New Year's, the Mohawks and settlers carried on the tradition of calling on each other and sharing food and drink, but bad feelings over the land festered.[59]

The local tensions over Oriske, Schoharie, and Canajoharie were felt at the great treaty council of 1768. Burdened with the expense of governing much of North America, the British Parliament had tried to raise revenue from the colonies with exceedingly unpopular taxes. It also sought to cut the cost of protecting the frontier by keeping the peace with Indigenous nations, which meant respecting their territory. They could stop white expansion, officials assured Native leaders, if they drew a clear boundary between their colonies and Native territory.[60]

New York assemblymen said it was "impossible to discover the true Owners of any Lands among unlettered Barbarians" who kept no papers. Not true, knew William Johnson. The Six Nations understood exactly where their boundaries were. Sir William also had learned who were the most formidable protectors of the land, which was why he had requested that the Haudenosaunee women stay away from a treaty council held a few years earlier. They came anyway. "It was always the custom for them to be present on Such Occasions being of much estimation amongst us, in that we proceed from them," explained Kanagweas to the man who lived with Molly Brant.[61]

The largest Indian treaty council ever held in colonial America took place at the Oneida Carrying Place, where the British had constructed the impressive Fort Stanwix. The Haudenosaunee came to preserve their territory, and the colonial delegates came for land. John Penn, governor of Pennsylvania, and William Franklin, governor of New Jersey and son of Ben, were there. A Virginian represented the speculators George Washington and Thomas Jefferson. Sir William arrived with twenty boatloads of presents. He followed the Haudenosaunee protocols of making opening addresses of thanksgiving, which Europeans found tedious. On the third day, they got down to business.[62]

The Oneidas were the major obstacle. Five hundred of them, almost half of their entire population, attended the council held on their territory. The sachems were willing to deal to fulfill their role as peacekeepers and receivers of gifts for their people in need. Being generous with their land, they believed, could earn them respect and reciprocity from the colonial government. Honyery and the warriors wanted to keep the Carrying Place. Through three days and nights of deliberation, Johnson promised more presents and cash. He said he would not be able to restrain settlers without a boundary line.[63]

In the end, the Oneidas gave up lands in the Oriskany Patent, with the proviso that the British and the Oneidas would share control of the Carrying Place and that Oriske would remain an Oneida town. For the first time, the Oneidas ceded territory at a treaty council. They did it because Sir William pledged to secure their remaining territory. He promised that Oriske, Canajoharie, and Tiononderogue would remain Indian towns even though they were on the British side of the boundary line.[64]

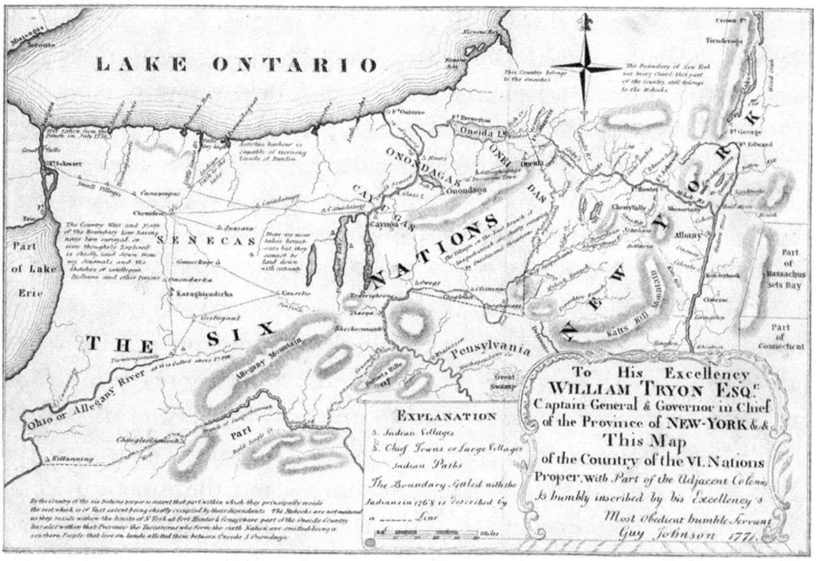

FIGURE 9. This 1771 map shows the Line of Property as the boundary between the Six Nations and New York. Guy Johnson, "To His Excellency William Tryon, Esq. Captain General and Governor in Chief of the Province of New York." New York State Library Manuscripts and Special Collections, Albany.

The Line of Property began four miles northwest of the Carrying Place, ran southeast to the Susquehanna, and then turned west. In return for money and goods, the Six Nations had protected their own land by giving away millions of acres in the Ohio Valley that belonged to other Natives. The Line of Property failed to stop westward settlement. "It is now worse than it was before," said a Mohawk of Canajoharie. Johnson himself invited four hundred Scots to settle north of Johnstown.[65]

By then, the inhabitants of the Mohawk Valley had blended in some ways and not in others. Guests dined at Johnson Hall with sachems who dressed like white people. Many farmers and trappers preferred to wear the soft, rugged buckskins and moccasins made by Mohawks and Oneidas. Some colonists had tattoos as the Haudenosaunee did, but they rarely painted their faces. Few adopted the fashion among well-to-do Europeans of whitening the face with lead-based paint and powdering their hair. For the people of the Six Nations, long, smooth hair, styled with bear oil, meant spiritual health.[66]

Sir William and Molly hosted a celebration in honor of newly created Tryon County. Named after the governor, it was set off from Albany County and bordered on the west by the Line of Property. Johnstown was designated the county seat, where the election of Sir William's supporters to public office was celebrated at the tavern owned by Sir William, who also owned the church, jail, and courthouse. Governor William Tryon, the Livingstons, the Van Rensselaers, Philip Schuyler, and Nicholas Herkimer attended the festivities. George Klock, who was not invited, made offensive remarks during the speeches. Joseph Brant complained to the governor about Klock, who later sailed on the *Sir William Johnson* to London to advocate his land cases and protest Johnson's ascendancy over the Mohawk Valley. George failed to obtain an audience, perhaps because Sir William had written ahead to warn officials against him.[67]

In July 1774, Sir William held a Six Nations council at a time of crisis in the colonies. The previous December, the radical Sons of Liberty had protested taxation without representation by dumping tea into Boston Harbor. Parliament had cracked down on the colonials and passed the Quebec Act, which was intended to restrict expansion by making the Ohio Valley part of the Canadian province. Land the American colonists believed should belong to them had been given to people they had defeated in the French and Indian War. In response, twelve of the colonies chose delegates to the First Continental Congress in Philadelphia, where they would consider uniting as Ben Franklin had urged twenty years earlier.

The Six Nations, situated between Canada and the unruly colonies, would play a decisive role in any conflict on the continent. At council, Sir William listened to complaints about George Klock as well as the presence of white squatters in Iroquoia. Wait patiently, he advised, and do not use violence. Feeling unwell, he ordered pipes, tobacco, and liquor for the Haudenosaunee delegates, adjourned the council, went away, suffered a stroke, and died. Kanagweas led the sachems in condolence for the great man.[68]

Sir William left most of his estate to his white son, Sir John Johnson, who had been knighted by George III. Obedient to the wishes of his father, Sir John had married a New York City heiress after removing his mistress, a Mohawk Dutch descendant of Marie du Trieux and Otstok, and their children to a tenant house. The new baronet sent Molly Brant back to Canajoharie, where Sir William had willed tracts of one to four thousand acres in the Royal Grant to his and Molly's children. To Molly, Sir William gave Lot 1 on the river next to the Timmerman family. Molly's lot, it appears, included a sliver of the tract granted to Margaret Timmerman by the Mohawks. The stories of these people on the land, it seems to me, illustrate how their lives were woven together and unraveling.[69]

Honyery's family and the Dennys saw the fracture lines. The Mohawks had agreed to share territory, especially with kinfolk, but, as the years went by, they felt that Europeans had taken too much, often by engaging in corrupt conduct regarding surveys, deeds, and patents like the ones claiming Canajoharie and Oriskany. With mixed results, the Mohawks and Oneidas appealed to the colonial authorities to obey their own laws. Honyery saw William Johnson and the British Empire ignore guarantees of Oneida land in their pursuit of Oriske and the Carrying Place. By the 1770s, the Dennys were about the only Native family left in Schoharie who still brought their babies to be baptized at the Dutch and German churches.

As for the Clements and Timmermans, they pursued the dream of generations to become owners of property. For most of the 1700s, these Mohawk Dutch traders and Palatine farmers were closer to the Mohawks and Oneidas than to the English authorities. As go-betweens, they participated in a colonial enterprise based on the European assumption of dominion over the Native peoples and their territory, but not always in a manner intended to advance the British Empire. After the defeat of France, they witnessed the rise of Sir William, the diminished clout of the Mohawks, and embittered rivalries over places of significance.

My forebears, I suspect, would have resented whoever came between them and their goal of land.

Some of my landless ancestors appear to have admired both the territory and the independence of the Six Nations. They were the indentured servants and tenant farmers of James Duane, an Indian commissioner of New York and one of William Johnson's distinguished pallbearers. Although he was a skilled lawyer, Duane had lost his case when he represented the Crown in a suit charging George Klock with defrauding the Indians. Duane, who lived at his country home called Gramercy in Manhattan, pursued his ambition of becoming a landed gentleman like Robert Livingston, 3rd lord of the manor and his father-in-law. He set about acquiring an estate between Schenectady and Schoharie called Duanesburg.[70]

Duane relied on tenants and indentured servants to clear his land and work in his potash plant, where timber was turned into ashes in demand in Europe for the making of soap and glass. The indentured boys believed the plant manager was a tyrant, and they threatened to run away. "I will rather neeaver sarve him an hour if I can posibel avoid it," wrote one of them, my fourth great-grandfather John Myers, who probably had limited schooling. Duane's overseer blamed John for his part in the resistance and withheld the "freedom clothes" due to him at the end of his indenture. John protested to Duane that he had earned the new suit that signified his status as a free man.[71]

The overseer faced another rebellion in the early 1770s when he ordered each of the tenant families to furnish a man to work at Duane's sawmill. A feudal tradition common in colonial New York land contracts required a tenant to pay part of his annual rent by doing a day of work for the landlord. The Dutch, German, and Scottish tenants, who constructed roads, hauled timber, or worked at the landlord's mills, despised this requirement of unpaid labor because it implied a permanent status of servitude. As Cadwallader Colden observed, these people had not uprooted their lives and ventured so far to be dependent on landlords. They viewed their indentures and tenancy as a temporary step toward someday owning their own land.[72]

The recalcitrant tenants, the overseer wrote to Duane, held a "grand council" like their Mohawk and Oneida neighbors did. They did not mind helping the miller, but they thought about what it would mean for the next generation if they accepted additional unpaid labor. They wanted to pass on freedom, not bondage, to their children. The tenants reached a consensus and delivered their decision to the overseer:

they refused to work for nothing at the mill. For their pretension to rule themselves, the overseer concluded, "Silly people, but in such things they must be humored."[73]

The people of the Mohawk Valley, both Natives and newcomers, associated land with home and freedom. The question of how to protect it was not an easy one to answer as relations deteriorated between rebellious colonists and their British rulers. At the Boston Tea Party, the protesters had dressed like Mohawks. With painted faces and war whoops, they assumed both a disguise and an identity as righteous disturbers, the authentic owners of the land who were free to govern themselves. They emulated the people they longed to displace.[74]

CHAPTER 3

For King or Country

"It is our fixed Resolution . . . to be free, or die," declared Mohawk Valley rebels in 1775. When war broke out between British troops and colonial minutemen in Massachusetts, Tryon County divided over allegiance to the king or the Continental Congress. Rebels like my forefather Henry Timmerman called themselves patriots or lovers of their country. Those who remained true to George III, like Sir John Johnson, were called Loyalists or Tories. The rebels objected to being ruled by one family, they said, and feared that Sir John would use his Mohawk allies to keep "us in Awe." When dozens of prominent Loyalists left to join the British in Canada, the rebels installed their own officials. "The River will be in Ashes," threatened the ousted Loyalist sheriff. The Indians, he declared, would burn it.[1]

I knew the Oneidas considered their role on the side of the United States during the American Revolution to be a turning point in their history and a key factor in their land claims cases. I wanted to understand their wartime experience, which I had grown up knowing nothing about. I wondered what happened to my ancestors in the Mohawk Valley and Polly Denny's extended family of Mohawks and Oneidas at Schoharie and Oriske. Did they encounter each other in the horrific and heartrending conflict that ensued?

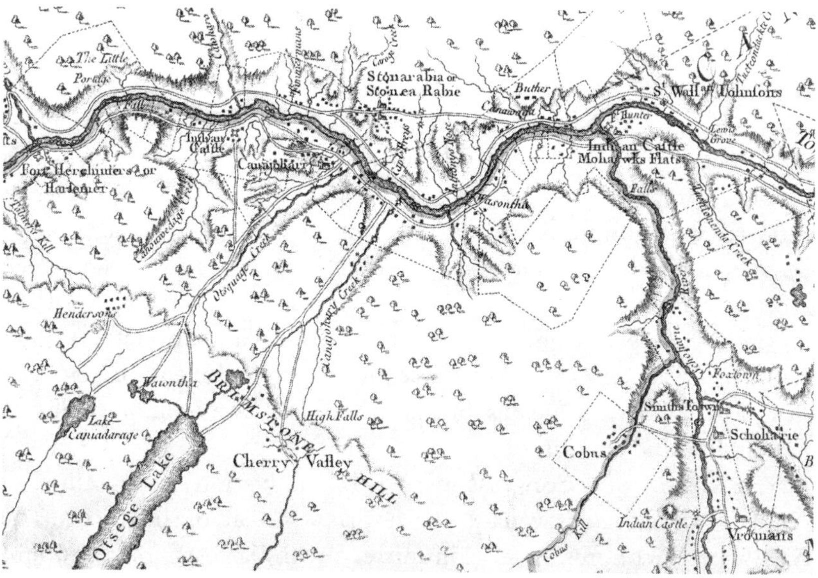

FIGURE 10. Detail from "Province de New York: En 4 feuilles." 1777. Drawn by John Montrésor, this map shows the home of Louis and Maria Denny at the Indian Castle on Schoharie Creek in the lower right-hand corner, and in the upper left, the Indian Castle of the Canajoharie Mohawks upriver from the settlement known as Timmermans. New York Public Library Digital Collections.

When the fighting started, everyone wanted to know what the Six Nations would do. At councils across Iroquoia, Haudenosaunee leaders deliberated over a course of action. There was no good choice. The Mohawks and the Oneidas on either side of the Line of Property, drawn in 1768 to mark the border between Indian and English territory, were in danger. Even as the sachems and clan mothers advocated neutrality as the best way to keep the peace, they feared their people would be in the middle of the clash to come.[2]

The warriors Honyery and Joseph Brant did not hesitate to take sides. Brant, a longtime friend of the Johnson family, was an ally of the Loyalists. He called on the Haudenosaunee to "defend their Lands & Liberty against the Rebels," who sought to be "sole Masters of this Continent." In early 1776, Captain Brant went to London to meet King George, attend balls, and advocate for the Six Nations. He complained about the Palatine trader George Klock to British officials, who promised to attend to the dispute over Canajoharie after they had finished putting down the rebellion.[3]

Honyery, who had objected to the British takeover of the Oneida Carrying Place, did not consider the king or the Johnson family to be allies. He was remembered as "quite a gentleman in his demeanor," according to the oral history interviews conducted years later with Oneidas who knew him or had been told about him. At Oriske, Honyery had become a wealthy man, the richest of the Oneidas, and the holder of property worth more than that of the average colonist. In accordance with Haudenosaunee practice, the warriors chose their own war chief. Elected war chief of the Wolf Clan, Honyery led the warriors of Oriske to join their rebel neighbors at militia drills in German Flatts. I don't know why Honyery took this consequential action ahead of any decision reached by the Oneidas, but he appears to have been preparing to protect his land and kinfolk.[4]

The Continental Congress invited the Six Nations to a council in Albany to renew the Covenant Chain with it instead of the British. The five-member congressional Committee on Indian Affairs was dominated by the New Yorkers James Duane, Philip Schuyler, and Philip Livingston, the son of the Philip Livingston who forty years earlier had acquired the controversial Canajoharie Patent. At the council, the congressmen relied not on local Mohawk Dutch interpreters but on the New Englanders Samuel Kirkland and James Dean, a recent graduate of Dartmouth College who as a boy had been sent by his missionary family to live with Oneidas as a sort of goodwill exchange student. Both men were trusted by the Oneidas and, like Joseph Brant, had attended Eleazer Wheelock's school.[5]

The congressmen did not make it easy for their interpreters. Their abstract speech, an observer recalled, sounded "like a chapter out of Locke." The English philosopher John Locke wrote that in contrast to "the wild Indian, who knows no enclosure," the civilized man owned and improved his property. In doing so, he enjoyed not only the material possession of it but also the freedom to think and act independently. The role of government was to protect the right to own property, Locke argued, not to deprive an individual of it without their consent by taxation without representation. This belief that individual ownership of property meant independence inspired rich and poor American colonials alike.[6]

It was not, however, a winning argument to present to the Haudenosaunee, who feared the loss of their territory and with it their freedom. Instead, congressional leaders described how the colonies had held a great council fire and agreed to unite as one. They promised to keep the roads open and free for their Iroquois brothers "as long as this Earth remains." The Six Nations pledged neutrality, and, in return, the Americans promised to reopen trade and call for an investigation of disputed land claims. The policy of neutrality preserved the unity of the People of the Longhouse and satisfied the colonials who did not want to take on both the Six Nations and the British Empire. The congressional delegation was as impressed by Haudenosaunee diplomacy and treaty making as the Dutch and English had been. "It is amazing with what exactness these people recollect all that has been said to them," noted a Maryland man.[7]

The Mohawk Valley rebels, meanwhile, learned that governing themselves was not easy. They created the Tryon County Committee of Safety, which was responsible for raising money, supplying the militia, and suppressing Loyalist activity. After months of meetings, the committee members established basic rules of conduct: Everyone must take his seat and stay there. Each man may give his opinion, but only one at a time, while the rest must be quiet. There was to be no discussion of private affairs. This was not the time to sell a horse.[8]

The Oneidas, expert at holding council and mobilizing for war, helped the rebel colonists to focus on the crisis at hand. The sachems and warriors attended a committee meeting chaired by militia commander Nicholas Herkimer in German Flatts. They advised, the rebels recorded, "that we should not neglect to shut (in their manner of speaking) the Gate at Fort Stanwix, that nothing might pass and repass to the hurt of our Country." The Oneidas assured the committee that they would share any news and trusted the settlers to do the same. What the Oneidas did not say was that they would use these exchanges of intelligence as an opportunity to educate their rebel neighbors about strategy.[9]

As it organized the militia, the committee faced a challenge to its authority from the patriots of Canajoharie, who lived north of the river. The committee was "a parcel of great Rascals," declared Thomas Baxter, who operated the ferry at East Canada Creek. Anyone who tried to force them to appear before it would get "a good flogging," he said. The constable asked, "And who shall do it?" and Baxter retorted, "We and in particular Henry Timmerman can do it." He did not explain why Henry was their champion, although it is a safe bet that Henry, as the youngest of fifteen, knew how to handle himself in a fight.[10]

Upon deliberation, the committee resolved to forgive Baxter and his neighbor Christian House for their "mutinous pretentions" if they acknowledged their faults and promised to pay strict obedience to its orders in the future. Henry Timmerman stated before the committee that he and his neighbors had had no say over who would command them. They preferred to be enlisted in a company closer to their homes and wanted to elect their own chief. The committee resolved that the Timmermans and others should train under Christian House, their choice as militia captain, and serve in Colonel Jacob Klock's regiment.[11]

The more painful task before patriot leaders was sorting out who was for king or country. Some people made it easy. "I am a King's Man, who dare say anything aginst it," said William of Canajoharie, the Mohawk son of William Johnson who came to Colonel Klock's house wearing two pistols, a gun, and a broadsword. William declared, "I only pity the wives and children, for I shall come with 500 men, which I have ready, to cut off the whole river and burn their houses this fall yet."[12]

Lewis Clement, the surviving son of Joseph and Anna, was also a king's man with close ties to the Mohawks and Sir John. Lewis was the proud owner of three houses, an orchard, sixty acres of cleared land, woods, a share in a sawmill, and three enslaved people. The rebel Jelles Fonda reported that after Lewis met with Loyalists at Oswego, he announced he had twelve guns at home that he might soon be using. "Is it not a pity," said Lewis to a neighbor, "that I being a man of a good Estate must go and leave the same for [the] sake of these damned Fondas, but I shall soon make up a good Number of Indians, and return with them to destroy and ruin such people all here about."[13]

Lewis Clement was "striving to do hurt to the Country," reported Nicholas Herkimer, whose own brother remained loyal to the king. The rebels held a secret trial where Lewis was found guilty and offered the choice of a fine or jail time. Lewis refused to pay a "single copper" and chose confinement. Little Abraham, the neutral sachem of Tionon-derogue, applied for the release and forgiveness of Lewis. The committee agreed, but only to please the Mohawks. Once freed, Lewis and his eldest son, Joseph, left for Canada to serve as officers in His Majesty's Indian Department. They were joined by Sir John Johnson, who formed 1,300 Loyalists into the King's Royal Regiment of New York.[14]

The Clements, like many families, split apart. Lewis's rebel nephew, my fourth great-grandfather Lambert Clement of Johnstown, enlisted at age eighteen in the Tryon County militia. I don't know why Lambert was a patriot. People chose a side for all sorts of reasons. Religion, class, race, or ethnicity was not a clear indicator. To find out what happened to my rebel forefathers Lambert Clement, Henry Timmerman, and John Myers, I relied on histories as well as eyewitness testimony included in pension applications submitted by Revolutionary War veterans. These testimonies, made decades later, contain clear and foggy memories and must be used with care. Lambert stated that he was serving at Fort Stanwix, guarding the Oneida Carrying Place, when the United States declared its independence in July 1776.[15]

That summer the British prepared a successful attack on New York City, and pressure grew on the Oneidas to abandon neutrality. Onondagas and Cayugas warned that if the white people at Albany defeated the king, they would push the Indians out of their lands. Joseph Brant assured the Oneidas that the king's troops were victorious. If this was so, the Oneidas answered, the king did not need them. At the end of the year, General Philip Schuyler, commander of the Continental Army's Northern Department, sent news of rare American victories in New Jersey along with six barrels of rum to the People of the Standing Stone. Schuyler, who knew what mattered most to the Oneidas, pledged that the United States would respect their territory by honoring the Line of Property.[16]

As consensus among the Haudenosaunee disintegrated, the Onondagas covered the council fire in early 1777. Each of the Six Nations could go its own way. Seneca, Cayuga, and Onondaga warriors joined the Mohawk supporters of the British. The Oneidas and Tuscaroras supplied intelligence to the rebels. British general John Burgoyne planned to move south from Canada to seize Albany. His force was to be joined by Colonel Barry St. Leger and Sir John, who prepared to head east from Oswego, vanquish Fort Stanwix, and take the Mohawk Valley. By controlling the waterways of New York, the British aimed to cut off the patriot stronghold in New England and force it to submit.[17]

In June, the men of the Mohawk Valley held a last council when General Herkimer marched several hundred militiamen to the Unadilla River to meet Joseph Brant and his Loyalist force. At first everyone was polite. Henry's nephew Jacob J. Timmerman recalled that Captain Brant and General Herkimer agreed not to cross Oriskany Creek into the other's territory. If so, that meant Oriske straddled the front line. Civility collapsed when Brant asked whether Colonel Ebenezer Cox was the son-in-law of George Klock. Everyone, including Brant, knew that he was. Cox, described by his admirers as a bold man and by others as a hothead, cursed at Brant. The allusion to the feud over land at Canajoharie brought the council to an end. An invasion was coming from the west, Brant told Herkimer, and he and his men would join it.[18]

General Schuyler ordered General Herkimer to send two hundred militiamen to Fort Stanwix. Herkimer sent one hundred. "We are but few," he wrote to Schuyler, as he explained that no one wanted to leave their families unprotected. Without more troops, he added, "I fear the Indians will make a Ravage of our Frontier Country." No reinforcements were available, replied the New York Council of Safety, as Burgoyne moved south and took Fort Ticonderoga on Lake Champlain. The people of the Mohawk Valley, said the council, should show bravery becoming the character of freemen and defend themselves. The message, in other words, was, "You are on your own."[19]

Holding the Ground at Oriskany

Fortunately for the rebels, they were not alone. The coming invasion of their nation convinced many Oneidas to stand against the British. This decision, made in agony because it divided them from most of the Six Nations, had practical justifications. The Oneidas had been promised by Congress and General Schuyler that their land would be preserved. They had sent some war chiefs, including the impressive Skenandoah (The Deer), to assess the fighting capacity of the Continental Army and be welcomed by its commander, George Washington. Honyery and the warriors of Oriske knew they could not protect their home by themselves.[20]

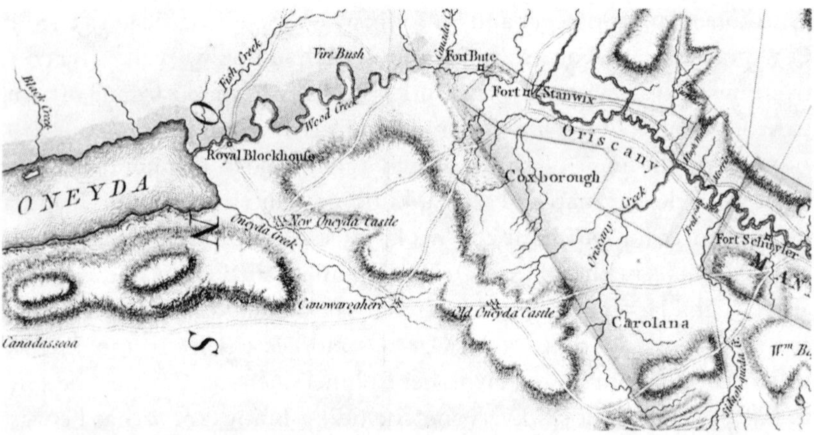

FIGURE 11. Oneida towns in the 1770s included Old Oneyda Castle and Canowagohere or Kanonwalohale (present-day Oneida Castle). Oriske, on the New York side of the Line of Property, was not shown on this map made by Claude Joseph Sauthier. Detail from "A Chorographical Map of the Province of New York in North America, Divided into Counties, Manors, Patents, and Townships," published in London by William Faden in 1779. Courtesy of the Norman B. Leventhal Map & Education Center at the Boston Public Library.

"Brothers, I therefore desire you to be Spirited," entreated Bear Clan sachem Thomas Sinavis. Thomas, the intrepid leader of reconnaissance missions to Canada made at the request of General Schuyler, knew the strength of the invading force. Speaking before the Tryon County Committee of Safety, the sachem called on the militia to march to the assistance of Fort Stanwix. "Save your Country before it is too late," he warned. If the enemy took the fort, they would all be destroyed. He urged the rebels to block the Carrying Place by filling Wood Creek with trees. Men of Captain House's company helped to clog the narrow stream.[21]

Oneida scouts alerted the twenty-eight-year-old Colonel Peter Gansevoort, the commander of Fort Stanwix, that 750 British regulars, Hessians (the German troops hired to serve King George), and Sir John's Loyalists, accompanied by about 800 Senecas, Cayugas, Mohawks, some Onondagas, and a few Tuscaroras and Oneidas, were four days away. While the defenders prepared for attack, they scrounged around for red, white, and blue fabric to make a striped flag. With a "general Exhilaration of spirits," recorded Lieutenant Colonel Marinus Willet of Long Island, they raised their banner on the morning of 3 August 1777. To the rebels, the flag meant that the fort, situated on the Oneida homeland, belonged to the United States. Around the fort, Oneida warriors positioned themselves as lookouts.[22]

The first Oneida to engage with the enemy was one of the nation's fastest runners, Paul Powless, or Tegahsweangalolis (The Sawmill), of Kanonwalohale. The young warrior saw Joseph Brant approach with an advance party. Brant tried to recruit Powless by saying that the great power of the king would crush the Oneidas. Powless replied that he and the Oneidas "had joined their fortunes with those of the Americans and would share with them whatever good or evil might come." He sprinted away to warn his fellow scouts, while Sarah, Honyery's wife, notified General Herkimer that the enemy had arrived. It took the British troops nine days to clear the debris out of Wood Creek so they could get their weapons and supplies near the fort. St. Leger knew his artillery was inadequate, but he was confident that his professionals would prevail over amateurs.[23]

Sergeant Conrad Timmerman, his sons Lieutenant John C. Timmerman and Private William C. Timmerman, and Captain Christian House were mowing wheat when they were hailed by their neighbor, Colonel Jacob Klock. The enemy, Klock said, was at Wood Creek on its way to

Fort Stanwix. He ordered the men to march immediately. Ensign Henry Timmerman and his nephews Jacob J., John G., Jacob L., Conrad L., and Henry L. joined them. Henry left behind his wife, Margaret, and their nine children. The youngest, my fourth great-grandmother Anna Rosina, was Henry and Margaret's first child to be born in the United States.[24]

The Tryon County militia, called out by General Herkimer, gathered at German Flatts. Every free and healthy man between sixteen and sixty was expected to report with his own musket, bayonet sword or tomahawk, and ammunition. Those who were too old or too ill or too lame to march presented themselves armed and ready to defend those left behind. Captain House, concerned that they were about to leave their families without protection, ordered Lieutenant John C. Timmerman to take some men and return home. Their job was not simply to guard against any surprise attack. They were supposed to prevent the "Tory women" from passing on information about troop movements to the enemy. Lieutenant John's detail failed to stop Molly Brant of Canajoharie from warning her brother Joseph that the militia was on its way to relieve Fort Stanwix.[25]

On the second day, the relief column crossed the Mohawk River at a ford near Old Fort Schuyler (present-day Utica) and camped that night near Oriske. There they were joined by at least sixty Oneidas led by Honyery. The warriors included Kanadolock (Peter Bread) and Louis Atayataghronghta, a Wolf Clan war chief from Kahnawake, a Mohawk town on the St. Lawrence near Montreal. Louis, the son of an African father and an Abenaki mother, had earned a reputation for bravery when he fought against the British in the French and Indian War. He had assured General Washington that he was eager to fight the British again.[26]

From Oriske that night, General Herkimer sent a message to Fort Stanwix. He asked Colonel Gansevoort to send out a diversionary force to distract the enemy as the militia approached and to signal that he had done so by firing off a cannon shot. While Herkimer waited for the signal, his troops grew impatient. Colonel Ebenezer Cox and others accused the general of being a coward, or a Tory like his brother. When Herkimer gave in and ordered the militia to march, the men cheered.[27]

Colonel Cox's First Regiment from the Canajoharie District led the way, followed by Colonel Klock's Second Regiment from the Palatine District north of the river. The Oneidas came next, led by Honyery, with Sarah and their son Cornelius, Honyery's brother Plattcop, and his sister's husband, Shagoyontha (Drag Him in the House), also known as

Cornelius Shagoyontha or Henry Cornelius. Honyery was too old for military service, one of his young warriors later recalled, "yet used to go fearlessly into the fights." Next marched Peter Bellinger's Fourth Regiment from the German Flatts District, followed by the wagons carrying ammunition and provisions, and the Third Regiment from the Mohawk District, which included Tiononderogue and Johnstown.[28]

When they learned that eight hundred men of the Tryon County militia supported by Oneida warriors were on their way, the British officers, Loyalists, and war chiefs conferred. Sir John and his father's longtime agent, Major John Butler, knew that many of their men had friends and relations in the militia. They wondered if they should hold a parley and try to convince the militia to turn back. The Senecas approved of this idea. They were there to protect their land, not to fight their Oneida brothers. Captain Brant disagreed. He knew how stubborn the militia was and dismissed the Oneidas as traitors. The thirty-four-year-old Mohawk offended the Seneca chiefs with his take-charge attitude, but Brant won the debate. St. Leger agreed with the plan for an ambush.[29]

Five hundred Loyalists, their Six Nations allies, and a detachment of Hessians hid in the densely wooded high ground. They waited until the militiamen at the head of the column began to climb out of a ravine and then caught the rebels in a crossfire. Colonel Cox fell. General Herkimer, at the lead, turned back to the ravine. A bullet struck his horse and came out through the general's leg. His men dragged Herkimer up the ridge and leaned him against a tree, from where he calmly issued orders. Brant and his men attacked the supply carts and killed drivers and oxen. At the other end of the column, some men of the Third Regiment fled and others "feariously engaged" the enemy.[30]

Holding the middle were the Oneidas and the men of Klock's and Bellinger's regiments. After firing, it took twenty seconds to load a musket and a minute or more to load a rifle. The warriors waited for these moments to rush the line with tomahawks and knives, hacking into the militiamen. Some ran, while others, using their muskets as clubs, drove the attackers back. It was hard to tell friend from foe. The Senecas later complained that some of their warriors were killed by Loyalists. Others knew the enemy too well. The militiaman Abram Quackenbush was urged to surrender by his boyhood friend, a Mohawk from Fort Hunter, and when Abram refused, the Mohawk shot and missed Abram's head by an inch. Abram fired back and killed his friend.[31]

Honyery, armed with musket, tomahawk, and sword, killed nine men. After he was wounded in his right wrist, his musket was loaded by Sarah, who put aside her own gun. Their son Cornelius killed two men. Plattcop ran through the middle of the fight three times, slashing his tomahawk right and left against enemy fighters. He survived the day with a broken arm and would be remembered as a "very famous warrior." Louis Atayataghronghta noticed that an enemy Indian was a crack shot. When the warrior next rose to take aim, Louis fired. "That fellow will do no more harm," declared Louis, who went to take the dead man's scalp.[32]

The combatants had been fighting for six hours when a runner alerted the Loyalists and their Indian allies that their camps were being ransacked by troops from Fort Stanwix. The warriors pulled back, and British forces followed. Their losses included thirty Loyalists and thirty-six Senecas killed. "Completest victory," reported Colonel St. Leger to General Burgoyne. "The militia will never rally." Around 150 rebels walked away. Most of the several dozen men taken prisoner were executed out of retribution. Sarah rode off to tell the valley the outcome of what would be called the battle of Oriskany.[33]

Henry lay as though dead with a bullet through his side. He was hauled back to Oriske by his nephew John G. and three comrades, who set down Henry's litter and collapsed to the ground. If anyone tended to Henry that night, my guess is that it was probably Oneida women. The survivors carried away about fifty wounded, including General Herkimer, who later bled to death when a surgeon amputated his leg. There was no one to bury the dead. Asked later about the missing, neighbors would say, "He went away and did not come back." The militia did not give up, people remembered. The men had held the ground.[34]

Joseph Brant and Sir John proposed to follow up the battle by attacking the valley and breaking the back of the rebellion. Colonel St. Leger instead used the threat of an attack to try to convince Gansevoort to surrender. When Gansevoort refused, the British laid siege and bombarded Fort Stanwix with mortar shells and sniper fire while Oneida runners delivered the news to General Schuyler in Albany. "The militia are entirely cut to pieces," the general informed John Hancock, the president of the Continental Congress. Schuyler, who had sent troops north to face Burgoyne, decided to risk dividing his force to rescue Fort Stanwix. He gave Major General Benedict Arnold nine hundred Continental troops, which he knew wasn't enough. He told Arnold the Oneidas "must be cherished" and sent a handsome cash present for them.[35]

The rebels improved their poor odds with a trick. St. Leger had sent Major Butler's son Walter to deliver a proclamation threatening the people of Tryon County. If they did not persuade Fort Stanwix to surrender,

Britain's Native allies would "put every soul to death." Butler and his party were taken prisoner, tried as spies under the order of General Arnold, and sentenced to be hanged. One of the prisoners was Honyost Schuyler, the son of Peter D. Schuyler and Elizabeth Herkimer, who has been described in some accounts as an easily manipulated half-wit and in others as "crazy like a fox"—someone who, if caught, always got away. I think the latter description is a better fit.[36]

Honyost Schuyler, who had grown up with Mohawks and was said to have married an Oneida woman, was willing to play both sides. Most of the Mohawk Valley Schuylers were rebels, but Honyost had gone off with one of William Johnson's Mohawk sons rather than join the militia because "he did not like to fight," said his brother. After his brother and mother pleaded for his clemency, the rebel commanders offered a deal. In return for his freedom, Honyost would pretend to have eluded his captors and warn the Indians with St. Leger that a powerful rebel army was fast approaching from the east. Two Oneidas volunteered to come from different directions with the same report. General Arnold approved the plan, but he held Honyost's brother as a hostage to ensure his cooperation.[37]

Honyost Schuyler's coat was shot through as though he had been fired on while escaping. He and the Oneidas delivered their "news" to St. Leger's Native allies, who, already demoralized by their losses, began to leave. The false rumors that General Arnold was coming with two to three thousand men and that General Burgoyne had been defeated reached St. Leger. With his force diminished by more than half, the British commander decided to retreat. A few days later, Arnold's troops marched past the dead at Oriskany and arrived at Fort Stanwix.[38]

"The Oneidas and Tuscaroras have been exceedingly friendly to us in the present dispute," reported General Arnold. For that, the Oneidas of Oriske would pay. The men were away when an enemy war party attacked and burned the town while the women and children hid in the woods. Honyery lost his frame house, barn, wagon, sleigh, tools, kettles, and plates, along with fifteen horses, six cows, sixty hogs, two sheep, and one hundred chickens. His crops of oats and wheat were destroyed. His one hundred bushels of corn stored for the winter went up in flames. The log house of his sister and Shagoyontha was ashes. The horses and livestock of Plattcop were gone. Their town, which the warriors of Oriske had fought to protect, was the first in the valley to be ravaged.[39]

Peter Dygert of the Committee of Safety urged the Oneidas to make up their losses by confiscating the belongings of Canajoharie

Mohawks aligned with the British. Take two cows for every one you lost, Dygert told Honyery. The Wolf Clan war chief instructed David Schuyler, the son or grandson of the early settler David Schuyler, to deliver two hogs to nearby families. David and Honyost Schuyler harvested the corn in the Mohawk fields. They delivered barrels of flour to a neutral Mohawk leader at Canajoharie. The Oneidas and the militiamen looted the house of Molly Brant, who had fled to Canada with her children and two enslaved women. They divided up furniture, jewelry, fine china, and wagonloads of crops. One of Molly's silk gowns was seen on Peter Dygert's daughter. Honyery moved his homeless family into Molly's house. He was on familiar ground near the Klocks and Timmermans.[40]

Captain Honyery and the Oneida Allies

The Oneidas and Tuscaroras declared their alliance with the United States when they accepted the war hatchet at General Schuyler's council held in Albany a few weeks later. They would use it against the British, they said, but not against their Haudenosaunee brothers. The warriors headed north to the US headquarters of General Horatio Gates, whose forces now were strengthened by the Oneidas, militiamen, and soldiers who had deprived General Burgoyne of St. Leger's support. At the crucial Battle of Saratoga, Honyery served as head warrior and Sarah as messenger. The Oneidas, recalled the Mohawk Valley man Daniel Hadcock, "fought like Bull dogs till Burgoine surrendert." In gratitude for the service of her family, General Gates ordered that Sarah be presented with a winter's supply of three gallons of rum. A turning point in the war, the rebel victory at Saratoga not only stopped the British offensive. It convinced the French to join the American colonials against their mutual enemy.[41]

While recovering from his wound, Henry Timmerman represented the Palatine District on the county Committee of Safety. The committee, which had lost several members at Oriskany, engaged in infighting. It condemned Colonel Klock's adjutant for yelling, "Run, boys, run!" at the battle and questioned the integrity of Major Jelles Fonda, who had advised Henry not to fire on the Indians. If Fonda had hoped to keep the Six Nations out of the quarrel between the rebels and the British, he was at best deluded as far as Henry was concerned. Fonda took depositions from eyewitnesses of the theft by Oneidas and militiamen of property belonging to Molly Brant and Nicholas Herkimer's Loyalist brother. Charges of looting and cowardice were dropped by officials, who urged the demoralized rebels of Tryon County to unite. The Committee of Safety disbanded when the first state legislature of New York was established in 1778.[42]

Representatives of the US government came to Johnstown to praise the courage of the Oneidas and assure them of "our Friendship and Protection." Congressman James Duane was there in his dual role as the New York Indian commissioner and chair of the congressional Committee on Indian Affairs. The Oneidas welcomed the new French allies, including the twenty-year-old Marquis de Lafayette, who held the rank of major general in the Continental Army. The Oneidas impressed the French officers, who hoped the local militiamen could fight better than they looked. Grasshopper, the dignified warrior from Oriske who held the Wolf Clan sachem title of Odatshedah, spoke at the council. Do not be ruled by the rage of combat, he urged the Oneidas, as he called on them to remember that the Haudenosaunee traditions of peace and unity were in the best interests of the people. I wonder what Honyery thought of these wise words.[43]

General Washington asked the Oneidas to come to his winter quarters at Valley Forge, northwest of Philadelphia. He wanted two hundred warriors, but the Oneidas could spare only fifty. On the day they arrived, Washington hosted Honyery at supper. The Oneidas were "stout-looking fellows and remarkably neat for that race of mortals," said a soldier from Connecticut, who added, "but they were Indians." According to Oneida tradition, an Oneida woman, Polly Cooper, accompanied the warriors and taught the troops how to make corn soup. In gratitude, Washington and his wife, Martha, presented her with a shawl. The performance of the warriors earned the accolade of the Prussian drillmaster Friedrich von Steuben. Several weeks later, Honyery, Honyost, Plattcop, Shagoyontha, and others left for the 250-mile trek home. They came back without the inspiring Thomas Sinavis, who was killed in battle. Little Abraham came from Tiononderogue to conduct the condolence ceremony for the fallen sachem.[44]

The Oneidas returned in time to face attacks on the Mohawk and Schoharie Valleys led by Captain Brant. As he raided, Brant recruited a hundred Mohawks and white Loyalists who lived off the land and dressed and painted themselves as Indians. Their mission, as intended by the British command, was to quash the rebellion by destroying the mills, farms, and crops of the patriots and their Native allies. As the men and women of Oriske knew, it took only minutes to set a town ablaze.[45]

In Schoharie, only a few Mohawks, like the Turtle Clan warrior known as Schoharie John, along with the Oneida Louis Denny, supported the rebels. Schoharie John, probably a close relative, had sponsored the baptism in 1775 of Louis and Maria's daughter Maria, called Polly, whose earliest memories would be of war. Louis served as a spy, soldier, and interpreter in the Fifteenth Regiment of the Albany County Militia, made up of rebels from Schoharie and Duanesburg and led by Colonel Peter Vrooman. Louis was "a France man" and "a friend to the Cause," noted Vrooman, as he passed on Denny's report that the enemy was on its way to Schoharie. The intelligence reached New York governor George Clinton along with a request for troops to defend the valley. The first elected governor of New York State, Clinton shared the name of his distant relation who had been colonial governor. Clinton, who was also a general in the Continental Army, knew that troops were needed everywhere.[46]

John Myers served with Louis Denny in Albany County's Fifteenth Regiment. John, who a few years earlier had been an indentured servant on the estate of James Duane, was now a lieutenant in the militia following his service at Saratoga. John and Louis may have met, as they were known to be in the same place at about the same time at least once or twice. For the families of the best land, the war was becoming a blur of destruction interspersed with sights that were hard to forget. John marched ten miles west of Schoharie to the smoldering settlement of Cobleskill, where raiders had strung the intestines of a dead rebel soldier from his hand to the limb of a big tree.[47]

In October, rebel troops from Pennsylvania leveled Oquaga, the prosperous Oneida town on the Susquehanna in present-day Broome County, which Captain Brant used as a base. "It was the finest Indian town I ever saw," said the officer who ordered the home of pro-British, pro-American, and neutral Oneidas burned to the ground. An attack in November on Cherry Valley in the Canajoharie District sealed Captain Walter Butler's reputation as the most hated man in the Mohawk Valley. The Loyalist, who had escaped imprisonment, oversaw the killing of thirty-two civilians and twenty-six soldiers by Loyalists, Mohawks, and Senecas. The men of Captain House's company had been on their way home from guard duty in German Flatts when they were ordered to march to the relief of Cherry Valley. They arrived too late to rescue anyone. Instead they helped to bury the dead families of their fellow militiamen.[48]

Join us against the Americans, the Cayugas urged the Oneidas, or give up your land, move south, and resume neutrality. If not, they warned, you will be crushed by the king's people. The Oneidas deliberated at council. Everyone had a chance to state his or her position. Those who wished to join their Haudenosaunee brothers with the British could go freely. The rest pledged to stand together "in Defense of their Lives and Liberty," reported James Dean to General Schuyler. In recognition of their valuable service, Congress granted US military commissions to Oneida warriors. Honyery became a captain, Honyost Thaosagwat a lieutenant, and Louis Atayataghronghta a lieutenant colonel.[49]

As much as the defenders of the Mohawk Valley counted on the Oneidas, they at times questioned their loyalty. In pursuit of a raiding party, soldiers suspected that their guide, "Henry Flathead," or Plattcop, had yelled to warn "his red brethren" as they came upon the enemy's campfire. The rebels found meat still cooking in the fire, but no raiders. This account fits the Oneidas' stated position. They would fight the British, but they preferred not to engage the Six Nations. The bitterness of the rebels is understandable too. They were after Loyalists and Indians who had hit the Ephratah settlement, located between the Timmermans' mill and Johnstown. Members of Captain House's company found the body of a four-year-old scalped and thrown into Caroga Creek still clutching a spoon in his hand. After this raid, several rebel families abandoned their homes.[50]

"The only way of preventing Indian ravages is to carry the war vigorously into their own country," announced General Washington. For months James Duane had agitated for an invasion of Iroquoia. He wanted Continental troops to subdue the Six Nations. Otherwise "we may as well hunt the Eagles of the air as the Indians in the woods," he wrote to Governor Clinton. "They have only two points in war—an ambush, and the nimbleness of their Heels," enhanced by "a perfect Knowledge of our extensive Forests." Duane, who spent much of the war with Congress in Philadelphia or on his untouched estate at Duanesburg, was not only wrong about the Haudenosaunee. He was getting ahead of himself when he referred to "our" forests.[51]

The US offensive known as the Sullivan Expedition took place in the summer of 1779. General John Sullivan of New Hampshire and General James Clinton, the governor's brother, led 4,500 troops. The expedition was joined by a few Oneidas, including Lieutenant Honyost Thaosagwat, who was described by an officer as "an Anyder Indian of considerable note." Sullivan disregarded the Oneidas' request that the troops refrain from burning the crops of the Cayugas. As directed by General Washington, US troops destroyed forty Haudenosaunee villages, acres of orchards, and fields of "the best corn that I ever saw," recalled one soldier. Members of the expedition took scalps of slain Natives, and two of them skinned the legs of dead Indians to make leggings. While guiding a scouting party near the Seneca town of Geneseo, Honyost was captured and executed, as was the lieutenant in charge. The sight of the lieutenant's grossly mutilated body shocked US officers who reviled the atrocities committed by the other side.[52]

Almost all the now homeless Cayugas and Senecas sought shelter with the British at Niagara. They were joined by Onondagas, who had fled an attack by US troops on their territory. As they ran, Onondaga women had snatched up precious seeds to preserve from destruction heirlooms of the past as well as hope for the future. Rebel troops burned, looted, raped, and killed Onondagas whether they were pro-American, pro-British, or neutral. They torched the big longhouse where the Onondagas kept the council fire that represented the unity of the Six Nations. On their way to Onondaga and back to Fort Stanwix, the attackers most likely marched past the best land. When they returned, an Oneida asked the commanding officer if some awful mistake had been made at Onondaga. No, answered the officer. "I was ordered to do it," he said, "and it is done."[53]

General Sullivan instructed US troops to destroy Tiononderogue and take the Mohawks prisoner. The US force again failed to distinguish between friendly, neutral, and enemy Natives. Sullivan made an exception for Canajoharie. Inhabited by "our friends" the Oriskes, the upper castle was not to be disturbed. John Jay, the New Yorker who at the time presided over the Continental Congress, wanted to claim the western Haudenosaunee territory for his state. "Would it not be proper for New York to establish Posts in that Country," he wrote to Governor Clinton, "and in every respect treat it as their own?"[54]

Concerned about the threat to the Mohawk Valley following the Sullivan Expedition, Colonel Klock warned Governor Clinton that the Indians would want revenge and could very easily get it here. In May 1780, a Loyalist force burned Caughnawaga (present-day Fonda) and attacked Tribes Hill. While Lambert Clement guarded boats carrying supplies up the river, his Loyalist cousin Lieutenant Joseph Clement raided with Captain Brant. In July, Brant and Lieutenant Clement oversaw the burning of Kanonwalohale to the ground. They destroyed the Oneidas' meeting house, their newly constructed fort, seventy-three homes, food stores, and livestock. Brant's party did not bother Old Oneida, the home of neutrals, elders, women, and children.[55]

With Brant and Lieutenant Clement were the prisoners Skenandoah and Good Peter, the Christian convert from Oquaga also known as Agwelondongwas (Breaking of the Twigs). The previous February, General Schuyler had sent the two Oneidas, along with Little Abraham and another neutral Mohawk, from Tiononderogue to Fort Niagara to try to persuade the Haudenosaunee to abandon the British. To his brethren, Little Abraham said, "What has happened to us is calamitous! There is now no Long House where you and I can safely tell each other our fears." Think about returning, he pleaded, "so that all our people will live again upon our former firesides and plantations, and smoke will rise again from our former cabins and all will enjoy the lordship of their lands again."[56]

To Little Abraham's call for a resumption of neutrality, angry Mohawk and Seneca spokesmen retorted that the conduct of the Oneidas had not been neutral. The elderly emissaries were imprisoned for five months in a dungeon called "the black hole," where Little Abraham died. Skenandoah and Good Peter had been brought back to convince the Oneidas to return with them to Niagara. A few hundred, including the families of Skenandoah and Good Peter, accepted the protection of the British. Their homes at Kanonwalohale and Oquaga had been wiped out, one by a pro-British force and the other by US troops.[57]

About six hundred Oneidas remained on the side of the rebels. Some sought safety at Schenectady, which was crowded with refugees from Cherry Valley and German Flatts. They moved into grim camps outside town with little food, heat, or clothing. An outbreak of smallpox took lives. According to church records, Honyery and Sarah and Louis and Maria Denny were in Schenectady at this time. It is possible that their wives and children remained there while Honyery and Louis returned to defend their valleys. General Schuyler told Congress that the Americans might lose their best fighters if they did not take care of the Oneida families. In Quebec, Governor Frederick Haldimand, Britain's commander in chief of the Northern Department, was pleased to learn of the destruction of Kanonwalohale. He considered the Oneida warriors to be far too effective. He wanted them eliminated.[58]

Conflagration All around Fort Timmerman

Captain Honyery and his warriors teamed up with what remained of the militia around Canajoharie. The Mohawk Valley rebels constructed forts by building stockades around twenty-four houses at strategic

FIGURE 12. This stone house on the Mohawk River was built in 1750 by Johannes Klock, the brother of George Klock and Colonel Jacob Klock. It is an example of a fortified dwelling with loopholes or gunports in every wall so that muskets could be fired from the inside during an attack. Fort Klock Historic Restoration, St. Johnsville, NY. Brewer Collection.

locations such as the Timmermans' mill. Each fort was intended to hold ten to fifty families. The firing of one signal shot meant that the enemy had been sighted and that people should rush to the nearest stockade. Two or three shots fired quickly meant that the enemy was close and it was too late to reach the fort. Every family had a designated hideout, a deep thicket or hollow with brush ready to pull over the top. Typically, the father and older sons answered the alarm, while the women and young children would hide until all was safe.[59]

It was risky to fetch water, pick apples, or collect firewood. Farmers plowed and planted fields in armed companies. Families would go to the nearest fort at night to bed down in safety and return the next morning to milk the cows, feed the stock, and tend the crops. Every evening, Henry and Margaret and their children moved to the fort a mile away from their house. One night they were appalled to realize that they had left behind the baby. Henry strode back to retrieve his youngest, who lay asleep in her cradle. Years later, two Indians told Henry that they had watched him go by that night with a rifle on one arm and an infant on the other and decided not to bother him.[60]

Captain Brant and Lieutenant Clement, with a force of five hundred, attacked Canajoharie in August 1780. The raiders set one hundred houses on fire, killed fourteen people, took fifty prisoners, and confiscated three hundred cows, horses, and pigs. Captain House's men were at Fort Stanwix shouting hurrahs because the boats they had been guarding reached the fort safely. On the way home, they heard news of the raid and began to run. As they grew closer, they could see the smoke rising. Some families were all right, some were dead, and others were gone. The raiders spread out to Schoharie, where they killed five members of the Vrooman family.[61]

Determined to destroy General Washington's food supplies and avenge the Sullivan Expedition, Sir John led an ambitious attack on the Schoharie and Mohawk Valleys in October. Several hundred raiders traveled from Canada through Oneida territory into the upper Schoharie Valley. Sir John laid siege to the Middle Fort, where Schoharie John and Louis Denny lived during the war. The rebels refused to surrender, although Colonel Vrooman's hair stood on end when he saw how little ammunition they had left. The defenders captured a French-speaking Indian interpreter who berated his captors until Louis, who could understand what he was saying, knocked him down. John Myers joined Vrooman in pursuit of the raiders, who torched fields of grain as they moved north. People from the outskirts of Albany could see the "great smoak" rising above Schoharie.[62]

Sir John's force reached Fort Hunter and moved on to Stone Arabia in the Palatine District. They overwhelmed the resistance put up by Oneidas and soldiers, killing five warriors and forty rebels. The Oneidas and militiamen crossed the river to meet the enemy with the expectation that General Robert Van Rensselaer's troops from Albany County soon would follow. When Van Rensselaer did not arrive until several hours later, Colonel Louis expressed the outrage felt by many when he shook his sword at the general and called him a Tory. The general, later exonerated, was remembered with bitterness by Tryon County militiamen.[63]

From Fort Timmerman, members of Captain House's company marched to join General Van Rensselaer's troops in what would be known as the battle of Klock's Field. Sixty Oneidas teamed up with militiamen to confront Sir John's force. The combatants heard Brant's Mohawks give their war yell and the Oneidas answer with their own. As it grew dark, rebels fired at rebels and units of the Albany militia broke and rallied and broke before Sir John's men retreated west. The battle of Klock's Field wasn't a US victory, concluded Governor Clinton, but he believed that the militia and the Oneidas had prevented Johnson from destroying the entire county.[64]

The valor of the Oneidas at the battle of Klock's Field won the admiration of rebel officers. Their performance reinforced Governor Haldimand's frustration. It was impossible, the British commander concluded, to effect "anything against the Enemy in the Quarter they Inhabit." In the coming months, the British shifted their strategy to concentrate on pacifying the southern colonies. By then, hundreds of Mohawk Valley farms had been abandoned. Two-thirds of the inhabitants had become refugees. Colonel Willett, who now commanded the defense of Tryon County, informed General Washington that the militia was down to eight hundred fit for service. Their position was made more precarious by the abandonment of Fort Stanwix, damaged by flood, fire, and desertions, in the spring of 1781. New York State was on the "Verge of Ruin," Governor Clinton told Congress.[65]

To James Duane, the governor wrote, "Schenectady may now be said to become the limits of our western Frontier." Forty-seven miles west of Schenectady, Lieutenant Henry Timmerman led the defense remembered as the time of "conflagration" and "desolation" all around Fort Timmerman. Forced to abandon their farms, the Timmermans crowded into the fortified family homestead. They shared it with militiamen and Oneidas, some of whom stayed nearby at the stone house of George Klock, the onetime home of Honyery and Plattcop.[66]

On August 4, Colonel Willett ordered Fort Timmerman to supply six men for a scouting party. Henry chose his nephews and a neighbor to accompany him. Lieutenant John's wife watched her husband lift down his gun from the beam and hold it while he awaited the others. John turned to his father and said, "I believe I will put my gun back again." Conrad answered, "I wish it were so, my son, that you could lay by your gun." The men departed and had not gone far when they were fired on by hidden Loyalists and Indians. Henry and Private Adam Timmerman escaped, Private Jacob J. Timmerman and the neighbor were taken prisoner, and John and Sergeant Jacob L. Timmerman were mortally wounded and scalped. Militiamen responding to the sound of gunfire found Jacob L. dead and carried John home to die.[67]

There was no time for grieving. The Oneidas and the militiamen posted at Fort Timmerman were ordered by Colonel Klock to report to another fort three miles away. They left behind the Oneida and Timmerman women and children. An enemy force struck on August 14. The Oneida women held off 150 raiders. One eyewitness, a small boy named

David Welch of Native and African descent, watched his mother and Dolly Cobus of Oriske defend the fort by firing through the loopholes. Another child who probably was there was my foremother Anna Rosina. The Oneida women may have saved her and Fort Timmerman, but they had to look on helplessly as the attackers set fire to the surrounding houses, barns, and stacks of wheat. By then they had seen many harvests go up in flames.[68]

Soon after the raids on Fort Timmerman, several Oneidas, led by Grasshopper and Colonel Louis, traveled to Philadelphia to be honored by the US Congress. The congressmen expressed their sorrow over the loss of Kanonwalohale and promised that the Oneidas soon would be "restored to the peaceable enjoyments of your land." Some of the Oneida delegation decided to travel south to visit Generals Washington and Lafayette, who were with the US and French forces confronting Lord Cornwallis and the British army near Yorktown, Virginia. Others returned to defend the Mohawk Valley.[69]

The British surrender at Yorktown in October did not end the attacks on the New York frontier. A raiding party of 630 Loyalists and 130 Indians, with Walter Butler as second in command, came to destroy rebel property and wipe out the Oneidas. After burning seven miles along the Mohawk River, the raiders clashed with Colonel Willett's four hundred militiamen at the inconclusive battle of Johnstown. The rebel force, which included Henry Timmerman, Lambert Clement, and several defenders who were not yet sixteen years old, suffered heavy losses. As the raiders retreated, Willett's men, led by sixty Oneidas, followed in pursuit. In a skirmish with the rearguard, the warriors killed the despised Butler. Willett's after-action report praised the Oneidas.[70]

Enemy attacks on the Mohawk Valley continued through 1782, although there was not much left to burn or loot. Governor Haldimand gave Captain Brant permission to lead a strike against Honyery and the Oneidas at Canajoharie as long as no settlers were harmed, but Brant could not persuade other Haudenosaunee warriors to join him. Forty-five years old and disabled by his wound, Henry Timmerman hired a substitute to serve in the militia in his place. New York was running out of troops and funds to pay the ones it had. The state passed legislation to compensate soldiers with land. The bounty land, as it was called, referred to Six Nations territory except that belonging to the friendly Oneidas and Tuscaroras.[71]

General Washington wanted to see the place where the Americans had turned the war around. In June he sailed up the Hudson, was feted in Albany, and toured Saratoga with Governor Clinton and General Schuyler. In Schenectady, he thanked the magistrates and military officers. "May the complicated blessings of peace soon reward your arduous struggles for the independence and freedom of our common country," he wrote. There, he greeted one hundred Oneida warriors. Their presence was a reminder that if not for the Oneida and Tuscarora allies, the Americans would have confronted the full force of the Six Nations. Colonel Willett was distressed that so little had been done for the Oneidas who had done so much.[72]

The news arrived in April 1783 that the war was over. The "blessings of peace" would be complicated indeed. The Six Nations had ruptured. Across Haudenosaunee territory, towns and fields were in ruins. In the Mohawk Valley, families had been torn apart. The deaths of militiamen had left 380 women widowed and 2,000 children without fathers. Oriske, Cherry Valley, Oquaga, German Flatts, and Kanonwalohale were destroyed. The population of the Oneidas had been cut down to somewhere between 600 and 1,000. Honyery and Sarah, Louis and Maria Denny, and Henry and Margaret Timmerman had lost friends and relations, their houses and barns, their crops and livestock. The families of the best land, I found out, had fought side by side to defend their homes and freedom.[73]

The Oneidas believed they made the right choice. The United States, New York State, and Generals Washington and Schuyler had promised that their lands were secure. That summer they welcomed Washington, who returned to tour the Carrying Place and Oneida Lake as he viewed "the vast inland navigation of these United States." He was, he wrote, "struck with the immense . . . importance of it, and with the goodness of that Providence which has dealt his favours to us with so profuse a hand." The general longed to explore the western country. "A new empire," he called it. Washington was not alone in his ambition. Thousands of American soldiers had seen the richness of Haudenosaunee fields. The way to them was through the best land.[74]

Chapter 4

As Long as the Grass Shall Grow

It was time to go home. Around Fort Timmerman, the children collected spent bullets, while their parents made do without tools, seeds, arms, medicine, tea, and sugar. Henry and Margaret's daughters remembered dressing in rags, while girls from a nearby settlement untouched by raids had petticoats to wear. A young neighbor, who had been taken captive at age nine, walked back from Canada five years later. "There's an Indian coming," someone called out. "No, that's my boy," said his mother. For the weary inhabitants of the Mohawk Valley, peace meant reconstructing their farms and families if they could.[1]

Honyery, the Wolf Clan war chief, led his family back to Oriske. The Oneidas, scattered, divided, and impoverished, began the restoration of abandoned communities. The deprivations of the conflict showed on their bodies, which appeared thin and aged. "We returned to our Country where Ruin and Desolation had spread over our Fields and Villages," said the Oneidas to New York State legislators. "We rejoiced however that we could return in Peace, and please ourselves with the Hopes of the peaceable and quiet Enjoyment of our Country, for which we had fought and bled, in the common Cause together with you." This communication would be published decades later in *Proceedings of the Commissioners of Indian Affairs, Appointed by Law for the Extinguishment of Indian Titles in the*

State of New York. For the Oneidas, going home would be one thing; keeping it would be another.[2]

I remember believing that, following the American Revolution, the Oneida Indians disappeared along with the rest of the Six Nations. After finding out how much my ancestors owed their survival of the war to Oneida men and women, I wanted to learn what happened afterward. How did Polly's family and mine recover from the devastation? What did my rebel ancestors do with their hard-won independence? How did the People of the Standing Stone conduct relations with the new governments of the United States and New York State, which had promised to respect the Oneida lands they viewed as the way west?

Not all homecomings were happy. When the prisoners of war Good Peter and Skenandoah returned, Good Peter was welcomed by everyone, but Skenandoah, accused of assisting the British, was not. In the Schoharie Valley, Polly Denny's relation, Schoharie John, and Peter C. Vrooman quarreled with a Mohawk ally of the British, who was not seen again. Most of the Indians of Schoharie vanished after the war, recalled a white landowner who had been a friend of the Dennys: "Several of them had been met in places by citizen hunters, and were possibly mistaken for bears. A few disappeared, and the rest took the hint and left the country."[3]

Even though they had fought alongside the rebels to defend their home, the Denny family left Schoharie. They followed the eldest son, John Denny, described as "a smart handsome fellow," to Oriske. John had married Dorothea, called Dolly, the only daughter of Honyery and Sarah, and moved in with her family. John and Dolly took their children downriver to be baptized at the Fort Herkimer Church in German Flatts. Their daughter Sarah was sponsored by her grandparents Honyery and Sarah.[4]

Some months later, Honyery took his son Peter to the Fort Herkimer Church to be baptized. Peter's mother was Dolly Cobus of Oriske, who had defended Fort Timmerman in 1781. It is not known when or if Honyery married Dolly Cobus, who, like Sarah, was known for her wartime bravery. In any event, both Dolly Cobus and Sarah were part of Honyery's life in the 1780s. Honyery's family preferred the "old way" of baptism, as done in Dutch and German settlements where the parents did not have to convert to Christianity.[5]

To the Dennys, the mixed Oneida, Mohawk, and European community at Oriske was familiar. A trader from New Hampshire named Ephraim Webster, who had a Native wife, resided there. Abraham Van

Eps of Schenectady set up a trading post, an important source of goods for people who had lost everything. Polly's brothers married Oneida women. Many of the young Oneidas adopted European surnames in the patriarchal tradition understood by their white neighbors. Honyery's children took the surname of Doxtator. The children of his brother Plattcop went by Schuyler. The children of his sister and Shagoyontha used Cornelius as a last name.[6]

Colonel Honyery, as he was called after the war, was known for his hospitality. A French immigrant who stopped at Oriske wrote, "We were received with a cordiality we have not found in any other part of America, and which is not always found in France." The visitors were given salmon, beds, and blankets. "These Indians show nothing of the savage except in dress," recorded the Frenchman, who noted that many of them conversed in English with "spirit and ease." Oriske would grow to a population of two hundred, but it never fully recovered. In the early months of the peace, the Oneidas needed time to rebuild their towns and revive their councils, deliberate on matters of importance to their nation, and reach consensus, but time they did not have.[7]

A cavalcade of sachems, chiefs, federal and state officials, foreign dignitaries, speculators, and spies arrived at the Oneida Carrying Place in 1784. The Senecas, Cayugas, Onondagas, and Mohawks came to make peace with the United States. The British and the Americans had not included the Six Nations in the Treaty of Paris, which transferred to the United States the Crown's self-proclaimed right of preemption to Native territory east of the Mississippi River. That meant the United States assumed the right to dispossess Indigenous people of their land. In the meantime, officials believed that the Indians had the right of the soil, meaning the right to occupy their ancestral land and the right to refuse to sell it. Even so, they intended to take over Iroquoia. "We are now Masters of this Island," said General Philip Schuyler. It was just a question of when.[8]

George Washington believed in gradual acquisition. The "extension of our Settlements will as certainly cause the Savage as the Wolf to retire," he assured James Duane. New Yorkers, Washington observed, were impatient. The state was anxious to deny the claim of Massachusetts to Iroquoia based on a charter from the English monarch that predated its own. It already had lost a disputed northeastern section to Vermont seceders whose leader, Ethan Allen, had declared he would rather eat mouse meat than live under New York. To dispel any notion that New York's western border was the 1768 Line of Property, the state was in a hurry to claim Haudenosaunee territory and fill it with New Yorkers.[9]

Governor George Clinton arrived at Fort Stanwix before the US delegation to hold his own council with the Six Nations. He had been advised by James Duane, who, like many Americans of the day, put his state before his country. Duane had signed the Articles of Confederation, the first US constitution, ratified in 1781. It gave the federal government the sole right to manage the affairs of Natives who were not members of any of the states. That presented a "great difficulty," thought Duane, but he had a plan. He urged Clinton to treat the Haudenosaunee as "[ancient] dependents on this state." He knew that the Six Nations did not see themselves as dependents. Indeed, Duane observed, "they assume a perfect equality." It will take "skill and delicacy" to reconcile the tribes "to the idea of being members of the state," he informed the governor.[10]

Duane recommended that the governor express concern about the security of the Six Nations at a time of "resentment and animosity" against them. He advised that when in council, Clinton should recall a happy and not entirely accurate history of how the Dutch and their successors always fought for their protection and never deceived them. Clinton, he said, should remind the Haudenosaunee of the steady friendship of "their own countrymen, born in and inhabiting the same soil which they themselves inherited." Then Clinton should suggest that "for the advantage and comfort" of all, a border line must be established "between the settlements of the white people and the lands to be reserved for the use of the Indians within our state." There it was: "within our state."[11]

Duane believed that New York could render the Six Nations dependent by treating them as dependent. Don't call them "brethren" and don't conform to their ceremonies, he wrote, but make them adopt our way of doing business. He objected to treaty making as it had been conducted by the colonial government, and even to using the word "treaty," because it implied equality between sovereigns. He recommended that the governor not use wampum but only signed and sealed written communication. In that way, the Haudenosaunee method of recording agreements would cease.[12]

At Fort Stanwix, Clinton was met by Colonel James Monroe, who had been sent ahead by Congress to keep an eye on the New Yorkers. The Virginian had no way of knowing the loyalties and vendettas concealed in the hearts of those present, including Honyery and Joseph Brant. There was plenty of intrigue. Clinton instructed the interpreter James Dean to undermine Brant's influence while encouraging the Six Nations to trust New York State. The missionary Samuel Kirkland warned the Oneidas that New York State wanted their land.[13]

Clinton adopted Duane's suggestions but not his recommendation to ignore the traditions of the council fire. "By this string," said the governor, "we wipe your eyes, console your breasts, and open your ears that you may hear what we have to say." Clinton expressed his gratitude to the Oneidas and said, "We have no claim on your Lands." Then he proclaimed the state's authority over Oneida territory. The governor informed the Oneidas that the state constitution forbade them from disposing of any of their lands to individuals without the legislature's consent. That the Oneidas had no part in the writing of the state constitution went unsaid. The New Yorkers asked the Oneidas to trace out their boundaries so that the state would not infringe on the territory of its friends.[14]

Grasshopper, the Wolf Clan sachem who had fought alongside the rebels, thanked Clinton for his address and offered condolences for the state's losses during the war. "You have come to inform us that our land is our own," he said with civility, and perhaps a bit of sarcasm, although it is impossible to know for sure. He raised the status of Oriske as a matter of importance. Oriske possibly had been sold, said Clinton, neglecting to mention that he himself was interested in the disputed Oriskany Patent. It would not be right to take away someone's property, added the governor, making a statement worthy of ironical response. General Washington had assured them that they should keep their lands, said the Oneidas. They showed Clinton a letter from the US Indian commissioners saying that the governor was not authorized by Congress to hold treaties with them.[15]

As the New York delegation withdrew, Clinton left behind Major Peter P. Schuyler with instructions "to counteract and frustrate" the representatives of Congress if they did anything that may "prove detrimental to the state." Major Schuyler, a nephew of Philip Schuyler, was conversant in Mohawk. Supplied with dozens of kegs of rum, the major got himself banned by the US commissioners, who prohibited alcohol at the council. This prohibition proved unpopular with almost everyone, including the congenial Irishman William Colbraith, a veteran of the siege of Fort Stanwix who was there to sell liquor. As a compromise, the commissioners tasked the Reverend Kirkland with managing the distribution of intoxicating spirits.[16]

While the New Yorkers and US officials sparred, a solemn delegation of Oneidas led by Grasshopper approached the dwellings of the visiting Senecas. Although the sachem had supported the alliance with the rebels in response to the invasion of Oneida territory, he believed the Six Nations should resume a policy of unity and neutrality. He and the Oneidas stopped and waited. The Seneca leader came out to receive them. After exchanging courtesies, the men sat, talked, and smoked the pipe of peace. For the Haudenosaunee, a treaty council was a time to condole over losses, address injustice, and heal hearts and minds. Otherwise, wounds festered, and peace was denied. The Oneidas and Senecas repeated the ritual of reconciliation the next day.[17]

During the Fort Stanwix council, the Oneidas hosted General Lafayette and the diplomat François de Barbé-Marbois of the French delegation. "The fertility surpasses anything that can be imagined," Marbois wrote, amazed at soils that were twelve to fifteen feet deep. Bemused by the sight of Grasshopper wearing the embroidered court hunting costume given to him by the French ambassador during the war, Marbois did not understand that to the sachem, the fancy coat symbolized friendship and reciprocity between France and the Oneida Nation.[18]

Marbois was astonished when an Oneida who wore bones hanging from his nose spoke to him in excellent French. It was Nicholas Jordan, who like Louis Denny was an adopted French captive. As he was about to be tortured, Nicholas recounted, he was invited to gain his freedom by marrying a sachem's daughter whose husband had died. Such a marriage would give him the greatest pleasure in the world, he had replied. Although he missed France, especially a beautiful woman from Picardy, Nicholas was content. His family, like the Dennys, would produce generations of interpreters.[19]

The Oneida men and women were most attentive at the council, Marbois thought. They heard the US commissioners, accompanied by James Madison of Virginia, express their gratitude. The Oneida and Tuscarora Nations "shall be secured in the possession of the Lands on which they are settled," stated the 1784 Treaty of Fort Stanwix. The United States confirmed its promise with presents, wampum belts, the symbolic burying of a hatchet and breaking of a sword, and the smoking of a pipe of peace. In contrast, the commissioners dealt roughly with the Mohawks, Onondagas, Cayugas, and Senecas, from whom they demanded tracts of land at Forts Oswego and Niagara along with all Six Nations territory west of the mouth of Buffalo Creek at present-day Buffalo.[20]

At Fort Stanwix, Oneida land was guaranteed by US officials who promised to protect a crucial territory they expected someday to call their own. Madison complained to Monroe about the aggressiveness of New Yorkers, but he concluded that the issue of federal authority should not be pressed. He thought the status of Indians as members of a state remained perplexing, although he had no trouble believing that Virginia should control the Native land within its borders. Besides, after his trip to the New York frontier, Madison noted privately, "the vacant land in that part of America opens the surest field of speculation in any of the U.S." Madison and Monroe bought nine hundred acres next to Oriske, while George Washington and Governor Clinton partnered on the purchase of six thousand acres along the Mohawk River not far from the Carrying Place.[21]

The Land of Promise

Oneida land became a refuge for Onondagas, Cayugas, and Lenapes. To the Stockbridge Indians, as the Mohicans of western Massachusetts were known, the Oneidas had given a tract known as New Stockbridge, six miles by six miles, on Oneida Creek south of Kanonwalohale. The Brothertowns, who were Christian Algonquins from Long Island, Connecticut, and Rhode Island, settled along Oriskany Creek south of Oriske. The Oneidas welcomed these people as a shield against white encroachment, but their homelessness was a warning. Indians with land were important, observed Good Peter, but Indians without land were not.[22]

With their prestige as US allies, Honyery, along with Good Peter, Colonel Louis, and Nicholas Jordan, attended Six Nations councils and met with Indian commissioners. When Grasshopper died, the clan mothers named Honyery as counselor to the boy they chose to be raised up as Odatshedah. Honyery's family had an influential friend in Major Peter Schuyler, state senator and Indian commissioner, who served as sponsor at the baptisms of Honyery's son and grandson.[23]

Privately, Major Schuyler complained to Governor Clinton about the inconvenience of daily visits from Indians who expected him to provide food and liquor at his expense. He hosted Molly Brant, who came from Canada to recover property in the Royal Grant willed by William Johnson to their children. Molly rightly asserted that her minor children were too young to forfeit their inheritance. She received financial compensation for these properties but not the land.[24]

Joseph Brant achieved similar results regarding Canajoharie. To the end, Brant condemned George Klock and his claim to the upper castle, but he said his people in Canada needed cattle and so he would take part payment in cattle. The state extinguished the Mohawk claims to Canajoharie in 1789. A newcomer to the Mohawk Valley thought Captain Brant was a "very conversible, well-informed man," and at least one old-timer tried to kill him. As for George Klock, he lived long enough to see Sir William's Royal Grant confiscated by New York State.[25]

Governor Clinton supported the distribution of former Loyalist properties and Six Nations land to ordinary white people. His policies were opposed by the great landlords led by James Duane, Philip Schuyler, and Schuyler's sons-in-law, Stephen Van Rensselaer and Alexander Hamilton, who felt that government, run by men like themselves, should protect the property of men like themselves. Both factions endorsed the state land laws introduced by Duane, which provided that the governor should proceed at once to buy "unappropriated" land from the Indians.[26]

Clinton's policies appealed to veterans, poorly paid or not paid at all, who were in debt and growing restless for their bounty lands. At Duanesburg, tenants fell behind on their rent. Michael Hetzel, my fifth great-grandfather, informed Duane that he had to give up the farm he had worked for two decades. Michael's son George, a militia veteran, put aside his dream of his own place and offered to work his father's if Duane would allow it. "It will be imposbal for me ever to clear up the debt on this farm," George warned. "I have no mony." Duane permitted George and his sister Mary to work the farm for four years without paying rent, while George labored on the Duane estate to pay off his father's debt. After twenty years on Duane's land, the Hetzels had little to show for it. Mary married George's lieutenant, John Myers, and had a daughter named Catharine, my third great-grandmother.[27]

John, now known as Captain Myers, was hired by Duane to be his land agent and overseer in 1785. Back when John was an indentured youth, he begged Duane to help his parents, who were about to lose their living because the lease on their land had expired. If Duane would take care of them, John pledged to "satisfy him for it." John worked for Duane for the rest of Duane's life. He sent regular reports to New York City, where Duane was mayor from 1784 to 1789. From John, Duane heard about a hailstorm that damaged the crops, a flood that took out the mill, and the eagerness of New Englanders to lease farms in Duanesburg.[28]

New Englanders swarmed west into the Mohawk Valley, "seeking the land of promise," wrote Elkanah Watson of Rhode Island. The Oneidas reminded Governor Clinton of William Johnson's promise that Oriske was theirs. Honyery, Plattcop, Shagoyontha, and John Denny sent a petition to the New York legislature. From their ancestors, they wrote, they knew that the Oriskes should retain their land. They had demonstrated their attachment to the United States and "suffered in common with their American Brethren all the inconveniences of the Late War." Addressing "the Honorable Legislature," they requested a secure title to their lands.[29]

The Oneidas planned to earn revenue by leasing land to settlers in the manner "done by the White People." The rents, Good Peter pointed out, would provide an income for the children to come. Governor Clinton was insulted by this idea. Leasing would elevate Indians to the status of the great landlords and would, he protested, make the state a tributary of the Oneidas. When Clinton offered to buy a large tract, the Oneidas said no. "The United States have informed us that the soil of our lands was our own," said Good Peter, who asked the governor to stop his people from trying to take it.[30]

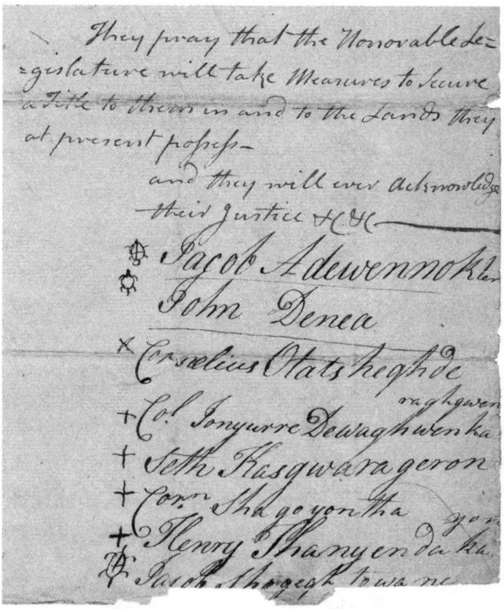
They pray that the Honorable Le-
gislature will take Measures to secure
a Title to them in and to the Lands they
at present possess—
and they will ever acknowledge
their Justice &c &c—
Jacob Adewennokta
John Denea
Cornelius Otatsheghde
Col. Jonyurre Dewaghwenka raghgwen
Seth Kasgwarageron
Corn. Shagoyontha
Henry Thanyendaka yon
Jacob Thogeghtowane

FIGURE 13. On this petition asking for justice for Oriske, John Denny made his Turtle Clan mark. His name is followed by Cornelius Otatsheghde, Honyery as Col. Jonyurre Dewaghwenkraghwen, Cornelius Shagoyontha, Plattcop as Henry Thanyendakayon, and others. Detail, Oriskany, NY, petition, undated [after 1783], AHMC–Oriskany, New York Historical Society.

Clinton told the Oneidas that unless they ceded land to the state, he would not protect it. The Oneidas reluctantly agreed to sell over three hundred thousand acres along their southern border (parts of present-day Broome, Chenango, and Tioga Counties) in the 1785 Treaty of Fort Herkimer. There would be no more land cessions, they said. The Oneidas granted a tract to the interpreter James Dean on their eastern border at present-day Westmoreland in the hope that this friend would be a safeguard between them and white settlement. Not mentioned in the treaty were 320 acres set aside for Samuel Kirkland, who in the past had denied any interest in Oneida land. The state made a substantial profit by selling for $125,955 three-quarters of this cession purchased from the Oneidas for $11,500 and provisions.[31]

The Oneidas, still hoping to earn revenue through rents, were interested in the offer made by Colonel John Livingston to lease all their land for 999 years. Livingston, a younger son of the 3rd lord of Livingston Manor and James Duane's brother-in-law, had organized the New York Genesee Company of Adventurers to acquire as much land as possible. Leasing allowed him to get around the law that prohibited the purchase of Indigenous land without the express authority of the state.[32]

The Adventurers told the Oneidas that they represented New York State. They did not, although many of them held office. Samuel Kirkland, James Dean, Major Peter Schuyler, and William Colbraith encouraged their Oneida friends to accept. The Adventurers paid Colonel Louis, Nicholas Jordan, and a proud but unreliable warrior turned schoolteacher named Jacob Reed in cash or shares for their support. The Oneidas, who thought it easier to deal with "one great man" than hundreds of tenants, signed the Livingston lease.[33]

The Oneidas were told by a French merchant who claimed to represent Louis XVI that the Livingston lease was a bad deal. Peter Penet asked the Oneidas to name what presents they would like from "their Father the French King." When the presents did not arrive, Penet said they were delayed by shipwreck. In the meantime, he pledged to protect Oneida lands from rapacious Americans. The offer appealed to the Oneidas, who hoped that the interest of France meant a return to the time when they had the power to play off one imperial nation against the other.[34]

New York State took advantage of the confusion created by the schemes of the Adventurers and Peter Penet. The legislature annulled the Livingston lease, but it led the Oneidas to believe they were on the verge of losing their country. The state Indian commissioners knew the

Oneidas were starving following a summer so cold and rainy that the corn failed to ripen before the frost got it. They sent two boatloads of provisions and invited the Oneidas to a council at Fort Stanwix.[35]

The Carrying Place looked like a fairground. An uninvited guest was the French minister to the United States, who treated Peter Penet as a fellow representative of Louis XVI. To visitors, the Indians appeared "fantastically dressed," some in the richest silks and others in fine scarlet cloth covered in brooches. When Elkanah Watson observed the polished Peter Otsequette drinking rum and whooping, he concluded that the young Oneida demonstrated "the Folly of attempting to civilize an Indian." At age fourteen, Peter had gone with Lafayette to France. Now, after an absence of four years, he had returned home and felt, he said, "distressed at the wretched situation of my Nation."[36]

Honyery, with the Bear and Turtle Clan leaders, informed the commissioners that the Oneida Nation was ready to speak to them. Governor Clinton began his remarks by saying he did not want to purchase any more land because there was more than enough for his people. Good Peter was skeptical. "As long as any spot of our excellent land remains," he said to the governor, settlers "will covet it and . . . never rest till they possess it." Peter Otsequette reminded Clinton of former days when the governor's people first landed in New York. "You were then small and we were great," said Peter. "We then took you under our Protection." Now the Oneidas had sunk down, he said, "while you are so risen that your hands extend over the whole island and reach the stars." He asked the governor to prevent their ruin.[37]

Honyery listened as Good Peter insisted that the Oneidas could remain at Oriske as long as they pleased. Clinton replied that he had found the patent, which meant the land had been sold. "These poor People of Oriske fought with you," protested Good Peter. "[L]et them possess that small spot of land at Oriske." Clinton replied that it was private property. Good Peter knew that not all private property was sacred. He reminded Clinton, "When the War was over you laid Hands upon the Property of those who took side with the king of Great Britain." Good Peter was on target with this point. Investors, including Clinton, had acquired sections of the Oriskany Patent confiscated from Loyalists.[38]

Throughout the council, Clinton let the Oneidas think that he was there to save their territory for them. The Oneidas believed they agreed to lease five million acres to New York State and keep for themselves a three-hundred-thousand-acre reservation, which consisted of parts of present-day Oneida and Madison Counties, including the best land. The treaty guaranteed the Oneidas and their posterity forever the right to hunt and fish on the ceded lands and set aside land along the north shore of Oneida Lake for their use. The Oneidas remembered the speeches made by state officials. "The Governor of New York said to us," recalled Good Peter, "'You have now leased to me all of your territory, exclusive of the reservation, as long as the grass shall grow & the rivers run.'"[39]

"The Oneidas do cede and grant all their lands to the people of the state of New York forever," began the 1788 Treaty of Fort Stanwix, as written by state officials. It gave New York five million acres for $5,500 in cash, clothing, provisions, a sawmill, a grist mill, and an annuity of $600. The treaty set aside the three-hundred-thousand-acre reservation and allowed the Oneidas to lease land in a four-mile-wide strip along their southern border. Although Good Peter requested that all negotiations be done in the open, officials conducted nighttime deals with a few Oneidas, including Colonel Louis and Peter Otsequette, who received tracts of land. Before signing the treaty, Good Peter expressed his thanks: "My Nation are now restored to a Possession of their Property which they were in danger of having lost." No one disabused him of this misunderstanding.[40]

The sachems Odatshedah and Kanagweas signed the Treaty of Fort Stanwix first by making a mark next to their names. They were followed by Peter Otsequette, Honyery, Paul Powless, Good Peter, Shagoyontha, Plattcop, Skenandoah, and others. Oneida women signed. Good Peter later explained that it was wrong to reject the counsel of the clan mothers. "It is an acknowledged Truth," he said, "that our Sisters are the principal Inhabitants of the Earth." On the parchment were thirty-five seals, the white man's symbol of validity, and attached to it was a string of wampum made of blue and white beads two inches wide and two feet long, the Oneida guarantee of words and deeds.[41]

Clinton made closing remarks about the clarity of understanding that comes from open council. "You have a very large Tract of Country for your own Use and Cultivation; you are to have the Rents of a very large Tract," and $600 annually, he said. "You have therefore more than sufficient for the comfortable support of yourselves and your posterity if you are prudent and sober." Clinton warned, "Do not suffer any of our people who lead disorderly lives to come and reside among you." If you are unable to keep out these people, said the governor, alert us and we will oblige them to move.[42]

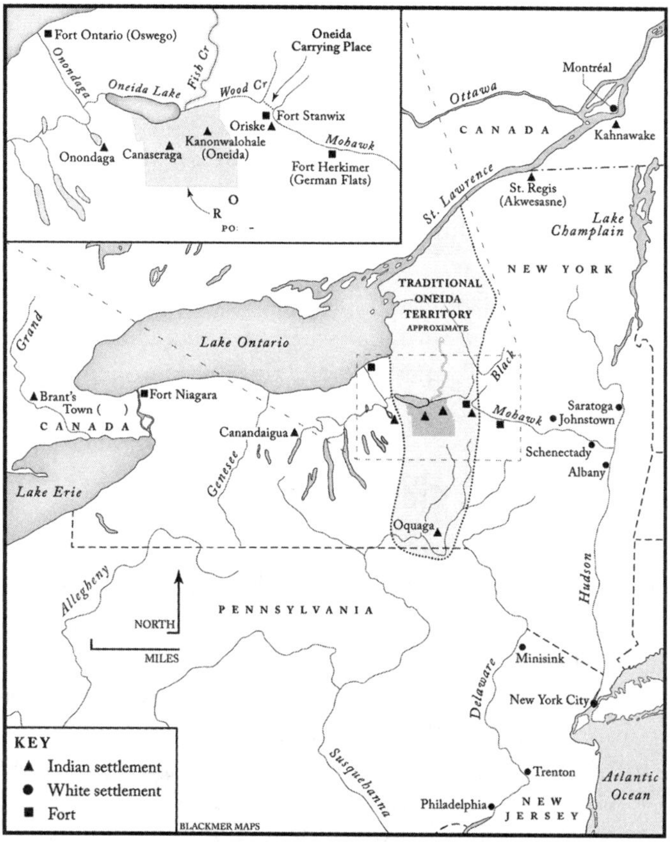

FIGURE 14. Oneida territory in the late 1700s. Following the Treaty of 1788 made with New York State, the Oneida Nation was reduced to a reservation of three hundred thousand acres southeast of Oneida Lake. Reprinted from *The People of the Standing Stone*. © 2011 by the University of Massachusetts Press.

The Oneidas approved a plan to support themselves by leasing their land. They knew every inch of their territory, but they didn't know what an inch was. Many of them were not familiar with the surveyor's measures of rods, links, and chains, or rendering calculations in arabic numbers, or practicing concepts of debt and interest. Few white people, admitted one official, understood the legal jargon used in deeds and contracts. The Oneidas needed someone to advise them. They appointed Peter Penet as their agent, but they began to lose confidence in him. Honyery and the warriors asked the governor whether Penet truly represented the French king. Clinton replied that Penet represented only himself.[43]

The Oneidas were on edge. When they went to Fort Stanwix to receive their annuity payment, they reported that white people had moved onto their reservation. State officials assured them that they would remove any intruders as soon as the surveyors completed their work. Colonel Louis complained that the boundary lines drawn by the surveyors were too generous to the state. Honyery was concerned because settlers who had killed the hogs of their white neighbors blamed the crime on young warriors. The Oneidas held council after council to discuss what to do about hunger in their towns, their supposed French friend, the state's actions, and the onslaught of settlers, but they could not agree. The Oriske families, according to Kirkland, were at odds with the rest of the Oneidas. I wonder whether, situated as they were, the Oriskes felt the most vulnerable despite their extraordinary service during the Revolution.[44]

"Be Obedient to Your Great Chief"

While the Oneidas struggled with their differences, New Yorkers split over the ratification of a new US Constitution. Federalists, led by Alexander Hamilton, wanted a centralized government strong enough to set up a reliable financial system and conduct foreign policy. The United States was in debt and its money was a mess. Hamilton's proposed reforms found support in the seaboard counties, which needed a trusted currency for international trade. Antifederalists led by Governor Clinton feared that Hamilton's policies would benefit the rich minority. Farmers in the backcountry worried that a more powerful government might limit their access to Indigenous land, raise taxes, and infringe on freedoms. James Madison's promise to add a bill of rights did not win them over.[45]

James Duane supported the Federalists, but his tenants did not. They already objected to New York State's voter eligibility laws based on property ownership. The tenants, reported John Myers, resented laws that prevented veterans, who had defended the state when called out again and again but were in debt or without sufficient property, from voting in all elections, while some who had served King George had full voting rights. John would have known the case of Peter Brewer, a fellow militiaman of the Fifteenth Regiment of Albany County and my fourth great-grandfather. The Brewers had been tenants on Vought's Patent, two thousand acres next to Duanesburg, owned by John Christopher Vought, a well-known Loyalist of Hunterdon County, New Jersey. Although Vought's New Jersey property had been confiscated, he retained his property near Schenectady and settled there when his family returned from Canada around 1787. As a major landowner, Vought therefore had voting rights that Peter Brewer did not. "If that be the rights of america," protested John to Duane, "then it maks no mater who was for king or country."[46]

Instructed by his boss to promote the new Constitution, John informed Duane that he had "a grate deal of trubel." He reported that most people in Schenectady, Schoharie, and Montgomery County (formerly Tryon County) opposed it. The New York State convention, with Duane as a delegate, voted for ratification without any yes votes from north of Dutchess and Ulster Counties. In addition, Duane pushed through a state law that made Duanesburg an independent political entity, thereby securing his family's control over their estate. For years, Duanesburg voters elected Duane's son-in-law and son to represent them in the state legislature.[47]

"Terabel cry for bread—as ever I seen," observed John in 1789. Many have nothing, he wrote. "The one cant healp the other." Pressed by Duane to collect his rents, John said that many tenants were too poor to pay. Smallpox went through the estate, he reported, "as some are for nokelaten [inoculation]" and others were not. To attract tenants, Duane built new mills, a school, and a church he thought necessary "to prevent the Inhabitants from running wild." While new tenants leased farms, others left to seek a place of their own on former Haudenosaunee territory taken over by the state, now routinely referred to as "government land." As John Myers had noted, "the rights of America" were tied to property, even though that property belonged to someone else.[48]

During these hard times, the Oneidas heard a terrible rumor that they had sold most of their territory to New York. When they questioned Indian commissioner John Tayler, a witness of the 1788 treaty, Tayler avoided a direct answer. They found someone to explain "the writings" to them. "We find our Hope and Expectations blasted and disappointed in every particular," the stunned Oneidas wrote the governor. Honyery was part of the delegation, accompanied by Kirkland, that went to New York City in 1790 to see Clinton. The Oneidas wanted an annuity that reflected the true value of their land and redrawn survey lines. "The several Matters of Complaint and Request contained in the messages from the Oneidas are without foundation," concluded state officials. The governor assured the Oneidas that the state had their "interest and happiness at heart."[49]

The delegation spoke for Oriske. The chiefs could not find any writing or recollect any agreement regarding its sale, they explained. William

Johnson had promised that they would remain the proprietors. General Schuyler, they said, told them that if they conquered the common enemy, the Oneidas should be happy and retain their property. "We never deserted," said the warriors. "We love our land." They asked for "some writing" to secure their claim to Oriske. Instead, Governor Clinton took Honyery to the secretary's office to show him the deed for Oriskany, which was interpreted for him by Kirkland. According to the state's account, Honyery "appeared to be satisfied that the Indian Rights to the soil had been extinguished."[50]

What was this moment like for Honyery as he looked at the paper he could not read? Did he recall Oriskany, Saratoga, Valley Forge, and the defense of the Mohawk Valley? Did he picture the rebuilt village on the paths and the river that could take him anywhere he wanted to go? Did he think about the warriors who followed him, the women who tended the crops, or the children born there?

What Honyery did, according to the records, was to ask that he and his tribe might remain at Oriske until they could prepare to move and that they be compensated for the improvements they had made to the land. The officials gave the delegation blankets and cash. What the Oneidas wanted was justice. "We are free People," they said. "We choose to regulate our Affairs and to conduct our concerns by the Rules and Maxims of our Ancestors," they concluded with dignity and, again, possibly sarcasm, "without being governed by the Laws of our Brothers, the White People, which are not calculated for a People so little civilized as we are."[51]

As the Oneidas prepared to leave Oriske, investors came to marvel over the Carrying Place. It was the "only water communication with the immense regions in the west, which are destined to bless millions of freemen in the approaching century," pronounced Elkanah Watson. He had moved to Albany to speculate on the military tracts, the almost two million acres of Onondaga, Cayuga, and Seneca lands acquired by New York State and set aside for veterans. Watson was investigating routes for Philip Schuyler's Western Inland Lock Navigation Company, which planned to build a canal to connect the Hudson River to Lake Ontario. As he was rowed across Oneida Lake, Watson looked to the south. "The country lies flat, for 8 to 10 miles, and then swells into waving hills," he noted. It was "at present inhabited by the Oneida Nation of Indians," but not for long, he assumed. "Our western country," he exulted, was unsurpassed for its "luxuriance of soil, mildness of climate, and easy access to markets."[52]

In contrast to the new arrivals on the New York frontier, the recently elected President Washington was not in a hurry to remove the Haudenosaunee. He wanted the Six Nations to serve as a buffer between the United States and the Indigenous people to the west and the British to the north. For a nation low on funds, there were the expenses to consider. The cost of taking Ohio by force, for example, would total about $200,000, whereas purchasing it from the Indians might run the government around $16,000 in cash and presents. Besides, Washington felt that recognizing the Native people's "right to the soil" and buying it from them was the honorable thing to do. The Constitution decreed that all treaties, defined as "the supreme law of the land," had to be ratified by the US Senate and signed by the president.[53]

At a council with the Six Nations in Philadelphia in 1792, US Indian commissioner Timothy Pickering expected the magnificent entertainments to "excite [the] reverence" of the Six Nations. Instead, the unhappy Oneida delegation told Pickering how New York State had deceived them out of over five million acres. The governor did not say, "I buy your country," Good Peter recalled. "Nor did we say—'We sell it to you.'" The consequences of the Oneidas' attachment to the United

FIGURE 15. Miniature of Good Peter, or Agwrongdougwas, at age seventy-five, painted in Philadelphia in 1792. The artist, John Trumball, described him as a great orator. Trumball Collection, Yale University Art Gallery.

States, concluded Pickering, "have not been 'good' unless it is good for them to lose almost all their lands for a trifle." Philadelphia held a lavish funeral for Peter Otsequette, who died during the council. The wise and trusted Good Peter passed away some months later.[54]

On the latest maps, Kanonwalohale, located at the geographic center of New York State, looked like the site of buried treasure. Any major route west had to go through Oneida lands, as the mapmaker Simeon DeWitt knew better than anyone. DeWitt had served as surveyor general to the Continental Army, where he supervised mapmaking at Washington's headquarters. When President Washington asked DeWitt to become surveyor general of the United States, DeWitt declined. He preferred to be an architect of the Empire State. As surveyor general of New York for fifty years, he played an instrumental role in the acquisition of Haudenosaunee lands. According to the geographer Jo Margaret Mano, DeWitt's 1802 map of New York State "set the standard for the new American school of cartography." On it there was no clearly marked Oneida Reservation, although DeWitt had been there.[55]

The state made DeWitt an Indian commissioner and sent him to Kanonwalohale in 1793 to negotiate another land cession. The Oneidas refused to sell. The Turtle Clan sachem, Captain John, reminded DeWitt of the rewards the Oneidas were supposed to have received after the Revolutionary War. He asked whether the "mighty benefit" promised by the state was "to root us out of the country and reduce us to nothing." In response, DeWitt warned that the legislature would be displeased if the Oneidas were ungrateful. "It is beneath the dignity of the State to use any intrigue to deceive and cheat you out of your lands," he said.[56]

The Oneidas were unconvinced. Captain Peter, the eloquent and volatile son of Good Peter, called out New York for not protecting Oneida lands from individuals, as it had promised. "Here is P[eter] Smith creeping about us to get lands," he said about a young fur trader. Captain Peter waved a copy of the Indian Trade and Intercourse Act of 1793 in front of the state officials. The Indian Trade and Intercourse Acts, passed by Congress in 1790 and 1793, prohibited Natives from selling land without the supervision and approval of Congress and the president. "Be obedient to your Great Chief George Washington," said Captain Peter.[57]

Honyery's family and the Dennys relocated to Canaseraga, on the western border of Oneida territory. Canaseraga was not as important as Oriske, but it was more than good. Described by Samuel Kirkland as "the best land in all their territory," it was located where the main trail west, known as the Genesee Road, crossed Canaseraga Creek. Haudenosaunee runners, veterans moving to the military tracts, and tourists on their way to see the great falls at Niagara stopped at Canaseraga. Honyery's son Cornelius Doxtator ran a tavern out of a log cabin, and John Denny established an inn.[58]

Canaseraga, like Oriske, was a mixed community. Travelers, perplexed that white families lived there, did not know that the Mohawk Dutch families from Canajoharie and the Oneidas from Oriske had grown up together, gone into battle together, and looted Molly Brant's house together. Many of them, including David Schuyler Jr., had been prisoners of war in Canada. With them was David's infamous cousin Honyost Schuyler. These POWs may have returned home to find their farms in ruins or taken over by relatives or newcomers. Unable or unwilling to rebuild their old life, they made a fresh start in an advantageous location where the Schuylers had kinship ties to the Oneidas.[59]

The legality of their residence in Canaseraga was uncertain. Some settlers leased land from Peter Penet, who, in turn, had leased it from a few Oneida sachems. About this time, Penet, who had failed to pay the rent he owed the Oneidas, took off for good to the West Indies. When Honyery protested Penet's lease to the governor, Clinton, who was eager to see the Oneidas of Oriske located elsewhere, took action. He ordered William Colbraith, now sheriff of Herkimer County, and his posse to burn out the squatters. Colbraith arrested Honyost Schuyler, whose theatrics once had helped to rescue him and the defenders of Fort Stanwix. I do not know what happened following this arrest, but Honyost Schuyler had gotten out of worse fixes. He would come to the end of his eventful life two decades later in nearby Canastota.[60]

While Colbraith's posse set fire to the squatter cabins, the Oneidas stood by with "hearts more full of sorrow for the white man than joy for justice secured them by righteous laws," according to nineteenth-century local histories. In these accounts, the Oneidas took pity on the homeless settlers and provided them with lands on Chittenango Creek south of the Genesee Road. The records show that the Oneidas, however sympathetic they may have been, were doing business. They leased land to the Schuylers and others, who paid their rent to Jacob Reed. Honyery's son Jacob Doxtator, John Denny, Skenandoah, and others visited their tenants to discuss a survey of the lots.[61]

The Oneidas also welcomed members of the Klock family to their territory. Conrad Klock, the brother of the "old rogue" George Klock and Colonel Jacob Klock, had been a prisoner of war in Canada for three years. He and his sons, who would spell their name "Clock," leased from the Oneidas three hundred acres south of the main road at present-day Clockville. About "old Mr. Clock," the Oneida chiefs told Sheriff Colbraith, "We esteem him a clever, harmless, old man, and he is of service to us when we are out that way a hunting. He supplies us with milk and such things as we want."[62]

The Oneidas at Canaseraga, who dressed like white people, kept some Dutch customs. On New Year's Day, they fired guns into the air. On Sundays, they went to church, ate, drank, and made merry. Although Kirkland acknowledged that the people from Oriske had considerable abilities and were decent farmers, he did not approve of them. They "could not bear the restraints of the Christian religion, nor love its doctrines," he observed. Many of them belonged to what Kirkland called the Pagan Party. The word *pagan*, which was from the Latin and meant "of the countryside," had come to refer to those who practiced the old religions of gods and spirits on the land. Kirkland proposed a formal division of Oneidas into Christian and Pagan communities. Kanonwalohale was to be civilized, agricultural, Christian, and without ardent spirits, and Canaseraga not. The Oneidas rejected the proposal.[63]

At his new home, Honyery was concerned about the threat to Oneida land posed by Peter Smith. In 1788, the fur trader had opened a store at Old Fort Schuyler, where he sold goods shipped from New York City by his partner, John Jacob Astor. Smith learned to speak Oneida; sold merchandise to Indians on credit, which made them indebted to him; cultivated a friendship with Skenandoah; and made a secret deal with Jacob Reed. Without state or federal approval, he secured from some of the chiefs a lease to lands in the present-day townships of Cazenovia, Fenner, Smithfield, Stockbridge, and Augusta. Smith sent in surveyors to measure lots on land that belonged to the Oneidas.[64]

By this time, it appears, Honyery had given up asking state and federal authorities to protect Oneida land. In 1793, the old war chief led a party that included his sons and Captain Peter. They broke the compass and the chains of Smith's surveyors at work north of present-day Peterboro. Someone threw a hatchet at the surveyor Joseph Annin. "In warding off the weapon from a more vital spot," Annin was struck in the hand and seriously injured, reported the local historian William H. Tuttle. Annin made his way back to his lodgings at the home of the Clocks. The sachems deplored the attack, which turned out to be the great warrior's last fight. Honyery died soon afterward when a sickness swept through the Oneidas, taking some forty to fifty lives. The Oneidas never forgot Honyery.[65]

"We Are Nothing but a Wreck of Bones!"

Honyery did not live to see the Oneidas attend the momentous Six Nations Council held in Canandaigua in 1794. In a time of war on the frontier and in Europe, the United States and the Six Nations revived their commitment to peaceful coexistence. The US government pledged federal protection of Oneida, Cayuga, and Onondaga lands, guaranteed hunting and fishing rights, and returned a million acres to the Senecas. The Six Nations surrendered claims to land outside New York and agreed that US citizens could pass freely through their territories. The United States confirmed the Treaty of Canandaigua with wampum known as the George Washington or Covenant Chain belt, presents worth $10,000, and the promise of treaty cloth to be delivered every year.[66]

Something more must be done for the Oneidas, said Commissioner Pickering. At Oneida, a lengthy list was made of wartime losses. The late Honyery had lost the most. Louis Denny had lost a cow, two large hogs, two brass kettles, and a harness. With the Oneida Veterans Treaty, ratified by Congress in 1795, the United States "acknowledged their obligation to these faithful friends" and paid $5,000 to compensate their losses. What the Oneidas really wanted was their land back. Its restoration, they believed, would reunite their nation. Pickering assured them, "The land is yours and the State cannot take it from you without your own consent." He reminded them to make sure a federal treaty commissioner was present at any transaction. "Follow this advice, and nobody can hurt you for the United States will protect you."[67]

Although the Oneidas had lost a great deal of their territory to the state, they kept the most valuable section along the main road, which included the best land. New York saw a chance to acquire some of it when the People of the Standing Stone asked for help. The Oneidas wanted the state to overturn the disputed lease to Peter Smith and appoint their friends General Philip Schuyler and James Dean to oversee the leasing of their lands. The state asked Schuyler to serve as the state's commissioner and Dean as the state's interpreter. Schuyler had a personal incentive for taking on this duty. He needed Oneida land to build his canal near the Carrying Place.[68]

The Oneidas declined to sell any territory. "We are nothing but a wreck of Bones!" said Captain John. "Our lands are almost all gone from us, for almost nothing." According to Samuel Kirkland, the Turtle Clan sachem had a "very discerning mind, at least for an Indian." Captain

John wanted a federal treaty commissioner present, but the legislature voted down an amendment to request the presence of a federal commissioner when it authorized the purchase of Indian land. It mandated a rock-bottom purchase price that even Governor Clinton thought was unfair. This legislative act was "a Stain on our public Records," protested the lawyer Jonas Platt, the Herkimer County Clerk.[69]

Pickering, now secretary of war, sent the New York State government and Captain Israel Chapin Jr., the federal agent to the Six Nations, the legal opinion of the US attorney general. Aboriginal title, said the opinion, "cannot be extinguished but by a treaty holden under the authority of the United States, and in the manner prescribed by the laws of Congress." Chapin delivered the warning, which General Schuyler urged the Oneidas to ignore. "We act perfectly agreeable to the law," the general told them. When Captain John opposed the sale of a large tract, he was removed from the treaty negotiations. The dejected sachem turned to alcohol. "We drink and we drink again," he once said. "By and by, our hearts grow light." When Captain John, a veteran of Valley Forge, died in Albany while the treaty was being concluded, the state commissioners insisted on finishing their business. There was no time for condolence.[70]

The Treaty of 1795 ceded about 132,000 acres, over half of the Oneida Reservation, to New York State. The signers included Jacob Doxtator and John Denny, who were assured by the state that the Oneidas would retain possession of Canaseraga. For their support, Skenandoah, Kanadolock, and Jacob Reed received cash payments ranging from $50 to $250. These amounts were not insignificant at a time when an unskilled worker made about a dollar a day. New York State paid $2,952 to the Oneidas outright and added $2,952 to the annuity. It spent around $0.50 per acre for land it sold for seven times that. The federal government, informed after the fact of New York State's violation of the law, decided it was too late to do anything about it. Instead it secured the promise of newly elected Federalist Party governor John Jay to obey US law in future land deals.[71]

The biggest individual beneficiary of the treaty was Peter Smith, who now could buy the land he leased from the Oneidas. The cession also included the Wood Creek property Philip Schuyler wanted. James Dean and Abraham Van Eps, who helped to persuade the sachems, chiefs, and clan mothers to agree to the treaty, received substantial parcels. The two square miles granted to Van Eps included the site of Old Oneida near present-day Vernon. Van Eps opened a store, built mills, and had no difficulty selling lots. He could tell prospective buyers that while visiting

Nicholas Jordan's place on Sconondoa Creek one evening, he had seen a fishing party spear half a cord of salmon.[72]

By the late 1790s, prominent New Yorkers had assumed the role of gatekeepers of Oneida territory. They guided the tour of Jeremy Belknap and Jedediah Morse, two ministers from Massachusetts, who came to investigate Kirkland's mission. Disgruntled Oneidas had complained of their missionary's neglect as Kirkland, in ill health and frustrated by his flock's lack of devotion, had turned his energies to founding the Oneida Hamilton Academy (later Hamilton College), named in honor of Alexander Hamilton. In Albany, Belknap stayed at the home of Lieutenant Governor Stephen Van Rensselaer, the ninth patroon, while Morse lodged with Elkanah Watson. The ministers traveled to the Carrying Place with Philip Schuyler, who was on his way to supervise his canal project. On the journey, Schuyler talked about the communal land practices of the Oneidas and how these traditions discouraged the men from advancing themselves.[73]

At Whitestown, near what had been Oriske, Belknap and Morse stayed with Assemblyman Jonas Platt. From there they rode on horseback through the property at Westmoreland granted to James Dean, who served as interpreter for the two men. At Kanonwalohale they stayed with Skenandoah, as Schuyler had recommended. At the chief's two-story house, the ministers dined on salmon, corn cake, fried eggs, and strawberries. On their return trip they visited James Duane, who had retired to his Duanesburg estate.[74]

While other visitors commented on the harmony of Oneida singing and the playing of a vigorous game "which consists of making a ball fly," Belknap and Morse focused on matters of God and the land. The Oneidas, they reported, had embraced neither Christianity nor civilization, despite Kirkland's efforts. There were only eight professed Pagans among them, but the whole nation was still influenced by traditional beliefs. The ministers visited Oneidas from Oriske who had settled southwest of Vernon at an orchard of hundreds of ancient apple trees. They saw the standing stone outside the home of an elder who told them he believed the rocks and winds had spirits. The Oneidas, reported the ministers, believed that "the Great Spirit gave the White man a plough, and the red man a bow and arrow, and sent them into the world by different paths, each to live in his own way."[75]

Belknap and Morse described Oneida agriculture as being "in its infancy" with the "labor being performed almost wholly by the women." The people may fence and cultivate as much ground as they please, noted the ministers, "but the land is the common property of the nation." A family that grows more than it needs is expected to feed the others. The ministers, echoing Schuyler, wrote that this practice discouraged individual ambition. The Oneidas "have a large tract of the most excellent land extremely well situated with respect to lakes and streams of water" with access to good markets, reported the ministers. "But they are insensible of these advantages and attached to their ancient habits." The Oneidas, they suggested, were not capable of becoming civilized nor did they deserve such fine land.[76]

White squatters believed they deserved the fine land of the Oneidas. One of them was my sixth great-grandfather Conraeth Moet, known as Conrad Moot, from Columbia County. Conrad's father at age sixteen had indentured himself for seven years to pay his passage from Germany in 1750. Father and son had served in the Albany County militia, led by General Robert Van Rensselaer. In contrast to the Mohawk Valley, where the rebels fought against the landed gentry, the rebels of Columbia County fought under them. Perhaps Conrad, like many veterans, felt owed for his military service and wanted payment in land, which to him meant security and freedom.[77]

Conrad left behind a tenant rebellion that had broken out on the large estates along the Hudson River. To protest the eviction of delinquent tenants from Livingston Manor, angry farmers dressed up like Indians. In the tradition of the Boston Tea Party, they assumed an identity as the true owners of the land who had been deprived of their rights. Governor Jay called out the militia to put down the tenant uprising. Leasing was demoralizing, said a missionary who sympathized with the tenants. "If men do not possess the right of the soil," he thought, "they never will nor can feel independent."[78]

Conrad chose a location near the Clocks. To be there on the ground was a way that poor men could beat out wealthy and well-connected speculators. Squatters gambled that the state would give them legal title to the land. They presented officials with a dilemma: the state could make more money selling land to rich men, but it also wanted the land settled. It chose not to evict these people despite its promise to protect Oneida territory. Governor Jay ordered out the militia to enforce the landowner rights of the Livingstons but not those of the People of the Standing Stone. A few of my forebears, I found out, were small-time crooks taking part in a major theft.[79]

It was the Oneidas who now felt bewildered on their territory. Federal officials said one thing, state officials said another, speculators manipulated the law, and squatters ignored it. Greed and ambition overrode pledges of eternal gratitude for their wartime sacrifices and guarantees of their territory confirmed by treaty. The Oneidas saw old friends and allies profit from their poverty and dispossession. Grasshopper, Good Peter, Captain John, and Honyery had tried to stop the loss of their territory. More often than not, they failed. They nevertheless left an enduring legacy about the land, rights, and sovereignty in the treaties they negotiated in good faith and in the protests they made against deceit and injustice. Their children inherited a much diminished nation. Some of them felt the key to survival was cooperation with white authorities; others believed in keeping to their own path. In Canaseraga, the Doxtators and the Dennys tried to do both.[80]

Back in the Mohawk Valley, the families of my ancestors Lambert Clement and Henry Timmerman spread out on the former Royal Grant. Henry had the satisfaction of purchasing a lot that William Johnson had left to one of his and Molly Brant's sons. There some of his children raised their families. The confiscation of Loyalist properties may have caused mixed feelings for Lambert Clement. New York State sold the Tribes Hill farm that had been the home of his grandparents Joseph and Anna. It was seized from the family of his Loyalist uncle Lewis Clement, who had died during the war. Lambert's cousins, along with many Loyalists and Mohawks from the Mohawk and Schoharie Valleys, settled in Canada.[81]

The Mohawk and Oneida towns of Tiononderogue, Canajoharie, and Oriske no longer existed, but the Timmermans often met Indians on the road. Oneidas and Mohawks still stopped by for food and news, although the custom was derided by newcomers as begging. One visit in the early 1800s left a vivid impression on a Timmerman boy. "I remember a squaw all dressed in silk and attended by another Injun woman who came by the house one day," he recalled years later. "I thought she was a princess." The passing of Henry Timmerman in 1807 was recorded in German in a family Bible. The father of nineteen, Henry had over one hundred grandchildren who would have to find somewhere to make a living. In his memory was inscribed a verse from the Book of Genesis: "And Israel said unto Joseph, Behold I die; but God shall be with you, and bring you again unto the land of your fathers."[82]

CHAPTER 5

"We Shall All Be Americans"

The Story of Polly and Angel

In the early 1800s, the best land became the home of Polly Denny's Oneida and Mohawk family and a haven for an exiled Frenchman named Angel Deferrier. It was time, said President Thomas Jefferson, for Indians and settlers to "become one people." The Haudenosaunee once had invited Europeans to be "one people" in the land of the longhouse. Now Jefferson told Native leaders, "We shall all be Americans." He said, "You will mix with us by marriage, your blood will run in our veins, and will spread with us over this great island." If not, he believed, Indigenous people would be driven out.[1]

For the best land, the most significant marriage was of Polly and Angel. Although they are well known in local history, the couple left few records. I rely on what others said about them, but not without questions. How did Polly and Angel become the owners of valuable Oneida land? In what ways did Polly's family and the Oneidas deal with the myriad of demands on their remaining territory made by New York State, developers, and settlers? What happened to my ancestors who were squatters on Oneida land? For all of them, the era of the early republic was one of relentless transformation, good and bad.

Local histories describe Polly as either Indian or civilized. She was "one of the most charming and beautiful Indian maidens that ever lived in this section of the country," wrote George Russell. "She could ride a horse, use a bow and arrow, shoot a gun and do all the things which an Indian girl in those days could do." Mrs. L. M. Hammond, author of *The History of Madison County*, was having none of that. Polly was "a respectable young woman, with pleasant manners and civilized habits," she wrote, "said by some to be very beautiful, and resembling the race to which her mother belonged but very little." Polly probably could do all those things—ride and shoot and have civilized habits, whatever they were.[2]

A glimpse of Polly's life is provided by the recollections of a young traveler. Fourteen-year-old Helen Burrows sailed up the Hudson from New York to Albany in 1796. She was amused to hear people speaking Dutch along the Mohawk River and felt afraid of the first Indian she ever saw at Old Fort Schuyler. As she headed west beyond the log cabin of James Dean at Westmoreland, the driver walked beside her carriage to keep it from falling over on the terrible road. After a stop at Kanonwalohale to feed the horses, Helen crossed the best land and spent the night

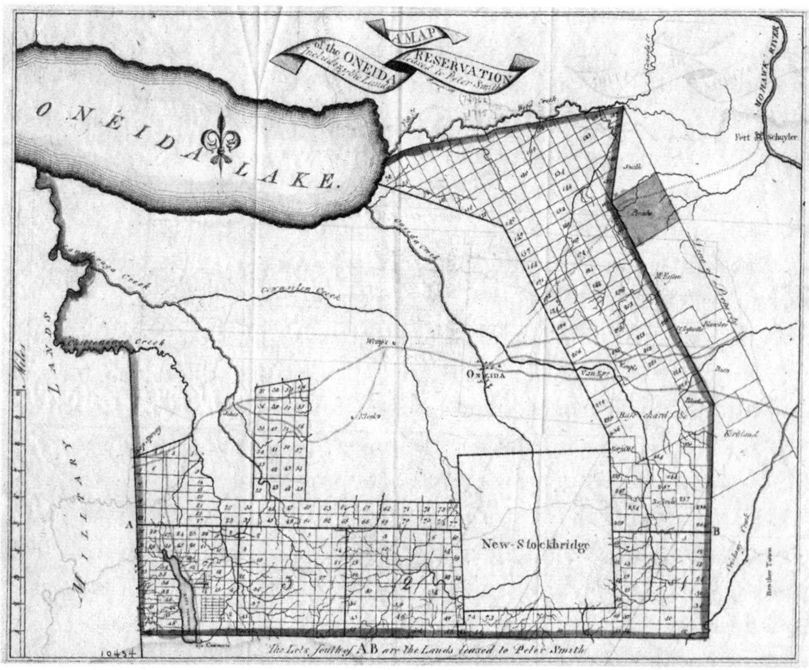

FIGURE 16. By the late 1790s, the best land was in the middle of the Oneida Reservation, surrounded by a grid of lots. Located on the Genesee Road was John Denny's inn on Canaseraga Creek, Wemp's near Cowaselon Creek, and Oneida, or Kanonwalohale, on Oneida Creek. Klock's place was to the south of Wemp's. "A Map of the Oneida Reservation including Lands Leased to Peter Smith," ca. 1795, New York State Library Manuscripts and Special Collections.

at the log inn of Myndert Wemple, who was from a Schenectady family with long-standing ties to the Six Nations. The next day, Helen stopped at John Denny's inn in Canaseraga. She met Polly, who took Helen to her own room, which Helen thought was fancifully furnished, and gave her a drink of cold water, a rare treat for frontier travelers. So began an acquaintance that would last five decades.[3]

That afternoon, Helen reached her destination, the new settlement called Cazenovia, which was a headquarters of the Holland Land Company. The company's agent, John Lincklaen of Amsterdam, named the village after his boss, the Dutch financier Theophile Cazenove, who had learned how to grease the wheels of the New York State government. After Cazenove failed to persuade the legislature to lift its restrictions on alien land ownership, he had been encouraged by Alexander Hamilton to invest $250,000 in the Western Inland Lock Navigation Company, run by Hamilton's father-in-law as the way to make things happen. Cazenove made a better deal with Assemblyman Aaron Burr, who accepted a $5,000 "loan" in return for managing the passage of an alien landowners act in 1798. By placing their funds in the hands of trustees, the Dutch investors already had acquired the one hundred thousand acres ceded by the Oneidas in the Treaty of 1788 and four thousand acres bought from Peter Smith under Lincklaen's management.[4]

Helen, an orphan, had come to live with her uncle Major Samuel Forman, one of several members of her family who held positions with the Holland Land Company. They would develop the Haudenosaunee territory so admired by Helen's father and other US troops during the Sullivan Expedition. On land "that exceeds any I have ever seen," Major John Burrows of New Jersey observed corn, beans, cucumbers, melons, and pumpkins "in such quantities . . . almost incredible to a civilized people." Major Burrows died before he could return to the home of the Six Nations, but his relations made their way there.[5]

Major Forman ran the store set up by Lincklaen, who sought to entice a more affluent, respectable class of settlers to Cazenovia with such amenities as roads, mills, and a well-stocked emporium. One day, Lincklaen took Helen to Oneida Castle to visit Skenandoah, "a very handsome fine looking old Indian," she thought. Of the white people she preferred the village residents to the rough folks back in the woods. I wonder if she was referring to my ancestors squatting nearby on Oneida land, who, I suspect, were not the type of people Lincklaen hoped to attract to Cazenovia.[6]

Helen later married her uncle Samuel's friend, Samuel Sidney Breese, who went by Sidney. A Yale University graduate and a lawyer who included Aaron Burr among his clients, Sidney worked for the Holland Land Company as Lincklaen's clerk. He also served as justice of the peace as well as the county clerk of Chenango County, created in 1798 and comprising present-day Madison and Chenango Counties. Sidney specialized in property cases, managed the sale of lots, and recorded deeds. When he had traveled to Cazenovia from New York, possibly along the same route taken by Helen, he was accompanied by the Frenchman Angel Deferrier.[7]

Angel's tombstone says he was born in Niort in western France and was at the royal palace of Versailles at the time of the French Revolution. I wondered whether Angel was the man he claimed to be. Yes, he was, I learned. Angel came from an ancient noble family, which displayed its connection to the New World on its coat of arms, consisting of a black lion with red claws, tongue, and crown rampant on a silver field bordered in black with eleven gold bezants, and a helmet on the crest, all supported by two "savages." The city of Niort long had depended on North America as the source of animal hides needed for its tanning industry as well as a market for its cloth. The hard times following the loss of Canada as well as the failure of his family to pass on wealth to go with its land made the decision by Angel's father to marry an heiress a practical one.[8]

Angel's mother had been born in Quebec, where her father, the colonial official Jacques-Michel Breard, made a fortune in furs and shipping. When Breard brought his family back to France, he purchased a manor house southeast of Niort. Although Breard's enrichment of himself while in service to the king was standard practice, he was arrested for defrauding the state, imprisoned in the Bastille, tried, fined, and banished from Paris. By 1771, when he was exonerated by Louis XV, he had married off his daughters, with their large dowries, to poor noblemen. On 8 January 1769, the vicar of the church of St. Andre in Niort recorded the baptism of "Ange César Theophille born at three o'clock this morning Legitimate son of my lord Charles César d'Algret d'Olède, Seigneur de Ferrierre and the lady Marie Angelique Breard."[9]

As a boy, Angel spent the winters in Niort, with its canals, markets, and imposing fortress built by Henry II and Eleanor of Aquitaine. In the summers, he lived at the nearby *seigneurie*, or manor, called Ferrieres, which he was to inherit as his father's eldest living son. At Ferrieres, the inhabitants plied the trades of the woods, the earth, and the vine.

In return for ten bushels of oats delivered by the feast of Saint Luke, two cattle, and chores done with oxen and carts for the house of Ferrieres, the peasants were permitted, according to an agreement between their ancestors and Angel's, to graze their livestock in the lord's woods and pastures. A mill built by Angel's great-great-grandfather was called the Bird Singing Mill because the countryside was so quiet that you could hear the birds sing. It was a way of saying that Ferrieres was in the middle of nowhere.[10]

As the son of a provincial noble, Angel was expected to serve the king. After attending military school, he became at age eighteen one of Louis XVI's Guarde du Corps, or bodyguards. The aristocratic regiment, better known for its courtly manners than its military prowess, had not seen action for decades because it took the field only when the king did. Two years later, Charles César, a *chevalier* (knight), attended the assembly of nobles held in Poitiers to elect deputies to the Estates General, which had been called to deal with the national crisis of 1789. Niort's wheat crop had perished, and all of France suffered the worst harvest in decades. Charles César died soon after, which meant that Angel would have succeeded him as lord of Ferrieres, if not for the revolution.[11]

Angel was with the king when the National Assembly voted to do away with feudalism. Led by reformers, the assembly approved the Declaration of the Rights of Man and of the Citizen, drafted with advice from Thomas Jefferson, the US minister to France. While people starved, the bodyguards at Versailles hosted a lavish banquet. They cheered the king and his queen, Marie Antoinette, and made a fuss over their son, the four-year-old Prince Louis (known as the Dauphin), the heir to the throne. Rumors of an orgy of feasting and treason spread to Paris. A mob yelling, "Kill the bodyguards!" stormed the palace two days later. Some of the guards locked themselves in the guardroom, while others held the doors to the royal apartments to protect the king and queen until the Marquis de Lafayette arrived to stop the bloodshed. I don't know how Angel conducted himself. My guess is that at age twenty, he was hoping to see twenty-one.[12]

The mob, carrying the heads of two bodyguards on pikes, forced the royal family to return to Paris. Angel joined the newly founded National Guard, or citizen's militia, commanded by Lafayette. The Guardsmen watched as the king swore to uphold the new constitution before an enormous crowd on the Champ de Mars. The king and queen held up the Dauphin dressed in a little Guardsman uniform.

After the royal family was caught attempting to escape, the revolution grew more radical. All titles of hereditary nobility and the monarchy were abolished, war broke out, and Louis XVI was executed for treason. During the reign of terror that followed, the government put to death tens of thousands deemed enemies of the revolution. Royalists and nobles fled.[13]

Angel left for Amsterdam, where he contacted investors in the Holland Land Company, who provided him with letters of credit to their bankers in the United States. Theophile Cazenove financed the relocation of many French aristocrats to the young republic. Angel may have hoped to follow in the footsteps of his maternal grandfather by seeking his fortune in the New World. He reportedly was not impressed with New York City and sought adventure on the frontier in Cazenovia, where he lived with Lincklaen. At Forman's store, Angel bought flour, tea, pork, and silk, which suggests that he had not given up entirely on the finer things. He was said to exhibit symptoms of mental derangement. Feelings of depression and despair were common among French exiles.[14]

New York and Pennsylvania provided a temporary home for many of the twenty thousand French men and women who sought refuge in the 1790s. Several émigrés settled near the Oneidas. At Asylum on the Susquehanna River in present-day Bradford County, Pennsylvania, they built a three-story log house for Marie Antoinette. After the queen's execution, they awaited the Dauphin until they learned he had died in prison. The émigrés, who tried making a living as farmers, chefs, or dance instructors, were at times so hungry they ate robins and tadpoles. They revived their former glamour at a resplendent celebration of the wedding of their highest-ranking resident, the Marquis de Blâcons, a former liberal member of the Estates General who had dined with Lafayette and Jefferson in Paris and now ran a haberdasher shop. In gratitude to the Oneidas who helped them to survive, the marquis and his wife named their baby Marie Madeleine Adélaïde Alexandrine Oneida. Her family would pass down the name Oneida in memory of kindness in the forests of the United States.[15]

When France's new ruler, Napoleon Bonaparte, gave the exiles permission to apply for repatriation and restoration of their property, most returned. Angel did not, because he had met the French-speaking Denny family in Canaseraga and married Polly. The couple moved south to Delaware County for a few years, and when they came back to Oneida territory with two small daughters, they lived in a log cabin at the village called Cowaselon (Skawagslea), after the creek that crossed the main road. Oneidas who had sought shelter with the British during the American Revolution, along with refugees from Oquaga and the dispossessed from Oriske, had settled there. Angel called himself Colonel Deferrier, using the typical military rank for young French noblemen and the name of the seigneurie of his ancestors.[16]

Compagnie of the Oneida Chiefs and Warriors

By marrying Polly, Angel had allied himself with an important family of property who were well-known go-betweens on the edge of Oneida territory. Canaseraga was vulnerable, however, because New York State wanted to develop the Genesee Road. Although Jacob Doxtator protested the sale of the western side of Oneida territory, the state gave itself permission to extinguish the Oneidas' claim to their reserved land that "may be convenient for public roads." The Doxtators and the Dennys did not sign the Treaty of 1798, in which the Oneidas ceded thirty thousand acres on their borders, including tracts on the main road through present-day Sherrill and Canastota.[17]

The treaty allowed Honyery's widow, now known as Sarah Doxtator, her sons Cornelius and Jacob, her son-in-law John Denny, and Louis Denny to remain on the land they had cultivated and improved, in lots limited to fifty acres. This provision, however, may not have reassured those who had lost Oriske. They worried that some chiefs or sachems might be persuaded to sell their new residence out from under them, as they believed had happened before. Even though Governor Jay followed US law by having a federal commissioner present, getting US Senate approval, and having President John Adams sign the Treaty of 1798, the state previously had ignored such protections put in place by the federal government.[18]

The Doxtators and Dennys adopted a new strategy. They petitioned to be subjected to the same laws and enjoy the same rights as the white inhabitants regarding the possession of their land. They informed the state legislature that they wished to keep their rights to the "common and unappropriated lands" of the Oneidas and remain eligible for their part of the annuities. The state granted Sarah, Jacob, and Cornelius Doxtator the right to "sell and dispose of their Lots as the White People do." It granted Dolly Doxtator's husband, John Denny, 250 acres for a dollar an acre. John leased his lots to white tenants who improved his lands, which rapidly rose in value. I wonder if Polly's family recalled the observation of Good Peter: Indians with land were important. Indians without land were not.[19]

The Doxtators and Dennys were right to be concerned. The Oneidas, facing hunger after a spring flood drowned their crops, decided they may as well get something for sections of their territory illegally inhabited by white people. Accompanied by Myndert Wemple, a group traveled to Albany to negotiate the Treaty of 1802, which ceded four thousand acres along Fish Creek and seven thousand acres south of present-day Canastota occupied by squatters and leasers, including my ancestor Conrad Moot and the Clock family. The surveyor Joseph Annin, whose encounter with Honyery's last war party had left him with a mutilated hand, served as a witness. In this treaty, Governor Clinton, recently returned to office, followed federal law. Although the US Senate approved the treaty, President Jefferson for some reason never signed it.[20]

The Treaty of 1802 would be the last made with the Oneidas in which New York State obeyed US law. It granted one hundred acres for one hundred dollars to Myndert Wemple, who now owned the land where he lived. The Mohawk Dutch families, who had leased land near Canaseraga from the Oneidas, petitioned to buy it from New York State. The gamble taken by squatters like Conrad Moot paid off when they received from the state preemption rights for the ceded land they had begun to clear and farm. New York rewarded the intruders and itself as squatters turned into property owners and taxpayers. I wonder whether Conrad felt absolved of any wrongdoing.[21]

The property strategy of the Dennys and Doxtators appears to have been accepted by some and resented by others. It positioned these useful multilingual people between white settlement and the reservation, while it also undermined communal tradition. The Oneidas and the state agreed to set aside 320 acres, for a dollar an acre, to Louis Denny and his sons Louis Jr., Jonathan, and Martinus Denny, the tribal interpreter, on the Genesee Road between Wemple's tavern and Canastota. Local histories say that when Angel and Polly married, the Dennys gave the bride and groom a gift of this property. The records show that Angel in 1804 paid Polly's father and brothers $580 for their 320 acres.[22]

Angel and Polly's new property was enhanced by the improvement of the Genesee Road. The state chartered the Seneca Turnpike Company and its commissioners, including Captain Chapin, who combined this position with his job as federal superintendent of Indian affairs, to develop the road through private capital. Sidney Breese, John Lincklaen, and Peter Smith invested in the turnpike, which was completed through to Buffalo in 1809. In addition to the Seneca Turnpike, with its fences, gates, and tollbooths, the Cherry Valley Turnpike (present-day Route 20), which connected Cherry Valley to Cazenovia, and the Peterboro Turnpike, which ran from Vernon to Cazenovia, crisscrossed Oneida land.[23]

The Oneidas felt the decline of prestige and the sting of racial discrimination. "The White Skin race as a body have become proud," said Captain Peter a few weeks before Angel acquired his first 320 acres. "You glory in your riches . . . and despise us Indians for our indigence, our poor huts, our scanty food." Feeling abandoned by old friends as they struggled to reorient their lives on their remaining land, the Oneidas needed new allies. They hoped that Angel, with his education and his Turtle Clan wife, would be an asset to them. The former royal bodyguard may have reminded the Oneidas of their distinguished French friends. They adopted Angel into their nation and gave him one hundred acres where he and Polly lived at Cowaselon.[24]

Beginning in 1805, Angel replaced Samuel Kirkland as a witness of the annuity payments made by New York State to the Oneidas. The elderly missionary credited Angel with fomenting the division between the Pagan and Christian Parties, although Kirkland a decade earlier had advocated a separation between those Oneidas who held traditional beliefs and those who converted to Christianity. When Christian Party leaders asked Angel to take charge of the Oneida mills, the Pagan Party objected.[25]

The two parties, which had tried for years to reach consensus and failed, formalized their disunion in 1805. In a treaty, they split their remaining fifty-thousand-acre reservation in two. Angel witnessed the partition, which the state supported. Cornelius Doxtator, Plattcop, Shagoyontha, Colonel Louis, and Captain Peter signed for the Pagan Party. Skenandoah, Louis Denny, and Kanadolock, now known as Peter Bread, were among the Christian Party signatories. The larger Christian Party was assigned the northern section along the Genesee Road. The Pagan Party received the smaller, hilly section to the south. Although the Oneidas had asked for a federal commissioner to be present, the state conducted the treaty without one.[26]

The splintering over land and tradition divided the Doxtator and Denny families. Dolly Denny, like her brother Cornelius Doxtator, belonged to the Pagan Party, while Louis Denny and Jacob Doxtator belonged to the Christian Party. Converts to Christianity found solace in their faith, but they wondered why it was that Native Christians must be punished for their sins while white Christians, who drank, sinned, and cheated Natives, appeared to enjoy "blessings of every kind." White people viewed Christian Oneidas as on their way to becoming civilized, while the Pagans, as Kirkland explained, held four-day ceremonies of feasts with games of chance, sacrifices of animals, and attention to dreams.[27]

Most of the Pagans were from Oriske, noted Kirkland. He described these once prominent people as "generally proud, self-conceited, envious." They were a "mongrel breed," he wrote, explaining that most of them had some mixture of French-Dutch or African blood. Blood was the way Americans defined who was Oneida, not the way Oneidas did. Talk of the last of the "full-bloods" made it sound like Natives were dying out. "These Indians are all of mixed blood," Jedidiah Morse wrote in the *American Gazetteer*. "[T]here has not been a pure Oneida for several years past." Considered an authority on the Oneidas, Morse misleadingly implied that the People of the Standing Stone no longer existed.[28]

Newcomers to Oneida territory did not understand that for generations the Dennys and the Doxtators, as well as their Mohawk Dutch neighbors, the Schuylers and the Van Slycks, had benefited from the advantages of a blended heritage. Three of John and Dolly Denny's children married spouses from local white families. Mrs. Hammond noted that when their daughter Sarah, called Sally, married handsome John Garlock, her wealthy father gave the couple a bushel of dollars. Mrs. Hammond did not mention the marriages of the Dennys' "good looking" sons Abraham and John to white women, possibly because such unions were considered more disturbing to white society and therefore not to be discussed.[29]

As John Denny's hospitality enterprise flourished, he replaced his frame structure with a large brick building. There was a spacious entryway and four "lofty and well furnished" rooms upstairs, reported an English traveler, who was impressed with the craftsmanship of the Indians who built the inn. At about eighteen by twenty feet, a room at "Indian John's," as it was called, was bigger than a typical pioneer cabin. Frontier taverns welcomed European tourists, locals stopping by to catch up on the news, and the uprooted who were cut off from opportunity for advancement or property ownership. They were known as places to swindle Indigenous people out of land and timber releases, or, in the case of Myndert Wemple's place, the site of auctions held by the state to sell lots of recently ceded Oneida territory. Taverns held "communal binges" at election time, during public hangings, and on the Fourth of July, a day of "national intoxication."[30]

At a militia training held at Canaseraga in 1807, John Denny was killed during a wrestling match with a Mohawk Dutch neighbor. There was no indication of foul play, but John's death created an opening for local white men to seize his property. Dolly Denny refused to be pushed aside. As administrator of John's estate, she hired Sidney Breese, who handled property cases for Angel, John Lincklaen, and Peter Smith. Many of these cases involved trespass, the failure of tenants to pay rent, and boundary disputes. Sidney successfully secured John's properties, amounting to almost six hundred acres, for Dolly and her children. Dolly, the most active Oneida woman in real estate, made her mark on deeds witnessed by her literate son Abraham Denny. Although most Natives left Canaseraga as more white people arrived, she and her family remained.[31]

The Dennys' home at Canaseraga became part of the town of Sullivan, named in honor of the general who had led the expedition to destroy Iroquoia a quarter century earlier. Cazenovia was made the county seat of Madison County, named after James Madison, and was created out of the northern section of Chenango County in 1806. Cowaselon was renamed after Myndert Wemple. Letters came from Old Fort Schuyler, now called Utica, addressed to "Wampsville on the Seneca Turnpike, about 3 miles west of Oneida Castle." Wampsville was in the town of Lenox, set off from the town of Sullivan in 1809. Bordered by the town of Smithfield, named after the universally disliked Peter Smith, to the south and Oneida Lake to the north, the town of Lenox was home to Christian and Pagan Oneidas, Polly and Angel, my ancestors, and the best land.[32]

"Compagnie of the Oneida Indians chiefs & warriors" was how Angel identified himself. In French, the word *compagnie* means companion, escort, military unit, and business firm. Angel accompanied Oneidas to Albany, where he witnessed treaties made by the Christian Party in 1807 and 1809. As James Duane had recommended, New York State replaced traditional councils with business transactions. The Oneidas, who feared that individuals might be bribed or deceived, objected to a process that disregarded their system of government, but they had no power to change it. The state paid out awards to individual Oneidas, as it did with eighty dollars each to Jacob Doxtator and Louis

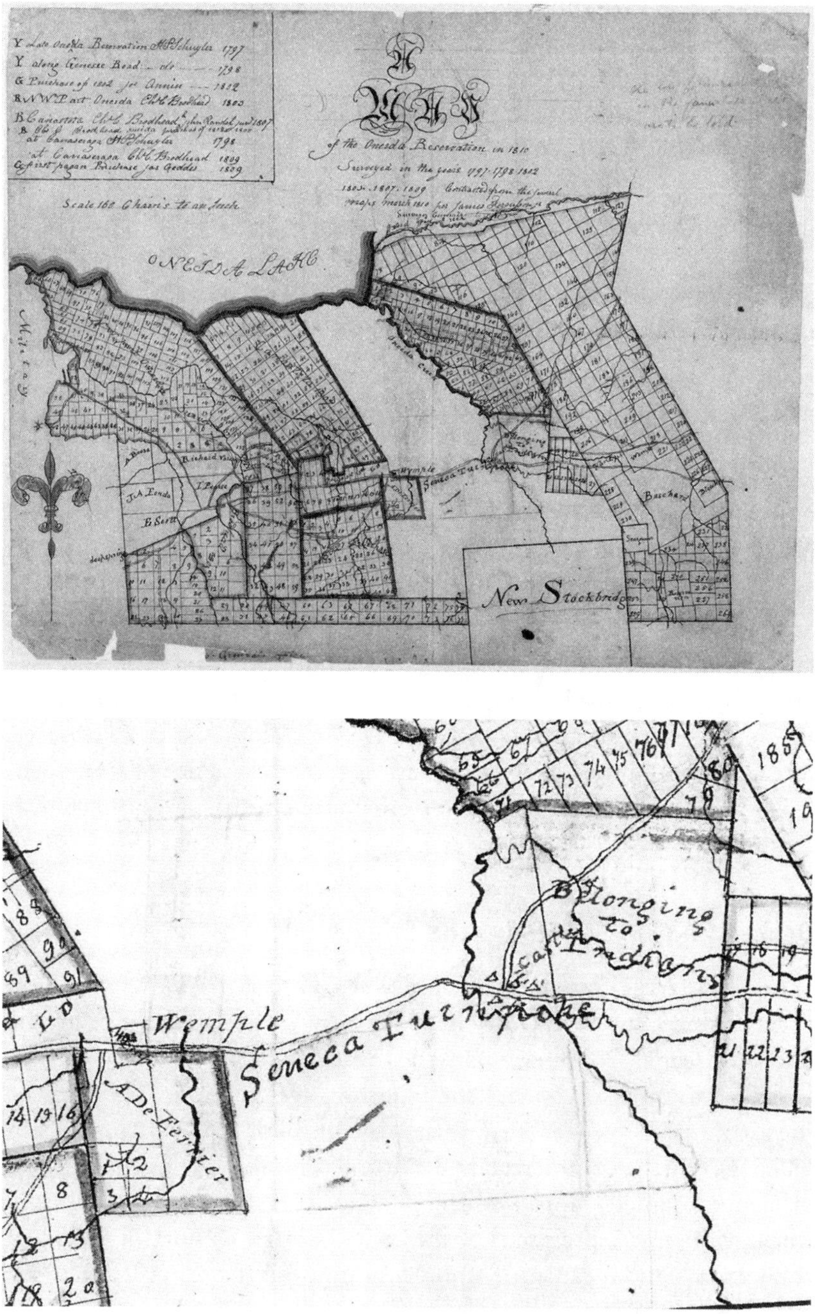

FIGURE 17a and b. Map of the Oneida Indian Reservation in 1810 and enlarged detail. The property granted to Angel Deferrier juts out to meet the Seneca Turnpike. The best land, to the north of Angel's grant, remained in Oneida hands. Series A0273-78, New York State Archives Digital Collections.

Denny in 1809. The governor asked Angel to deliver cash bounties to Skenandoah and others.[33]

Angel was the greatest individual beneficiary of these treaties. The Christian Party granted him a total of 1,544 acres south of the turnpike. To this day, the property stands out on the county tax map because it was never divided into lots on a grid. Angel and Polly sold land on the turnpike worth about $100 to $125 an acre, while the land a mile or so south went for $8 to $25 an acre. Angel turned over three-quarters of an acre on the hill alongside the turnpike to the school trustees, including Myndert Wemple and himself. My grandfather, my father, and I would go to school there on land that had been the burial ground of the people of Cowaselon.[34]

On the turnpike, where wagon trains of forty teams headed west, Angel and Polly built an inn considered the "best tavern on the road." For a time, they rented it to Dr. Benjamin Stockton of Princeton, New Jersey. An Englishman was astonished to find such an "elegantly furnished" inn hundreds of miles from Philadelphia or New York, situated amid the Oneidas. It had an excellent bed, good carpet, and the latest window and bed curtains "of a smart Manchester print." He observed brawny Indian men sitting calmly in the barroom. Their sobriety, he assumed, was a credit to Dr. Stockton. Visitors, I observe, often attributed the behavior of Natives to the influence of white people, as though Indigenous people were not in control of their own lives or destiny.[35]

DeWitt Clinton Scouts for the Erie Canal

"The most fertile country in the universe," proclaimed DeWitt Clinton as he toured Oneida territory in 1810. New York State had set up the Board of Canal Commissioners to investigate the possibility of constructing a canal to connect the Hudson River to Lake Erie. Clinton, the astute mayor of New York City, was confident that the canal would make his city the commercial and cultural capital of the world. The son of General James Clinton and nephew of Governor George Clinton, who was then vice president of the United States, DeWitt Clinton had connections and a career of embracing innovations, from Robert Fulton's steamboat to free schools for poor children. The journal he kept of his tour across the state is one of the most informative sources on Angel and Polly, although he never said whether he discussed the canal with them.[36]

"1700 acres of the best land" belonged to Deferrier, discovered Clinton. He noted that the Frenchman had a great influence over the Oneidas and "prevailed on them to confer on him donations of valuable land—which have been sanctioned by the State." Angel, he learned, had been among the Indians for twelve years. His mother was rich, Angel told Clinton, and had written for him to return to his country, but he declined on account of his "red wife." Here Clinton may have been quoting Angel about Polly or putting the conversation in his own words. He described Polly as "a well-behaved woman of civilized manners and habits, and resembling an Indian in nothing but color." He thought Angel "a man of genteel manners, sensible, and well-informed."[37]

Polly's father, Clinton observed, was "quite proud of his opulent son-in-law." Clinton thought that Louis Denny, although born a Frenchman, had become "a perfect Indian in dress, manners, and behavior; his color is somewhat whiter." Louis was not very intelligent, noted Clinton: "He prefers the savage life; his character is good, and what he represents he believes." Louis's wife, he wrote, "retains her primitive manners, and is decent and clean." Clinton referred to the deceased John Denny as "a hybrid, or half-Indian" and to Dolly as a "half blood." Their children, he wrote, owned the fine flats at Canaseraga and were "the worst-tempered of any in the nation." This characterization may have been true after everything that had happened. At the same time, it reflected the belief that mixed-race people, especially those with fine flats, were trouble.[38]

At Oneida Castle, Clinton noted that the Christian and Pagan Oneidas were "entirely separated in their territory, as well as in their God." He thought the morals of the Pagans were better than those of the Christians. He described Captain Peter as a "very sensible man" and visited Skenandoah at his home, where a large kettle of corn was boiling on the fire. Salmon ran up Oneida Creek as far as Stockbridge, and a beautiful Oneida girl sold apples at the bridge. To Clinton, signs of "incipient civilization" included Oneida men wearing feathers while plowing with oxen, and women milking cows. "Incipient civilization" came with hard times. The cattle of white men broke their fences and ate their wheat and corn, protested the Oneidas. The deer once had been as thick as leaves in Schoharie, recalled Louis Denny, but now the game was gone.[39]

While Clinton and the commissioners plotted canal construction, the state and local people exploited the divisions among the Oneidas over their land. Peter August of Cowaselon was anxious and rightly so. On the best land, Peter had become the premier farmer of the Oneida Nation. With their increased dependence on agriculture, a bad crop year meant famine for the Oneidas. When they needed money to buy food, they had only one possession of value to sell, and that was land. Peter feared that Christian Party leaders might sell his farm. He traveled to Albany with a plea written for him by James Dean. Peter, Dean noted, had made handsome improvements on his land, including a comfortable house and good barn. Dean, who at this point in his life tended to view Indigenous people with contempt, described Peter as "an example of Industry, frugality and Economy so rarely found in a Native Indian."[40]

The Oneidas sold land, but not Peter's farm. In 1810 and 1811, the Christian Party ceded about twelve thousand acres on the southern shore of Oneida Lake already occupied by squatters. Angel, who witnessed the 1810 treaty, received two hundred acres on the lake at present-day South Bay. The Christian Party complained that the white men they had employed to protect their rights and property had deceived them. They named Angel Deferrier and Myndert Wemple and asked that the legislators "not hear them." The controversies over Oneida land involved not only Angel but also members of Polly's extended family.[41]

Wemple, for instance, had bought two hundred acres set aside for Dolly Denny, which he turned around and sold to Sidney Breese. After work with the Holland Land Company had wound down, Sidney became a law partner of Jonas Platt in Whitestown. He noted that cotton goods were in demand. Before the Revolution, the British had banned the manufacture of cotton cloth in the colonies, and cloth shipped from England remained pricey. Platt, Stephen Van Rensselaer, and DeWitt Clinton already had invested in cotton production at the Oriskany Manufacturing Company. "I am going on with the cotton factory at Oneida, home of the Indians," announced Sidney. On the Denny lot, where the road to Fort Stanwix (present-day Route 365) crossed Sconondoa Creek, Sidney built a new home and business. Located a mile north of Oneida Castle, the place became known as the village of Sconondoa. Their Oneida neighbors came to their kitchen, remembered the Breese children, and ate in silence as they warmed themselves by the fire.[42]

The Pagan Party, meanwhile, criticized Cornelius Doxtator for promoting his own interest to the detriment of the nation. Cornelius and his wife, Skenandoah's daughter Jenny, sold one hundred acres set aside for him on the turnpike at present-day Sherrill to Peter Smith for $1,000. Cornelius also made $50 by deeding to Smith the interest he would inherit in one hundred acres reserved to his mother in 1802. This deal went wrong for Smith when Sarah Doxtator outlived her son, but she did not retain control over her property west of Clockville. Already living on Sarah's land, the surveyor had discovered, was a squatter from the Mohawk Valley named George Harp, my fifth great-grandfather. Unabashed about being caught illegally on Oneida territory, George said that he wanted to be granted preemption on another lot as compensation for the improvements he had made on the land set aside for Sarah.[43]

A few years later, the legislature passed an act "for the relief of Sarah Doxtader," which allowed the state to pay Sarah for her land and then sell it. I don't know what role Sarah played in giving up her lot. Did she need the money? Was she pressured by white people? Was this property too far away from her family? George Harp could not afford the state's asking price of $1,000, but the newcomer Sylvester Beecher could. Harp and his sons continued to work Sarah's former lot on Beecher's behalf until Beecher later sold him a section of it. What happened to the lots reserved to Sarah and her children illustrates the tangled way in which prominent Oneidas, the state, the developer Peter Smith, the early settlers Sidney Breese and Myndert Wemple, the well-off newcomer Sylvester Beecher, and the squatter George Harp played a part in the diminution of Oneida territory.[44]

Settlers like George Harp typically arrived in loosely organized groups of several families or as a single, often extended, family. In George's case, his wife's relatives may have been directed to valuable Oneida land by her distant cousin, the storekeeper Abraham Van Eps. Pioneer families came in caravans of wagons piled high with spinning wheels, trunks, feather beds, and children, trailed by livestock. During the first years, known as the starving years, they cut underbrush, chopped trees, built shelters, planted crops, and hunted and fished to put food on the table. A few got a head start by living in log huts left by the Oneidas on clearings made by the Oneidas. So much could go wrong. Injury, illness, a hailstorm, or early frost could mean dire setbacks. Those who failed to make the payments on their land lost it to seizure by the sheriff, who would put it up for sale. Lots changed hands many times. Several would-be property owners gave up and left; others, including some of my ancestors, ended up as tenants on someone else's land.[45]

FIGURE 18a, b, c. For some early settlers in the town of Lenox, these nineteenth-century depictions of pioneer progress illustrated a dream rather than the reality. F. W. Beers, *History of Herkimer County, N.Y.*, 1879.

As they cleared the forests, settlers left millions of stumps and thousands of half-burned trees crisscrossed over one another. The scene would make a German forester cry, thought a visiting German geologist. The Oneidas tried to save Fish Creek, which was "extraordinarily rich in fish and especially salmon," he noted. They had stipulated that the woods for a half mile on either side of the creek should not be cut down, to preserve the creek and the fishing. Their stipulation ignored, the trees came down, the high banks eroded, and sediment filled the creek bottom. The fishing, essential to the Oneidas, declined as streams flooded higher in the spring and dried up in the summer.[46]

Settlers, I learned, had some things in common with the Oneidas. They adopted the practice of multiple plantings of corn, beans, and squash or pumpkin to produce a bountiful harvest. They wore a combination of buckskin and woven cloth and ate a cornmeal mush flavored with maple syrup. Neighbors, often connected by kinship ties, were expected to help each other at barn raisings or cornhusking bees and contribute to the community their skills as carpenters or midwives. Those of Dutch and German heritage, known as Yorkers, came from an oral tradition. They believed their word was their bond. This custom made them appear "simple and honest," according to the New Englanders, who, with their written contracts, developed a reputation for being cunning and crafty even though many people relied on their know-how. For example, it took years for two sons of Connecticut, Sylvester Beecher and Stephen Chapman, to clear the title to the Clock properties, because the Clocks never bothered to obtain a patent from the state for the land they had leased from the Oneidas.[47]

Settlers from New England, known as Yankees, felt superior about their public schools, wrathful God, and manly hands on the plow. To them, the Yorkers appeared cut off from progress. The Yorkers, who preferred a minimalist government, tended to be wary of civic reforms and ambitious internal improvements like the proposed Erie Canal. In state politics they supported the Democratic-Republican Party, which associated the rival Federalists with the great landowners, corrupt development, and the oppression of ordinary people. Lincklaen, reported Samuel Forman to Sidney Breese, was doing the Federalist party in Cazenovia no good with his aristocratic behavior.[48]

With his unusual standing as a popular Federalist from a Democratic-Republican district, the ideal man to introduce the state canal bill was state senator Jonas Platt of Oneida County, which had been created from part of Herkimer County in 1798. The backers of the Erie Canal project thought it too important to be entrusted to a private corporation. They persuaded the state to sponsor and finance the canal. The legislature authorized the commissioners to secure the loans, do the surveys, and acquire the land along the proposed route. It passed the canal bill in June 1812 on the day after the United States declared war on Great Britain.[49]

The country went to war to compel recognition of its rights as an independent nation, but it was not united. Easterners, who valued the Atlantic trade, wanted peace. Westerners wanted territory. In their way was a Native confederacy organized by the Shawnee leader Tecumseh, who allied with the British to protect Indigenous lands from Americans. The US government justified the War of 1812 as a fight for its sovereignty against Britain and its "savage allies." At the same time, it courted the Six Nations, who lived on both sides of the border. Six hundred warriors, including two hundred Oneidas, chose to fight alongside the Americans, while others supported the British. I wonder whether the Oneida warriors, many of whom were veterans of the Revolutionary War, fought not only to defend their homeland but also to remind the Americans of their obligation to such steadfast allies.[50]

New York was in danger because the Royal Navy controlled the Great Lakes. In 1813, the Oneidas, with the Lenox men of the Seventy-Fourth Infantry, captained by John Conrad Moot, my fourth great-grandfather, and Sylvester Beecher, prevented a British force from capturing Sacket's Harbor, the most important US shipbuilding yard on the lakes. A year later, the Oneidas, including war chief Cornelius Doxtator, Captain Peter, and Shagoyontha, escorted a supply convoy sailing from Oswego to Sacket's Harbor, still under British blockade. When the convoy, under pursuit by Royal Navy gunboats, pulled into Sandy Creek, Oneida riflemen and reinforcements from Sacket's Harbor overwhelmed the British force and made possible US supremacy over Lake Ontario.[51]

Louis Denny and Jacob Doxtator were among the 150 Oneida warriors who took part in the 1814 invasion of Canada. Twenty Oneida women participated as well. Polly Cooper, who was not the woman of the same name at Valley Forge, traveled to the Niagara frontier to serve as a cook. With the help of their Native allies, the US forces prevailed at the battle of Chippawa in July, but only temporarily. The next month, the Americans suffered a humiliating attack on their national capital, after which they blocked an invasion from the north at Plattsburgh and defeated an assault on New Orleans. Meanwhile the Royal Navy shut down the Atlantic trade. Confronted with a stalemate, the United States and Britain negotiated a peace.[52]

The War of 1812 was considered a draw by the British and Americans, a proud repulse of US invaders by the Canadians, and a disaster by the western Indians. I suspect that John Conrad Moot named his son William Harrison Moot, born in 1816, in honor of General William Henry Harrison, who defeated Tecumseh. As settlers rushed across central New York on their way west, the Oneidas returned home to celebrate their victories and mourn their losses, including the death of Cornelius Doxtator, who fell at the battle of Chippawa. With the help of the People of the Standing Stone, the Americans had fought the British Empire a second time and not lost.[53]

This war, declared DeWitt Clinton, proved the importance of the canal. It had exposed the difficulty of shipping arms and supplies over bad roads to the front lines. Besides, Clinton told the legislature, land and men were cheap and available. He acknowledged the fear of a collision between North and South over slavery, but he echoed George Washington's view that the real danger was a break between the coast and the mountains. A canal, Clinton asserted, would tie East to West with "an imperishable cement of connexion." And New York, "standing on this exalted eminence," both Atlantic and western, was the only state where this connection could happen. Thousands of New Yorkers signed in support of the project. To build the Erie Canal, the state needed one more piece of Oneida territory: the best land.[54]

"Papers Are Wicked Things"

Do not pay any attention to Angel Deferrier, wrote twenty-seven chiefs and warriors of the Christian Party to the state legislature in February 1814. He "has been in the habit of taking down Indians [to Albany] for the Express Purpose of cheating them out of their Land," they wrote. The wives and widows of the chiefs added their say. "They pity their children and grandchildren and fear they will be destitute of land," declared the women. "It is our wish to have all our land in common as was the case formerly. But it is not the wish of those Indians who have gone down to Albany to appropriate a part to themselves." The state ignored this petition.[55]

To negotiate the sale of the best land, Angel accompanied members of the Christian Party to Albany in February 1815. The Oneidas needed funds. Prices had soared during the war. While the warriors had been away fighting, more squatters moved in on their land. The state asked for tracts along the turnpike already inhabited by white people. When Governor Daniel Tompkins signed the Treaty of 1815 in March, no federal authority was present. Angel was the only witness who was not a state official. Twenty-eight Oneidas, including Louis Denny and Jacob Doxtator, signed the treaty. Peter August, who lost his farm, did not.[56]

New York State purchased 1,154½ acres for about a dollar an acre. The first tract contained the best land. It included over 650 acres north of the turnpike between Myndert Wemple's farm and Oneida territory. The second tract was next to Angel's lands south of the turnpike. The third and fourth tracts were on the eastern edge of the reservation and included part of Oneida Castle. Angel was rewarded with 50 acres on the north side of the turnpike where it crossed Cowaselon Creek. The treaty protected the home of Polly's brother Martinus Denny by reserving to him 20 acres where he lived on the hill overlooking the creek. The Oneidas received $562 at the time of the treaty, and Angel was given the remaining $600 to deliver to them.[57]

The state immediately sent in two experienced surveyors. Charles C. Brodhead, who took the first tract, was a survivor of risky assignments that included the capsize of a raft that went over the falls on Black River and the first recorded ascent of an Adirondack high peak. Known for his crochety temper, Brodhead also served as sheriff of Oneida County. John Randel Jr., who surveyed Oneida Castle, had apprenticed with Simeon DeWitt and was considered the top surveyor in the state. In Manhattan, Randel recently had completed an elegant grid of avenues and streets over twenty-five square miles. While carrying out this assignment, he and his crew had been chased by packs of dogs and bombarded with cabbages thrown by an old woman when they drew the line of an avenue through her kitchen.[58]

As surveyors, Brodhead and Randel had to keep detailed records, evaluate soils and timber, and be able to defend themselves from the inhabitants whose home they would change forever by defining it with degrees and measures. The Treaty of 1815 said that the Indians could not be dispossessed until they had been compensated for their improvements up to twenty dollars. In the English colonial tradition, improvements meant cleared forests, established fields of crops, fences, and "proper" houses. "Must I add the value of the improvements to the Lots or are white squatters entitled to be paid for them?" Randel wrote Simeon DeWitt. In the margin of the original Randel map was drawn an Indian on the hunt and a white man holding a document saying, "The Indian has his bow and arrow and I have the land deed and all papers!"[59]

Brodhead and Randel stayed with Sidney and Helen Breese while they valued the Indian improvements. Sidney assumed that after the state paid the Oneidas it would sell the land, which would mean new neighbors. He paid $1,000 for fifty acres that belonged to John Cornelius, probably the son of Shagoyontha, across the creek from the Breese homestead. "My place increases a little–like a small Indian village," reported Sidney, who wrote that he would be happy to welcome a visitor to his wigwam with a good fire and a blanket.[60]

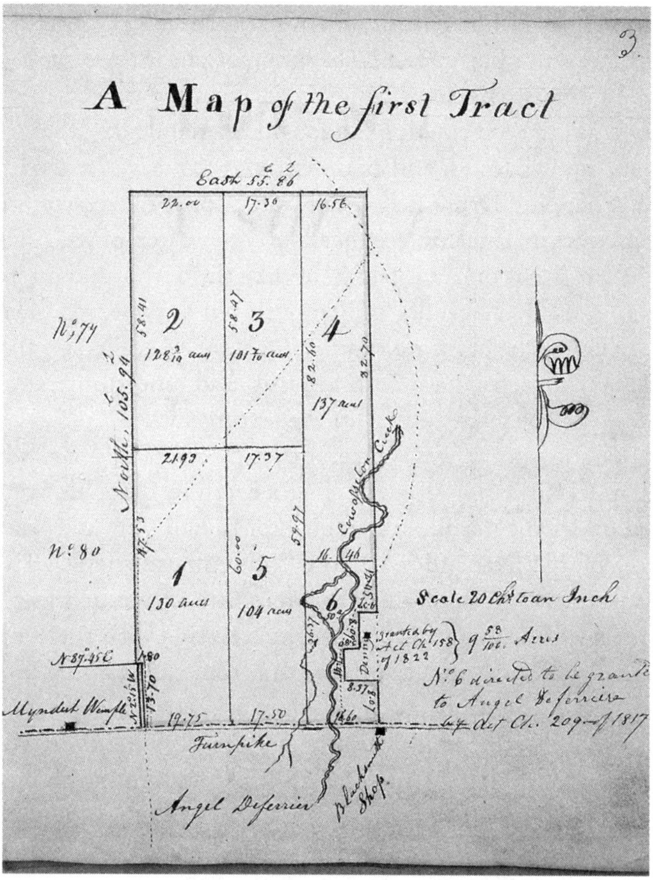

FIGURE 19. The first survey of the best land. The land reserved to Martinus Denny was cut out of Lot 6, which was, as noted, granted to Angel Deferrier in 1817. "A Survey of the Lands Purchased of the Christian Party of Oneida Indians, the 3rd of March 1815," A4019, vol. 14, Land Survey Field Book, MU1, reel 16, New York State Archives.

Brodhead divided the first tract of land into six lots. He set aside Lot 6 for Angel and 1.6 acres for Myndert Wemple, a grant that had not been mentioned in the treaty. The best land included Lots 1 through 5. About Lot 5, containing 104 acres, the surveyor remarked, "This is an Excellent Lot, soil gravelly loam all cleared and improved by Peter August an Oneida Indian and his Tenants, a small framed House and Barn on it, the House is not well finished." Brodhead valued the lot at $30 an acre, making Peter's place worth $3,120. According to the treaty, Peter was entitled to receive $20 for his improvements. For the time being, the state held on to Lots 2, 3, and 4, through which the canal would be routed.[61]

The Treaty of 1815 broke the heart of Skenandoah. "The news that came last night by our men from Albany made this a sick day in Oneida," the chief announced at council. He spoke of cheating whites and the weakness of chiefs who signed papers. "Papers are wicked things," he declared. With the loss of this land, said Skenandoah, "the graves of our fathers are destroyed, and their children are driven away." He had warned his people, "Drink no strong water, for it makes you mice for white men, who are cats. Many a meal have they eaten of you." The aged warrior recalled that once his feet were "like the deer's, and his arm like the bear's," but now he could "only mourn out a few words." His voice, he said, "will soon be heard no more in Oneida." He called on the Oneidas to remain peaceful, have faith in Jesus, and send runners "to carry our sorrows" to the great council of the setting sun.[62]

Skenandoah's speech was written down by the missionary who succeeded Samuel Kirkland. After the chief's death in 1816, his words were published under the headline "Instances of Indian Genius." Newspaper articles celebrated Skenandoah as the "white man's friend." The story of his conversion to Christianity and rejection of liquor was told. He was credited with influencing the Oneidas to side with the Americans during the Revolution and saving settlers from the scalping knife and massacre. Left unmentioned was the chief's frequent cooperation with land cessions up to the point where they came close to home. The story of his past glory and sad demise made Skenandoah the symbolic last of the Oneidas.[63]

The publication of Skenandoah's speech was part of a trend in the early republic. Newspapers printed orations by Native leaders, and schoolchildren memorized them to recite. In this way, Americans honored the image of the vanishing Indian while carrying out the national policy of dispossession. Speaking before the New York Historical

Society in 1811, DeWitt Clinton acknowledged the injustice of it all and described the degradation of the once mighty Iroquois. The mankind of Europe, he said, "has contaminated their morals, destroyed their population, robbed them of their country, and deprived them of their national spirit." Clinton predicted that after this generation passed away, not a single Haudenosaunee would be left in the state. We have reason to fear, he said, that the extermination of millions of "red men" and the enslavement of Africans will be met by "the retributive justice of the Almighty." The "calamities which we have so wantonly and wickedly inflicted upon others," Clinton warned, might soon burst upon European America.[64]

Simeon DeWitt, meanwhile, proceeded with the paperwork that deprived the Oneidas of their homes. Immediately after the Treaty of 1815, a settler named William Sternbergh had been granted the right to buy two hundred acres of the best land on which Jacob Doxtator, Peter August, and an unnamed Oneida woman had improvements. Sternbergh's wife, Peggy, knew the Oneidas well. Celebrated in local history as the first white child born in the town of Sullivan, she was the daughter of Honyost Schuyler and his second wife. Sternbergh, who had been instructed by DeWitt that he must purchase releases from the Oneida owners of the improvements, said he had acquired one from Jacob Doxtator. DeWitt arranged for compensation to be delivered to Peter August and the Oneida woman and asked Angel to find out about Jacob's papers.[65]

Angel replied that he went to see Jacob about the papers in question. "But I did find that he could not tell me what he has don with them," wrote Angel. "He has showed to me all his writting which I have examined very carefully and I am very satisfait that none of those notes are among them." Angel consulted Jacob's family and learned that Jacob had sold a note worth $20 to a tavernkeeper for $10 and that the tavernkeeper had sold that note to Sternbergh for $10. Angel sent the contract between Jacob and Sternberg to DeWitt with the request that the surveyor general keep it in case either man demanded it. He wrote that he felt himself responsible to both parties in the matter. Angel promised to keep DeWitt informed if he learned anything new.[66]

It is easy to see how Jacob could lose control of his property. An interpreter, he had speaking skills, but not good bookkeeping habits or the ability to read or write in English. Jacob was taken advantage of by the tavernkeeper who sold his note to Sternbergh who wanted Jacob's land. It's not clear whether Jacob's compliance mattered in any event. "If Jacob Doxstader should refuse to sign a release with the other Indians," instructed DeWitt, "the paper which he has signed as a Receipt may be considered in the nature of a release of his right in the improvements he owned." The legitimacy of Jacob's release, after all, was a minor issue for state officials who had big plans for this property. For Jacob Doxtator, the Treaty of 1815 would mean the loss of his home for a third time.[67]

By then, several members of Polly's extended family resided around her on the best land. Their controversial strategy regarding property had given them status and income but not the comfort of permanence. Perhaps they hoped to find security near her and her husband. Maybe Angel, who, like Myndert Wemple and Sidney Breese, had benefited from friendships with Oneidas, seemed a better ally than no ally at all. Polly may have been thankful to be in a position to provide shelter for her relatives. Her nephew Abraham Denny, who along with his mother and brother had sold their lots at Canaseraga during the war, selected a place to live on the Oneida Reservation close to Polly and Angel. He located his family on a rise east of Cowaselon Creek that someday would be the home of my great-grandparents.[68]

My ancestors saw Oneida territory as a land of opportunity, but many of them endured years of grind-it-out subsistence before they would be able to call a piece of it their own. I wonder what they thought of the people of Cowaselon at their advantageous location. To them, I imagine, Polly and her family appeared to enjoy a good life. James Dean, who remembered the wife of Martinus Denny as "the most beautiful woman he had ever seen of any nationality whatever," recalled her daily routine. In the morning the Oneida woman would hoe corn, taking care to blacken her face to protect it from sunburn, and in the afternoon, she would bathe, dress in gay colors, and entertain company. Along the creek, Denny and Deferrier cousins grew up together.[69]

The Dennys and Doxtators continued to choose spouses from white, Native, and African and Native communities. Such marriages, which long had been an asset to these families, were looked down on by certain white people. Indians of mixed blood, opined Jedediah Morse, intermarried "with the lowest classes of white people and negroes." Such distinctions regarding race and class were at odds with the old notion of "one people." Polly's marriage to a gentleman like Angel was considered mysterious by white people but not by Oneidas.[70]

"One people," of course, was not a category on the 1820 US Census. By then, Angel no longer owned an enslaved girl named Gin whom he had bought for $175 when she was about thirteen years old. "Free male colored" was the designation for Abraham Denny, the grandson of Honyery, Sarah, Louis, and Maria. Abraham's children were identified as free male and female "colored persons," while his wife, Catharine Nellis, was identified as "free white." At the next-door household of Polly and Angel, the census taker identified Angel and Angel and Polly's children as "free white" and Polly as a "free female colored person." The census taker may have chosen to place the children in the same category with their fathers, or he may have defined the children by the way they lived. On the 1830 federal census, Polly was identified as white.[71]

Were Angel and Polly the blended Americans envisioned by Thomas Jefferson? Both the Frenchman and the Turtle Clan woman had survived revolutions that overturned the worlds they knew as children and rendered them homeless. As go-betweens, they acquired property by serving the interests of the Oneidas for a time, then New York State, and ultimately themselves. Polly and Angel enhanced the value of their lots and attracted settlers by constructing mills, a brewery, a distillery, a store, and a blacksmith shop. Over Cowaselon Creek, which at the time was much deeper and wider than it is now, a stone bridge was constructed with a tablet inscribed, "Erected 1817. De Ferriere's Bridge." Known for a time as the "great bridge west of Albany," it was crossed by waves of Americans heading west. On a foundation of broken law and betrayed trust, Polly and Angel built a prosperous life on the best land.[72]

CHAPTER 6

Making Way for the Erie Canal

The interpreter Martinus Denny was worried about his home. The Treaty of 1815 had reserved to him twenty acres on the Cowaselon where he and his family lived. The official survey, however, carved out only ten acres for Martinus. When New York State in 1817 granted the entire lot to his sister Polly's husband, Angel Deferrier, the patent made no mention of Martinus or his land. The interpreter petitioned the state to secure his property. Surveyor General Simeon DeWitt noted that Martinus Denny "lives in the manner of civilized man and is reputed to be fully competent to prudent management of any property he possesses." The state set aside less than ten acres for Martinus as designated on the survey, not as guaranteed by the treaty. That was not enough to support his family, said Martinus.[1]

By then, the remaining territory of the Oneidas consisted of about twenty thousand acres bordered by Cowaselon Creek to the west and Oneida Creek on the east. The Oneidas had cleared their land, enlarged the cornfields, built comfortable houses, and founded an Agricultural Society dedicated to the promotion of farming. They displayed a spirit of industry and ambition, reported their Indian agent Jasper Parrish, especially noticeable in the current generation of young men. Their achievements made settlers, including my ancestors, covet their territory even more. Just as some Oneidas began to prosper in "the manner of civilized man" advocated by white political and religious leaders, New Yorkers began to construct the Erie Canal through their ancestral homeland. The canal would transform the territory of the Six Nations, the state of New York, and the entire country. What, I wondered, did the building of an artificial river through the best land mean for Polly's extended family and mine?[2]

The state proposed to dig a canal over 350 miles long from the Hudson River to the Great Lakes and do it fast. Officials feared that after the War of 1812, western New Yorkers might develop stronger trade ties to Canada than to Albany and New York City. The ceremonial first dig took place on Independence Day 1817 at the Oneida Carrying Place, where the town around Fort Stanwix was named Rome after one of the most famous imperial cities in history. The builders began with the middle section, which crossed the relatively flat land between Utica and the settlement near Onondaga later called Syracuse. They hoped to figure out what they were doing before they tackled the locks at either end. This middle section, known as the Long Level, was about to become the longest level canal without locks in the world.[3]

That year the Oneidas of the Pagan Party ceded land along Cowaselon Creek in a deal that involved the Denny family and a Kahnawake Mohawk named Eleazer Williams. The Oneidas had invited Williams to be their missionary because they wanted someone to preach in their own language. The charismatic Williams was the great-grandson of Eunice Williams of Deerfield, Massachusetts, who at age seven had been taken captive during a French and Indian raid. When Eunice refused to return home, her Deerfield family stayed in contact with her Mohawk family and supported Eleazer's education. After he arrived in Oneida, Eleazer earned praise and publicity when members of the Pagan Party converted to Christianity. The new converts called themselves the Second Christian Party, remained a separate political entity, and continued to control the land designated for the Pagan Party.[4]

Williams had arrived at a difficult moment for the Oneidas. In 1816, which locals called "eighteen hundred and froze to death," there had been frost and snow every month thanks to clouds of ash from a massive volcano eruption in the Dutch East Indies, now Indonesia. When the crops failed, the Oneidas asked Williams to go to Albany to request an advance on their annuity. In addition, the Oneidas agreed to the construction of a new church. The Second Christian Party paid its share with proceeds from the sale to the state of over 4,226 acres known as the Cowaselon Tract.[5]

FIGURE 20. Eleazer Williams (ca. 1792–1857). George Catlin, artist. 1836. Wisconsin Historical Society, WHI-3021.

In Albany, someone in the secretary of state's office noted that, according to the US Constitution, the federal government held the exclusive right to make a "treaty, alliance or confederation" with the Indigenous people. In that case, the bureaucrat suggested, treaties between the state and the Indians should be called "grants, conveyances, or cessions." In the years to follow, it became more common for New Yorkers to refer to the "Purchase of 1817," for example, rather than the "Treaty of 1817." Meanwhile, the state continued to officially record these transactions, made in violation of federal law, as treaties.[6]

The Treaty of 1817 granted to Eleazer Williams 150 acres south of Wampsville. It also granted 200 acres to Dolly Denny, 100 acres each to her sons Abraham and John, and 50 acres to her daughter Sally. Dolly's lot, which included a waterfall on Limestone Creek, was a potential mill site. The Oneidas again had situated the Dennys between themselves and white settlers. In return for these lots, said the treaty, the Dennys agreed to relinquish all rights and claims to the annuities paid to the Second Christian Party. I do not know what happened regarding the annuities, but the deeds show that the Dennys turned this land into income.[7]

The chief beneficiary of the Treaty of 1817 was the Lenox Iron Company. Founded by my ancestor Conrad Moot and others, the company operated a furnace that used the timber cleared by settlers to burn fires hot enough to smelt iron ore, which was made into potash kettles, stoves, and castings for plows. The company immediately bought from Eleazer Williams fifty acres of his tract, as well as timber rights on an additional twenty-five acres. It later acquired from Dolly and Abraham their lots in purchases made before Stephen Chapman of Clockville, who was the county commissioner of deeds as well as a founder and trustee of the Lenox Iron Company. The highest-valued incorporated company in the county, the Lenox Iron Company was responsible for the development of a bustling hamlet called Lenox Furnace, built in part on land bought from Angel a mile south of his house.[8]

A mile north of Angel's house, work crews cut the Erie Canal through the town of Lenox. The workers, almost all local, were joined by Welsh and Irish newcomers. "The land is a desolate wilderness," William Thomas warned his folks back in Wales. Don't think of coming here. The men staked off a width of forty feet for the canal and ten feet more on each side to accommodate the towpath. Then they commenced "grubbing and clearing." Masters of innovation on the job, they used levers, gears, wheels, chains, and teams of horses to rip out thousands of trees and stumps. With spades and plows, the workers carved out a ditch four feet deep.[9]

From the Carrying Place, the canal crossed the best land at Mile 17. The commissioners reported that this section was "very flat country" with a sandy loam soil, some gravel, and a cedar swamp. The canal builders transported limestone and sandstone quarried from the hills to the south. Local contractors and scientists invented a waterproof cement that sealed wet masonry joints. Five of the aqueducts built between the Mohawk and Seneca Rivers were constructed of stone, including the one that carried the canal over Oneida Creek. The eight wooden aqueducts, like the one over Cowaselon Creek, consisted of timber-framed boxlike structures supported by stone piers, designed by the Clockville farmer and inventor Asa Cady. By draining the low, wet ground at its northern end, the Erie Canal had made the best land even better for farming.[10]

Did the builders realize that there was a problem where the canal crossed Cowaselon Creek? That sliver of the best land north of Abraham Denny's farm still belonged to the Oneida Nation. The canal commission's map only identified Oneida Lake. On it, the Oneida Reservation did not exist. I don't know whether Abraham was aware of the mistake.

If he had been, would he have followed the example of his grandfather Honyery and confronted trespassers on Oneida territory? For the time being, the northwest corner of the Oneida Reservation had become extremely valuable.[11]

The celebration of the completion of the Long Level was held in Syracuse on the Fourth of July in 1820. Governor DeWitt Clinton rode on the canal boat *Oneida Chief.* Elkanah Watson returned to the Carrying Place, where, he wrote, "savage tribes" had "roamed" thirty years earlier when he attended the Fort Stanwix treaty. He did not recall the oratory of Good Peter or the trickery expended to acquire Oneida territory. Instead, he praised the transformation of the region, with its "vigorous and intelligent population, fine turnpike roads, . . . beautiful towns, . . . excellent and highly cultivated farms, matured orchards, and above all, the Erie Canal."[12]

Angel was away during the festivities. Leaving Polly in charge, he had gone back to France to settle family affairs. On the trip he escorted a troupe of Oneidas. Show business, the Oneidas had learned, could mean travel, income, and recognition. "Highly satisfactory and civil," reported the *Columbian Register* of New Haven about a performance of a war dance by Oneidas at Williamstown, Massachusetts. "[W]e wish we could say that the civility of some of the spectators equaled that of the Oneida Indians." The veteran warrior Shagoyontha, now in his eighties, recently had returned from Britain, where Oneida performers had appeared in Liverpool and at the Royal Circus and Surrey Theatre in London. He, along with four Oneida men and three Oneida women, left for France with Angel.[13]

In Bordeaux, the Oneidas excited "considerable curiosity," reported a Parisian newspaper. Shagoyontha had a strong desire to visit France, he said, and indicated that he hoped to make some money. He explained that he received only a scanty pension from the United States, probably from his service in the War of 1812. "It is presumed that he will find in our country a kind of hospitality not so simple, but much more profitable," said the newspaper. Angel may have hoped to make money on the troupe as well. He financed their passage to France, but something went wrong.[14]

Five months after their arrival, the Oneida women and one man became separated from the others and were left abandoned in the interior of France. A kind family helped them return to Bordeaux, where they turned to the US consul, who advanced them the funds to reach Paris and reunite with the troupe. In Paris, the Oneidas performed at

FIGURE 21. Oneida performers in Paris, 1819. From left to right: Shagoyontha, his son John Cornelius, John's son John Cornelius, and Baptist Canada. Their costumes appear to have been made in France. Courtesy of the Bibliothèque Nationale de France, Paris.

the Theatre Comte, run by Louis Comte, the "King's Conjurer," believed to be the first magician to pull a rabbit out of a hat. The earnings from their performances did not cover their expenses, and they ran out of money. They wanted to go home.[15]

The Oneidas asked for assistance from Albert Gallatin, the respected former US secretary of the treasury who was minister to France. The Swiss-born diplomat had an unusual problem on his hands. Who was responsible for the Oneidas? They weren't subjects or citizens of the United States, but they were under US protection, according to treaties. Gallatin blamed Angel for abandoning the Oneidas, but he understood that Angel may not have had enough money to send them home. Supposing Angel was perfectly honest, wrote Gallatin, he probably had hoped that the earnings of the Oneidas would reimburse him for the cost of their journey.[16]

Worried that Angel might desert the Oneidas again, Gallatin alerted Marquis Dessolle, the minister of foreign affairs and prime minister of France. He explained that the Oneidas were very intelligent but were ignorant of business affairs. Gallatin may have hoped that Dessolle would compel Angel, identified as a Frenchman who lived in Oneida country, to pay up. Instead, Dessolle referred the matter to the French Department of the Interior. Gallatin then had Angel brought before a justice of the peace, who decided the case in Angel's favor. He considered a lawsuit against Angel, but that would take time, and there was the issue of how the Oneidas would support themselves while awaiting a verdict.[17]

In the end, Gallatin decided to cover the costs of the Oneidas' journey home himself, because he was uncertain about the legitimacy of using State Department funds for such an expense. He purchased seats for the Oneidas in the public coach from Paris to Havre de Grace. He bought woolen jackets, mattresses, blankets, and tobacco for the travelers. He paid for their lodging and the cost of the doctor who treated Shagoyontha when the old man fell ill. Before he did all this, he required Angel to promise to repay him within a year's time. Deferrier, Gallatin informed Secretary of State John Quincy Adams, had considerable real estate in Madison County, New York. Angel did not return with the Oneidas. He headed to Niort to conduct family business with his two sisters, who were his surviving siblings. When Angel came back to Lenox in 1821 with family silver, china, jewelry, books, paintings, and $5,000, he appeared to have acquired the funds to reimburse Gallatin. Whether he did so is another question. Angel did not go to France again.[18]

The episode in France may have fueled the animosity between Angel and Eleazer Williams, who seem to have been rivals for influence with the Oneidas. If so, the debacle of the French tour may have sunk Angel's standing, already damaged by his part in land cessions. "Williams hated [Deferrier] cordially and was always cautioning the Indians against him," remembered Albert Gallatin Ellis. A young printer's apprentice who assisted Williams as a teacher, Ellis was a local boy whose parents must have admired Jefferson's treasury secretary. Deferrier regarded Williams "as a fraud, living on the credulity of the Indians," recalled Ellis. "The men were at swords' points while I was there." Ellis may or may not have been literal about the swords, but Angel certainly had one and knew how to use it.[19]

Bustle and Noise

Around this time, Eleazer Williams began to promote a grand future out west for the New York Indians, including the Oneidas, Brothertowns, and Stockbridge Indians. However sincere he may have been about this plan, he advocated it with the backing of state officials, church leaders, and land speculators. New York legislators blamed alcohol and squatters for the problems on Native land. Their solution was to remove the Natives. The assembly declared that the state's Indigenous population "ought to yield to the public interest." The senate called on the governor to act on removal with or without the cooperation of the federal government.[20]

The US secretary of war, John C. Calhoun, supported the peaceful removal of Indians out of the way of roads, canals, and settlement. With this end in mind, in 1820 he asked the Reverend Jedediah Morse to investigate Indian affairs throughout the country. Morse's publication of geography textbooks had earned him the title "father of American geography," but he still needed to borrow $1,000 from his brother-in-law Sidney Breese. As he had been back in 1796, Morse was escorted through New York by the most prominent of guides. He traveled on the Erie Canal with Governor DeWitt Clinton and the ninth patroon, Stephen Van Rensselaer, who is still ranked as one of the richest Americans of all time. On his journey, Morse took notes about the tremendous economic advantages created by the canal. A raft carrying 446 tons of timber covered eighteen miles in a day and a half at a cost of $50. To haul such a load the same distance on land cost $1,200.[21]

In Oneida, Morse thought that the People of the Standing Stone had improved in education, religion, and agriculture. He concluded, however, that they had not met expectations. He blamed the "influence of low and depraved white people." The Oneida leaders were "unsettled" regarding removal, noted Morse, who saw great anxiety in their faces. Most of them wanted to stay on their homelands. They believed, Morse wrote, that they could "be civilized where they are." He disagreed. The Oneidas would be better off in the Northwest Territory, he told Calhoun in a report that validated the national policy of removal.[22]

The Oneidas mounted an articulate resistance. The sale of their treasured land to raise funds to build a church showed their commitment to staying put, they said. The chiefs of the Second Christian Party were outraged to learn that Eleazer Williams, already in trouble over missing church funds, misrepresented them as somewhat favorable toward removal. They made their position public. "All this bustle and noise about our emigrating," they posted in the *Albany Gazette and Daily Advertiser*, "has arisen from designing and interested men, whom we esteem our enemies." They announced they were sending a deputation to "inform the government against the designs of our missionary and his associates, and implore its protection."[23]

When the deputation, including Martin Denny and Moses Schuyler, the son of Plattcop, arrived in Washington, President James Monroe and Secretary Calhoun were not there. This Martin Denny was most likely Polly's nephew, then in his twenties and a leader in the Second Christian Party, rather than the interpreter Martinus Denny, Polly's forty-four-year-old brother, who was associated with the First Christian Party. The young men left a message: "Our Reservation is already diminished to a very small space; but we calculate to keep what we have got, and we think much of it, we intend it shall go down to generations after us." The secretary of war sent word that the Oneidas would not be removed by force. Oneida leaders assured the president that if they planned to move, the chiefs would come to see him in person. He was not to trust Mr. Eleazer Williams or any written communication on such an important issue.[24]

Although Williams did not have the authority to speak for the Oneidas, he negotiated treaties with the Ho-Chunks and Menominees in 1821 and 1822. These people thought they were agreeing to share their land to the west of Lake Michigan, but the treaty, which would be contested for years, called the deal a sale. Williams began to receive payments from the Ogden Land Company. Its founder, David A. Ogden, a former counsel to the Holland Land Company and investor in western New York properties, aggressively pushed for the relocation of the Six Nations. His company put Indian Agent Parrish, who worked for both the federal and state governments, on its payroll.[25]

As agitation for removal grew, the US Supreme Court delivered what is considered the landmark decision on Indian title. *Johnson v. McIntosh* (1823) held that private citizens could not purchase land from Native people without the permission of the United States. In his ruling, Chief Justice John Marshall revisited the doctrine of discovery. In their eagerness to appropriate as much of the American continent as they could, noted Marshall, "the potentates of the old world found no difficulty in convincing themselves that they made ample compensation to the inhabitants of the new, by bestowing on them civilization and Christianity." Their claim of sovereignty over their colonies, "however extravagant the pretention," wrote Marshall, had passed to the US government. To overturn it would invalidate property titles across the nation. The United States therefore owned all the land, while Indigenous people retained the right to remain on their aboriginal territory.[26]

Considered by many the greatest Supreme Court justice in US history, Marshall is worth quoting a bit more on this precedent-setting decision. Indians, he ruled, are "to be considered merely as occupants, to be protected, indeed, while in peace, in the possession of their lands" by the federal government in its role as benevolent guardian. He described dispossession as justified, however, because Indigenous people at the time of European arrival were "fierce savages, whose occupation was war, and whose subsistence was drawn chiefly from the forest." It was impossible to mix with them or govern them as a distinct people, he said, "because they were as brave and as high spirited as they were fierce, and ready to repel by arms every attempt on their independence." He concluded, "To leave them in possession of their country was to leave the country a wilderness." The history cited in this landmark ruling, it seems to me, contains layers of fictions.[27]

For the Oneidas, who had the right to remain on their land, the decision to go or stay was made even harder by the eloquence of respected leaders on both sides. Daniel Bread, the son of Kanadolock and member of the First Christian Party, advocated removal. He felt it was impossible to thrive on their ancestral land. Out west, they could make a fresh start, build an Indian Christian community, and establish a good place for their children. Moses Schuyler and Martin Denny argued for staying. White people would crowd in wherever you went, they thought. There was no better place than our own home, where, said a chief of the Second Christian Party, "we wish to walk by ourselves and enjoy our own privileges in our own way."[28]

The only possession of the Oneidas valuable enough to finance a move west was land. The First Christian Party sold two thousand acres to the state in 1824. Those who left for Green Bay in what was then Michigan Territory were compensated for their orchards, houses, and barns with payments ranging from two dollars to one hundred dollars. Those who stayed received no compensation. The first tract, on the eastern border, included part of Oneida Castle and the village of Sconondoa. One "very good Lot, all improved, pleasantly situated on the Seneca Road," remarked the surveyor, "is well watered, has one frame house, formerly the residence of the venerable Chief Skanandoa and has the much admired butternut orchard." The treaty granted Eleazer Williams one hundred acres out of the first tract, which was occupied by Sidney Breese's Sconondoa Cotton Company and white squatters.[29]

The second tract, on the western border, included the last of the best land to be ceded by the Oneidas. The state acquired the remaining Oneida land along Cowaselon Creek north of the turnpike, including the corner crossed by the Erie Canal. One hundred acres of this tract, already the home of Abraham Denny, was set off for him. The lot, noted the surveyor, was an "excellent stand" and well watered. Another "very good lot" of one hundred acres north of the turnpike was set aside for Martin Denny, who, the treaty stated, "has exclusively devoted his life to the business of agriculture and purposes to continue the same on the land of his Fathers."[30]

As the first parties of Oneidas left their homeland, townspeople along the Erie Canal turned out to honor a visiting celebrity. The Marquis de Lafayette was on tour of all twenty-four states. In Utica in 1825, Lafayette reunited with his old but, he thought, surprisingly robust comrades from Oriske. "We sincerely love our white brothers, the Americans," said Shagoyontha, Jacob Doxtator, and a warrior referred to as Taniatakaya, who possibly was Plattcop Tonyentagoyon. "They permit us to live in peace near the bones of our fathers, which they have not obliged us to transport to a strange land; and the government often succours us when our harvests fail." Lafayette had not forgotten their valuable service, he assured them, as he gave the men presents of money. After Lafayette left Utica, his party watched a half-naked Oneida race along the canal bank, wait on a bridge, and gracefully jump down onto the Frenchman's barge. Anthony Otsequette had come to talk of the love of his father, Peter, for Lafayette.[31]

The official celebration of the completed canal started with cannon fire. Boats carrying eagles, wolves, raccoons, a black bear, and two Seneca boys journeyed from west to east. The trip from Buffalo to Albany, which had taken thirty-two days in 1810, now took less than five. In New York City, Governor Clinton took a keg of Lake Erie water from the *Seneca Chief*, poured it into the Atlantic, and declared, "May the God of Heavens and the Earth smile most propitiously on the work, accomplished by the wisdom, public spirit, and energy of the people of the state of New York."[32]

The Erie Canal, along with Saratoga Springs and Niagara Falls, became a sight to see on the American Grand Tour. "All hands upon deck," instructed the canal guide, to see the "grand, imposing, and highly picturesque" scenery at Little Falls. Less thrilled with nature, a young traveler deplored "swarms of mosquitos of a gigantic size." She thought the wooden aqueducts looked fragile and was not reassured when a canal commissioner said they should last at least a dozen years. On the Long Level, the aspiring author Nathaniel Hawthorne of Massachusetts saw "dismal swamps and unimpressive scenery." It was, he thought, "the very land of unsubstantial things, whither dreams might betake themselves, when they quit the slumberer's brain."[33]

FIGURE 22a, b, c. Portraits by Samuel Finley Breese Morse (1791–1872) of the Marquis de Lafayette (1757–1834) while on his American tour in 1824–25 and the artist's uncle Sidney Breese (1768–1848) and aunt Helen Breese (1781–1861), painted in Sconondoa in 1827. Morse, the son of Jedediah Morse, was a professor of painting and sculpture at the University of the City of New York (now New York University) and the inventor of an electric telegraph and the Morse Code. Marquis de Lafayette photograph by Glenn Castellano, Collection of the Public Design Commission of the City of New York. Samuel Sidney Breese and Helen Burrows Breese, Yale University Art Gallery, Gift of the Associates in Fine Arts.

Hawthorne's packet passed a boat manned by three Indians "who gazed at us in silence," he wrote. "Perhaps these three alone, among the ancient possessors of the land, had attempted to derive benefit from the white man's mighty projects, and float along the current of his enterprise." Traveling through the swamp past Rome, another passenger saw Onondaga and Oneida Indians. We "diverted ourselves for miles in making the children run after the packet by tossing out a cent," he recalled. "We could not prevail upon them to converse by the offer of any bribe whatever." These accounts, I noticed, rendered as mute the Native people seen along the engineering marvel of the age. No doubt the Denny children ran down the creek and along the canal, the first to do so of generations of children on the best land, who, in my experience, were far from quiet.[34]

The canal turned Wampsville into a little boomtown of cooks, mule drivers, smiths, hostlers, repairmen, hotels, shops, and taverns supplied with food and hay by local farmers. Described by Hawthorne as a "dull race of money-getting drudges," the inhabitants along the Long Level now had access to markets and multiple jobs. After harvest, town of Lenox farmers manned the boats rushing their grain and produce to cities. Early on, when there were no rules regarding passing, the boat crews

FIGURE 23. "View on the Erie Canal." J. W. Hill, artist. 1829. New York Public Library Digital Collection.

determined with their fists who went first. The explosion of population and commerce along the Erie Canal, reported the *Niles Weekly Register*, increased the value of lands in the state by more than $100,000,000.[35]

A grateful New York State presented Angel with the best land. Governor Clinton granted seven hundred acres of the first tract of the Treaty of 1815 to the Deferriers. This section, between the turnpike and the canal, included the former homes of Peter August and Jacob Doxtator. In addition, the state gave Angel land along the creek in Lots 2 and 3 of the second tract of the Treaty of 1824. All in all, treaties and patents awarded around 2,700 acres to Angel between 1809 and 1830. The Deferriers sold two to three lots a year while keeping most of the best land in the family. Polly, who never learned to read and write, was frequently present at these transactions and made her mark on numerous deeds.[36]

Angel and Polly entertained at their stately house. They rode in their carriage to the Breese home for tea. Sidney's nephew Edward Elbridge Salisbury, a professor of Arabic and Sanskrit at Yale University, recalled "the charming novelties" of his boyhood trips to Sconondoa. "Here, too, I first saw Indians, a remnant of the Oneidas," he wrote, "and visited the family of Col. de Ferrier, a wealthy refugee from France, in my uncle's neighborhood, who had married an Indian squaw, never quite weaned from her first habits of life."[37]

The story of the Deferrier family fascinated stagecoach travelers on the turnpike. After leaving Oneida Castle, reported the newspaper publisher and politician Thurlow Weed, "the passengers would talk of the devotion of Rev. Mr. Kirkland to the Oneida Indians, of the eloquence of Shenandoah, one of their aged chiefs, and a French officer, Colonel de Ferrier, who married an Indian wife at Oneida Castle, and whose sons and daughters were well educated ladies and gentlemen; and this topic would scarcely be exhausted when we were driven into the village of Vernon where we always changed horses." The accounts of Salisbury and Weed show what about Polly and Angel was remembered and what was not.[38]

Polly and Angel's son Charles and daughters Nancy, Sophia, Lucy, and Mary were part of a social set who attended concerts and supper parties. As a young boy, Charles was sent to the Fairfield Academy in Herkimer for two years. He later studied law in New York City, and by 1826, at age twenty-two, he had a law office in Utica. When Charles paid a call on the Breese family, he came "in great style like a true knight errant or more properly a dandy," wrote Sidney's daughter Margaret, who was the same age as Charles. Her sister Helen Platt Breese spent an afternoon at the Deferriers' with Charles, Lucy, aged nineteen, and their friend Abby Higinbotham, the daughter of the merchant Sands Higinbotham. "It was rather pleasant," reported Helen. "Lucy was very clever. She has gone to Utica to get some new things to dash in this winter."[39]

Removal from Land and Memory

Marriage to a Deferrier daughter meant influence with the Oneidas. Sophia's husband, Thomas T. Loomis, had come from Massachusetts as a boy and settled with his family in the town of Verona, located between Oneida Castle and Rome. Like his brother-in-law, Thomas had attended Fairfield Academy and studied law. Out of Angel's grant, Thomas acquired a profitable property on the canal. He assisted the Oneidas with business and legal matters. Anthony Otsequette, who led one hundred Oneidas to Green Bay, gave Thomas the power of attorney to accept his annuity of forty-two dollars. This transaction was witnessed by Nancy's husband, John Hadcock.[40]

John Hadcock assumed his father-in-law's old role. After the Treaty of 1815 and the trip to France, Angel no longer witnessed treaties or the distribution of the annuities to the Oneidas, but John did. John had been born on Oneida territory near the home of his maternal grandfather, Conrad Clock, in 1795. His father, Daniel Hadcock, had fought alongside Oneida warriors at the Battle of Saratoga. Many times, John had seen the handsome wampum belt given by George Washington to Kanadolock in gratitude for his outstanding service during the Revolutionary War. John and Nancy lived among the Oneidas in the Stockbridge Valley, where John ran a trading post.[41]

The Oneidas asked John Hadcock to accompany a delegation of their leading men to Albany in 1824. Years later, John recalled the meeting between chiefs and headmen Moses Schuyler, Jacob Doxtator, and Paul Powless, the orator Martinus White, the interpreter Martinus Denny, and others with Governor Joseph C. Yates and Simeon DeWitt. The Oneidas protested the plan to build a dam on the Oswego River. The state had promised them the right of fishing and hunting forever, they said, pointing to a copy of the Treaty of 1788 they had brought with them. The proposed dam, eighteen feet high, would block the salmon run. The Oneidas said they would accept a lower dam that the salmon could jump over. The officials replied that the engineers required the dam at the proposed height to feed the canals and promised that if the construction harmed the Oneida fisheries, the state would make it right.[42]

"Is our land all safe that is reserved to us along Oneida Lake?" asked Martinus White. DeWitt replied, "I have sold that land." White asked, "By what authority?" DeWitt answered that he had sold it under some treaty. "Show me the treaty," said White. For a few hours, DeWitt looked for the treaty. He showed them the Treaty of 1809 that sold land on both sides of Fish Creek. White said, "We know we have sold that about Fish Creek, but around Oneida Lake we never sold." DeWitt said he could not find a treaty, but again assured the delegation that the state would make it right. The chiefs and clan mothers never let Oneida children forget about the reserved land on the north shore of Oneida Lake. They spoke of it often, recalled Jacob L. W. Doxtator, the grandson of Jacob Doxtator, and Jacob Cornelius, the grandson of Shagoyontha.[43]

With the assistance of John Hadcock, the state acquired the last of the Oneida land on Cowaselon Creek, a hilly tract of 1,640 acres south of present-day Mount Hope Avenue that would be the home of my great-great-grandparents. The controversial Treaty of 1826 favored the Oneidas who planned to leave. The parcel belonged to the Second Christian Party, which protested the sale. In a petition to the state, the party charged that there had been no council held in public to discuss the treaty. There were accusations of forgery and bribery, including the charge that chief William Day signed the treaty in exchange for one hundred dollars and a suit of clothes from John Hadcock. A legislative committee responded to these accusations. Treaties were never made with the unanimous consent of all the Indians involved, it concluded. Out of this treaty and another in 1827, Hadcock received over 120 acres.[44]

Along Oneida Creek, John and Nancy Hadcock, the Stockbridge Indians, and the Oneidas were joined by my grandmother's ancestors. They settled at Five Chimneys, named after the tavern at the intersection of the Oneida Turnpike, or Peterboro Road, and the north-south trail to the Oneidas' fishing camp on Oneida Lake, now known as West Road or Route 46. Among the first of the new neighbors was John Gregg, my fifth great-grandfather, who leased Indian land on Stockbridge West Hill. Scots Irish families from New Hampshire like the Greggs and Boylans, along with Yankees like the Adams and Green families from Massachusetts, purchased, leased, and squatted on Indian land.[45]

When the Oneida and Stockbridge Indians complained to the state of trespass, the legislator Alexander Haring investigated. White invaders "of the most abandoned cast," reported Haring, took illegal possession of Oneida lands, abused and impoverished the outnumbered Indians, and "raise[d] themselves upon their ruin." I do not know whether Haring was referring specifically to any of my ancestors. In pointing out this wrongdoing, I observe, the sympathetic legislator positioned the state as a protector of Indians, although it had led the way in the illegal acquisition of Oneida lands and permitted squatters to crowd into Native territory. In any event, nothing was done about the invasion. White settlers objected to the cost to taxpayers of enforcing trespass laws on Indian land.[46]

Visitors reinforced the view that local white people and what Thurlow Weed wryly referred to as "the advantages of civilization" were not doing the Oneidas any good. "These advantages consisted in loafing about taverns and groceries, and in drinking bad whisky," Weed wrote. On his way to becoming one of the most powerful politicians in the state, Weed was not a disinterested observer but an advocate for the development of canals and railroads across New York. Heading west on the turnpike, the English traveler John Fowler saw nearly naked Oneida children running alongside the stagecoach asking for charity. He was told, he noted in his published journal, that the Oneidas were wretched farmers and neglected their lands to go hunting. "These Indians are a harmless, inoffensive set of beings," concluded Fowler, "but have lost much of their ancient spirit and energy."[47]

Such negative descriptions of the Oneidas in the 1830s contrasted with the portrayals of the "noble savage" of the past, then popular at theaters and in literature. In New York and Boston, Oneidas danced before urban audiences who did not know that some Native performers reenacted scalping maneuvers to raise money to oppose the trespass on their lands by white people. In celebrated novels set in Iroquoia, the author James Fenimore Cooper of Otsego County enthralled readers with the adventures of the white frontiersman Natty Bumppo, known as Hawkeye or the Deerslayer, and his wise companion, the Mohican Chingachgook. The French visitor Alexis de Tocqueville, whose observations collected during his tour of the United States in 1831 inspired his brilliant commentary on American democracy, had learned about Indigenous people from reading Cooper's *The Last of the Mohicans*. The ragged Oneidas he passed on the road, Tocqueville assumed, could not be real Indians.[48]

Stagecoach passengers, theatergoers, and readers of Cooper were unaware of the accomplishments of their Oneida Indian contemporaries, who had restored the size of their population to what it had been before the Revolutionary War. The travelers on the turnpike witnessed the poverty of Oneidas, but they did not see their successful farms, sawmill, schools, and churches. They did not see Indigenous people as good neighbors. When the barn of a white woman in Oneida Castle caught fire, Oneida Indian men and women carried water and mud to stop the flames from spreading to her house. Although the Oneidas had troubles, they were not as desperate as visitors claimed. Depictions of their degradation, however, reinforced the case for removal.[49]

With "a view of hastening and facilitating the emigration of the Oneida Indians," wrote Simeon DeWitt, the state legislature ordered that the Oneidas be paid a fair price for their lands. The First Christian Party sold Oneida land north and south of the turnpike in 1829, including the tract that would be the site of the city of Oneida. The Oneidas protested in vain when it turned out that the state's idea of a fair price was to pay eight dollars an acre for land it sold at twenty-two dollars an acre. Jacob Doxtator and Peter August, who already had lost their homes on the best land, again gave up their improvements. Purchasers of lots included my fourth great-grandfather Christian Harp, son of the squatter George Harp. This sale funded the removal of 110 Oneidas, led by Daniel Bread, to present-day Wisconsin.[50]

Now that the Oneidas had sold their last land on the turnpike, the Dennys no longer were as necessary as intermediaries. Their property strategy was in jeopardy. Abraham Denny and his brother Martin petitioned the state legislature to pass a law that would authorize them to sell the valuable lots reserved to them. The brothers explained that they wanted to ensure the validity of their deeds. But that was not the real reason for the request, said Abraham's family. In an opposing petition, Catharine Denny and her children stated that Sylvester Beecher, who held mortgages on Abraham's property, had induced Abraham to apply for rights to sell his land. In the two decades since he had bought the property of Abraham's grandmother Sarah, Beecher had become one of the wealthiest men in the town of Lenox. Abraham's family protested that an act by the legislature would deprive them of their "sole dependence" and be contrary to the intent of the treaty that had set aside their home.[51]

The state made it possible for Abraham Denny to sell his one hundred acres. He did so in 1831, and his property was bought and sold twice before it was acquired by his cousin Charles Deferrier and William Cobb, a former agent of the Lenox Iron Company. After Abraham's home became the Cobb estate, he and his family resided in diminished circumstances next to Polly and Angel. Martinus Denny gave up on his ten acres, which he and his wife sold to Angel. Although Polly's brother and nephews lived as "civilized" on land reserved for them by treaty, they had not been able to hold on to their property.[52]

"The cholera is now amongst our poor Indians," reported Helen Burrows Breese in August 1832. "Six have died, 2 yesterday, and they could scarcely get any person to go out and bury them." Abraham Van Eps was raising money to pay for a doctor and provisions for them, she wrote. Gerrit Smith, the heir of Peter, came from Peterboro to donate twenty-five dollars. During a global pandemic, cholera had spread along the Erie Canal, where in Utica, seventy people perished. At Oneida, the losses included Shagoyontha, warrior, counselor, and international performer.[53]

Angel may have been a victim of the disease when he died a few weeks later. He was laid to rest at the burial ground by the school. Later Polly had him interred in the small graveyard on her property. The family ordered a tall stone marker shipped by canal and hauled by six oxen up the knoll above the creek. "Charles has erected a beautiful monument at the head of his father's grave," wrote Helen Platt Breese. Another sort of monument to Angel was the surrounding landscape. With its cleared fields, wooded hills, and big sky, Lenox now looked like the *seigneurie* Ferrieres. But no mill on Angel's land, crossed as it was by wagon trains and canal boats, would be called the Bird Singing Mill because the place was so quiet you could hear the birds sing.[54]

The deaths of their elders convinced some Oneidas to go, while others were determined to stay. Jacob Doxtator died at Oneida Castle. Possibly intoxicated, he fell during a scuffle and broke his neck. It was a sad end for the warrior and interpreter who had lost his homes at Oriske, Cowaselon, and Oneida Castle. Jacob's enterprising sister Dolly and his extraordinary mother, Sarah, died in 1833 within weeks of each other. Four hundred more Oneidas left for Green Bay. Their leave-taking was not as deadly as the forced relocation of the southeastern Indians known as the Trail of Tears, but it was full of difficulty and heartache. In Dolly Denny's last years, her great-granddaughter was born a thousand miles away. The oneness of land and family had been sundered.[55]

The era of removal coincided with dimming memories of the American Revolution and the promised guarantees of Oneida territory. In 1832, Congress offered pensions to veterans and their survivors if they could provide written evidence or eyewitness testimony of their service. Elderly militiamen admitted that it was difficult to recall details regarding the wartime chaos in the Mohawk Valley. Not one of us, explained the seventy-three-year-old William Bellinger, can account for the exact number of times we were called out, the precise duties performed, or the names of all our superior officers, or produce written discharges. Raiders had stolen his cattle, killed his brother, and taken his father prisoner, he said, while he had kept himself "always in readiness at a moment's warning."[56]

The Oneidas had an oral history of their Revolutionary War service. It was not customary to keep paper records, explained Henry Powless in a pension application regarding his father, since his parents could not read or write. The Oneidas could not count on testimonies from their former militia comrades, who, I noticed, vividly and not surprisingly recalled the terror of attacks made by enemy Indians and their Loyalist allies. They less often acknowledged the part played by the Oneidas. When they did, they rarely named individuals but instead referred to "our Indians" or "friendly Indians" or "American Indians."[57]

For the Oneidas, pension applications resulted in disappointment and denial. Peter Doxtator reported a fraudulent application for his father, Honyery, submitted by local white men, one of whom went to jail. In other applications, Oneida families provided testimony about years of service as scouts, messengers, defenders of forts, and fighters in battle. But however valuable the Oneida warriors were to the common cause, determined the pension commissioner, they were ineligible under the law. "He did not serve in any regularly organized corps, nor by virtue of any competent [military] authority," said the letter rejecting the application made on behalf of Shagoyontha, who had seen action with Generals Herkimer, Lafayette, and Washington.[58]

The Home Party

The coming of the railroad reinforced the belief among white residents that it was time for the Oneidas to go. Sands Higinbotham, who had purchased land west of Oneida Castle, gave the railroad company a free right-of-way across his property as long as the train stopped there. He cleared a site for a hotel and a restaurant. To connect the train station to the turnpike, he improved the trail now known as Main Street. A feeder canal that brought water from Oneida Creek to the Erie Canal north of the tracks was enlarged to allow boats access to the railroad. Higinbotham sold lots at low prices and then supplied lumber from his mill in Vernon for the construction of houses and shops. His friend

Sidney Breese, who was one of the appraisers of purchased Indian land, lent money to buyers of property and builders of homes. The village of Oneida was born as a railroad depot.[59]

The railroad meant a jump in the value of the Deferrier property. The Syracuse and Utica Railroad naturally wanted to build on the same level terrain already occupied by the Seneca Turnpike and the Erie Canal. Polly signed an agreement witnessed by Higinbotham that allowed the railroad to cross her land in return for $10 a year for her life, a five-foot-high fence, and two swing gates in good repair. Her 153-acre property was now assessed at $7,500, up from $5,600 the year before. Abraham Denny's former property, now owned by Charles Deferrier and William Cobb, doubled in value. The new tracks soon would become part of the famed New York Central Railroad.[60]

Members of the Denny and Deferrier families may have been among the crowd that gathered to see the first train go through Wampsville on the Fourth of July 1839. According to Mrs. Hammond, a few Oneidas joined the adventurous passengers on the first railroad coaches. She imagined their sadness at this latest "inroad of a scarcely understood civilization on the domain of their ancestors and their own homes." Perhaps she was right about the sadness, but not about the lack of understanding of transportation technology among the Oneidas, many of whom traveled far and wide. In Wampsville, a plank road (present-day Court Street) connected the canal, the railroad, and the mills at Lenox Furnace. At the intersection with the turnpike, an elegant house in the popular Greek revival style was built across the street from the store where Thomas T. Loomis, as justice of the peace, held court upstairs. Indians, white residents assumed, did not belong in such a modern place.[61]

"We do not wish to remove from the lands given us by the good spirit and secured to us by different treaties," Moses Schuyler wrote to President Martin Van Buren. Over six hundred Oneidas, or more than half of all of them, had stayed on their ancestral land. Following a bad crop year in 1835, the First Christian Party requested an advance on its annuity from the state. Its request made in June, I noted, was marked paid in December. In addition, the federal government, the Oneidas complained, had been withholding the payment of the annuities it had promised.[62]

John Denny, Polly Deferrier's nephew and interpreter for the Oneidas, asked the state for a portion of the funds left over from the sale of Oneida lands not used to support the move west. He and his family, he said, had been educated according to the customs of white people and preferred to live among whites rather than go to Green Bay. The Senate Committee on Indian Affairs acknowledged that John and his family were moral and respectable, but it denied his petition. The state policy, it said, was to encourage emigration out of "the most paternal regard for the welfare of the Indians themselves." In addition, said the legislators, "it has always been a governing principle to deal with the Indians in their national capacity, and not as individuals." John's response to this statement of principle so at odds with practice is unknown.[63]

John and his brother Abraham decided to accept the federal government's offer of land in the Kansas Territory. As part of the national policy of removal, the United States negotiated the Treaty of Buffalo Creek with the Six Nations in 1838. The goal of the treaty, which was conducted by corrupt officials in partnership with the Ogden Land Company, was to move the Haudenosaunee out of New York. The treaty said that $2,000 would be paid to Oneida chief William Day for expenses in Green Bay, but William Day was not present at the treaty and did not plan on moving. The New York Oneidas objected to the treaty and issued a written statement that they were not a party to it.[64]

For the Oneidas who did go to Kansas, the US government failed to provide an annuity, a blacksmith, mills, a schoolhouse, tools, and teams and cows for widows, as promised. "None of these things have ever been done or furnished," declared Lewis S. Denny, John's son, whose claim was jumped by a white man when the United States opened Kansas to white settlement. John Denny was among the Oneidas who returned to their New York homelands. Abraham Denny died at Little Osage, Missouri.[65]

It was time for the remaining Oneidas to become civilized, believed William Seward, the new governor of New York in 1839. A member of the Whig Party, Seward did not support the removal policy of the Democrats. He viewed the state as guardian of the Oneidas and felt it should encourage the Oneidas to assimilate. For those who thought assimilation meant that Indigenous people would vanish into American society, the policy was another way to achieve the goal of removal. The Oneidas should give up communal ownership of their lands, Seward maintained, and become individual owners of private property like everyone else. This policy, called severalty, had been opposed by the Haudenosaunee for years. "Holding our lands in common, as we now do, keeps us together," explained a Seneca chief.[66]

Confronted with the prospect of severalty, Moses Schuyler changed his mind about staying on the Oneida homelands. Known as a wise man with good judgment, Moses described how the policy of individual ownership would make a bad situation worse. We already have lost most of our land, he explained. When the people need money, they will sell what little land they have left and end up poorer than ever. Then when they are low on funds, they will buy goods from white people on credit. If they have difficulty paying what they owe, their land will be taken to cover their debts. With severalty, Moses predicted, we shall lose all our land.[67]

Moses Schuyler concluded that the government had forsaken the Indians. The traditional system had its headaches, he knew. His own brothers intrigued against him out of jealousy over his influence as a leader. Even so, Moses believed in preserving the Oneida way of life. He and others preferred to leave rather than assimilate. To finance their removal, the Oneidas sold their last major tract of territory. In treaties made between 1840 and 1842, they gave up three thousand acres along Oneida Creek where most of them lived, farmed, and operated their mill. By the time this series of land cessions was finished, the Oneidas had left less than two thousand acres.[68]

The witness of two of these treaties was Sands Higinbotham, the railroad developer, who, like the turnpike and canal promoters before him, had been appointed Indian commissioner by the state. His fellow witness Nathan Burchard, the state-appointed attorney to the Oneidas, surveyed the ceded land. He wrote a glowing appraisal of beautiful lots with rich soils, bountiful orchards, stately forests, and valuable Indian improvements. When he delivered the payments due to the Oneidas for their improvements, he charged hefty fees. Burchard, the Oneidas said, was our "lawless Lawyer Agent."[69]

The Oneidas split into emigrating parties provided with thousands of dollars by New York State to help with moving expenses. Many headed to Wisconsin. Others went to live with Onondagas, Senecas, and Tuscaroras. Moses Schuyler led a few hundred people to Canada. Moses acknowledged that part of his nation had allied with the Americans during the Revolution, but he claimed those people went to Green Bay. "Our party never spilled the blood of the British, we were called the peace party," said Moses as he diplomatically neglected to mention the valiant performance of his father, Plattcop, at the battle of Oriskany. At Thames River, the Oneidas performed ceremonies of condolence and reconciliation with their brothers and sisters of the Six Nations.[70]

The Oneidas who stayed were called the Home Party. The state treaties authorized the commissioners to set aside tracts to be held as private property by Oneida families who could combine to make up the numbers needed to entitle them to more than fifty acres. Officials had to confirm that the heads of families were "prudent, industrious & capable of managing & taking care of such lands." Women headed many of the families, but the state made the adult male "liable on contracts, and subject to taxation and to the civil jurisdiction" of state courts "whenever he shall become a freeholder, to the value of one hundred dollars." The Oneidas, said the state, could sell their land to a third party as long as the sale was overseen by a local superintendent.[71]

These rules allowed members of the Home Party to own real estate in the same manner as a citizen but without the rights of citizens. Most New Yorkers, Governor Seward believed, would oppose citizenship for Indians because of widespread racial prejudice. The Oneidas had reasons to accept severalty. They could sell land if they wished to emigrate. With a title to their land, it could not be signed away by others or claimed by Oneidas who left but might return. Most of all, the Home Party wanted to stay. "This is where we always lived," said an elderly Oneida woman when asked why her grandparents had not moved to Wisconsin. "[I]sn't this Oneida?" Her grandfather, she said, "couldn't see no benefit to going to a strange place when everything he knew or wanted was right here." By 1845, there were 185 Oneidas left on their ancestral land.[72]

Most of Polly Deferrier's relations left. Her brothers, Louis and Martinus, followed the Oneidas to Wisconsin, as did many of her nephew Abraham's children and their mother. Polly's own children stayed close. Her youngest daughter, Mary, and Mary's husband, Nelson Cobb, farmed the best land. Sophia lived in Wampsville, Nancy in Stockbridge, and Lucy in Herkimer. Charles was married by the mayor of New York City to Theresa Bedlow, a great-niece of the philanthropist Henry Rutgers. When Charles and Theresa divorced, Charles returned, he said, to be close to his beloved mother. He built a house known as "The Cottage" next to the family graveyard. During the Van Buren administration, Charles delivered annuity payments to the Oneidas, as his father once had done.[73]

By the 1840s, the Erie Canal had brought thousands of people to Lenox and taken thousands away. Newcomers flocked to factory jobs along the towpath. In Wampsville, workers made wagons, sleighs, harnesses, and shoes as New York became the number one state in industrial production. Others left, including most Oneidas. Settlers headed west to start over because they failed to make payments on their property or could not compete as subsistence farming gave way to commercial

FIGURE 24. Charles Deferrier (1804–90). Detail from undated photograph. 2005.P002.03, Madison County Historical Society.

agriculture. Many moved on because the farm they owned or leased could not support an entire family. The scattered sons of the Clockville man who operated Sylvester Beecher's farm, for example, would die in Michigan, Wisconsin, Illinois, Iowa, western New York, Peterboro, and the Union Army.[74]

The dispossession of the Oneidas begun by state officials, speculators, and canal and railroad developers now was carried out by local people. Even supposing these men to be perfectly honest (as Albert Gallatin had said regarding Angel), Sidney Breese, Sands Higinbotham, Sylvester Beecher, and Angel Deferrier, among others, prospered as a result of illegal and unethical actions carried out by officials high and low. So did my ancestors, who had positioned themselves to take advantage of newly available Oneida lands. In 1831 the state legislature passed "An Act Directing the Sale to John Gregg of 250 Acres of Land, in the New Stockbridge or Oneida Reservation." Acts like this one allowed New York State to hand out Native land to white people while still claiming to protect Native land by banning any direct sale to individuals. On land reserved to the Home Party, Christian Harp settled next to the Antone,

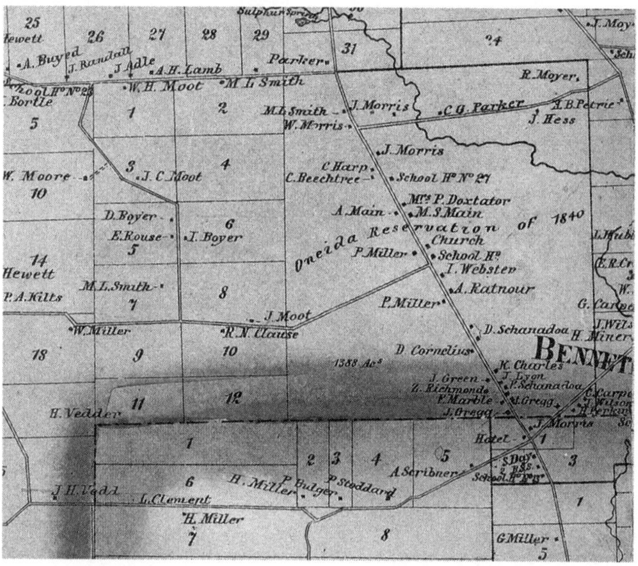

FIGURE 25. Detail showing the Oneida Reservation of 1840. Alongside the Oneida families of Beechtree, Doxtator, Webster, Schanandoa (Skenandoah), Cornelius, and Charles lived my Harp, Ratnour, Green, and Gregg kinfolk, with my Moot and Clement relations close by. From *Gillette's Map of Madison Co., New York: From Actual Surveys.* 1859, Library of Congress, Geography and Map Division.

Beechtree, and Doxtator families, while the Green family moved alongside the Cornelius and Skenandoah families.[75]

Perhaps Lewis and Dorothy Clement read the advertisement in the *Albany Argus* about the "very fine land" for sale in the town of Lenox on Stockbridge West Hill, "which for its healthy situation and fertility of soil, is probably second to none in the country." The Clements came from the Mohawk Valley with their four-year-old son, William, my great-great-grandfather, in the early 1830s. Lewis was the son of the Revolutionary War veteran Lambert Clement, the great-grandson of Joseph Clement, and the great-great-great-grandson of Marie du Trieux. His wife, Dorothy Vedder, now lived up the road from the grandsons of Honyery and Shagoyontha, the wartime comrades of her grandfather Henry Timmerman. Her new home was on the same hill her forefather Harmen Myndertsz Van den Bogaert had climbed two hundred years earlier after he had been greeted by an Oneida woman with her gift of baked pumpkin.[76]

CHAPTER 7

Squatters, Tenants, Owners

Polly Denny Deferrier added to her wealth and property in her last years. Her portrait, painted by the respected local artist Frederick Spencer, shows the distinguished Haudenosaunee woman of mid-nineteenth-century Wampsville that she was. When Polly died in 1853, she left almost everything to her son Charles and her daughter Mary, who had stayed on the best land. To Charles, Polly bequeathed 193 acres, the farming tools, the window curtains, and the set of mahogany chairs from the parlor. To Mary, she left her pleasure carriage, her horse, Lana, the parlor stove, and the high-post bedstead. She instructed Charles to erect a stone wall with an iron railing around the small family cemetery where she was buried next to Angel.[1]

Polly Deferrier was "a most exemplary woman," stated an article in the *Oneida Democratic Union*. It then discreetly addressed her origins: "Few indeed would have been able to overcome the taint of early education and associations as she did, and occupy so gracefully the position she afterwards filled." I think it is more likely that the so-called "taint" prepared Polly for such a position. Angel was known to have credited his success to "the wise counsel and prudent management" of his wife. Polly, whose early memories were of war and dislocation, had watched her Mohawk and Oneida relations make their way as entrepreneurs, landowners, and interpreters as they rebuilt their lives at Oriske, Canaseraga,

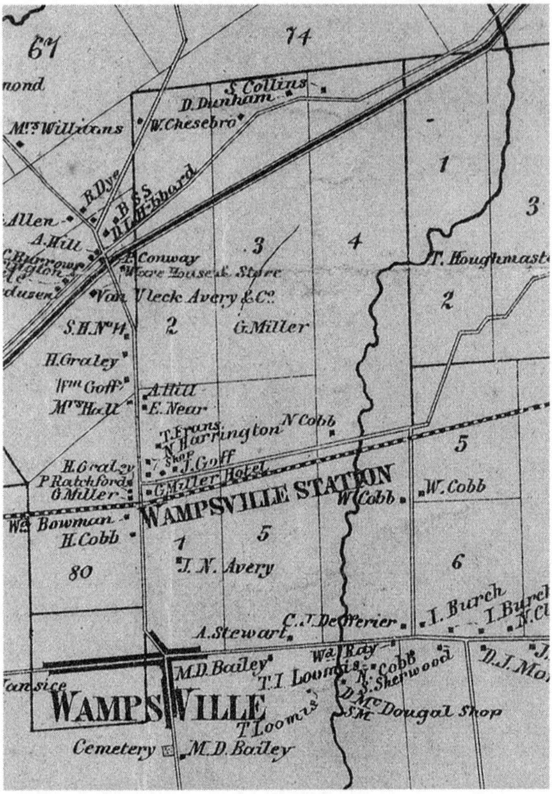

FIGURE 26. Detail of the best land crossed by the Erie Canal, the New York Central Railroad, and the Seneca Turnpike. Charles Deferrier and his sisters Sophia Loomis and Mary Cobb lived near each other on the turnpike, while Mary and her husband, Nelson Cobb, farmed Lot 4 along Cowaselon Creek. From *Gillette's Map of Madison Co., New York: From Actual Surveys*. 1859, Library of Congress, Geography and Map Division.

and Cowaselon. Then she said goodbye to most of them, while she remained on the best land for fifty years. What she thought about all of it, I do not know.[2]

In the year of Polly's death, the Deferrier family made the news thanks to the sensational story of the "Lost Dauphin." The Mohawk missionary Eleazer Williams claimed to be the son of Louis XVI. Magazine articles told how the young prince had not died in prison but was rescued, transported across the Atlantic, and secreted with the Mohawks. The presence of Colonel Deferrier in Oneida was cited as confirmation. Deferrier, reported the *Plattsburgh Republican*, was "one of the Body Guard of Louis XVI, married and resided among the Indians, at Oneida, where a considerable part of Mr. Williams' life was spent."

This story offered a fascinating explanation for what was regarded as Angel's peculiar behavior. Why else would a French nobleman marry a Native and settle on the New York frontier?[3]

Numerous people refuted Williams's claim. Most notably, the Mohawk woman Mary Ann Williams insisted that she, not Marie Antoinette, had given birth to Eleazer. The Prince de Joinville, the son of Louis Phillipe, king of France from 1830 to 1848, denied that he had asked Williams to abdicate the throne during a meeting on a steamboat from Buffalo to Green Bay. One of Angel and Polly's daughters recalled that Angel knew Eleazer Williams, but they were not friends. "As to the Rev. Mr. Williams, I can say that he came to our house often," she said. "As to his being anything more than the Reverend, I think my parents never considered him;—for he never was a favorite with them."[4]

Williams's former assistant, A. G. Ellis, debunked the story that Deferrier knew that Eleazer Williams was Louis XVII. He recalled that the Frenchman had married a sister of the tribal interpreter, Martinus Denny, and owned a good farm with mills west of Oneida. Ellis rejected the claim that Angel had returned from a trip to France in the 1820s with riches given to him by the royal Bourbon family as a reward for his care of young Eleazer. "He had a handsome property when he went, and it was not, as anybody knew, much increased on his return," stated Ellis. Besides, Deferrier and Williams detested each other. Eleazer Williams died in 1858, but the fantasy of the Lost Dauphin lived on.[5]

So did tales of Skenandoah. The *Southern Literary Messenger* published the story of the noble chief Skenando, whose love, "a beautiful and proud Indian girl," spurned him and then knifed him as he was about to be married to another. Pursuers chased her to the highest rock over a ravine, where, with eyes glaring with the fire of a maniac and her long black hair streaming in the night wind, she stabbed herself in her breast and leaped to her doom. Years later, the story concludes, Skenando was found dead by her grave. The old chief was immortalized in a folk song about Shenandoah, his daughter, and her love, the white trader who goes away across the wide Missouri. In songs and stories, passionate Indian maidens did not enjoy a comfortable old age as Polly Deferrier had.[6]

In the years following removal, romantic stories about the Indigenous people of central New York proliferated. One of the challenges to understanding Polly's family in the nineteenth century has been sorting out fact from fiction. I wanted to find out more about Polly's children, who lived as white people, and her relatives in the Home Party, who, in the face of enormous pressure on their land and culture, had to find a way to remain Oneida in Oneida. How did my family, I wondered, make the move from being squatters and tenants to owners of the best land?

To commemorate the Oneidas, white people removed the standing stone to a graveyard. The stone was "the symbolical record of their very nationality," explained the ethnologist Henry Rowe Schoolcraft, who had interviewed Abraham Denny about its location. With the permission of the landowner James Gregg, a boulder on Stockbridge East Hill was taken to Forest Hill Cemetery in Utica in 1849. It was installed on a pedestal with a bronze tablet reading, "Sacred Stone of the Oneida Indians." At the dedication, a local dignitary told the 150 Oneidas and Onondagas in attendance that they were welcome to bury their dead around the stone of their fathers.[7]

The Oneidas "still cling with great tenacity to the homes and haunts of their ancestors," wrote Nathaniel T. Strong, a Seneca who served as a New York State census taker in 1855. "Their lands are now in the possession of the people of the State, and the Oneidas are as aliens in the land of their fathers." About thirty families of the Home Party, with a total population of 160, lived on two reservations. The one on West Road consisted of some 750 acres called the Windfall. The 190-acre reservation known as the Orchard, on Marble Hill, was a few miles west in Oneida County. At the reservation schools, eighty children studied reading, writing, arithmetic, geography, drawing, and bookkeeping. At the annual school exhibition, reported a local paper, the Oneida children "were especially remarkable for their good elocution and self-possession."[8]

The Oneidas were Christians and maintained a pleasing appearance, stated the census report. The three chiefs, Thomas Cornelius, Daniel Skenandoah, and Christian Beechtree, who received the annuity to distribute among their people, were all prosperous farmers. "The houses of these Indians are generally much better than the log houses of the whites, being constructed of hewn, even joisted logs, with shingle roofs and good windows," wrote a fellow census taker. According to this report, William Doxtator, the son of Jacob Doxtator and Polly Antone and stepson of Turtle Clan chief Christian Beechtree, lived in a nicer house than his next-door neighbor, Christian Harp, and his daughter Caroline, my third great-grandmother.[9]

The Oneidas combined old and new ways to make a living. Families farmed their acres in common, while a few leased small parcels to their white neighbors. Oneida men worked as craftsmen in Utica or as day laborers. Some brought in cash by hunting. Catherine Skenandoah

Burning, Chief Skenandoah's great-granddaughter, was housekeeper at the home of the Higinbotham family. Oneidas of the "Indian Minstrel Company" performed war dances and sang hymns in New York City. John Denny, Thomas Cornelius, David Johnson, Peter Doxtator, and Henry Jordan earned income as interpreters. Jordan was married to Sophia Denny, a great-niece of Polly Deferrier and one of the few members of Polly's family who still lived in Oneida.[10]

Another was Polly's nephew, John Denny, the son of John Denny and Dolly Doxtator, known as Dr. Sundown. In addition to his work as an interpreter, he made a living as a medicine man, or root doctor. The secrets of the medicine, he said, had been handed down by his ancestors. Driving a rickety buggy, he traveled around former Oneida territory and beyond to Kahnawake, Onondaga, and Cooperstown to sell his remedies made with herbs, roots, and bark. His trade, reported a newspaper, was as heavy among the whites as it was among Indigenous people. Newspaper advertisements for products called "Indian Hair Restorer" and "Indian Vegetable Blood Purifier" suggest that "Native" cures had popular appeal among Dr. Sundown's contemporaries.[11]

Oneida men and women wove baskets and made moccasins. They sold their crafts at the railroad depot, in towns along the New York Central Railroad, and all around their ancestral lands. The women wore their straight black hair long and loose and donned short calico dresses that showed their beaded leggings. In Otsego County, Oneida women peddled their goods at the home of James Fenimore Cooper's daughter Susan. These people, felt Susan, had a strong claim on those "who have taken their country and their place on the earth."[12]

The basket maker Dolly John of the Turtle Clan did not conform to her white neighbors' notion of marriage. "So, who cares what the man is!" said one Haudenosaunee woman. "We have clans and we go by the mother. There's no bastards in this world." Dolly had nine children with five different Oneida men. She was thought to have married Jake Antone and went by the name of Dolly John Antone. Her children took the last names of their fathers and lived with her. The father of her son Louis Doxtator, for example, was William Doxtator. Dolly John had been raised by her mother, Margaret Cooper from Oriske, who had remained at Oneida with her children while her husband, the War of 1812 veteran Captain John (Ha Yank), had gone to Kansas. He, like John Denny, had returned home to land maintained by the women.[13]

Oneida Indian territory continued to shrink thanks to the policies of Indian removal and severalty that benefited local white people, including my ancestors. My third great-grandfather, John Moot, had a rocky beginning as a landowner. The substantial property acquired by his grandfather Conrad Moot had gone to the children of Conrad's second wife. John's father, Captain John C. Moot, left a tiny estate valued at less than one hundred dollars. As a young man with a young family, John had failed on a farm south of Clockville. Like the Oneida Indians who were unable to pay mortgages, John lost his land. In contrast to the Oneidas, however, John did not lose national territory.[14]

The ability of John Moot to start over illustrates one way in which money made off Oneida land cycled through the local economy. Throughout his career, John borrowed money from the Canastota merchant Daniel Crouse, the son-in-law of Sylvester Beecher whose real estate affairs had included land reserved to Sarah Doxtator and Abraham Denny. Crouse invested in property, the New York Central Railroad, and the Western Union Telegraph. He later served as a director of the Oneida Valley National Bank along with Samuel Breese, John Hadcock, Absalom Gregg, and Niles Higinbotham, the sons and sons-in-law of men who had prospered off the dispossession of the original inhabitants. Esteemed as founders of Oneida, they made investments that were associated with progress and development. The loans to John Moot, for instance, made it possible for him to become a man of property. So did New York State when it issued patents to John for two lots of recently ceded Oneida land on Stockbridge West Hill overlooking the Windfall.[15]

The widowed Catharine Myers Brewer, my third great-grandmother, led her family from Duanesburg to the same hill in 1839. I wonder if the Brewers sought a new life in Madison County filled with hope or desperation. With Catharine were her eight children and her mother, Mary Hetzel Myers, who received a pension as the widow of the Revolutionary War veteran John Myers. Catharine had married Abraham Brewer, the son of the veteran Peter Brewer, who, according to tax records, had been one of the poorest men in Duanesburg when Abraham was young. Abraham, a tenant farmer, recently had died in debt to the Duane family. After four generations of working Duanesburg land, Catharine's family still had little to show for it.[16]

Catharine and her family left behind another tenant rebellion. This one exploded into the Anti-rent War in the 1840s. It was triggered by the death of the last patroon, Stephen Van Rensselaer, in 1839. On his estate, three thousand tenants paid rent with bushels of wheat, four fat fowls, and a day's work with a team of horses or oxen. Once a farmer paid the rent and his bills, he had little, if any, profit to show for the year. Many tenants believed that they and their fathers and grandfathers had paid more in rent than the land was worth. When Van Rensselaer's will called for the collection of back rents, the tenants refused to pay.[17]

Calling themselves "Indians," insurgent tenants, wearing sheepskin masks and calico dresses adorned with raccoon tails, carried tomahawks and pitchforks. They saw themselves as liberators of their homeland for its true heirs, the farmers who had a natural right to the land they had worked. As "Indians," they harassed rent collectors, burned eviction notices, and tarred and feathered a sheriff. Some law enforcers and bystanders were killed. Governor Seward sent the state militia to subdue unrest. The landlords blamed outside agitators for stirring up their tenants with radical notions. Their critics condemned feudal traditions as undemocratic and bad for the economy.[18]

After arrests and imprisonments quieted the protests, the anti-rent movement spread into politics. As wealthy New York landowners had feared, the extension in 1821 of voting rights to white men without property diminished their control. Anti-rent candidates swept local elections in Duanesburg and in Albany, Rensselaer, and Schoharie Counties in 1845. Anti-renters charged that landlords had benefited from corrupt deals made by their ancestors. They asked the state to examine the title of the Duane family, investigate the fraudulent Oriskany Patent, and challenge the legitimacy of the Van Rensselaer properties. If the Van Rensselaer title was ruled invalid, warned uneasy legislators, no title in the state was good.[19]

In *People v. Van Rensselaer* (1853), the court of appeals affirmed that there were imperfections in the paper title, but it ruled that the statute of limitations barred the state from challenging it. The statute said it was unfair to punish certain crimes committed so long ago that evidence was lost, memories had faded, and no witnesses existed to testify. The landlords won the legal battle, but the resistance prevailed when the tenants refused to pay rents. The Van Rensselaers and Livingstons decided to sell most of their estates. The victory of the tenants was bittersweet. After they bought out the landlord's rights and paid off their debts, the tenants had spent more on their farms than they were worth. The anti-renters had to be satisfied with winning the right for men like themselves to own their land.[20]

The Brewers therefore came to the town of Lenox with a long-denied desire for property of their own, but they did not prosper. Catharine's eldest son, James, took out a mortgage from the Lenox Iron Company on two of its lots. He ran a store, possibly the company store, in Lenox

Furnace, and married the daughter of the company manager, Calvin Avery, who two decades earlier had witnessed the purchase of the site from the Dennys and Eleazer Williams. The Lenox Iron Company closed soon afterward, because by then it had exhausted the available timber that fueled its furnace. James sold his land and died young. His brother, Abraham Brewer, my great-great grandfather, was left to support his four little sisters. Abraham became a tenant farmer like his fathers before him.[21]

Burned Over in Oneida

The Brewers arrived in Madison County at a time when demand for land, and with it freedom, was one of many reform movements sweeping through upstate New York. The region crossed by the Erie Canal was called the Burned-Over District because the fires of the spirit led to so many people being converted. There was "a great awakening" in Rome, wrote Helen Burrows Breese, and a "great engagedness in the cause of religion not far from here in Vernon Center." New sects emerged, while Protestant denominations like the Baptists, Methodists, and Presbyterians, which splintered over slavery, united in opposition to the Roman Catholic faith of the Irish immigrants who came to build more canals and railroads.[22]

The Oneidas hosted one of the first Methodist missions. Circuit riders preached at outdoor worship services, called camp meetings, about how a sinner could save him- or herself by repenting and following Jesus. The tall and dignified Thomas Cornelius, the grandson of Shagoyontha and Honyery's sister who impressed Mrs. Hammond with his "magnificent individuality," became a minister. As Methodists, the Oneidas were early backers of the temperance movement, a reform movement motivated by religious and social concern over excessive alcohol consumption, considered a serious problem in the rural United States. For the Oneidas, alcohol had served as a tool of dispossession as well as a balm for the "soul wound" of land loss, pressure to assimilate, and family breakups. They also were promised by the Methodist Conference, the organization that set church policy, that it would protect their houses of worship. The Home Party had lost a church at the Orchard on land sold by an emigrating party over their objection. A rebuilt Orchard Church and the mission house at the Windfall, Mrs. Hammond reported, were now in the care of the Methodist Conference and "are never more to be sold from them, for which the Indians are heartily glad."[23]

The Oneidas got on well with the newly established utopian religious society that took their name and called itself the Oneida Community. The followers of the radical preacher John Humphrey Noyes believed it was possible to create heaven on earth by living without selfishness. To practice what they called Bible Communism, members gave up their personal wealth and possessions to the group. Men and women shared leadership roles and rotated jobs. They engaged in what they termed complex marriage, where "each is married to all." They lived in a large building called the Mansion House and raised the children, who belonged to everyone, in the Children's House. Local people, who deplored the Community's views on marriage, respected it as an economic force.[24]

The Community saw their society as the inheritor of Oneida Indian communal life and land undefiled by private ownership. It thought their courteous Indigenous neighbors had not been treated well and employed Oneidas among the two hundred people who worked at its farms, mills, and factories dedicated to the manufacture of luggage, sewing silk, and steel traps. In honor of the Oneidas and their visiting kinfolk from Green Bay, the Community held a strawberry festival in the children's playground. "Many of them are fine looking persons," remarked a member about the Oneidas. "Their singing was really delightful."[25]

The new ideas about religion, culture, and politics did not impress Lewis Clement and John Moot. Lewis was active in the local Democratic Party, which advocated land policies that benefited ordinary white men. He distrusted big government and, as befitting a descendant of Joseph Clement and Marie du Trieux, opposed temperance. John expressed his partisanship by naming one of his sons Franklin Pierce Moot, after the Democratic president from New Hampshire who feared that the antislavery movement would tear apart the union. In their neighborhood, the only subscriber to the reform-minded Whig newspaper was James Ingalls, the husband of John Moot's aunt Nancy.[26]

In Madison County, the Whig Party, the successor to the defunct Federalist Party, held the southern townships. The northern half of the county, crossed by the canal and the railroad, was home to new parties called the Free Soil Party, the Liberty Party, the Prohibition Party, the Anti-rent Party, and the Native American or Know-Nothing Party. The Native American Party, the fastest-growing party in the country, had begun in the 1840s in New York City as a secret society whose members, if asked anything about it, were to say, "I know nothing." The party blamed the economic dislocation and social upheaval of the times on immigrants, especially Roman Catholics.

In Lenox, the supporters of the Native American Party included Christian Harp, who may have been born on Sarah Doxtator's lot and now lived next to her grandson William on West Road. Although he had resided among the Oneidas his entire life, Christian somehow saw himself as the rightful native of the place. When the Know-Nothings won the towns of Lenox, Vernon, Cazenovia, and Stockbridge in the 1855 elections, disgust was the response of the local newspaper, the *Oneida Sachem*, an advocate of Free Soil and temperance. The question before the people, the Know-Nothings said, is whether Americans would rule America. The question should be, declared the *Sachem*, Shall slave owners rule us?[27]

Radical politics in Madison County found a backer in Gerrit Smith, the largest landholder in the state. Educated at Hamilton College, Smith took over the land business when his father, Peter, retired. Gerrit said he had no moral right to his money and gave away millions. He believed working-class people deserved their rightful heritage as citizens, and that heritage was land. When elected to Congress in 1852, Smith supported a homestead bill advocated by Free Soilers. "The right to the soil is as natural, absolute and equal, as the right to the light and air," he declared. But when the bill was amended to limit the grant of government land to white persons, he opposed it.[28]

The Smiths recognized that they owed something to the original owners of their property. Peter, who had been instrumental in depriving the Oneidas of significant territory, said he felt "greatly indebted to them . . . for the enlargement of my worldly possessions." Echoing the old notion of spreading Christianity in return for taking land, he considered the possibility of promoting religious instruction among them. For his part, Gerrit welcomed the Oneidas, whenever they were passing through Peterboro, to stay the night rolled up in blankets in the back room of his mansion on Oneida Creek. Respectful of the old hospitality traditions, he invited the chiefs to dinner.[29]

Gerrit Smith funded the antislavery Liberty Party and ran as its presidential candidate in 1848, 1856, and 1860. Enslaved people should not be given Bibles, he believed, but pistols and compasses. Harriet Tubman, who had freed herself, escorted runaways to Peterboro, a station on the Underground Railroad, or on to Gerrit's colleague Frederick Douglass, the fiery abolitionist who lived in Rochester. Elizabeth Cady Stanton, Gerrit's cousin who had spent the summers of her girlhood in

Peterboro, dedicated her career to demanding equal rights for women as voters, property owners, income earners, and parents. Viewed as "deviant visionaries" by their contemporaries, Elizabeth Cady Stanton and Frederick Douglass only later would be honored as "prophetic leaders," observes the historian Michael Kammen.[30]

At this time, I realized, diverse groups of women living along Oneida Creek spoke as equals and dressed for action. Gerrit's daughter Elizabeth Smith Miller wore loose trousers under a knee-length skirt, as did Oneida Indian women and Oneida Community women. This fashion, promoted as healthy and liberating, was widely ridiculed. In 1845, the popular women's magazine *Godey's Lady's Book* referred to the skirt over leggings worn by Oneida Indian women as a "half-civilized costume." I remember learning while on a visit to the Mansion House that Community women kept traditional dresses to wear when they traveled, to avoid harassment. I wonder how the farmwomen of my family felt about these expressions of freedom made by their neighbors.[31]

When Gerrit Smith ran unsuccessfully for governor of New York in 1858, he spoke in Oneida before a large audience "of men and women and politicians of every stripe," reported the *Sachem*. The urbane Charles Deferrier, a Democrat, fielded questions for the controversial candidate. Smith declared he would use state troops, if necessary, to oppose the execution of the Fugitive Slave Act, which made the federal government responsible for returning escaped slaves to their owners and compelled state and local officials to cooperate in the capture of runaways. Smith believed women should be able to vote, hold office, and fight in war. He was in favor of prohibiting the sale of intoxicating liquors (with a gooseberry wine proviso) and making individual property up to the amount of $1,000 free of tax. This platform, opined the *Sachem*, was part commendable and part "very visionary and objectionable."[32]

During the Civil War, support for the Union was strong in Madison County. Many former Whigs, antislavery Democrats, Know-Nothings, and Free Soilers joined the newly organized Republican Party. Charles Deferrier remained a Democrat, while his sister Mary's husband, Nelson Cobb, and his nephew Angel Deferrier Loomis became Republicans. Mary donated a heavy blanket to a fundraiser for the Oneida Independent Company of Cavalry, a group of local volunteers who served as couriers and escorts at Antietam, Gettysburg, the Wilderness, and Appomattox. I wonder how Charles and Mary felt about the tirade against race mixing made by the antislavery campaign. Abolitionists, who condemned the separation of families sold on the auction block, routinely denounced miscegenation as the evil result of sexual violence and promiscuity. Charles and Mary were identified as white on the federal census, but was that how they saw themselves?[33]

Several Oneida Indian men served in the Union Army. Jacob Cornelius, possibly Thomas's son, was killed at the Second Battle of Bull Run in 1862. Dolly John Antone's son, Aaron Antone, went into the Sixteenth New York Heavy Artillery. Martin Powless served in the United States Colored Troops along with several Black, white, and mixed-race men from Madison County. Nick Honyost, who was seventeen the year the war ended, climbed the hill to enlist in Peterboro, but after three days decided the army had not fed him enough and walked back home. Abraham Elm went with some Oneidas to Vermont to enlist as substitutes because they heard they could get more money there.[34]

Many of the Lenox men who went to war were poor. William Moot, the son of John Moot, served in the 157th New York Infantry, while his better-off cousins hired substitutes. In September 1862, the 157th Infantry set up camp at Arlington Heights, Virginia, on the estate of Confederate general Robert E. Lee. They dismantled the general's fences to build campfires and ate his peaches even though they were not quite ripe. General Lee soundly defeated them at their first battle at Chancellorsville in May 1863. The 157th suffered ninety-eight killed, missing, and wounded, including Christian Harp's son Barney, a drummer.[35]

The worst war news to reach Madison County came two months later from Pennsylvania. At Gettysburg, the 157th New York took the field with over 400 men and suffered 307 casualties. "Many fell to breathe no more," reported Captain Charles Van Slyck. Early notices placed William Moot on the list of the missing. His family later learned that William had been wounded on the first day of the battle. Hospitalized until February 1865, he mustered out weeks after General Lee's surrender and, like many veterans, never fully recovered his health. Abraham Elm, for instance, was left behind when a cannon backfired and rolled over him. Rescued by Confederate soldiers, he returned to Oneida disabled in body and strong in spirit.[36]

Work with a Vengeance

Civil War veterans came home to a changed economy. New York State led the nation in the value of its farm produce, but its farmers couldn't compete with the cheap grain grown on the fresh soils of the prairie and shipped back east by canal and railroad. They responded by diversifying production for urban markets and adopting scientific methods of rotating crops and using fertilizer, as advocated by the new agricultural school at Cornell University in Ithaca. The US government had set aside federal land in each state for a public university that offered education in the liberal arts as well as training in agriculture and engineering for young people of the working class. This land-grant system allowed many Americans to benefit from the dispossession of Indigenous people, such as, in Cornell's case, the Cayugas of the Six Nations.[37]

To learn about typical Madison County farm life, I consulted the diaries kept by my great-great-grandfather William Clement of the town of Lenox, along with those of Edmund Adams of the town of Sullivan and James Holt of Morrisville, the county seat on Route 20 south of Stockbridge. The tenant farmer Abraham Brewer, who never learned to read or write, left few records, but according to the state agricultural schedule of 1860, he grew wheat, rye, Indian corn, and oats and raised seven milk cows, four horses, eight pigs, chickens, and forty-six sheep on one hundred acres that did not belong to him. During the war, sheep provided the wool in demand for military uniforms.[38]

After the war, many farmers shifted to the more labor-intensive dairy business. Gerrit Smith Miller, the grandson of the abolitionist, imported Holstein cows from Holland because of the breed's ability to produce large quantities of milk. It was impractical to ship fluid milk, so much of it went to cheese factories, including two along Cowaselon Creek. The cheese factory, like the mill before it, served as a store and meeting place where farmers caught up on the news and their boys wrestled to see who was strongest. Dorothy Clement, a talented weaver like her great-grandmother Margaret Timmerman, still made wool blankets soft as flannel, but many farmwomen put their looms in the attic and bought factory-made cloth. Freed up from spinning and weaving, they milked cows, churned butter, and made cheese.[39]

Lewis and Dorothy Clement had replaced their log cabin with a substantial frame house and acquired good horses, nice glassware, and fine clothes. They helped their sons William and Lewis H. get a start on parcels of land ceded by the Oneidas in the 1840s. William had married Lizzie (Elizabeth) Moot, the daughter of John Moot and Lucy Bortle, and had four daughters. As was common in farm and middle-class households, a teenaged female servant lived with them. Often the daughters of less well-off neighbors, they assisted with housework and childcare. Many farm families also had male hired hands living with them, but William and Lizzie did not. In 1872, William and Lizzie Clement acquired their own farm by buying fifty acres on Lot 12 of the Cowaselon Tract overlooking the Stockbridge Valley. William spent much of the winter chopping trees to clear the land.[40]

If it was sixteen degrees below zero and a farmer said it was too cold to work, he meant he would do only the chores. No matter what, the animals had to be fed, the cows milked, the stables cleaned, and the firewood carried into the house. William cut wood to sell "down to Oneida" and delivered logs to Lizzie's brother William Moot. Winter was a time to do the butchering and cut and haul ice. A trip to town might require "breaking the road." When a Clement grandchild died during a heavy snow, a neighbor hitched his team to a cauldron kettle and dragged it up and down the hill so the mourners could take the casket for burial. Diversions included sleigh rides and performances of *Uncle Tom's Cabin*, based on Harriet Beecher Stowe's famous antislavery novel.[41]

In March or April, after the sugar maples were tapped, Lizzie and her daughters collected and boiled the sap. Farmers and Oneida men cut hop poles and sharpened them. Nick Honyost, known as the "strongest man from Oneida Castle to Cobleskill," could set the long hop poles into the ground with one hand. Hops, a tender crop, were shipped by canal to breweries to be made into beer. By 1859, New York State produced seven-eighths of the hops in the nation, with Otsego, Madison, Oneida, and Schoharie Counties leading the way. Later in the spring, farmers drove the cattle to pasture and commenced plowing and sowing. William sheared sheep, split rails, and plowed his father's garden.[42]

After the Fourth of July celebration, farmers mowed hay with scythe and machine, cocked it, tossed it into wagons, hauled loads of it back to the barn, and pitched it into the mow. After the haying came the wheat harvest and then the oats. "Work with a vengeance," wrote Holt. "So awful tired." Farmwives canned fruits and vegetables. Oneida Indian women collected the root of sweet flag and cooked it in a syrup to make a breath-freshening candy that smelled like clove. Twenty to thirty thousand people attended the annual picnic hosted by the Local Hop Growers Association at Fish Creek on Oneida Lake (present-day Sylvan Beach). The last Saturday in July might as well be a legal holiday in central New York, observed the *Canastota Bee*, since no one went to work anyway.[43]

Baseball had become popular by 1874, when Oneida hosted a gala tournament. In local competition, the Oneida Castle Uniques beat the Wampsville Farmers 23–7. At a lacrosse match held between ball games, spectators watched the "wild and rapid movements" of the contestants dressed in tribal costume as the Oneida Indians lost to the Onondagas 5–7.

The paper reported that the Indian baseball club defeated "the colored men's club" 25–14. Racial segregation at the tournament was not surprising given that the hometown team was called the Ku Klux Klan, the name of the secretive white-supremacist terrorist organization founded in the South at the end of the Civil War. The Ku Kluxers of Oneida took third place behind the Flyaways of New York City and the Nassaus of Brooklyn.[44]

The hop harvest began in late August. Hop pickers, mostly young people, came by train to Oneida or Canastota, where the hop wagons would pick them up at the station and bring them to lodgings provided by growers. Eight to ten pickers bedded down at the Clements' house. When the Onondagas came for hop picking, they stayed with Sophia Denny. At night, the pickers held dances and listened to ghost stories. Worship services at the Indian Mission Church on West Road were packed with Oneidas and white people. Some sang hymns in Oneida, and some sang in English, men on one side of the aisle and women on the other.[45]

In a good year like 1882, the sale of a thousand pounds of hops for $5,000 put a town of Lenox farmer "on easy street." One season, Lizzie's brother John J. Moot was fined $150 for maliciously cutting down fifteen hills of hops belonging to Lucius Ingalls, the husband of William's sister. As soon as the hops were picked, dried, and pressed, the corn had to be harvested and husked. When the threshers came to harvest grains in October, farmwives took pride in pulling off the marathon of cooking and baking required to feed the hungry crew. With cash to spend, William and Lizzie acquired a parlor stove and a wash machine. A local shopkeeper advertised that he had switched from a system of long credit to ready pay and awaited the immediate settlement of all accounts. "He has our prayers," dryly commented the *Oneida Democratic Union*.[46]

October was fair time. "Some beautiful beadwork by Miss Hannah Webster; canes by D. Skenandoah; and axe handles by Thomas Cornelius comprised the donations of our aboriginal friends," reported the *Sachem*, which soon would be renamed the *Dispatch*. Nelson Cobb, an organizer of the Town of Lenox Fair, won for best plowing, and Mrs. Daniel Skenandoah won for best white quilted bedspread in 1861. Cornelius Doxtator, the son of Peter and Lucretia Doxtator, won for best pair of matched three-year-old colts, and Samuel Breese, the son of Sidney and Helen Breese, won for best summer squash in 1867. These awards must be considered hard won, because everyone was up against the Oneida Community, which dominated the prizes year after year—best

Ayrshire Bull, best steel traps, best cherry wine. When it came to canned and bottled fruits, the judges gave up. "No use of talking," they said. "Oneida Community can't be beat."[47]

After the fair came political meetings, torchlight parades, and Election Day. Nelson Cobb held local offices for the Republican Party. His son Charles Cobb and his nephew Angel Deferrier Loomis organized a young men's club to help reelect President Ulysses S. Grant in 1872. Abraham Elm, a descendant of Good Peter, made history when he and Louis Doxtator were arrested for voting in the congressional election held in Lenox in 1876. By voting, Elm, the Civil War veteran, and Doxtator, a twenty-one-year-old railroad worker, were making some point about their rights and status, but I don't know what that was. The authorities said that the two Indians were not citizens and therefore not eligible to vote. It was understood that the trial concerned a test case

FIGURE 27. Louis Doxtator (1855–94). Karst Collection

of importance. The judge ruled that only one man should be tried, and that no punishment would follow if the court found that the Oneida men were not entitled to vote.[48]

At Abraham Elm's trial, the federal judge stated that Indian nations with distinct political communities were sovereign. As such, they were not in the jurisdiction of the United States within the meaning of the Fourteenth Amendment, which said that persons born in the United States were citizens. He determined, however, that the twenty Oneida families who resided near their original reservation were mixed in with the rest of the population in terms of religion, customs, language, and everything "but the color of their skins." In *United States v. Elm*, the judge ruled that the Oneidas of New York had not maintained their tribal integrity and therefore were citizens with the right to vote. The court decided that Abraham Elm was no longer Oneida, while Abraham was sure that he was.[49]

The temperance movement, which had died down during the Civil War, revived. The open-minded James Holt attended the hop growers' convention in late November and a "maskerade festival" held by the temperance folks in February. At the convention of the National Christian Temperance Union of Madison County in 1878, Stockbridge reported not a single backslider. The Oneida Indians organized the Skenandoah Lodge dedicated to temperance, but Nick Honyost and Dr. Sundown, who was known to advise taking his remedies with whiskey, did not join.[50]

For William Clement, farming came with misfortunes. The neighbor's cattle got into his oats and destroyed them, his cow died, and his equipment broke down. William also suffered from illness, referred to as headaches and "fits" (probably some sort of seizure), but he had little time to rest. With shaky handwriting or in diary entries made by his daughter Ellen, he recorded that he made a fence, sowed oats, hoed potatoes, cultivated corn, harvested hops, and threshed grain. Relatives and neighbors occasionally helped out, and the Clement sisters did chores in addition to housework. After two years of running his own place, William died at age forty-six of sunstroke, according to the family Bible.[51]

A few years later, his mother, Dorothy, a believer in omens and dreams, was sewing by an open door when a bird flew in over her head and out another door. "That means bad news," she said. Someone came to tell her that her husband, Lewis, had been fatally stricken while on business in Oneida. It was important to both Lewis Clement and John Moot that their farms pass to their male heirs. It was considered

Figure 28. The Clement sisters. Top row, left to right: Jennie (1866–1926), Lucy (1861–95). Bottom row, left to right: Eva (1854–96), Ellen (1857–1920). Brewer Collection.

right and proper that Lewis's farm would go to his only Clement grandson, so that it would stay in the family name. I remember hearing this sentiment expressed when I was a child. I wonder whether William's daughters, who were left five dollars each in their grandfather's will, ever questioned it.[52]

Lewis's granddaughter Jennie, my great-grandmother, was eight, and her sister Lucy thirteen, when their widowed mother made a go of running the farm. Lizzie hired their neighbor Charles Snyder in 1880. Here is their contract as written:

> For one year. Agreement between Elizabeth Clement and Charles Snyder to work her farm on shares [he] is to have half of the grain he raises he is to do all the work draw the stone off build the fence she boards him does his washing for one year for ten dollars he is to furnish half the seed grain of all kinds they both furnish feed for the horses he is to pay for horseshoeing he is to cut all the fire wood fodder is to be fed on the place the grain is sold and money divided ecept wat is wanted for the horses throw the winter the hay is to bee left on the place he is to do the work in workman

> like maner and in good season. She pays the taxes he is to work the road tax the horses must not be drove of the place without she says they should.

While Lizzie managed the farm, Jennie went to school. For good scholarship at age fifteen, she received from her teacher an autograph album, which her friends filled with compliments, including this tribute: "May your virtues ever spread like butter on hot gingerbread."[53]

Lucy and Jennie Clement knew grief and hardship, but they were better off than their friends the Brewers. Abraham Brewer relied on his eldest daughter, Mary Adelia, called Deal, to keep house after his wife died. His son Frankie, my great-grandfather, was around twelve, Mary ten, Jennie eight, and Willie four. Deal's husband, a canal boatman and farm laborer, came to live with the Brewers. Young Frankie was listed among the weavers who worked at the Cady Woolen Mills. The owner, George Beecher Cady, had bought the old Lenox Iron Company property with his inheritance from his grandfather Sylvester Beecher. Most area textile mills relied on female and child labor.[54]

Frank Brewer, at age eighteen, and his sister Mary were farm laborers. Unlike many tenant farmers in the neighborhood, Abraham did not move from place to place. He remained on what is still known as Brewer Road, where it took him years to turn their log cabin into a frame house. When he was about sixty, Abraham became a property owner of one acre. For ten dollars he bought the site of his house from the farmer Luther Ingalls. Abraham's daughter Jennie went to work for the Oneida Community. A job there was a step up from being a farm laborer like her sister.[55]

The Oneida Community had become a capitalist enterprise thanks to internal problems and public pressure. Some members objected to the eugenics experiments begun in an attempt to breed a spiritually superior human. John Humphrey Noyes, accused of becoming authoritarian, left. The members created a joint stock company for the manufacture of flatware and traps, entered into conventional marriages, and settled around the Mansion House. The end of the Community's "peculiar social practices" was greeted with relief. "These Communists have long enjoyed the reputation of being good neighbors and citizens, and thoroughly trustworthy in all business transactions," wrote the local historian James H. Smith, "and now that the single avowed cause of offense is removed, their growth and prosperity will be welcomed by all classes."[56]

The Land Belongs to the Women

The Oneida Indians were under pressure to give up their communal ways and female leadership. "The men in the old days had nothing at all to do with deciding things," recalled Melinda Skenandoah John. "The land and the children were not theirs but the women's." The clan mothers continued to select the chiefs. Asked in the 1880s what a chief had to do, William Doxtator said, "Well, nothing now much." He had to be present when the government agent delivered the cloth in accordance with the 1794 Treaty of Canandaigua.[57]

William, a day laborer and Methodist Sunday school superintendent, was "powerfully built and had an extremely pleasant face," recalled a local white woman. He was beloved by children, "who were not afraid of him as they sometimes were of other Indians." When William married Mary Chrisjohn, he moved into her home. He, Mary, and their daughters made baskets, bows and arrows, and purses and pincushions decorated with sparkling glass beads to sell at resorts like Saratoga Springs and Sylvan Beach.[58]

Chiefs William Doxtator and Daniel Skenandoah walked in the parade at the 1887 centennial celebration of the village of Clinton, the home of Hamilton College. The newspaper identified them as the descendants of the Indians who had given the site of the village to its founders. This story of the Oneidas giving away their land, I noted, was a common one. A decade earlier, the Oneidas had marched at the centennial commemoration of the battle of Oriskany. On the stage sat Daniel Skenandoah and Honyery's grandson, John "Dr. Sundown" Denny, who listened to orations recalling the bravery of the Tryon County militia. One speaker briefly mentioned that a band of Oneidas had taken part in the fight.[59]

While Oneidas participated in commemorations that did not celebrate the past as they remembered it, one scholar of the era actually asked the Oneidas about their history. Lyman C. Draper of the Wisconsin Historical Society collected invaluable interviews of Oneida men and women, but he was not successful in his effort to learn more about Dr. Sundown. He questioned B. F. Burleson, postmaster of Oneida Castle, who had seen John Denny on the stage at the Oriskany Centennial.

There was nothing important to learn from "this Indian," the postmaster informed Draper. "He is an old Indian aged I presume about 80 years. I should say judging by his looks that he was not yet seventy, however," Burleson said of Dr. Sundown, who was then eighty-six years old. "He is extremely poor and manages somehow to get a scanty living by gathering roots and herbs and doctoring those who believe him to be wise and are willing to trust to his untaught skill." Burleson added, "I don't think that any of the Oneidas living here would give you any early historical information aside from the old doctor and I doubt if he could." Dr. Sundown, he wrote, "delights in extorting facts and making them appear more than they really are." I wonder how much Burleson knew about John Denny, who had been born in Oriske and raised in Canaseraga, held property on the turnpike near his aunt Polly, lived among the Senecas, and tried making a home in Kansas.[60]

Along with Daniel Skenandoah and Thomas Cornelius, John Denny sent requests to Congress for compensation for Oneida land lost in Kansas. In addition, the Oneidas repeatedly petitioned New York State for title to homeland they had never ceded and for compensation they never received. They complained that the fish and game reserved to them by treaty had been destroyed. Only a few times did legislators recommend a favorable response. The Oneida claim was just, said an 1829 committee, as it pointed out that the state had paid "a mere trifle" for land that had made it rich. In 1865, legislators acknowledged the service of Oneidas in the Union Army and declared that the state should aid these loyal Indians so they "may spend their last days in happiness and comfort."[61]

State officials usually recommended the rejection of Oneida claims. Four decades after the orator Martinus White had demanded, "Show me the treaty," the lieutenant governor and others admitted that no treaty ceding Oneida land north of Oneida Lake had been found. The treaty must be lost, they stated in 1866, because they could not believe that Surveyor General Simeon DeWitt would have said there was such a treaty if it were not true. As for hunting and fishing rights, these had never been denied but rather were overborne by settlement. "If the Indians with whom the treaty was made had represented an educated and civilized people," concluded state officials, they would have understood that their ceded territory would be transformed by white inhabitants who would have exclusive control as property owners.[62]

The Oneidas did not give up. They sent more petitions, and the assembly created more commissions. "But the answer of the four commissioners is all wrong," said Daniel Skenandoah in response. A commission created in 1878 rejected the notion that the Oneidas must have ceded land north of Oneida Lake in some lost treaty. Improbable, concluded the commissioners. "The white man . . . is the custodian of the history and of all the treaties." If no treaty existed, there was no cession of this land. The commission noted that the persistent Oneidas justified their claims by treaty and "the testimony and memory of their oldest chiefs." It concluded, "The State cannot and should not . . . resist these claims." The state resisted.[63]

In 1888, the New York State Assembly launched an investigation of what it called the "Indian problem." It charged a special committee with examining the condition of Indigenous people, assessing the allotment of tribal land, and analyzing treaties made between the state and the Indians, and the United States and the Indians. The goal of the committee's chairman. J. S. Whipple, was to assert the sovereignty of New York State, not the federal government or Natives, over Indian Affairs. The Whipple Committee held hearings across the state. In Oneida, it interviewed several white men about the Oneida Indians but interviewed only one Oneida Indian.[64]

The committee asked William Doxtator which Indian owned the most land. William answered that Daniel Skenandoah had forty-two acres, but that it really belonged to his wife and children because Daniel had sold his land to go to Green Bay and then didn't go. "All the men them days sold out," explained William. The land, he said, "belongs to the women." He named several Oneida women who owned land. "All the women own that tract of land," he repeated. The men sold out to go to Green Bay and came back. The committee was perplexed. "They sold out and left the women with the land?" asked a member. "Yes, sir," William replied, as he joined the long line of Oneida men stretching back to Kanagweas and Good Peter who tried to explain to white men about Oneida women and the land.[65]

The Whipple Committee found that the New York Oneidas were an industrious people who produced abundant crops on their four hundred acres of fertile soil. It was unable to distinguish farms owned by these well-to-do Indians from farms owned by whites. The committee credited white farmers with setting a good example. Although it knew that the Oneidas already were successful farmers, the committee recommended severalty to encourage thrift, industriousness, and self-respect. It ignored William Doxtator's concern that when the land was divided up, it was sold. It quoted William A. Duncan, a Sunday school administrator from Syracuse, who said, "The Indian will never be civilized until he ceases to be a communist."[66]

The "Indian problem," concluded the Whipple Report, will be solved when "the Indians of the State are absorbed into the great mass of the American people." It was time to "exterminate the tribe and preserve the individual." This position was in line with federal Indian policy. Natives "have got as far as they can go, because they own their land in common," said Senator Henry Dawes of Massachusetts, sponsor of the Severalty Act of 1887. "There is no selfishness, which is at the bottom of civilization." Dawes spoke of a civilization that depended on the short-term exploitation of land and its resources for profit, rather than one based on stewardship for the generations to come.[67]

Assimilation was too moderate a policy for some. "Our only safety depends on the total extermination of the Indians," wrote the South Dakota newspaper editor L. Frank Baum in 1890 in response to the massacre of 150 Lakota people by the US Army at Wounded Knee. Baum, who had been born in Chittenango, was a decade away from publishing his beloved *The Wonderful Wizard of Oz*. As Americans weighed policies of extermination versus assimilation of Indians, they agreed on the goal of access to Native land.[68]

To push assimilation, the Whipple Report stated that New York Indians "should now be educated to be men, not Indians." Asked what Oneida children excelled at, N. L. Tilden, the white superintendent of Indian schools, answered, "Geography" and "Something they can commit to memory." He contradicted William Doxtator's complaint that the

FIGURE 29. Oneida children attend public school at Five Chimneys, 1898. Lyman John (1889–1972), son of Louisa Day and Martin John, far left, and Elizabeth "Lizzie" Skenandoah (1888–1941), daughter of Mary Denny and Thomas Skenandoah, and great-great-niece of Polly Denny Deferrier, fourth from left. Karst Collection.

dilapidated school was unfit to use, but he still recommended that the Indian schools be closed. The Whipple Committee agreed. Some of the Oneida children went to local public schools. where they learned that Christopher Columbus discovered America.[69]

Other Oneida children went away to boarding schools. Reformers argued that young Indians, if taken from their tribes, could be taught to be good citizens, value private property, and be dutiful workers. This policy removed the children of the Home Party from their land and families. William Doxtator's granddaughters did not like the Thomas Indian School at the Cattaraugus Reservation of the Seneca Nation. They were fed bad food, not allowed to speak Oneida, and punished often. At age sixteen, Stella Doxtator was placed with a family to do housekeeping. Laura Cornelius, a Wisconsin Oneida of Stella's generation, later denounced the boarding schools for training a girl who might have become a teacher or a business manager to instead be "the servant of the race which has oppressed her people."[70]

At boarding school, the Doxtator sisters were taught to prefer "white people's ways," while back home they listened to Haudenosaunee stories told by their grandmother Dolly John Antone. From their aunts,

FIGURE 30. The Doxtator sisters, in a photograph probably taken while they were at boarding school. Top row, left to right: Stella (1884–1949), Anna (1885–1966). Middle row, left to right: Emily (1888–1984), Lucy (1893–1986), Electa (1889–1937). Bottom row: Ellen (1895–1918). Karst Collection.

they learned about traditional beliefs in dreams and witches. At New Year's, Oneida children and their mothers still called on their Native and non-Native neighbors and were invited in to feast on fried cakes, which is what my grandmother called doughnuts. There were fewer Oneidas around to celebrate the old custom. As William Doxtator feared, Oneidas lost their land through sales and foreclosures. By 1893, they were down to one hundred acres. Many of those who stayed now lived as tenants on their ancestral lands. At a farm on West Road that no longer belonged to Oneidas, William's grandson helped a young cousin of Jennie Clement learn to ride her first bicycle. Dr. Sundown spent his final years at the Honyost place, believed to be the last of the original Oneida territory.[71]

Of Dr. Sundown's Deferrier cousins, only Mary Cobb and her children remained on the best land. Most of Polly and Angel's grandchildren had moved elsewhere in New York or out west. A few lived in Oneida. Angel Deferrier Loomis left farming to become a city sewer contractor. His cousin Dewitt C. Hadcock, a founder of the Madison County Historical Society, left a colorful mark on local history with sketches like the one titled "More or Less True." One of his less true stories was about how his grandfather had invited Lafayette, while on his Erie Canal tour, to stop by the Deferrier residence for roast pig and champagne. The two men "belonged to the same line of royalty in France," wrote Hadcock, who sometimes elevated Angel to the rank of marquis.[72]

Dewitt Hadcock may have borrowed some of Angel's biography from a new version of the Lost Dauphin story. A novel by Mary Hartwell Catherwood published in 1901 called *Lazarre* told the tale of a white-skinned Indian boy who was the real king of France. The boy thrived in the "primeval and vigor-giving" life of the aborigines under the guidance of the exiled Marquis de Ferrier and the educated Oneida Skenedonk. In contrast to Catherwood's stilted romance, Mark Twain's classic *The Adventures of Huckleberry Finn* turned the Lost Dauphin into the con man Looey the Seventeen. "Yes, gentlemen, you see before you, in blue jeans and misery, the wanderin', exiled, trampled-on, and sufferin' rightful King of France," Looey tells a skeptical Huck and Jim.[73]

While Angel's memory was glamorized, Polly's identity was erased. Mrs. Hammond tried to "de-Indianize" her. From her history of Madison County, Lyman C. Draper learned that Angel Deferrier "married a Miss Dennie, possessing a tinge of Indian blood." Mrs. Hammond implicated the Dennys in dismissing their Native heritage. Her only anecdote about Martinus Denny quoted the interpreter as saying, "Me no Indian, Me

French and squaw." Local newspapers often ignored Polly. She even went unmentioned in the obituary of her daughter Sophia Loomis in 1864. Sophia, it said, "was the daughter of Col. DeFerrier, an excellent and elegant French gentleman who was . . . one of the most prominent citizens in this section of country."[74]

An article about Charles Deferrier from an unidentified newspaper also said nothing about his mother. It recounted the story of his father, Chevalier De Ferrier, who fled the Reign of Terror, settled among the Oneidas, and acquired three thousand acres in Wampsville. Charles lived in the family homestead, where hung "paintings by Murillo, the celebrated Spaniard, and others of equal interest by famous Europeans," said the article. It noted that Mr. Deferrier, "a gentleman of means and education," had made extended visits to Paris and London. Charles, who died in 1890, instructed that he was to be buried in the family cemetery on the north side of the grave of his dear mother. In his will, he left his house, his paintings, and his sixty-six acres to his nephew Charles Cobb.[75]

Charles Cobb needed a tenant to farm the best land that he and his sisters inherited from their parents in the 1890s. Frank Brewer took on

FIGURE 31. DeVerne (1899–1978), Harry (1897–1974), and Hazel Brewer (1900–1996). Brewer Collection.

the job. He had married William and Lizzie Clement's daughter Lucy. For a time, Frank and Lucy and their two children lived near Abraham on Brewer Road. When Lucy gave birth to a boy in 1895, both mother and baby died. Lucy's younger sister Jennie came to take care of the bereaved family. As was not uncommon in those days, Frank and Jennie married. In 1899, my grandfather DeVerne Franklin Brewer was born in the tenant house of the Cobbs on Cowaselon Creek.

Frank purchased the farm from Angel and Polly's grandchildren in 1904. The crash of the hops market in the late 1880s had been followed by a nationwide depression. For farmers across the United States, hard times in an era transformed by industrialization and urbanization caused feelings of being discounted, as though they were "strangers in their own country," notes the historian David B. Danbom. For Frank, it meant that a property formerly priced at $5,500 was now within his reach. He offered $1,500 for it and agreed to pay a mortgage of $2,200 taken out by Nelson and Mary Cobb. The farm, described as part of the Oneida Purchase of 1815, maintained the original east and west lines of Lot 4 and was bounded on the north by the Erie Canal and on the south by the New York Central Railroad. Frank's father, Abraham, who passed away in 1903, did not live to see Frank and Jennie, descendants of squatters and tenants, become the owners of the best land.[76]

CHAPTER 8

Realms of Orchards

Frank and Jennie Brewer named their farm the Orchard Place Dairy. They planted apple, plum, cherry, peach, and pear trees. Frank harvested hay, oats, barley, and wheat, sold milk to the creamery, and delivered peas, corn, and pumpkins to canning companies in Lenox Furnace and Oneida. Within a few years, Frank and Jennie moved the old tenant house to the east side of Cowaselon Creek and built a new farmhouse with a large dining room, a pantry, and a porch off the parlor. With help from Jennie's mother, Lizzie Clement, they raised six children.[1]

For a long time, I could find out very little about Frank and Jennie's life. Then my cousins contacted me to say that while cleaning out their mother's house they found Frank's old diaries. The diaries, beginning in 1901, contain a poorly spelled but detailed record of his move from being the tenant farmer of Charles Cobb, the grandson of Polly and Angel Deferrier, to property owner. In 1904, Frank recorded that Charles's sister, Irene Cobb, had killed herself. Although the timing may be a coincidence, it is striking that she ended her life days after Frank filed his deed to the best land. The original property of the Deferriers had dwindled to a few dozen acres.[2]

The diaries show that Frank viewed Jennie as an essential partner. Jennie washed, ironed, cleaned, and sewed clothes for the family.

On Saturdays, she baked loaves of bread, pies, and cookies. In the summer and fall, Jennie canned tomatoes, corn, cherries, and peaches. When Frank butchered the hog, she made sausage. She raised chickens and sold dozens of eggs. Sometimes Jennie did the chores, delivered the milk, picked up the seed corn, paid off loans at the bank, or went to town for supplies.

The location of the Orchard Place Dairy was an asset. Frank earned income by selling over a thousand tons of gravel from his property to the superintendent of the Erie Canal. This stretch of the canal, now in its eighth decade, was about to be made obsolete by the completion of the bigger Barge Canal that connected Rome to Oneida Lake. Meanwhile, the railroad lines expanded. The New York Central carried salesmen from Chicago and honeymooners to Niagara Falls. The West Shore line specialized in freight. The local third rail line, which Frank hired on to help build, ran trolleys that stopped near his house.[3]

Wampsville successfully campaigned to become the county seat in the early 1900s. Morrisville was too isolated, people complained, and the jail had been condemned. Wampsville offered itself as a compromise candidate between the contenders Oneida and Canastota. It was not a cow pasture, as some claimed. With seventy trains a day passing through, a person could arrive at or depart from Wampsville every fifteen minutes from six o'clock in the morning to midnight. Frank delivered ice to the new courthouse, which was designed as a "temple of justice" and faced the tracks.[4]

Madison County celebrated its centennial in 1906 with a pageant held in Oneida. Now officially a city, Oneida had a new high school, where the town kids called the country kids sodbusters, and a bustling downtown, which was decked in red, white, and blue bunting for the festivities. The attorney Edwin J. Brown, president of the Madison County Historical Society, made welcoming remarks. For the parade, the Cazenovia delegation brought a float carrying a log cabin from the Lincklaen era, guarded by men dressed as pioneers and armed with muskets. Another float featured an Indian cabin, reported the *Syracuse Post-Standard*, "accompanied by a number of real Indians in the paint and feathers of the aborigines."[5]

On view at the Cherry Street School were the former possessions of Angel Deferrier. According to the newspapers, Deferrier had fled France, settled in Wampsville, and married a woman described either as an Indian princess or as "a full-blooded squaw." Visitors saw his shoe buckles inlaid with gold and brilliants that belonged to Charles Cobb and his double-barreled shotgun, broadsword, silver spoons, and French china owned by the granddaughter of the prominent early settler Stephen Chapman. Also on display were the spectacles worn by old chief Skenandoah, the key to his cabin door, and one of his kettles. By this time, many of Angel and Skenandoah's belongings had passed out of the hands of their descendants and into the homes of the local gentry and relic collectors.[6]

Indigenous artifacts belonged in museums, believed the authorities. The New York State legislature passed the Wampum Law, which first allowed the State University of New York and later the legislature itself to be named Wampum keeper, with the responsibility to protect and study such curiosities. An anthropologist paid $5.84 to Daniel Webster, the oldest Oneida at the Windfall, for an ancient string of wampum that had belonged to Chief Christian Beechtree. The string went to New York City to the American Museum of Natural History, known for its dioramas of Indigenous people behind glass.[7]

The centennial speaker was William D. Hoard, the publisher and former governor of Wisconsin known as the "father of modern dairying." He spoke of the great improvements to the beautiful Stockbridge Valley, where he had been born in 1836. "It was settled originally by the choicest blood of New England," he recounted. "Out of their poverty they laid the foundations of railroads and canals and of great business enterprises." These people of genius, declared Hoard, "followed in the footpaths of the Six Nation Indians, the bravest, most enterprising and sagacious in government and war of all the tribes that have peopled this mighty Continent."[8]

Hoard recalled growing up with the Skenandoahs, the Websters, and the Johnsons. He recounted the "splendid lesson" taught to him by Thomas Cornelius at a camp meeting. "You see all these trees—birch, maple, basswood, elm, ash, hemlock. . . . Every tree different. God like it so; trees like it, too. Every tree mind his own business," Cornelius had said. "All grow on same ground; All point up. Why not men so good as trees?" I don't know if Cornelius spoke English this way or if Hoard was employing what passed for "Indian talk" in plays and literature. Hoard told this story in the tradition of honoring the wisdom of dead Indians.[9]

The centennial program also included a "charming talk" by an Oneida Indian who was decidedly alive. The audience at the First Baptist Church gave an ovation to Miss Laura Cornelius of Wisconsin, who delivered "a message from the Oneidas." The newspapers did not report on what that message was. Instead they focused on the glamorous young woman who delivered it. This "Indian maiden" had attended Stanford University and was the granddaughter of the chiefs who were the creators of the new Oneidas, said the *Oneida Union*. Her witty address attracted more attention than the talk delivered by William M. Beauchamp, noted authority on the Iroquois.[10]

The Oneidas of the Windfall and Marble Hill did not speak at the centennial celebration, although the family of Abraham Elm's son, Simeon Elm, and Sylvia Honyost had been the "real Indians" in the parade.

FIGURE 32. Sylvia Honyost Elm and Simeon Elm with their children, Ray, Andrew, Alda, and Winifred, at the Madison County centennial parade, 1906. 2005.P021/2008.P021. From the Collection of the Madison County Historical Society.

Their children helped to raise money for the Madison County Historical Society with benefit performances of "The Song of Hiawatha," the epic poem by Henry Wadsworth Longfellow that blended Iroquois and Ojibwe tradition. The performances in Oneida and Cazenovia were a success, reported the *Evening Courant* of Canastota, which noted that the cast members were the grandchildren of Nick Honyost, who recently had been acquitted of a charge of murder. It was ruled that he had killed a man with an axe in self-defense.[11]

Routinely referred to as "the remnant," the Oneidas lived east and west of the Oneida Community neighborhood on Oneida Creek. "The squaws no longer sew pretty beads on bright-colored clothes, nor do they make baskets," reported the *Oneida Dispatch* in 1909. "All the picturesque features of their lives have disappeared." Many of the Oneidas—including the farm laborer John Denny, the son of Dr. Sundown, and the domestic servant Lydia Doxtator, the daughter of William Doxtator—worked out for wages A few of them farmed small parcels. "They are not yet first-rate farmers, but are improving," said the *Dispatch*. "They were too poor to buy the best land, and are not scientific enough to make the most of what they have."[12]

This writer may have been unaware that twenty years earlier, the Oneidas had farms superior to those of their white neighbors, which they since had lost to sale and foreclosure. The *Dispatch* also printed a speech given at the historical society, which accused white people of acquiring Native land through "legalized larceny" and observed that if the Six Nations had been paid anything close to what their land was worth, they would be "among the richest on the face of the earth." Solomon John, the proprietor of a downtown cane chair repair business, always maintained that as an Oneida Indian he was entitled to land on Oneida Lake. Known as King Solomon, he was considered a local character.[13]

The last of Oneida territory at the Windfall was in trouble. The thirty-two acres was the home of the Honyost family, headed by Mary Honyost Skenandoah, or Gargeajunttar (Plucking Flower). Mary held the farm through her mother, grandmother, and great-grandmother, who was the War of 1812 veteran Polly Cooper. The Honyost place was considered the "sentimental capital" of all Oneidas. It was land held communally under their own government, where the Oneidas gathered for ceremonies.[14]

The Honyost property was about to be lost, thanks to a disputed mortgage and confusion over female ownership. Mary's brother Isaac

Honyost had taken out a $1,250 mortgage on the place in 1887 from the local landowner Philander Spaulding, who had acquired Oneida properties at the Windfall through foreclosure. Mary, who did not speak English, said her mother had not signed any deeds that would make it possible for the land to be put up for security for such a mortgage. Members of the family did not agree on all the details, but they were sure that the Honyosts never saw anything like $1,250. The Honyost debt was transferred to a local woman, Julia Boylan, who filed an action to foreclose on the property with the intent of recovering the $1,250 plus $400 in interest owed. The legal battle that followed was known as the Boylan case.[15]

Mary's son Chapman Skenandoah tried to help save the land. An inventor and mechanic, he worked in Schenectady for Thomas Edison's Illuminating Company, later known as General Electric. In 1897, he enlisted in the navy to see the world and send home wages to make payments on the mortgage. When he learned of the threatened foreclosure, he asked for leave and was refused. He deserted in Buenos Aires, traveled back to the Windfall, and then turned himself in at Washington, DC. The press coverage of Chapman's court martial mentioned his poor mother and his ancestor "Skenando," the great chief who aided the Americans during the Revolution. That and his "distinguished service in the Spanish-American War" led the navy to restore him to active duty.[16]

Chapman assured Julia Boylan that his uncle Isaac would make payments on the mortgage when he and the rest of the family received their Kansas claims. Following years of petitioning, the Six Nations had won compensation for the broken 1838 Treaty of Buffalo Creek. The US Supreme Court ruled that the US government must award the New York Indians $1,967,056 for the land promised in Kansas. The Oneidas did not receive as much compensation from the Kansas claims as they expected. Edwin J. Brown, who had been appointed to distribute the payments while preparing for the county centennial celebration, subtracted a hefty fee for his services. Mary Honyost Skenandoah, for example, received $122 out of the $200 she was entitled to.[17]

After the Oneidas lost, won, and lost the Boylan case, a Madison County deputy sheriff in 1909 led a posse to evict the Honyost family. When the Honyosts refused to go, a deputy carried Mary out of her house and set her down on West Road. The seventy-one-year-old woman got up and walked back to her house. The deputies carried her out again and she returned. Mary and her brother William were removed over and

Oneidas and Onondagas Called in Land Suit

Front row, left to right—William Honyost, William Rockwell, Mrs. Mary Shenandoah, Albert Shenandoah. Back row—Webster Thomas, Alex Verning, Nicholas Honyost, Chapman Shenandoah.
This photograph was taken yesterday at the Court House.

FIGURE 33. Mary Honyost Skenandoah and her family and friends (including her son, Chapman Skenandoah, and her nephew William Rockwell) outside the courthouse where they testified before a federal judge. "Indians Plead for their Land," *Syracuse Post-Standard*, 28 July 1916. From the Collection of the Onondaga Historical Association, Syracuse, NY.

over until the two of them were too exhausted to walk back to the house. The officers put Mary's possessions on the street and padlocked her front door. The cast of "Hiawatha" had lost their family home.[18]

The Oneidas turned to the US government for help. To everyone's surprise, they received it. Local people were baffled by such a development, while the Oneidas, who knew their nation was entitled to federal protection, had not received any for over a century. In *United States v. Julia Boylan*, the United States sued for recovery of the Honyost property, which it declared to be unalienable by individuals.[19]

The lawyer for Julia Boylan argued that the Oneida Nation no longer existed. He asked Mary's nephew Chief William Honyost Rockwell how the Oneidas could be regarded as Indians if they worked and dressed like white people and did not live by hunting and fishing. The Oneidas, according to this line of questioning, faced losing their land because they were not considered "real Indians." Perhaps it was experiences like this one that inspired Chief Rockwell to don the feathered war bonnet of the Plains Indians when he posed for newspaper photographs. White people would recognize him as a Native if he looked like the Indians they saw in the movies.[20]

It did not matter what the Oneidas wore or how they made a living, said Judge George W. Ray. He found that the New York Oneidas "were a separate nation" under the protection of the federal government. That right to protection existed "so long as a single Indian entitled thereto invokes it and remains on the reservation . . . whether that reservation has been reduced from thousands of acres to 1 or 100 acres." The state did not have the power or authority to terminate the tribe or authorize the Oneidas to hold their land in severalty. The Boylan title was invalid; the land belonged to the Oneidas. Litigation continued.[21]

"Court Gives Back Land to the Indians," reported the *Dispatch*. What about the other properties on West Road that had been divided up by the state in severalty? The newspaper raised the possibility that the US government, on behalf of the Oneidas, might start ejectment actions on a thousand acres in the First Ward of the city of Oneida. Was it possible that white people could lose their land? At the historical society, Edwin J. Brown, now Judge Brown, told concerned residents that he disagreed with the ruling. He thought the state treaties were valid and that white residents could not be dispossessed.[22]

Give Us What Is Right

The Boylan case inspired activism. Wilson Cornelius, a Bear Clan medicine man from Canada who married a New York Oneida, agitated for an investigation of Oneida land claims. Wilson wrote letter after letter to the Bureau of Indian Affairs (BIA) at the US Department of the Interior. When asked for evidence to back up the claims, Wilson answered, "What the oldest members of the tribe say" and sent hand-drawn maps. Wilson either had come across some early treaty that he assumed was still in force, thought one official, or he was a crackpot.[23]

Federal officials replied that the Oneida Reservation no longer existed. A few times they acknowledged that the Boylan decision had "intimated" that Indians could not transfer their lands in New York State without the consent of the federal government. Even if so, warned Assistant Indian Commissioner Edgar B. Meritt, at any time Congress could wipe out the Oneida land claims by ratifying past transactions between the Indians and the state. From Washington came the word that there was no path back to the land.[24]

While the Boylan case made its way through the courts, the United States in 1917 entered the Great War against Germany. John Denny's stepsons, Sergeant Baptist Powless and Lieutenant John Powless, went into the infantry. "Lafayette, we are here!" declared a US officer at the general's tomb in Paris. The arrival of US troops on the Western Front, he indicated, was a tribute to their French Revolutionary War allies. Back in New York, the descendants of Oneida Revolutionary War allies were in danger of losing the last of their ancestral homeland.[25]

DeVerne Brewer, aged eighteen when the United States declared war, registered for the selective service, received a high draft number, and was never called. Frank expanded his holdings by buying a second farm. The heirs of William Cobb had sold their property to the farmer Myron Peebles, who kept the land north of the railroad and sold Frank the forty-acre section to the south, which once had belonged to Charles Deferrier and before that Deferrier's cousin Abraham Denny.[26]

Frank and Jennie moved to the former Cobb estate. Their daughter Hazel and her husband lived next door on what was then called Cobb Avenue and later Hubbard Place. Their sons Harry and DeVerne stayed on the large farm on West Elm Street. After Lizzie Clement died, Frank obtained a patent from the state for her hill farm with the help of the law firm Coville & Santry, which had both Julia Boylan and the Brewers as clients. Frank used the Clement farm as a wood lot and summer pasture. By then he and Jennie had a telephone, a McCormick mower, and a Buick with 22.5 horsepower. The Brewer family prospered in the early 1900s, known as the golden age of agriculture in the United States.[27]

Frank's daughters, brother, sister, and nieces worked for Oneida Community Limited, which produced quality silverware. Oneida Limited offered its workers good wages, health and life insurance, stock ownership, pensions, a visiting nursing service, a bowling alley, and swimming at Sunset Lake. In its company town, called Sherrill, it paid for utilities, fire protection, and garbage collection. "This company is different from any company you have ever heard of in their treatment of their employees"—like "human beings," wrote a visiting labor organizer. When out at restaurants, people from Oneida turned over a spoon or fork to look for the Oneida stamp, a custom referred to as the "Oneida flip."[28]

DeVerne met Mabelle Greene at the sheriff's reception in Wampsville. Their names made them part of regional tradition. By the end of the nineteenth century, Puritan names such as Welcome and Deliverance, as well as names out of the Bible, like Hephzibah and Eliphalet, had fallen out of fashion. French names or names that sounded French remained popular, as families associated their children with the memory of elegant allies and émigrés. Madison County boys were called Lafayette, LeGrand, DuVerry, Chevalier, and Montsier. Girls were named Marquise, Chiffonette, Alfaretta, Saffarine, and Charaloise. The name Mabelle, which she sometimes spelled Maybelle, the way it was pronounced, was one of many variations on Belle. At some point her family added an *e* to the end of Green to make it fancier.[29]

DeVerne and Mabelle began married life on the best land in 1922. He was wiry and quiet. She was plump and lively. He was a graduate of Mor-

FIGURE 34. DeVerne Brewer and Mabelle Greene Brewer in 1922, the year of their marriage. Brewer Collection.

risville College, the only one of his siblings to obtain higher education. Mabelle graduated from Cazenovia Seminary and took a ten-month course at Central City Business School. For a year she worked as a secretary in the Oneida law office of Brown & Woolever. She remembered Edwin J. Brown as a lonely man whose wife and daughter had died. He invited Mabelle and DeVerne to go to church with him on Easter Sunday and attended their wedding.[30]

Unlike Judge Brown, state officials were worried about the Boylan case. The court had ruled that New York had no jurisdiction over the original inhabitants. It had defined Indians as wards of the United States and as aliens who had never surrendered self-government. Where did that leave the state? To find out, the legislature in 1919 set up the New York State Indian Commission, called the Everett Commission after its chair, Edward A. Everett, a Republican assemblyman from Potsdam in St. Lawrence County.[31]

Everett believed that the democratic spirit the United States had shown to the world during the Great War called for justice to be done at home for Indigenous people. Back when the Indians were stronger than we were, he said, we treated them as equal, and when we became the greater power, we treated them as wards, foreigners, and aliens. "We must not do that," he argued. "We don't want to hand down to our children what our forefathers handed to us. This has gone far enough and we will have difficulty enough in settling now." Everett revealed his reckless side when he declared, "Let the matter of financial result drop where it will."[32]

Everett told the US Board of Indian Commissioners that he wanted to discover the "true history of what was done" in New York. Did the whole state belong to the Indians? asked the chairman. "If that is the case, the State of New York and the United States will have exceeding difficulty in unscrambling the eggs." No one in the federal government wants the New York Indians, pointed out the secretary of the board. No member of Congress seemed to know much about them or care. The Department of the Interior proposed that Congress could solve the problem by making all the Indigenous people of New York citizens of the United States and then putting them under the jurisdiction of New York State. But that, objected Everett, would mean compelling a man to become a member of a nation that was now in possession of the country it had taken from him.[33]

At hearings held across the state in 1920 by the Everett Commission, spokesmen for the Six Nations expressed their belief that it was white people, not they, who were the aliens. They insisted that New York State had no jurisdiction over them and that they remained under the protection of the US government. Everett presented the question at hand: what was the status of the New York Indians? He wanted to hear their version of their history to help answer this question. He was aware that they did not have written records, but he asked them to share what they knew from oral accounts.[34]

The Oneidas, whose home territory remained in dispute, testified at the Onondaga Reservation, where many of them now resided. Chapman Skenandoah recalled how, in the fur-trading days of Henry Hudson and Peter Stuyvesant, "a perfect government of the Iroquois" made peace with the Europeans. Then during the Sullivan Expedition, American soldiers made leggings of Indian skins. The Oneidas "never fought against the Stars and Stripes," he told the committee. They helped in every war the United States had. Chapman, who had witnessed the Americans' treatment of Cubans, Filipinos, and Hawaiians, was skeptical of US promises of "self-government." If Indians had equality, they could be citizens, he thought, but that was impossible given the relations among the races.[35]

"You can call me a Bolshevist or whatever you want; but I am an American," said Joseph Johnson. "I live in the same land that my fathers and forefathers were born in and possessed thousands of years ago and still I am classified as an alien." State officials, said Johnson, "say the Indians are dying because they don't know how to take care of themselves." They were wrong. The death of his people was connected to the loss of their territory. Johnson accused the state of hastening their demise by allowing the county courts to uphold fraudulent land transactions. Even though Indians were not citizens, he pointed out, they had volunteered to defend the country. "Give us what is coming and what is right and we are willing to be satisfied," he said.[36]

It had been so many years since the Oneidas had held a council with state officials that this is new for us, said Chief Marshall John, the son of Melinda Skenandoah John. "Us Indians would not have written records of our matters," explained Marshall John, "and have to rely upon what we gained from older heads." Marshall John knew of thirty-two treaties made by the Oneidas with the United States and New York State. He didn't remember many dates, he said, but he was off by only two days for the signing of the Treaty of 1795. The Oneidas had asked the state for written copies of the treaties and received nothing, he added. John observed that local white people had been courteous to the Native children who now attended public school, but they still tried to take over Oneida land. The ongoing litigation over the Honyost property was just one example.[37]

In his report, which Everett rightly assumed would end his political career, he concluded that the Indians of New York State still owned the fee-simple title to their territory guaranteed by the US government at Fort Stanwix in 1784. The treaties made it clear that the Six Nations never had been conquered and that they rightfully possessed the soil. The federal and state governments were to blame for the illegal acquisition of aboriginal territory and owed the Haudenosaunee compensation for the land taken from them. The current landowners were not at fault and should not suffer.[38]

No one else on the commission signed Everett's report. A fellow commissioner accused Everett of "wandering in a swamp of delusion." Everett retorted that his colleague wallowed "in a swamp of dishonesty." He called on anyone who had evidence that disputed his conclusions to come forward, but no one did. The New York State legislature in 1922 refused to accept the Everett Report, and the suppressed report vanished for fifty years. Contrary to Everett's hopes, his generation would hand down to its children the legacy of injustice inherited from its forefathers.[39]

The Oneidas, meanwhile, in a rare and significant victory, won the Boylan case. The district attorney of Madison County had been slow to grasp the significance of the small property dispute on the outskirts of Oneida. When he did, he wrote to the clerk of the US Supreme Court, days before the deadline for appeal, "We are in trouble on this case." He pointed to the implications for all of central and western New York of a ruling that said the state had no right to make a treaty with the Oneida Indians for the sale of land. On the technicality of a late filing, the US Supreme Court in November 1921 declined to view the Boylan case. It let stand the decision in favor of the Oneidas.[40]

Oneidas from Wisconsin, Canada, and Onondaga, as well as Mohawks, Onondagas, and Senecas, came to the Windfall to celebrate. Chief Rockwell announced that they gathered to show respect for the laws of the United States. "We sought justice, not revenge," Rockwell said. Mary Honyost Skenandoah did not live to see the celebration held at her lifelong home. The *Democratic Union* published a bizarre account of her funeral. All through the night on the reservation, it reported, were heard "weird chants of the old-time braves wailing the 'Oy-sy-ana' around the bier of the squaw." The chant, scoffed Rockwell, was just a

Methodist hymn, probably one with a hosanna in it. "White men get funny ideas about Indians," said Rockwell, speaking words of caution to any of us who rely on newspaper stories for accounts of the past.[41]

The US attorney directed Chief Rockwell to take possession of the Honyost land on behalf of his people. By then, local whites had crowded out Oneidas at the Windfall, explained Marshall John. They had moved their fences inch by inch onto Oneida land "until in reality there is nothing practically left." They had taken over the Oneida mission house on West Road by locking the door. In 1925, reported the *Dispatch*, "seventy-five descendants of Jeduthan and Sally Gregg Green, pioneer settlers of Northern Madison County, assembled at the old Indian Church" for their annual reunion and picnic. Mabelle and DeVerne attended these family reunions held at the Oneida mission house under the shade of a magnificent elm tree. The Methodists, it appears, had forgotten their promise to protect Oneida Indian houses of worship.[42]

Blood and Land

Mabelle was proud of her New England roots. With her ability to trace her lineage to Revolutionary War patriots, she was eligible to join the Daughters of the American Revolution. Of DeVerne's family, nothing was known beyond the hardscrabble existence up in the hills. Mabelle's interest in family history was part of a national trend in the early twentieth century, one that the historian Gary Nash calls a "fetish of genealogy." Middle- and upper-class American Protestants invented a "comforting history of Anglo-Saxonism," writes Nash, to distinguish themselves from the millions of Jews and Catholics arriving from eastern and southern Europe as well as Mexican Americans, African Americans, and Indigenous people whose families had inhabited the continent for centuries.[43]

Scientific studies of the day confirmed a belief in the racial superiority of white people. Madison Grant, the author of *The Passing of the Great Race*, stoked fears that so-called white supremacy would be destroyed by racial intermixing. The children of such unions, he wrote, "would inevitably degenerate to the lower type." Attitudes about racial intermixing influenced a 1914 case regarding a land claim by Montauk Indians on Long Island. The court ruled that the Montauks had no right to sue because they were not living as a tribe, and that the purity of their blood had been "greatly impaired by miscegenation, particularly with the negro race."[44]

The Ku Klux Klan, which had grown into a national movement, was active in Madison County. Calling for the preservation of "American ideals and American institutions," the Klan supported immigration restriction and shutting down parochial schools like the one that had recently been opened by St. Patrick's parish in Oneida. Hooded marchers wearing white robes paraded on Main and Broad Streets. The KKK burned in effigy Tony Waldo, the mayor of Canastota, whose family, like many others in the area, had come from Italy. Canastota answered the Klan by reelecting Waldo for a decade. The burning of a large cross on Stockbridge East Hill was one of many signs of KKK activity around the Windfall and the Orchard.[45]

Without the consent of Native peoples, President Calvin Coolidge in 1924 signed a law that granted citizenship to all Indians born within the United States. According to US Supreme Court decisions, Indians now were both citizens and wards of the government. Chief Rockwell declared he would never vote in the white man's elections. At congressional hearings, Laura Cornelius, who had married the white attorney Orrin Kellogg, condemned Native health, education, and poverty as well as the incompetence of the BIA. In her book *Our Democracy and the American Indian*, she asked, "Is anybody's career in Congress worth the Indian's justice?" The hearings failed to clarify the status of New York Indians. They were "more or less" under state jurisdiction, testified Assistant Commissioner Meritt, but "there is a twilight zone there."[46]

Wilson Cornelius joined the ambitious land claims movement led by Laura Cornelius Kellogg, but Chapman Skenandoah felt the plan to sue for eighteen million acres of land in New York State on behalf of all Haudenosaunee was a pipe dream. When the Kellogg Party did not use the donations it collected to sue for the land, Iroquois leaders accused it of swindling poor people. The Kellogg Party wasn't listening to advice or producing receipts, said Katie Honyost John, the wife of Marshall John. The Oneida Council met every week to discuss strategies, but it made no headway. If the Oneidas hired a lawyer to pursue the land claims, she thought, he might just drag out the case to get his pay until we are all dead. It would be just as quick if they let the government see to it, which she knew would not be quick at all.[47]

The Kellogg Party's activism and the victorious Boylan decision did not help the Doxtator sisters save their land on Marble Hill. When Lydia Doxtator died, her niece Stella Doxtator Miller claimed her three acres. So did a town of Vernon man who said he had purchased the property from the Christian and Missionary Alliance Church, which had been given the property by Lydia in her will. The Oneidas, who knew that the non-Native minister of the church had rewritten Lydia's will and that he and his wife were the only witnesses to this document, denounced this purchase. They insisted that Lydia wanted her land to go to the women of her family.[48]

As the case went through the courts, Chief Rockwell wrote to Washington for help. The secretary of the interior replied that the case should be referred to the state. "I come to you for aid and relief from the intrusion of white persons upon our reservation houses," Rockwell wrote in vain to Governor Franklin D. Roosevelt. With no help forthcoming, Stella could not afford to appeal after five years of legal expenses. Her family returned home one day to find their furniture removed from the house. Her daughter Irma saw her wicker doll carriage on the lawn across the street, but she was forbidden to say anything about it. Everyone was upset, even though they would not speak about the eviction in front of her.[49]

With her painful memories of boarding school, Stella did not talk much about Oneida culture. This era, Oneidas recalled, was when the language died. Suppressed at school and treated as an embarrassment, it was viewed by many of the young people as a great burden, along with the oral history that came with it. "You can't live in the past," said an Oneida youth. Life in the present was difficult enough. Stella told Irma that Native children had to do better and try harder than other children because they were Indian. Irma often was the only Oneida child at her school. "You're just an old Indian," taunted the children. She felt ashamed, until she decided that she would not. I'm as good as they are, she told herself. Stella and her family eventually left. Pushed out by local hostility and pulled away by job opportunities, more Oneidas moved to the Onondaga Reservation or upstate cities.[50]

The Oneidas who stayed in Oneida felt they needed to blend in as much as possible. Stella's sister Electa Doxtator John was remembered by the neighbors as "always ready with a willing heart" to help anyone in need. Her husband, Lyman John, a silver plater at Oneida Limited, was kind and never drank. But Electa and her children knew tough times, made worse by Lyman's gambling. Her son Martin John remembered growing up poor and hungry. Some local white people did not want their sons and daughters dating the children of Italian immigrants or Indians. Martin's courtship of Ella Mae Staudt, a white neighbor of the Brewers, did not meet with the approval of her family.[51]

At the same time, an Oneida woman recalled, Oneidas felt pressure to try to pass as Italian or marry non-Native people to "get rid of that bloodline." Blood was the way the federal government defined who was Native. The "blood quantum" system formalized in the Indian Reorganization Act of 1934 recognized persons "of one-half or more Indian blood" as Indian. Senator Burton K. Wheeler of Montana wanted the "half blood" requirement because he feared that all sorts of people would claim they were one-quarter Indian in order to be put on the government roll. If Oneidas continued to marry people of mixed ancestry, as had John Denny's great-grandparents, they would cease to exist under blood quantum rules. That seemed to be the goal for some. "What we are trying to do is get rid of the Indian problem rather than add to it," said Senator Wheeler.[52]

On the best land, DeVerne had no idea that his Mohawk Dutch ancestors once viewed kinship ties to the Six Nations as an advantage. In his diary, Frank mentioned hiring "the Indian" at harvest time, but that was all he wrote about the presence of Oneidas in his life. The Brewers ran the Orchard Place Dairy as a farm-to-house business. Frank and DeVerne sold pasteurized and bottled milk, butter, and cream to customers on the north side of Oneida, the working-class neighborhood north of the railroad tracks. Sometimes people were unable to pay DeVerne during the Great Depression, but he delivered the milk anyway.[53]

Mabelle kept house and looked after Robert (Bob), who was born in 1928, followed by my father, Herbert DeVerne (Herb) in 1930 and Virginia (Ginny) in 1933. A sketch performer, Mabelle was invited to entertain at parties and club meetings. In the afternoons, she went to the movies, where she may have seen the short film *The King without a Crown*, from MGM's historical mystery series, shown in 1937. It told the story of the Lost Dauphin, in which a dignified Eleazer Williams learns his true heritage. After church on Sundays, DeVerne and Mabelle took the family on drives up into the hills to Stockbridge or Chittenango Falls to revisit the stomping ground of their grandparents.[54]

By the time Frank passed away in 1940, he was the proud owner of three farms. Years after Jennie had died, he sold the Clement farm, but he retained the rights to the timber on it for ten years. Frank left his hundred-acre farm to DeVerne with the proviso that he was to pay his brothers and sisters a one-sixth part as their share. He left his forty-acre farm to his son Leo with the same instruction. He said that his daughters Reta and Mae could stay in the house on Leo's farm until they married. Years later, Reta, who never married, would still have the farm.[55]

During recess at the Wampsville school, Bob, Herb, and Ginny played tag and found arrowheads. On the way home, Bob fished for trout in

Cowaselon Creek. He was allowed to work his way upstream past the Cobbs' to where "the old Indian" lived. Bob didn't know who "the old Indian" was; he knew just that he was not to bother him. DeVerne rented three or four little fields from his friend Dewitt Cobb, the great-grandson of Angel and Polly Deferrier. Dewitt worked as a janitor at the Episcopal church and was a nice guy who had trouble with vandalism, remembered Bob and Herb.[56]

When there was free time and a good day, the Brewer kids made for the canal. A section of the original Erie Canal, which once had trespassed across Oneida territory, had been abandoned when the canal later was straightened and enlarged. At this spot, which they called Clinton's Ditch, Bob, Herb, and Ginny built a corral and a hut where they kept their horses and camped. They fished in the canal, hiked along it, and, in the winter, skated on it. After they returned to the house from one of their expeditions, they looked down the field and saw smoke rising. The campfire they put out had spread underground through the dense organic matter in the soil.[57]

During World War II, there was plenty to eat on the farm, but gas was rationed and there was a labor shortage. Bob slopped the pigs and fed the calves and horses. Herb became the proprietor of the chicken house. As his flock grew, he sold eggs to stores and households on the north side of Oneida. As a girl, Ginny had no assigned farm chores. Tasked with dusting, ironing, and cooking, she escaped outdoors when she could. Around Halloween, Bob, Herb, and Ginny invited their friends to cornhusking parties held in the barn. Mabelle entertained the huskers with cider, doughnuts, and ghost stories. At over one hundred feet long and fifty feet wide, the barn housed the dairy, the horse stalls, and the granary. In the haymow, the kids climbed up on the twelve-by-twelve-inch beams and swung on ropes over the opening to the floor below.[58]

At Oneida Junior High School, Homeroom 2 reported that it was halfway to its goal of raising funds to cover the cost of a jeep. A controversy arose when girls asked to be allowed to wear pants instead of dresses. Slacks were warm, acknowledged the student Ann Marshall, but many boys objected to girls wearing them to school. Trousers, she concluded, should be worn by girls only for sports, lounging, and defense work, and she urged petitioners not to start trouble over such a small matter. "One of the most outstanding students in our homeroom is Herbert Brewer," reported Homeroom 8. "He has a high average, and received high marks in exams, including a 100% in his math. He also is a favorite among his classmates. Homeroom 8 is proud to have him in their room." This type

FIGURE 35. GIs during World War II. Martin John is in the center of the front row. Karst Collection.

of tribute inspired merciless teasing by Bob. Mabelle and DeVerne, who had thought their family was complete, had a baby in 1943 and named him Richard (Dick).[59]

Hundreds of the men and women who left Madison County to serve in the war did not return. They died in Pearl Harbor, Tunisia, Guadalcanal, China, India, Dakar, Anzio Beach, the Adriatic Sea, Normandy, Belgium, Iwo Jima, and Okinawa, and along the Rhine River. The Turtle Clan sons of Electa Doxtator John served. Private Martin John trained as a medic before he was sent to Officer Candidate School and made a lieutenant in the Seventh Armored Division. In 1944, he was assigned to Twelfth Army Company Headquarters under General Omar Bradley in London, where he adopted a stray fox terrier. Martin and Ella Mae began their fifty-two years of marriage separated by war.[60]

Did Martin know that the paratroopers of the 101st Airborne shaved their hair Mohawk style and donned war paint before they dropped into France on D-Day? A motor transport officer during the Normandy, Ardennes, and Rhineland campaigns, Martin was made captain, as his forefather Honyery had been. When Germany surrendered, the former star athlete of Stockbridge High School was ordered to Paris, where he played basketball for the army team. He returned home to his job at Oneida Limited, which after a few years of making bayonets and rifle sights had resumed the production of silverware. Martin rarely spoke about his military service, and no one knew what happened to the terrier.[61]

Martin's father, Lyman John, served as a chief along with Nelson Skenandoah and William Rockwell. They were named to their position by the clan mothers in the traditional manner and expected to work "for the good of the Nation." Chief Rockwell spoke out about Oneida land, which he said had been acquired "through a ruthless sham" by New York State. People around the world had sacrificed to "protect and preserve their sovereignty, so that they could rightfully stand on their home land, and joyfully say, 'this is my country,'" said Rockwell. "This is what we want too."[62]

Using a process promoted by advocates of assimilation, the Oneidas at Onondaga voted for their chiefs. They elected Rockwell's cousin Chapman Skenandoah as chief, for example. In addition, Mary Cornelius Winder, an activist like her father Wilson Cornelius, served as a representative. She explained to the Indian superintendent that Oneidas had shelter from the storms thanks to the kindness of the Onondagas. She did not add that the Oneidas still were viewed as pariahs by the Six Nations for their decision to ally with the Americans during the Revolutionary War, or that their kinfolk back at the Windfall and Marble Hill referred to them as the "aliens up at the Onondaga." She asked for the restoration of lands reserved to the Oneidas at the Treaty of Fort Stanwix made in 1788. Officials replied that nothing could be done.[63]

The Cloth and the Corn

At the New York State Fair, held in Syracuse at the end of every summer, Mary and her sister Delia Cornelius Waterman helped to plan performances of Haudenosaunee dances and band concerts as well as demonstrations of crafts and agricultural practices. At the fair, Iroquois leaders founded an "Indian Village," for which the state had allocated funds thanks to the lobbying efforts of the Agricultural Extension Service at Cornell University. Chapman Skenandoah, who had won first prize for reviving an ancient strain of Iroquoian maize, carved a giant ear of corn that became the symbol of the village. The Oneidas also displayed the shawl that Revolutionary War–era Polly Cooper had brought back from Valley Forge. Corn soup was served at the soup house, and visiting dignitaries were adopted as "blood brothers" in ceremonies officiated by Chief Rockwell and others. Mohawks, Oneidas, Onondagas, Cayugas, Senecas, and Tuscaroras attended the fair to have fun and enlighten New Yorkers about the history and traditions of the Six Nations. In the 1950s, they also gathered to discuss their survival.[64]

They were up against a policy called termination. The federal government wanted to end its recognition of about one hundred tribes across the country and compel the assimilation of Native people into US society. The policy would free the Indians, who were being held back by federal guardianship, officials claimed. Dillon S. Myer, who oversaw the concentration camps for Japanese Americans during the war and was now head of the BIA, said, "We must proceed even though Indian cooperation may be lacking in certain cases." The term "relocation," which had been used to describe Japanese American internment, was now applied to the national policy of moving Indigenous people off reservations and into urban areas and industrial jobs.[65]

Fully on board with termination was New York, the first state to get federal statutory authority for jurisdiction over "its" Indians. To pave the way, the state's Joint Legislative Committee on Indian Affairs held hearings. Chapman Skenandoah asked whether these hearings involved changing the wardship status of Native people. No, lied the committee attorney. The state, said legislators, only wanted to promote the "eventual social assimilation of the New York Indians into the general population." Over the protest of the Haudenosaunee, who suspected the state of wanting to take their reservations and destroy their tribal organizations, Congress transferred criminal and civil jurisdiction over the New York Indians to New York State.[66]

As a companion to the termination policy, the US government set up the Indian Claims Commission. "We stand ready to correct any mistakes we have made," said President Harry Truman about the violation of treaties, the illegal seizure of Indian land, and military campaigns of racial extermination. From the US government's perspective, the Indian Claims Commission was a "final accounting" to be carried out before wrapping up the federal trust responsibility and handing over the job to the states. Tribes were allowed to file claims against the United States for its failure to carry out treaty obligations. No land was to be returned to Indigenous people; the compensation would be financial only, and once made, it would forever bar any legal claim to the land.[67]

For many of the Haudenosaunee, the creation of the Indian Claims Commission initially meant a chance to assert their rights and seek restitution. Mary Winder and Delia Waterman, who helped to organize a land claims movement among the Oneidas at Onondaga, passed a hat to collect money to pay for stamps. The Oneidas submitted a claim in 1951. They stated that the United States had allowed New York State to buy their ancestral land in violation of the federal Trade and Intercourse Acts.[68]

Herb knew nothing about the Oneida land claims. When he graduated from Oneida High School in 1948, his proud family, filled with anxiety for him over his stuttering, listened to him deliver his valedictory speech on the dangers of Red Communism. Herb, the Madison County 4-H poultry champion, sold half of his nine hundred chickens to pay his way at the State College of Agriculture at Cornell University. There he studied botany, zoology, geology, bacteriology, meteorology, agricultural economics and engineering, agronomy, animal husbandry, history, government, and military science as a member of the ROTC during the Korean War.[69]

In the summers, Herb worked on the farm. The construction of the New York State Thruway in the early 1950s was a bonanza for the best land. The new toll road stretched from New York City to Buffalo, following much the same route past the farm as had the Seneca Turnpike, the Erie Canal, and the New York Central Railroad. At the opening ceremony, held in Syracuse in 1954, Chief Rockwell presented Governor Thomas Dewey with a wampum belt and suggested that the superhighway be called the Iroquois Trail. Instead, rest stops were named Mohawk, Oneida, and Seneca. DeVerne sold gravel from the north end of his property to the state, which needed to build up the marshy section between Durhamville and Canastota. With the money, he expanded the barn and built a silo that had a self-feeder. DeVerne no longer delivered milk door to door. He took it in milk cans to the creamery.[70]

After Herb graduated, he became a partner in the dairy farm. He and his siblings had grown up taking the ownership of property for granted, although they were the first generation born to landowners rather than tenants in the family of their father's fathers, going back to colonial Duanesburg. By then, Bob had left the navy, where he had trained to be a fighter pilot, and went to work for the state Fish and Wildlife Department after graduating from the New York State College of Forestry at Syracuse University. Ginny studied nursing at the University of Rochester. The littlest brother, Dick, was initiated into farm work. Herb started a 4-H Club for boys called the Wampsville County Seaters. His courtship of the new Madison County 4-H agent, he felt, was the object of unnecessary assistance from the sheriff, the county clerk, and club leaders.[71]

Mary Lou Sipperley, a graduate of Buffalo State University and my mother, worked for the New York State Cooperative Extension Service, directed by Cornell University in fulfillment of its role in the land-grant system. The extension service embraced "learning by doing" as it spread the latest research on best practices to rural communities. Mary Lou specialized in youth development and home economics. She and Herb scheduled their wedding to be held after the state fair, where Mary Lou supervised young exhibitors at the 4-H building next to the Indian Village.

Over time, the Brewers acquired the remaining farmland in the First Tract of the Oneida Treaty of 1815 that had been granted by New York State to Angel Deferrier. "Brewers Are Successful Dairymen," reported George W. Walter in a 1958 edition of the *Dispatch*'s farm news. "The Brewer farm is noted for its excellent corn." DeVerne was a Mason, a member of the Farm Bureau, and president of the Oneida City Schools Board of Education, reported Walter. Mabelle, "a noted monologuist," was active in the Order of the Eastern Star, which was affiliated with the Masons, and on church committees. She also served on the Election Board of the Fifth Ward. Their son Herb and daughter-in-law, with their baby daughter, Susan, had a new ranch-style home next door. My brothers Russell (Russ) and Thomas (Tom), and sister Elizabeth (Beth), followed.[72]

When I felt I wasn't getting enough attention at home, I crossed the field to Grandma's house. I asked her to tell stories about the olden days over and over so I would remember. When aunts and uncles came to visit, the cousins headed to the hayloft in the big barn to build forts out of hay bales and swing on ropes from beam to beam. We rode on tractors and swam in the creek. We were fond of our great-aunts Hazel and Reta, who believed that anyone doing chores or going to 4-H camp needed cookies.

When we played in the front yard, we waved at the engineer as the train went by. The New York Central tracks, which crossed the best land between our house and Aunt Reta's, were relocated to the back of the cornfields in the 1960s. This move was made to limit accidents and avoid blocking traffic, especially emergency vehicles, through downtown Oneida. The railroad, once the heart of the city, had become an obstacle. To acquire the land for the tracks, the state exercised eminent domain. DeVerne was served notice. He was waiting for the paperwork to be finalized when he saw the construction crews arriving. He stood at the boundary of his farm with his Remington rifle and said, "Until I sign papers, you are not coming through here." The papers were delivered, and the relocation of the tracks went ahead. It cost the farm a forty-acre field. Now trapped between the canal and the railroad, the lot was difficult to access.[73]

I attended the old elementary school, where third graders would be good out of love for Laura Ingalls Wilder. If we behaved, our teacher read us the Little House books after lunch. From Laura we learned how to put up with snobs from town like Nellie Oleson, and how Pa found his way through a blizzard by tying a rope from the cabin to the barn. I didn't understand why Ma warned Laura to put on her sunbonnet or else she would become "brown like an Indian." Was it a mother thing, I wondered, like no elbows on the table? I didn't know that the Ingalls family had squatted on Osage land in Kansas, just like I didn't know that my ancestors had squatted on Oneida land. I didn't remember the part where Pa explained why Indians must move on. "That's why we're here, Laura. White people are going to settle all this country, and we get the best land because we get here first and take our pick." When Laura asked, "Won't it make the Indians mad to—" Pa interrupted. "No more questions, Laura," he said. "Go to sleep."[74]

On Sundays, Mabelle liked to see her progeny filling the pews at the Methodist church. Afterward, the family sometimes went for drives in the hills that would bequeath to me a nostalgia (a word that in its Greek roots combines "return home" with "longing") for the landscape. As we passed their territory, there was no mention of the Oneida Indians. It was an unofficial reflection of official policy. The US government, which had defended the last thirty-two acres of Oneida territory in the Boylan case, had not been heard from again except for creating the Indian Claims Commission and sending discouraging replies to Oneidas regarding their land claims. New York State did not formally recognize the thirty-two acres as a reservation, but it provided school aid as though they were. As far as the authorities were concerned, the Oneidas existed in a twilight zone.[75]

Meanwhile Chief Rockwell handed out the treaty cloth delivered by the United States in fulfillment of the Treaty of Canandaigua. For years, he and other Haudenosaunee leaders had called on the US government to "review" all the guarantees made in that treaty by the Washington administration, not just the part about the cloth. Following Rockwell's

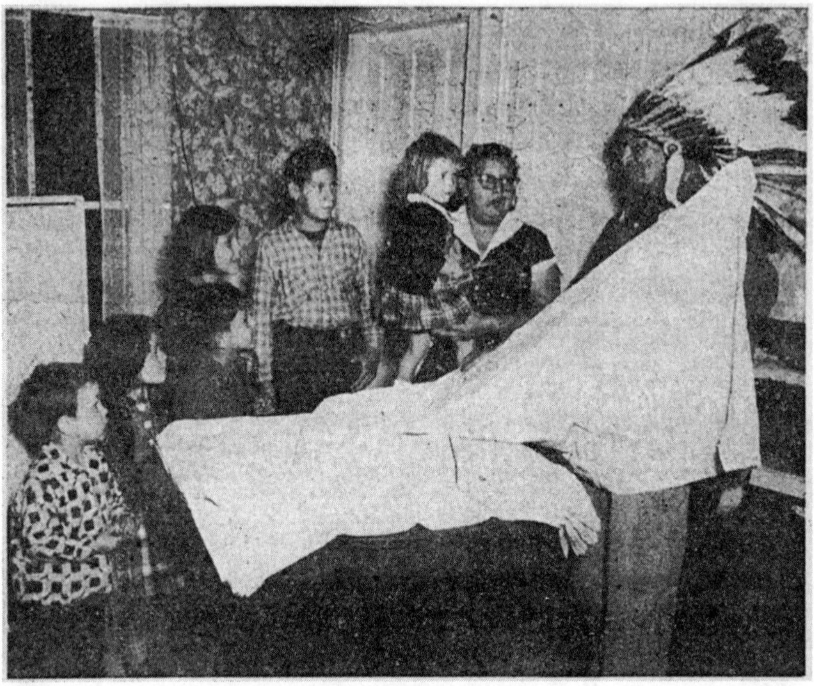

FIGURE 36. At his home on Oneida territory, Chief William Rockwell hands out the cloth delivered by the US government in accordance with the 1794 Treaty of Canandaigua. Pictured with him are Marion John Miles (daughter of Electa Doxtator and Lyman John), who holds her youngest daughter Penny, while the other children look on. Unidentified newspaper, October 1955. Karst Collection.

death in 1960, Emily Doxtator Johnson took over the distribution of the cloth. One of Dr. Sundown's great-granddaughters, for example, received a few yards of a flower print. Always claim the cloth, Mary Winder taught her daughters. It was proof that federal treaties were in force. About seven hundred enrolled Oneidas lived in central New York. Most were at the Onondaga Reservation. A few hundred remained on West Road, at Marble Hill, and around town.[76]

Richard Lynch, called Dick, knew next to nothing about the Oneidas. The Turtle Clan boy, who grew up on the north side of the city, thought everybody's grandparents spoke another language at home. At his friend's house it was Italian, and at his it was Oneida, as spoken by his grandmother, Rose Honyost Johnson. Dick remembers days of adventure when he and the neighborhood kids rode their bikes out West Elm Street to fish and swim in Cowaselon Creek. Dick pronounces Cowaselon as "Shkwaselon," as Samuel Kirkland wrote it.[77]

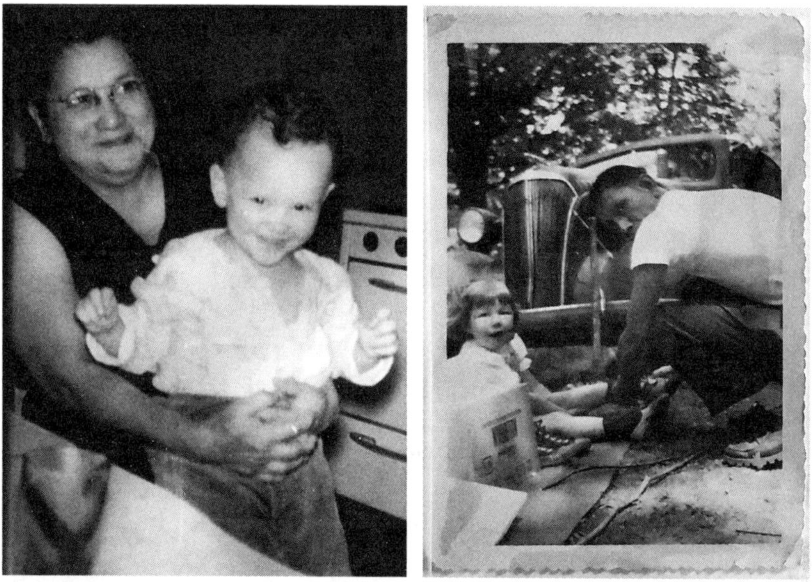

FIGURE 37A AND B. Rose Honyost Johnson with her grandson Richard "Dick" Lynch (Richard and Pamela Lynch Collection), and Rebecca "Becki" John Karst with her father, Martin John. Karst Collection.

Martin John didn't want anything to do with activism regarding Oneida lands. His fourteen-year-old daughter, Becki, heard him argue about it with his brother Lyman K. John after a Green Corn Festival she begged her parents to take her to on the reservation. When they came home, she heard her father say to Ella Mae, "Well, she's been to the Green Corn Festival," which sounded pretty final to Becki. It was not easy to grow up in Oneida with an Oneida father and a white mother, Becki recalled. More than once, because of some incident of discrimination, Martin called school administrators to demand that his children be treated fairly and with respect. Becki was not an enrolled Oneida, but she was named Rebecca Anna after her great-aunt, the Turtle Clan mother Anna Doxtator Skenandoah.[78]

Becki did not know the Oneida story of the corn husk doll, which goes like this: The Three Sisters—beans, corn, and squash—are the sustainers of life. The corn asked the great spirit if there was anything more she could do for her people. The great spirit said a doll could be made from her husk. The corn husk doll grew conceited because everywhere she went, she was admired for her beautiful face. The great spirit warned her not to think of herself as superior, but when she continued to do so, he took away her face. The doll without a face reminds children not to think or act like they're better than anyone else. When Emily Doxtator Johnson made her a corn husk doll, six-year-old Becki thought her great-aunt had forgotten to put on the face, so she drew one on herself. When she learned the story of the doll, she felt miserable about what she had done.[79]

My contemporaries Becki John and Dick Lynch were unaware that they descended from Catharine, the Wolf Clan woman who lived in the Mohawk Valley in the early 1700s. They were part of something they knew little about, because no one spoke much about their Oneida heritage. As a child, I thought that Polly Deferrier, the Native woman who was buried in the little cemetery up the road, and I were both princesses of the best land. A newspaper article about "Madison County's greatest love story" featured Polly as an Indian princess and Angel as a swashbuckling aristocrat who gave up his castle in France for love. While in kindergarten, I was in the queen's court in the Wampsville Volunteer Firemen's Parade. In my memory I am wearing white gloves as I wave from the back of a shiny convertible.[80]

Sometimes I rode with Grandpa in the truck or on the tractor. When it was milking time, I stood with him at the back of the barn as he called the cows to come in from the pasture. "Cah boss, Cah boss," DeVerne yelled, using a call from the Latin, as had his forefathers in Beverwyck. Grandpa hung a swing made out of a thick rope and notched board from an old apple tree that stood between his house and the barn. I could kick high or spin to twist the rope and twirl as it unwound. Out of the way and in the middle of everything, I watched over my kingdom.

Chapter 9

Fire and Water

In social studies class at Oneida Junior High School, I read about the longhouses of the once-great Iroquois Confederacy. I heard about injustice from a number-one song of 1971 called "Indian Reservation." The pom-pom girls did a routine to the Paul Revere and the Raiders hit at a game where we cheered on our team, called the Oneida Indians. "But maybe some day when they learn, Cherokee nation will return, will return, will return," the routine ended. "Here we go, Indians!" we yelled. "Let's go, Orange!" Our school colors, orange and blue, were the same as those of the guard companies in colonial New Amsterdam.

On the best land, my brothers, Russ and Tom, did chores after school and assisted our grandfather, who carried on with his seed corn business after he retired from farming in 1968. DeVerne and Mabelle moved to Wampsville. Uncle Dick and his wife, Joanne, who had returned from serving in the Peace Corps in Brazil, lived in the farmhouse. Herb and Dick expanded the farm operation now known as Brewer Farm. They built a free-stall barn, a milking parlor with sixteen milker units, and a milk house that held a bulk tank. The new setup required two hired men instead of three, allowed for an increased herd of two hundred cows, and cut chore time in half, reported *Successful Farming.*[1]

By then Herb had become active in local politics after a friend asked him to serve on a Republican Party committee. In 1960s Oneida, the political parties, while about to change, retained some Civil War–era characteristics. The Republicans tended to be pro-business, pro-government, and pro-reform, while the Democrats, in the old Yorker tradition, preferred small government that didn't interfere in people's lives with a lot of regulations and taxes. The Republicans dominated the middle-class south side of the tracks, and the Democrats held sway on the working-class north side.

Herb was elected alderman of the north side's Fifth Ward, where he and DeVerne had sold eggs and milk for years. He joined the other five aldermen who made up the Common Council chaired by the mayor. When the longtime mayor and West Road farmer Abraham "Abe" Williams, a First Ward Democrat, decided not to run for reelection, Herb ran and was elected in 1971. As dairy farmers, who numbered ninety-six out of the city population of 11,900, Herb and Abe could do the part-time job of mayor between morning and afternoon milking.[2]

Herb's tenure as mayor meant we had to answer the phone a lot. Calls came from city officials, reporters, constituents, and an elderly woman who insisted that strangers were watching her through her windows. Russ remembered that no youthful transgression involving a law enforcement officer was kept secret from our father when he oversaw the police department. Tom, to Herb's delight, sat through a few Common Council meetings at city hall to await his prize, a tour past the fire department trucks on the way out to the car. Beth liked riding with Herb in parades until she became bored. I remember dinner-table talk I did not understand about assessment and zoning boards.[3]

After constituents showed Herb a jar of city water that had worms in it, water became one of his top issues. Although we lived within the city limits, our water came from a well, which could run low in a dry summer. Like all farm families, we knew water to the cows and barn came first. The city water was carried by miles of leaky old pipes, which Herb planned to repair with a $10 million water improvement program that included a filtration plant. Also in need of attention was the antiquated sewer system, which dumped its overflow into Oneida Creek.[4]

When Herb became mayor, the Oneidas invited him to their reservation. A sign reading "Territory of the Oneida Indian Nation" now stood at the entrance to the thirty-two acres on West Road. Most of the forty families who lived there, including those of the sisters Mary Cornelius Winder and Delia Cornelius Waterman, recently had moved back from

FIGURE 38. This campaign ad for Herb included a photo of Beth and Herb at the farm office in the new barn (top left), Herb and a hired hand in the milking parlor (bottom left), Herb at city hall (center), Herb in the bunk silo (top right), and our family's least stiff publicity photo (lower right). When Tom refused to smile because he had lost his front teeth, Beth stuck out her tongue, and we all laughed. From left to right: Herb, Tom, Susan, Russ, Beth, Mary Lou. *Oneida Daily Dispatch*, 1975, Brewer Collection.

Onondaga. Many Oneidas lived in trailers originally provided by the federal government for homeless victims of Tropical Storm Agnes that afterward had been given to Native people.[5]

Although Herb had lived in Oneida his entire life, this was his introduction to the Oneida Indians, and it was interesting, he said. "The thrust of it was that they were the original inhabitants of the area and Mother Earth had supplied the water which was to be for everybody and to be free," Herb recounted. "I remember saying, after I listened to all that, well, I agree the water is here for everybody . . . but somebody has to pay to bring it down here, to get it here, to get it to everybody, including you." It sounds like Herb was privileged to hear the Oneidas talk about who they were and the land they lived on, as they had at councils for centuries. And he responded as generations of Europeans and Americans had before him. Let's get down to business, he thought. Mother Earth isn't going to pay to deliver the water.[6]

Herb was not aware that the Oneidas had filed a land claim case against Madison and Oneida Counties in federal court. Delia Waterman's daughter Geralda and her husband, Jacob "Jake" Thompson, first had to convince enough Oneidas that legal action was worth a try. Some thought the land claim was a legend. Others recalled being burned by the Kellogg Party. Many believed it was hopeless. "It's only going to make the white people around here mad at us," said an Oneida woman from Marble Hill. "That land's gone—why don't they forget it?"[7]

The lawyer George Shattuck saw the cloth given to Delia that spring in fulfillment of the Treaty of Canandaigua. "How strange," observed Shattuck, "that the United States saw fit to keep the promise to supply cloth for 180 years and yet to ignore the promise to protect their land." Shattuck found out that lawyers before him had believed the treaties were invalid but chose not to act. Perhaps, he thought, they were confounded by questions of jurisdiction, or they concluded that the case was not a moneymaker. Or maybe the idea of invalidating the treaties was just too fantastic to contemplate.[8]

The Oneidas sent petitions. Since 1634, when the Dutchman Harmen Van den Bogaert left Fort Orange and explored our homeland, wrote the Oneidas to New York State, there has been no conflict between our peoples. "For over 300 years our association has proven mutually beneficial," they added. The Oneidas said they had been paid inadequately by the state for five million acres of their land and asked for access to the state courts so they could sue for money damages. They wanted funds to reestablish a reservation of about ten thousand acres and to finance housing, agriculture, industry, arts, and the preservation of their ancient culture. Say no to the Oneidas' request, recommended the state attorney general. The cost of a potential damage claim, he calculated, might reach $858 million (about $6.5 billion in 2020). From Washington, DC, the BIA informed the Oneidas that there was no need for action because they had submitted a claim to the Indian Claims Commission. That claim, still pending after two decades, was limited to the historic land value, without interest or compensation for almost two centuries of use by others, including Van den Bogaert's descendants.[9]

The Oneidas continued to seek their day in court, but they were shut out. Ejectment cases to recover land belonged in the state courts, but cases involving Indian land claims were a federal matter. The Oneidas filed a test case in federal court in 1970. To circumvent the presumed restrictions against suing a state, Shattuck decided to sue Madison and Oneida Counties for the rental value of county property in 1968 and 1969. The Oneidas claimed they still owned one hundred thousand acres in Oneida and Madison Counties because the Treaty of 1795, conducted without federal approval, was invalid. Shattuck pleaded that the Oneidas had been deprived of due process because both federal and state courts refused to hear their claim. The court ruled that the federal government had no jurisdiction regarding ejectment cases and dismissed the case. The Oneidas appealed.[10]

The United States must obey its own treaties, laws, and promises, declared Shattuck before the US Supreme Court in 1973. He asked the court to allow the Oneidas to sue for redress of wrongs done them by New York State. The attorneys for the state asserted that New York was not bound by the Trade and Intercourse Acts. They argued that an Indian tribe out of possession of its land could not sue in federal court to get it back, because that was a state court matter. A decision against us, warned the state solicitor general, would upset titles all over the eastern United States.[11]

In a landmark decision later known as Oneida I, the US Supreme Court unanimously held that the Trade and Intercourse Acts were applicable to the original thirteen states, including New York. "Indian title is a matter of federal law," wrote Justice Byron White, "and can be extinguished only with federal consent." The court ruled that the Oneidas had the right to be heard in federal court. To Shattuck's surprise, the State of New York ignored the ruling and its implications. It rejected efforts by the Oneidas to negotiate a settlement.[12]

The Oneidas filed two more cases. They claimed their three-hundred-thousand-acre reservation, including the best land, in *Oneida v. Oneida County* (1974), which challenged the validity of treaties made with New York State after 1790. In addition, the New York Oneidas retained the Native American Rights Fund to sue for 750 acres on West Road. This case, called *Oneida Tribe of New York v. Abraham Williams et al.*, revisited the Boylan case over land that had been reserved by treaty in the 1840s for the Home Party and had been taken, the Oneidas said, through invalid tax foreclosure. The purpose of this case against landowners was to pressure the state to negotiate.[13]

When the man from Washington came to serve eviction papers, the West Road farmer Jack Curtin thought it was a joke. The man said he was a federal agent and he was going to take our land, recalled Jack, who replied, "Yeah, and I'm Wyatt Earp." The agent answered, "This isn't funny, sir. You better listen to what I'm telling you." After Jack moved to Oneida in the late 1950s, he had worked on Abe Williams's farm. Later, he and his brothers purchased two hundred acres across the road from the old Honyost place. "They didn't have anything, but they were all nice people," remembered Jack about his Oneida neighbors. "They all lived their own life and we lived next to them."[14]

The twenty-one property owners named in the West Road case elected as their chairman former mayor Abe Williams. They pooled their resources to hire legal counsel. "I am a citizen of the United States," said a West Road resident who worked at Oneida Limited, "but how can I deal with an Indian nation?" Our properties are now worthless, Williams told Herb and the Common Council. The city had received no word on the case from the federal government, responded Herb. His main concern, he said, was to keep feelings "as cool and calm as possible."[15]

The Standing Stone returned to Oneida territory after 125 years at a Utica cemetery. When the Oneidas asked for the stone back, the cemetery trustees acquiesced on the condition that the Indians present proof of their identity. Jake Thompson provided a letter from the BIA stating that the Indians living on the West Road reservation are the "true present leaders of the tribe." The Oneidas were not all in agreement regarding their leadership. Ray Elm, the son of Sylvia Honyost, had been named to succeed Chief Rockwell in the traditional way by the clan mothers. He had been a toddler when his family, as the "real Indians," participated in the Madison County centennial parade. He disputed Jake Thompson's election as president and promised to do his "damnedest" to prevent West Road residents from being evicted. His family, he remembered, knew what it was like to be evicted from their home.[16]

Incidents of vandalism on Native and non-Native West Road properties took on a charged significance. After responding to a suspicious barn fire, the Oneida City fire chief praised Oneida youths for helping to save machinery from the flames. Abe Williams reported that he heard someone on the reservation threaten to "burn every building on West Road." Who, people wanted to know, was responsible for law enforcement and fire protection on the Oneida territory? "Legally, no outside law-enforcement people can enter our nation without our permission," stated Thompson. We know the provisions of our treaties, he said, but with so many differences of opinion on the city, county, and state level, it would help to have the US government clarify matters. The City of Oneida attorney sent a letter to federal officials asking about jurisdiction, but he received no response.[17]

It was mostly Oneidas who listened as the test case was argued in federal court. Their attorney said that when New York State negotiated the Treaty of 1795, it acted in direct contradiction of federal law. "Did you just say that the State of New York acted not out of ignorance, but in direct contradiction to it?" interrupted Judge Edmund Port. That is correct, was the answer. The lawyers for Madison and Oneida Counties asserted that the case should be dismissed because the Oneidas had waited too long to bring suit. In response, the attorneys for the Oneidas showed decades of requests to the BIA for action on land claims and replies advising the Oneidas that they had no case for legal action. The arguments made, the Oneidas awaited a ruling on their case.[18]

Herb and Mary Lou took us on a summer cross-country tour. In South Dakota, we stopped at Laura Ingalls Wilder's home and Mount Rushmore. I don't recall if I was aware of the recent armed standoff at Wounded Knee between Native activists and federal officers. Around the country, Native militants and moderates had organized to resist US Indian policy. "We will not be terminated" was their message as they demanded the fulfillment of treaty rights. Russ and I teased Tom by telling him that a line of trees along a distant ridge was a row of Indians on the warpath about to attack us. What we knew about Indigenous people came from westerns on TV.[19]

Back home, where assimilation remained the expectation, we weren't aware of the Oneidas among us at church or school. To piece together what happened from the perspective of the families of the best land, I have relied on news reports and memories. Both sources are flawed. The newspaper coverage helps to untangle the complicated timeline of events that blur together in people's recollections. While the newspapers tried to be objective, they contained phrases like "last stand," "Indian Giver," and "circle the wagons." Such references are part of the story.

Oneida vs. Oneida

The notion that a collection of secondhand trailers on thirty-two acres constituted a sovereign nation seemed preposterous to many longtime residents. A *Dispatch* reporter noted that, according to the New York State legislative manual, "the Oneida Nation is no longer existent." The city followed the state's example. "The City of Oneida does not acknowledge the existence of an Oneida Indian Nation," declared a letter from the city to George Shattuck in 1975. At the same time, the Common Council voted to cover the legal expenses of the West Road residents, who ran out of funds to pay their lawyers. Fifth Ward alderman John Branigan agreed that the city should come to the aid of the property owners but added, "I wish we could get help from other forms of government." The Common Council then addressed street repairs.[20]

Becki John obeyed when her father told her not to go up to the reservation, where a power struggle was underway. Jake Thompson was removed as president, reinstated, and then replaced by David Honyost, who was part of the group known as the Warrior Society, which endorsed traditional ways and militant action. The divided Oneidas accused each other of crimes and assault. In December, thirty-five Oneidas who opposed the Warrior Society claimed they were forced off the reservation. City firemen responded to a fire that burned down the old Honyost place, by then used for storage. The next evening, the police were called because a shot had been fired, but they concluded the report was unfounded. Local officials feared that public safety personnel were being used as pawns in an internal dispute on the territory. The Oneidas complained of police harassment.[21]

The story of what occurred the next night would be told and retold. Officials said the police were sent to investigate a report of a break-in at the trailer of former president Jake Thompson. A standoff developed between Oneidas and the city police department, Madison County sheriff's officers, and New York State troopers. The police said they had the right to go on the territory and enforce the law. The Oneidas said they would defend their sovereign territory with firepower if necessary.[22]

Someone came out to the farm to pick up Herb and take him to see what was happening at the territory. I remember that Dad looked pale when he returned home. "The Indians had their guns out and the Oneida [City] police were behind trees aiming at the people on the reservation," he recalled. I felt grown-up because I understood why he was worried. Along with good cops, the police department had a few blowhards, who could not be trusted to be patient or cautious. "Get those guys the hell out of there," said Herb when he returned to city hall. "We're not going to have any battle up there."[23]

Herb, the police chief, Public Safety Commissioner Dr. Richard B. Myers, an orthodontist, and Madison County District Attorney William F. O'Brien held a meeting at the police department. The firemen reported that when they had responded to recent calls at the territory, they found themselves in the middle of an armed confrontation between Oneida factions. They had been harassed and their equipment damaged. They said they would not go to the territory without police protection. The Oneidas said their territory was off limits and threatened to shoot city personnel who tried to enter it, recalled Dr. Myers. Herb announced,

"The policy of the City of Oneida will be not to respond with police or fire to the 32-acre site."[24]

Beth, who was nine, remembered the incident as the time when the Oneidas said no police or firemen could come on their land and Dad agreed. Dick Lynch, the Turtle Clan man who was a year ahead of me at Oneida High School, recalled that his friends in the fire and police departments were confused about what was going on and how they were supposed to do their jobs. I did not understand until later that Herb would not say publicly that he was worried about a few officers. The city launched a search for a new police chief who could reform the department and had, as Herb put it, "experience with minorities." That qualification puzzled me. I think he meant someone who would interact respectfully with the Oneidas. That might be as close as Herb came to acknowledging the tension that David Honyost blamed on long-standing racism.[25]

I began to pay attention. I remember believing that the Oneida Indians were right about their land claims, while I could not imagine losing our farm. Growing up during the civil rights movement and the Vietnam War, I sympathized with struggles against discrimination and was skeptical of official pronouncements. My insistence that justice should be done was at odds with my father's focus on practical solutions, which meant that the best land was home to my coming-of-age recognition that I looked at things differently. Meanwhile my friends and I of the Oneida High School class of '76 waited for our lives to begin, which we were pretty sure was not going to happen in Wampsville.

A few days after graduation, I was about to leave for my summer job as a 4-H camp counselor when I answered the phone. Someone from the reservation shouted, "There's a fire! People are dying! Send help! Do something!" I remember feeling stunned and helpless, but I don't remember what I did. Mary Winder's son, Samuel Winder Jr., and his sister-in-law, Janice Winder, died in the fire. The Oneidas who first found the trailer enveloped in fire said they doubted that the man and woman could have been rescued. Even so, I felt what mattered was that the fire department had not tried. "I can't understand how human beings can say they are going to refuse an area fire protection," said David Honyost. Many people, including firefighters, agreed with him. The situation that Herb had hoped to defuse now exploded.[26]

The Associated Press reported that "the fire department was following orders from Mayor Herbert Brewer forbidding city police and fire agencies to respond to calls from the Oneida Indian Territory, a 32-acre trailer court within city limits." Oneida now had the attention of the US Justice Department. Federal officials met with Herb, Commissioner Myers, and representatives of the Warrior Society to work out an agreement on fire and police protection. In October, the Warrior Society's leaders unanimously ratified an agreement with city negotiators, which was to be presented to the Common Council for approval.[27]

The executive board of the Oneida Indian Nation, based on the Onondaga Reservation, insisted that it was the rightful government of the New York Oneidas. It accused the Warrior Society of excluding the nation's duly elected officers from participation in talks with the City of Oneida. The West Road territory, said Robert Burr, president of the executive board, belonged to the entire nation, not to any single group. He accused the Warrior Society of keeping the firemen off the thirty-two acres in the first place. It was a "confusing situation," said Herb, who responded that no one purposely had been excluded. "Our negotiations have been with the residents of the territory," he said. "We're dealing with the people that are there."[28]

Weeks later, the Civil Rights Division of the US Department of Justice launched an investigation of the City of Oneida. The complaint of possible civil rights violations was brought not by the Oneida Indians but by the Oneida County chapter of Rights of American Indians Now (RAIN). Chapter president Michael Monroe said that Senator James Abourezk of South Dakota, chair of the Senate Subcommittee on Indian Affairs, helped RAIN to file the complaint, naming Mayor Brewer. The Justice Department ordered a probe conducted by the Federal Bureau of Investigation. "It seemed rather strange," Herb told the FBI agent, "since we had been working very closely with the Department of Justice trying to negotiate a new agreement with the Indians, that suddenly this investigation comes along."[29]

That spring, the city threatened to shut off city water to the reservation after the West Road Oneidas failed to pay their bills over several months. On behalf of RAIN, Monroe parked his car over the water main and displayed a sign reading, "We remember when Oneidas carried corn on their backs to Valley Forge." The planned water shutoff was part of a "conspiracy to drive the Oneida people from their homeland," he told the area news media, "condoned and led by the mayor." The Oneidas said they appreciated the efforts of Monroe and RAIN on their behalf. They did not seek a confrontation, however, and asked Monroe to move his car and his sign and cancel his press conference, which he did. Asked about RAIN, Herb replied that he did not intend to negotiate with that organization. He wanted, he said, "to deal directly with the Indians." He hoped they would pay the water bill like everyone else.[30]

Gloria Winder Halbritter, a Wolf Clan businesswoman and activist like her mother, Mary Winder, came to see Herb at city hall. In a two-hour meeting that she described as "pleasant and friendly," Gloria explained that poverty and political turmoil on the territory made it hard to pay the water bill. She made a payment of $1,082 to cover the oldest bill and negotiated a payment plan of $200 a month on the remaining $2,585. Herb admired Gloria Halbritter for her forthright manner. Her visit was followed by that of a reporter from a Syracuse TV station who complained that she spent a long, cold day waiting for some blowup between the city and the Oneidas and nothing had happened.[31]

About the water bill, Gloria's son, Arthur Raymond "Ray" Halbritter, said that if they had the money, they probably would pay it. The real issue, he believed, was Oneida sovereignty. To the city of Oneida, he told the *Daily Press* of Utica, "we don't exist as Indian people." As an ironworker in Washington, DC, five years earlier, Ray Halbritter had witnessed the protest called "The Trail of Broken Treaties." A coalition of activists took over the BIA to demand that the United States honor its treaty commitments. Halbritter called the protest a "great awakening for many Native American people, and for me in particular." At age twenty-five, he emerged as the spokesman for the Warrior Society and the West Road Oneidas.[32]

Herb, Gloria, and Ray Halbritter, along with other local officials and Warrior Society members, were sued for $27 million in damages by the faction of Oneidas, who claimed they had been forced off the territory. The Oneida Indian plaintiffs said that the city fire and police departments had allowed the "criminal element," identified as the Oneida Warrior Society, to do whatever it wanted. Those who left did so at their own discretion, said Ray Halbritter, who accused Jake Thompson of blocking an accord on a fire and police protection pact between the city and the West Road Oneidas. Herb said he could not recall whether Thompson had threatened legal action against the city, but Robert Burr had done so. Herb felt the lawsuit involved a leadership question that should be settled by the Oneidas themselves. I remember thinking $27 million was a lot of money.[33]

"Oneida Nation Wins Case," reported the *Dispatch* about the test case in 1977. The state had not complied with the Trade and Intercourse Acts, ruled Judge Port, and so the purchase of Oneida land in 1795 was void.

Oneida and Madison Counties, it was understood, owed back rent to their landlords, the Oneida Indians. The state and the counties appealed the case. "Feds on Their Side: Indian Attacks Are Succeeding," declared a *Daily Press* editorial. The Indians, it noted, were attacking not with bows and arrows but through the federal courts. "One might almost think history is coming back to haunt us," wrote the editors. "And we thought our major problems were inflation, détente and neutron bombs!"[34]

History was commemorated that August by a reenactment of the battle of Oriskany on its two hundredth anniversary. The movie *Drums along the Mohawk*, made in 1939 and starring Henry Fonda, served as a reference for the participants, who suffered blisters on their hike to the site of the ambush. There was little mention of the Oneidas. Back-to-back with a newspaper article about the significance of the Revolutionary War battle was a photograph of a beaming Lyman K. "Jake" John and Ray Halbritter holding a map of Oneida and Madison Counties. "We don't want to take anybody's land—we're not that kind of people," said Halbritter. "After what we've been through, do you think we want to drive some farmer off a place he thought was his own for a hundred

FIGURE 39. This newspaper photograph of Lyman John and Arthur Raymond "Ray" Halbritter was accompanied by articles headlined "Tribe Wins in Courts" and "Indians Want Justice, Not Evictions." *Syracuse Herald American*, 7 August 1977. Karst Collection.

years or more?" The Oneidas wanted justice, "whatever cash award that is worked out," and maybe a "good-sized portion of a state forest," he explained.[35]

"If this land isn't safe, then what's all this stuff about the American dream?" asked Jack Curtin. West Road landowners, whose case had been pending awaiting Judge Port's ruling, reacted to the Oneidas' victory with dismay. Herb went to Albany for help and was told there was no issue. Although he thought Congress should act, he understood why it didn't. He had seen a map of Indian land claims spreading across the entire country. "That was quite an eye opener," he recalled. It was "going to take big bucks" to resolve that, he thought.[36]

Herb announced that fire and police protection would be restored to the Oneida territory. The Justice Department had threatened to sue the city for the "racially discriminatory use of federal monies" in violation of the General Revenue Sharing Act. Alderman William Matthews, an attorney at Oneida Limited, said, "I think the action of the Justice Department in raising this complaint stinks." The city maintained that the policy of nonresponse was the result of "overt aggressive acts of hostility on the part of all or some of the occupants" of the territory and "the threat of immediate deadly physical force to members" of the city fire and police departments.[37]

By then, the City of Oneida and the Oneida Indians told different stories about what had led to the no-protection policy. Both Herb and Ray Halbritter presented their "side" as much more united than it was, which enhanced the "us versus them" theme of their accounts. "The police, the district attorney, and the city officials were determined to force their way on our land," said Ray Halbritter. "[W]e just want to have the police ask permission to come on our land to preserve our old treaty rights for our children." He dismissed the notion that firemen would be endangered on the reservation. Herb stated that he always believed that the city had the right and responsibility to provide police and fire protection services on the Oneida territory. When he said that services had been withdrawn only because of the threat of violence, he left out his concern about the police officers he privately characterized as flamethrowers.[38]

The police agreed to enter Oneida territory "by invitation only," announced the new police chief. Some officers complained that the politicians had caved to the Oneidas' show of force. The newspaper reported that in accordance with federal laws recognizing the rights of Indian territories, the thirty-two-acre site was not subject to taxation and therefore did not pay for fire and police services. Politics as well as conflicting perspectives on equality, rights, and sovereignty shaped different versions of the same event. Looking back, said Dick Lynch, "it's hard to know where the truth is and where the truth isn't."[39]

"We've Got a Can of Worms Here"

Herb held a press conference in September to release copies of letters seeking action on the land claims. "We're asking the units of government that were responsible for the problem to get in there and solve it," he said. The state should take over the city's defense, he contended, because it had acquired the land from the Indians. Herb heard nothing from Albany. House Speaker Thomas P. "Tip" O'Neill turned his letter over to congressional committee. To President Jimmy Carter, Herb wrote, "The Indians and the property owners in these actions have been wronged and harmed because of inaction or action by the federal government." The White House referred the matter to the Justice Department's Land and Natural Resources Division, which passed it on to the Department of the Interior.[40]

In 1977, Herb ran for reelection against Abe Williams for the third time. The former mayor criticized the increased water rates and accused Herb of being a big spender. Herb argued that adequate water and sewer systems were necessary for economic development, a major issue in upstate New York as manufacturing jobs disappeared. Williams felt there should be more discussion of the $27 million lawsuit filed by Oneida Indians against the city. Herb deplored the inaction of the state on the land claims. "They're sitting back and letting us take it on the chin," he said. Brewer had "run into some pretty difficult problems," said the *Dispatch* editors who endorsed him. "He has wisely abstained from grandstanding" and shown he "will work hard to reach a fair solution." When Abe congratulated Herb on his victory, he said he had known the Brewer family for years.[41]

Herb and Mary Lou borrowed money to buy the Peebles farm next door when it came up for sale. The property included former Deferrier and Cobb land on both sides of Cowaselon Creek as well as land that once belonged to Abraham Denny. No one recalled any concern about the Oneida Indian claim to this land despite the court ruling in favor of the Oneidas. In the meantime, as had Frank and DeVerne, Herb acquired farm property adjacent to the best land when it became available. Uncle Dick had sold out to move to Arizona, and Herb had become sole operator of the 450-acre farm.[42]

Herb and Mary Lou kept the farmland and sold the Peebles house and barn to Becki John Karst and her husband, Terry. Terry ran a tree service and Becki worked for Carrier International Corporation in Syracuse. While growing up, Becki often had visited her mother's family farm down the road. Becki and Herb now lived across Cowaselon Creek from each other. They were the great-great-great-great-grandchildren of the Revolutionary War allies Honyery and Henry Timmerman, but they didn't know that. Only later did I figure out that Becki's ancestors and mine had lived next to each other at least since the 1760s.[43]

A few months later, in March 1978, the front page of the *Dispatch* featured a map showing the six-million-acre corridor of the original Oneida territory running from Canada to Pennsylvania. The map accompanied the news that the Oneida Indian Nation of New York had filed a claim for $12 million and all the state land within their aboriginal territory. The Oneidas cited the guarantee of this land made by the US government at the Treaty of Fort Stanwix in 1784. This claim was ludicrous, said the editors of the *Daily Press*. The Indians were "not going to help

FIGURE 40. Brewer Farm around 1977. Herb and Mary Lou purchased the Peebles farm that included land along Cowaselon Creek. They sold the house and the barn in the upper right-hand corner to Terry and Becki John Karst. Brewer Collection.

their cause by being so unrealistic," they warned. "There could even be a backlash."[44]

In Wampsville, the county board of supervisors decided not to appeal the ruling on the test case. The case "is a loser," said Madison County Attorney William L. Burke, ruefully noting that Madison County, created in 1806, did not even exist in 1795 when the state made its illegal purchase of the land in question. As officials began the process of identifying the county property on which they owed rent to the Oneidas, they found discrepancies regarding the boundaries defined by old treaties and maps. "There seems to be general confusion here," said a mapmaker from the Department of the Interior. Meanwhile, the county needed to borrow $3 million to replace the old jail, which no longer met fire safety standards. No one will loan us money because of the dispute over who owns the land, said the chair of the board of supervisors. "We've got a can of worms here."[45]

If you want to engage Mayor Brewer in conversation, ask him about Indian land claims, wrote the *Dispatch* reporter Doug Carroll. It would not be a quick chat, because Herb would lay out all the cases moving through the courts. There was the case pending at the Indian Claims Commission, the test case, the West Road case, the case regarding the three-hundred-thousand-acre reservation, and the case for the Oneidas' original six million acres. Some cases involved Oneidas from New York, Wisconsin, and Canada, and some involved only the New York Oneidas, who were split into factions. Herb knew the federal government honored old agreements by handing out "blankets," which he described as "peanuts." Throughout history, the claims issue had not been dealt with "promptly and with justice," he told Carroll. "Now we're paying the price."[46]

"Oneida Indians Win Claims Battle," read a *Dispatch* headline in October 1978. The Indian Claims Commission had ruled against the US government for failing to secure Oneida lands as promised. In his decision, Judge Oscar H. Davis recounted "the nature of chicanery" practiced by Governor George Clinton and the state commissioners at the Treaties of 1785 and 1788. "New York had only a right to purchase lands; it did not have a right to practice coercion or deception on the Indians," said Davis. Both the state and federal governments were at fault, concluded the ruling.[47]

We have a dilemma to be solved, wrote Doug Carroll. "What can be done now to compensate for injustices committed almost two centuries ago?" People wanted to know: did the Oneidas want land or money or both? There was talk that the elective faction wanted money and the

Warrior Society wanted land. Not true, said spokesmen for the elective faction. "Money alone is not our objective." It was the land that guaranteed a home for future generations of Oneidas. Ray Halbritter, speaking on behalf of the West Road Oneidas, said he wasn't all that interested in money. "Land is what's important to us," he declared. Land was the answer that frightened residents. Money could come from elsewhere; the land could not.[48]

It rankled local people that the Oneidas seemed to have the funds to launch multiple land claims cases but could not pay their water bill of $2,406.17. Herb said the city already had been more generous in working out a payment schedule with the Oneidas than it had with other property owners who were in arrears. There had been talks and letters of warning. Typically, when residents failed to pay their water bill, the amount owed was added to their taxes, recalled city water superintendent Rex Niles, but that was not an option for the Oneidas on the West Road territory, who did not pay property taxes. In November, a water department crew went on the thirty-two-acre territory and shut off the water supply.[49]

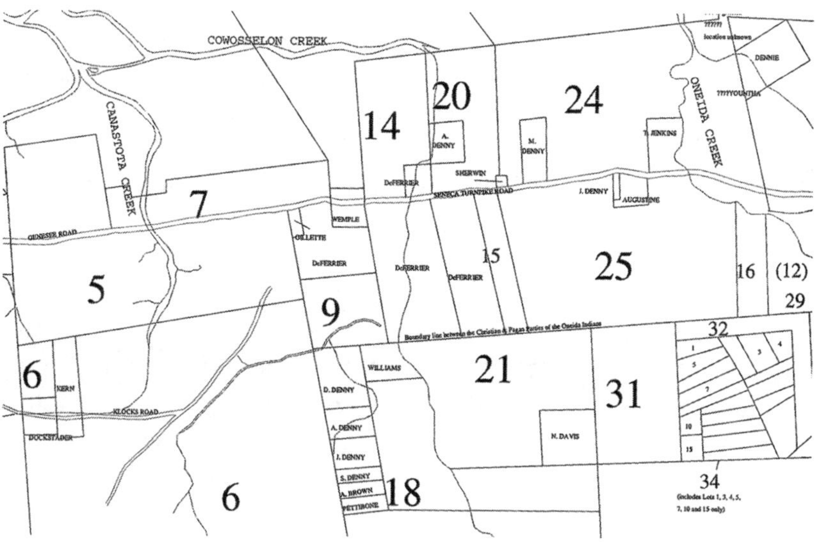

FIGURE 41. Detail from map of the parcels ceded in treaties made by the Oneidas with New York State from 1788 to 1846, including lots reserved to Angel Deferrier and members of the Denny and Doxtator families. The best land is located in numbers 14 and 20, designating respectively the Treaties of 1815 and 1824. "Oneida Nation Land Rights, Docket 301 Map 1," revised in 1973. Courtesy of the Oneida Nation of Wisconsin.

"Water will not be allowed to flow through Oneida land," announced the Oneida Indian Territory Council in retaliation. By this time, the Oneidas on West Road had set up a territorial council, a men's council, and a women's council. Rex Niles remembered that at the meetings he attended, he had the clear impression that the women were in charge. For the Oneidas, self-governance meant getting everyone to reach consensus. "It took us four or five days to agree," said an Oneida man. "But when we did, it was unanimous by the community." The Oneidas had the money to pay the bills, they announced at a press conference, but were postponing payment as a "matter of principle" until Brewer and other city officials met with them to discuss the right-of-way of the water pipeline. "We're always willing to talk," Herb responded, but he insisted that "the question about right of way has nothing to do with free water." Copies of all correspondence between the city and the territory related to the water bills, he said, had been forwarded to the Community Relations Service of the Department of Justice.[50]

What alarmed Herb was the threat by the Oneidas to block water to residents and farms south of the territory. The Common Council approved a plan to install a water pipeline on the other side of West Road. When the Oneida Indian Territory Council announced that they would not disturb the water line, Herb expressed concern that tribal leadership, which had changed at least four times in recent years, might change in the future and again threaten the pipeline. The Oneidas announced a plan to drill wells that would make the territory independent of the city. Their spokesmen added that a relocated pipeline across the road, while not on the reservation, still would be installed on land taken from them illegally.[51]

During this dispute, DeVerne was dying. Every day Mabelle read to him his favorite psalm, about green pastures and still waters. In her remaining years, she never recovered her spark. A few days after the funeral, Herb met with tribal council members on their territory. Everyone was polite, but they failed to resolve the water issue. The well dug by the Oneidas did not provide enough water, and, according to the state Health Department, it had a high bacteria count and was causing illness among the children. With the involvement of the Justice Department Community Relations Service, the city and the territory residents reached an agreement where the city would provide water and the residents would pay their back bills.[52]

From Onondaga, Robert Burr accused the city of refusing to negotiate with the elected government of the Oneida Nation, which, he said, owned the water meter on the territory but was not liable for the debt incurred by the current residents. He declared that Ray Halbritter had no authority to act on behalf of the Oneida Nation. "That's their argument, not ours," Herb said. "Ray lives out there . . . and he came forth as their representative." By then, Herb, as he conducted city affairs, repeatedly had reinforced the claim of the West Road Oneidas that they were the rightful leaders of the New York Oneidas because they lived on Oneida territory.[53]

"Let's settle the land claims!" demanded the *Dispatch* editors. That meant the question of who spoke for the New York Oneidas must be resolved. Two years earlier, the BIA had stated that it did not recognize "any faction as representing the Oneida Nation as a whole" and said that it was up to the Oneidas to decide who represented them. Now tasked with directing the formation of a government that represented all New York Oneidas, the BIA tried for months and failed. "We don't have to agree on who will lead now," said Robert Burr. "We've already won back our land with the Judge Port decisions. It took over 200 years so we can wait a while longer until the appeals process is completed." Waiting was not popular with city residents. Herb, like many local officials, felt the matter should not be resolved by the courts. Because the Oneidas are right about their land and the law is on their side, I remember saying.[54]

Local pressure on Congressman James M. Hanley, the Democrat from Syracuse whose Thirty-Second District included Oneida, mounted. In Wampsville, Madison County lawmakers voted unanimously to have the congressman sponsor legislation that would retroactively approve the treaties made between the Oneidas and New York State. The testimony presented to the Indian Claims Commission showed that the federal government was fully aware "that New York was abusing the Oneidas and virtually stealing their land," said Hanley. The burden, he argued, should be shifted from property owners to the federal government for its failure to exercise its trust responsibility to the Oneidas. "My constituents in New York are not interested in becoming pawns in . . . some penitential rite of national remorse for the sins of long ago," he said.[55]

Hanley introduced a bill that would extend federal ratification to New York State's treaties and extinguish all the aboriginal titles of the Oneidas. That bill will never get out of committee, said Robert Burr. "Every Indian in the country would be up in arms if they passed legislation extinguishing our rights in the courts." Suzan Harjo of the Native American Rights Fund explained that when activists at Wounded Knee had demanded treaty rights, they were told to work within the system, and so they were, by spending years in courtrooms to get the United

States to honor its own laws. "And if the government or anybody else is going to tell us—now that the system is working for us—that the system is wrong . . . well, I don't like to think of the consequences," she said.[56]

Herb approved of Congressman Hanley's legislation, and I did not. "I strongly feel that the constitutional rights of Americans should supersede treaty rights," Herb said. "We all agree that there were wrongs made against the Indians in the past, but we cannot have sovereign nations within a sovereign nation." I remember feeling like we lived in a swirl of contradictions. I thought it would be wrong for Congress to make the state's illegal action legal. Wouldn't that mean admitting that the Oneidas were right about their land and then depriving them of it again? How could Americans tell the Oneidas they must follow the rules and then change the rules? The legal quagmires of the land claims eluded me. I didn't know what title insurance was. I felt a vague sympathy for the West Road property owners. I didn't want to lose our farm.[57]

"This Has Always Been Ours"

"This has always been ours," said a member of the Oneida Territorial Council. The council invited Herb to meet under a tree at the territory entrance to discuss water bills and fire and police protection. The city had shut off the water again after the Oneidas failed to pay their bill. The proposal that, if called, the fire department would wait at the entrance until invited in was dismissed as ridiculous by a territory resident. She wanted to know that her house was protected by firefighters. It was the police the Oneidas wanted to enter only when invited. "The firemen would feel an awful lot better if one policeman could come down here with them," said a deputy fire chief.[58]

A few days earlier, city firemen had come to the territory to put out a trailer fire thought to have been set deliberately, but they had been kicked out by an armed and belligerent Oneida man. Ray Halbritter was criticized by some Oneidas for going to the police station to request the man's arrest for obstructing firefighting. When the man was shot to death by another Oneida Indian a few days later, the territory residents relied on the city police to handle the case. The West Road Oneidas for a time renounced Ray Halbritter as their spokesman.[59]

That summer, Herb ran in and lost the Republican congressional primary after Hanley announced he would not seek reelection. Herb enjoyed talking about the issues, but after hours of gladhanding, he liked to come home, pick up a hoe, and head to the garden to do what he called "honest work." In doing so, he confirmed my suspicion that life in Washington would have been tough on him. He was not the "world's greatest orator," said the *Dispatch*. "Brewer would take to the Congress expertise in what is possibly the most pressing issue for the district: resolution of the pending Indian land claims."[60]

That summer, I saw Dewitt Cobb outside his garage. "I'm DeVerne's granddaughter," I said. He looked at me and said twice, "I am ninety years old." Was this his way of telling me to get off his lawn, I wondered as I went on my way, or was he contemplating the passing of time? Some years earlier, Aunt Joanne had taken me to visit Dewitt, who lived in "the Cottage," which had been built by his great-uncle Charles Deferrier. I dimly remember a chipped linoleum floor and enormous dark paintings in gilded frames on the walls. Out in the carriage house, Dewitt showed Joanne an old sleigh upholstered in burgundy leather that had been chewed by squirrels. He was proud of the butternut tree next to Polly and Angel's grave.[61]

A recent news article had described the journey of Dewitt's great-grandfather Angel Deferrier from the fantastic richness of Versailles to a dirt-floored cabin outside of Wampsville and his marriage to Polly Denny, who was part French and from a nearby Oneida village. "I am their last living relative," Dewitt said. "We've lived on this land for nearly 200 years." Most likely there were descendants of Angel and Polly elsewhere, but Dewitt was the last on the original property. When Dewitt died, Mary Lou and Herb went to the auction at the Deferrier homestead. The antique dealers came out in force, Mary Lou said, because nothing ever had been moved out of that house. Some of the paintings and furniture went for thousands of dollars. Also sold were old letters and documents. It was a shame, Mary Lou felt, that they did not go to the historical society.[62]

As mayor, Herb had been contacted by the Countess d'Andigné, mayor of Condillac in southeastern France. She asked that her village of ninety-six inhabitants perched above the Rhone River become a twin city with Oneida. She explained that her family had taken refuge near Oneida during the French Revolution and that it had maintained the tradition of naming the eldest daughter Oneida ever since. Herb, who had never heard of this family, agreed. He wrote back about establishing new friendships and mentioned possible exchanges of emissaries between the city and the descendants of Mademoiselle Oneida.[63]

I was in graduate school in London when I became an emissary of sorts while traveling with my friend Linda. The countess, born Françoise Marie Therese Jeanne, Princesse de Faucigny Lucinge and Coligny, picked us up at the train station in her Volkswagen. She had married the late Charles d'Andigné, the great-grandson of the first Oneida, in Paris in 1935.

From the window of our rooms in the chateau, we observed a gardener raking the driveway gravel into straight lines. "We have never been anywhere like this before," said Linda. "We'll probably make mistakes, so let's go ahead and enjoy it." The elderly butler did his best to shepherd us through the visit. In front of a map left by the US general who made the chateau his headquarters in 1944, he formally thanked us for the liberation of his country, and we humbly accepted on behalf of ours.[64]

The countess said there were dungeons in the twelfth-century tower, but she did not show them to us. She pointed out the paintings of Greek myths on the walls and ceilings, restored by the first Oneida when she returned from the New World. The countess also wanted us to see the large murals that illustrated the family history. On one wall was a portrayal of the family in the Crusades. Another featured the Marquis de Blâcons standing before the Estates General. A third showed the family in the forests of the American frontier with their Oneida Indian friends.

The butler, who had changed into formal attire, served dinner. The countess asked about the great industrial city of Oneida and wondered if we wore evening dresses very often. She told us about coming home one day during World War II to find GIs guarding the gate. US soldiers still sent her Christmas cards, she said. She was surprised they remembered her, and we were not. Concentrating on the conversation, I failed to pay attention to the countess's lead on what to do and missed out on putting aside the finger bowl. The butler whispered instructions to me, but I did not understand, so I kept moving things until I finally relocated the right object. He nodded and we both smiled in victory.

The chateau was in a beautiful and lonely place. "One keeps it because one has a responsibility," said the countess. Herb told me that he had written to thank her for making a princess out of his farm girl. Not quite, Dad, I thought, remembering the finger bowl incident. A few years later, the countess's daughter, Oneida d'Andigné, visited Oneida. She presented the city with a portrait of the first Oneida and was given an engraved silver platter made by Oneida Limited. She said she hoped to bring her granddaughter, also named Oneida, to visit someday.[65]

The *Dispatch* reported that Oneida d'Andigné was named after the lake or the city, which had not existed when the first Oneida was born. It did not occur to me or my father or anyone else, as far as I can tell, to mention that the Oneida Indians might have been the more appropriate recipient of gratitude from this French family. Herb's letter to the countess on the Office of the Mayor stationery featured the seal of the City of Oneida—the profile of a Native man wearing a feathered headdress.

After all that had happened over fire and water, we still did not consider the Oneidas a part of our present with a real say rather a symbolic one.[66]

Being mayor of Oneida was a "total commitment," said Herb as he announced he would not run for a seventh term in 1983. The land claims cases remained unresolved, while the water and sewer projects were completed despite the "terrible bureaucratic process," he recalled. I once asked him what he was most proud of accomplishing as mayor. "The trees," he answered. In a citywide program, hundreds and hundreds of trees were planted to replace the great elms that had succumbed to Dutch elm disease.[67]

By then, Mary Lou had taken a job at Cornell University as assistant director of Cooperative Extension in charge of New York State's 4-H program. Although Herb talked with her about the problems and the people he dealt with as mayor, she doesn't remember many details given that her days were filled with a demanding job as Oneida County Extension coordinator and a busy household. Mary Lou was surprised when Herb encouraged her to accept the position. He said he would leave the farm and be a trailing spouse. Herb became executive director of the Tompkins County Chamber of Commerce. Asked whether he would run for office again, he answered, "No way!" It was a great experience, he said, but he didn't miss the long days.[68]

Tom and Russ took over running the farm as the United States was hit by the worst farm crisis since the Great Depression. Milk prices dropped and interest rates doubled. Farmers, encouraged by government officials and lenders to think big, had taken out risky loans that now they could not repay. In 1985, thousands of farmers occupied the National Mall in Washington, DC. At the US Department of Agriculture headquarters, they planted hundreds of black crosses for victims of foreclosure and suicide. Russ gave up the seed business he had taken over from DeVerne, because he didn't like to demand payment from struggling neighbors. The debt on the farm became a strain. Russ and Tom started milking three times a day. "The good thing and the bad thing about farming," recalled Russ, "is that there is always something to do."[69]

The Oneidas won the test case at the US Supreme Court in 1985. In another landmark decision, known as Oneida II, the court upheld the Oneidas' claim to one hundred thousand acres in Oneida and Madison Counties. It rejected the argument made by the counties that the Indians had not made a timely effort to sue and thus had forfeited their legal rights. The court suggested that, because of the enormous economic implications of the case, Congress should help settle the claims.[70]

"This decision," said Justice John Paul Stevens in his dissent, "upsets long-settled expectations in the ownership of real property in the Counties of Oneida and Madison, New York, and the disruption it is sure to cause will confirm the common-law wisdom that ancient claims are best left in repose." He warned, "The Court, no doubt, believes that it is undoing a grave historical injustice, but in doing so it has caused another, which only Congress may now rectify."[71]

To Oneida and Madison Counties, the ruling was a catastrophe. A "total victory for the Indians," said Allan Van Gestel, the attorney for the counties. "I've just read it and I'm picking myself up off the floor," he told a reporter. The chairman of the Madison County Board of Supervisors said he would seek relief from Congress. "The farmers are having a hard enough time without having to pay for a settlement," he said. "We're just innocent bystanders," protested a West Road property owner. "The state better come up with some bucks." Governor Mario Cuomo told landowners not to worry. "Government made the mistake," he said. "Government has to make it good." Noting that the Supreme Court ruled that it would be up to the state courts to determine whether New York State owed damages, local officials were skeptical as they awaited action.[72]

"It's significant for all Oneidas," said Ray Halbritter. "We can start anew," said Robert Burr. With the land, the rival Oneida leaders agreed, they would be able to build a future. The Oneidas wanted their children to learn about their heritage through living it, rather than merely reading about it in the white man's textbooks, explained Ray Halbritter and his aunt, the Wolf Clan mother Maisie Winder Shenandoah. "It's nice that we have all the legalities on our side," they said, but more important was being recognized as "a nation of Indian people who have a right to live here on their own land and decide for themselves what their life's work is going to be."[73]

Chapter 10

Ancestral Claims

The soil of the best land has a story. Around twelve thousand years ago, when the ice melted, a large body of water called Lake Iroquois collected on the Oneida plain. As Lake Iroquois receded, it left behind glacial till and organic deposits south of its remnant, Oneida Lake. The soil was enriched by minerals and nutrients from Cowaselon Creek and its watershed, which flows down over highly erodible shale and limestone. The deep silt loam, called the Wampsville series, makes up less than 1 percent of the soils in Madison County, according to a report my brother Russ wrote in college. "You could grow good crops in wet years and dry years," said Uncle Dick. "It is fantastic ground."[1]

Only my brother Tom and his family were still on Brewer Farm by the late 1980s. Tom had married after studying mechanics at SUNY Morrisville. Russ concluded that the farm could not support two families and decided to go to Cornell University to study agricultural economics, a subject he felt he needed to understand during a national farm crisis. Beth majored in early childhood education at SUNY Geneseo. "Much change is happening to the Brewer children," wrote Herb to me in London where I was doing dissertation research. Tom, he said, was carrying a heavy load. "I saw the animals a couple of weeks ago and they looked good—particularly the youngstock," he reported. "They

FIGURE 42. Brewer Farm in the 1980s. Brewer Collection.

have really done well in only a year's time." Tom was working too many hours on the farm, thought Beth.[2]

Tom's four children were the seventh generation of the family to be born on Oneida territory and the fourth to be born on the best land. To them the farm meant freedom. "You always had room to run," recalled Josh, the youngest. "You were never bored." You could ride bikes back and forth to the barn. You could jump on the hay bales and build forts. You could look for crawfish and skip stones in the creek and ride four-wheelers through it. You could help your dad do the milking, feed the calves, and ride along on the tractor. At the end of the day, you could head home triumphantly filthy.[3]

A fire devoured the old barn, built sometime in the 1800s, probably by Nelson and Mary Deferrier Cobb, and added on to by the Brewers. Tom was in the machine shop when he saw the smoke. He and a farm-hand chased the heifers out of the barn, but they lost two calves. "We just couldn't get back in there to get them," Tom recalled. "All the wires and stuff were popping." Firefighters from Oneida, Wampsville, Canastota, Sconondoa, and Oneida Castle battled intense heat to save nearby buildings. The fire marshal said he thought the blaze was caused by a water pump that had overheated. About three thousand bales of hay were lost. Tom had to round up cows scattered in the cornfield, he told a *Dispatch* reporter. "It's going to be a long day."[4]

On the Oneida Nation territory, the bingo hall was torched. Back in the 1970s, the Oneidas had decided to raise funds to buy their own firefighting equipment by holding bingo games like the Wampsville Volunteer Fire Department did. When tribal council members were arrested for conducting bingo games without a state license, their attorneys contended that the city court had no jurisdiction to hear the case. The Madison County assistant district attorney argued that under the US Code, passed in 1948, Congress intended to give the state and city jurisdiction over offenses committed by or against Indians on Indian land. The Oneidas responded that the state could not enforce its bingo laws in Canada or Switzerland or on their thirty-two acres of sovereign land.[5]

The bingo hall, built in the mid-1980s, brought in over $7 million its first year. On West Road, the Warrior Society splintered over profits and power. The hall became the site of clashes between rivals wielding baseball bats and firing shots. After a loud explosion followed by fire destroyed the hall, four Oneidas and a Mohawk man were convicted of conspiring to commit arson. "I've lived the land claims to see Oneida people come back here, but what's the sense of sovereignty if you can't be protected on your own land?" asked the clan mother Maisie Shenandoah. "I'm not against traditional people, but warriors carrying guns against their own people, there is nothing traditional about that."[6]

Some Oneidas blamed local public safety officers for failing to protect them, while city officials felt hamstrung. Mayor Army Carinci criticized the policy that permitted police officers to go on the territory only if invited. The city and the US Justice Department signed a memorandum pledging "equal protection" to the reservation. Madison and Oneida Counties concluded agreements regarding the new Oneida Nation police force, which had the authority to make arrests and investigate crimes on land owned or leased by the Oneidas. Tensions over jurisdiction persisted.[7]

With their bingo profits, the Oneida Indians bought forty-two acres, the first of their ancestral homeland to be reacquired. Within a few years, the Oneidas purchased almost a thousand acres from willing sellers. There was land available as area farms went out of business. I thought it was sad to see families, after years of work and dreams, lose their farms, but it also seemed unfair that the Oneidas had to buy land that rightfully belonged to them. Although I no longer lived in Oneida, my feelings about land, family, history, and justice remained conflicted.[8]

In 1989, the Oneidas of New York, Wisconsin, and Canada lost their claim for the six million acres of their original territory. Under the Articles of Confederation, said the US Court of Appeals, New York State did not have to get the permission of the national government to conduct treaties. "I think they're wrong," said Arlinda Locklear, the attorney for the Oneidas. The Oneidas had a "strong moral claim," she said, because the United States in the 1780s did not, as it had promised, protect the Oneidas in their dealings with New York State. James Madison, I suspect, would have agreed with her, but whether he would have done anything about it is another question.[9]

"Land is the issue," declared the Haudenosaunee faithkeeper Oren Lyons. "Original title is a problem for all of you," he said before the United Nations General Assembly in New York in 1992. Spain, the United States, and Canada initially had supported a plan to celebrate the five hundredth anniversary of Christopher Columbus's "encounter" with the New World as a time when Europeans brought gifts of civilization and Christianity to the people of the Americas. Indigenous peoples proposed a year of mourning instead. Their global activism on behalf of sovereignty and human rights led the United Nations to declare 1993 to be "The Year of the Indigenous Peoples." Lyons, an All-American lacrosse player, history professor, artist, and environmental activist, gave the opening address at the UN headquarters, located in the Turtle Bay neighborhood of Manhattan.[10]

Lyons spoke of the Great Law of Peace and how it instructed the people to share, respect freedom, and love Mother Earth. "Five hundred years ago, you came to our pristine lands," he said. "You brought us disease and death and the idea of Christian dominion over heathens, pagans, savages." Lyons talked about the degraded environment and broken treaties. "The catastrophe that we have suffered at the hands of our brothers from across the seas has been unremitting and inexcusable," he said. "[W]e share the same River of Life—what befalls me, befalls you." To survive, "we must join hands with the rest of Creation," he concluded before a standing ovation.[11]

On the best land, Tom struggled to keep the farm going. He tried to share cows and equipment with neighbors, but it did not work out. The herd numbers and the milk production declined. To make ends meet, he sold "really beautiful" topsoil from the pasture along the creek.

A cloud of volcanic ash created by the eruption of Mount Pinatubo in the Philippines caused global temperatures to drop, turning 1992 into a bad crop year during an economic recession. Unable to cover the bills and make loan payments, Tom negotiated an agreement with the West Road farmer Jack Curtin. It gave the Curtin Dairy an option to purchase the Brewer farm. In the meantime, the Curtins leased the farm and took over the debt. With sadness and relief, Tom went to work for the Curtin Dairy, while his family continued to live on the best land.[12]

Also in 1993, Ray Halbritter, on behalf of the Oneida Indian Nation, negotiated a gaming compact with New York governor Mario Cuomo, as required by the federal Indian Gaming Regulatory Act. Under the compact, the Oneidas did not have to share their revenue or settle the land claims. The state should not enrich itself on gambling profits, Cuomo later explained. "It's not good governance and it's not a good way to run a good economy." The governor felt that the income from gaming could make up for centuries of discrimination by the state and federal governments against Indians. "They had nothing," said Cuomo. "Halbritter came to us and made the case in our language." The Oneida spokesman had discussed economic development and self-sufficiency.[13]

Following the deaths of Richard Chrisjohn of the Bear Clan and Lyman K. John of the Turtle Clan, the Wolf Clan representative Ray Halbritter had become the sole spokesman for the Oneidas in Oneida. He had studied business at Syracuse University and completed a law degree at Harvard University in 1990. "I wanted to get the education that, in my opinion, the most powerful people in America have had," he explained about his decision to apply only to Harvard. "Before, I sat at the table and understood what I wanted but not what they wanted. Now I understand the complex world we all live in." From then on, Ray Halbritter usually was referred to in the national press as "Harvard-educated."[14]

The Oneida Indian Nation opened the Turning Stone Casino on a former cornfield at the thruway exit in Verona, located between the best land and the old Oneida Carrying Place. It was in the middle of nowhere, said a *New York Times* reporter, describing the first casino opened by Natives in New York State and the state's first legal casino since the 1870s. Within a year the Oneidas paid off the $10 million they had borrowed to construct Turning Stone. In addition, they built housing, set up a health department, offered after-school programs and college scholarships, and opened a language school. Joy as well as tears were part of the hard work of saving an intricate language. As she neared the end of her life, the Turtle Clan woman Marion John Miles turned to her youngest daughter and said words Penny Raymond could not understand. “My beautiful little baby,” translated Penny’s sister. With intensive training, Penny became fluent in the Oneida language, which she planned to teach her grandchildren.[15]

Descendants of the Home Party took part in the rebuilding of the nation, as it now was known locally. Dick Lynch, who had a business degree from Utica College, worked on economic diversification. He was excited about the opportunities for the Oneidas and everyone else in the depressed upstate economy. “You put five hundred people to work, or a thousand people to work,” they buy groceries, purchase cars, and build houses, and the benefits multiplied through the community, explained Dick. “All just very, very positive.” Becki Karst worked in a department dedicated to researching and preserving Indigenous culture. After years of campaigning by the Six Nations for the restoration of sacred objects, the Beechtree-Webster wampum string, one of the oldest documented anywhere, was returned to the Oneidas by the American Museum of Natural History.[16]

Becki witnessed the Oneidas’ exuberance as well as the rivalries among them. Some of the dissenters, as they were called, were joined by Haudenosaunee traditionalists in opposition to gaming, which they warned led to greed, corruption, and addiction. Some criticized the leadership of Ray Halbritter, who, not without controversy, had been named the federally recognized Oneida Indian Nation representative. They charged, for example, that Halbritter signed the casino compact with Governor Cuomo without formal consent from his people. Dissenters, who took part in a peaceful “March for Democracy,” were informed that they had “lost their voice” in the nation’s political affairs. Some lost their jobs at Oneida Nation enterprises or their share of profits.[17]

The Oneida Indian Nation became the largest employer in Madison and Oneida Counties. It ran gas stations and convenience stores, operated marinas on Oneida Lake, constructed championship golf courses, and opened a spa, a convention center, and luxury boutiques. The Turning Stone resort looked like Emerald City rising out of the land of Oz, thought two reporters from out of town. The Oneidas had built an upstate tourist attraction second only to Niagara Falls. Now known as the CEO of Oneida Nation Enterprises, Halbritter made no apology for the creation of an entertainment empire. “We tried poverty for 200 years; we decided to try something else,” he said.[18]

Turning Stone got around the state law banning slot machines, the most lucrative game, by installing the world's first video slotless machine. Although the Oneidas initially banned alcohol at the casino in acknowledgment of its damaging influence on their past, they applied to the state for approval to sell it. The casinos were turning everything around, noted the comedian Charlie Hill, a Wisconsin Oneida. "Remember a long time ago when the white man used to get the Indian drunk and take his money?"[19]

A Lot of Heartache

A fundamental right of sovereignty is not to be taxed. Although the Oneida Indian Nation paid about $25 million in payroll taxes for their local non-Native employees, it did not pay corporate tax or sales tax. It did not pay school taxes, but it voluntarily gave over $5 million in Silver Covenant Chain of Friendship Grants to local school districts. It did not pay property taxes on the more than four thousand acres it purchased in Madison and Oneida Counties. It was part of their reservation, the Oneidas claimed, with the backing of federal court rulings that held the Oneidas could reestablish their sovereign territory—at least within the land claim area—by buying it back.[20]

Local people complained about the increasing tax burden on the remaining property owners. A Peterboro man protested by suing the state for the taxes he had paid since 1985 when the US Supreme Court ruled that New York State had acquired Oneida territory illegally. If the Oneidas still own the land, he asked, "how come I'm paying New York state taxes on it?" A thousand residents signed a petition to the governor in opposition to Oneida Nation plans to build a truck stop, mini-casino, and hotel on property it had purchased next to the Canastota thruway exit. The state's compact with the Oneidas allowed them to conduct gaming on "nation land," but it did not spell out whether "nation land" meant the federally recognized thirty-two-acre reservation or the entire land claim area.[21]

Out on West Road, it had been two decades since the Curtin brothers had been threatened with eviction, and nothing had happened. The Oneidas told the brothers what they were doing, and they seemed to have a strong case, felt Jack Curtin. They intended to take the land, but they assured the Curtin family they would pay for it when they had the money. In their dealings, the Oneidas always had been "one hundred percent straight" with them, said Jack, who thought that Ray Halbritter was "smarter than all those fricking people at the state put together." In the meantime, the Curtins expanded. "We didn't care if the Indians had land claims," said Jack. "You have to buy a farm when it's for sale. You can't buy it when it isn't."[22]

As he did field work for the Curtins, Tom got to know the land around what used to be called Five Chimneys. The small fields created by his forebears were consolidated to accommodate big new farm equipment. Across the United States, larger farms prevailed, while farmers of smaller properties often sold out as young people left declining rural economies for other careers. At the close of the twentieth century, 1 percent of Americans lived on farms nationwide. Madison County, home to 4,600 farms in 1875, now had 700 active farms left. After Aunt Reta died, her farm, on land that once belonged to Abraham Denny, became a landscaping business run by my cousin.[23]

Becki Karst, Abraham's distant cousin, went to the auction of Aunt Reta's property in search of history. Becki believes the past is about putting together the pieces of family puzzles and making it mean something. Her father, proud of what the Oneidas were accomplishing, began to talk about his family following years of reticence. After Martin John's death, Becki wanted to find out more. She listened to elders, combed through old newspapers, volunteered at the county historical society, and collected names of Oneidas from the Kansas claim applications at the National Archives in Washington. She and Gloria Halbritter researched at the New York State Archives and attended the nation picnic where the treaty cloth was handed out. At yard sales, Becki bought antique Oneida baskets for a quarter. "People did not know what they had," she said.[24]

In the summer of 1998, hundreds of Native dancers in full regalia came from across the country to attend the Oneida Nation Cultural Festival. A few weeks later, Herb served as master of ceremonies at the fiftieth reunion of his Oneida High School class. He noted the changes from a half century earlier, when city life took place downtown with its movie theaters, stores, and railroad station. Now the shopping plazas, the YMCA, and the hospital were strung along Route 5 or Genesee Street, still sometimes referred to as the Seneca Turnpike. A Walmart Supercenter had opened next to the best land. He didn't mention that his aunt Hazel, who could see the sprawling parking lot from her window, felt the place formerly known as Cowaselon was "going to hell." Also new, Herb observed, were all the business enterprises of the Oneida Indian Nation.[25]

At the end of the year, the long-simmering land claims dispute boiled over. After almost three decades of court cases and mediation, nothing was settled. To put pressure on the state, the US government joined the Oneidas of New York, Wisconsin, and Canada in their claim regarding the three-hundred-thousand-acre reservation set aside in the Treaty of 1788, the one Good Peter believed had secured Oneida land for "as long as the grass shall grow." The federal government and the Oneidas expanded the lawsuit by naming Madison and Oneida County property owners as defendants. They insisted that they did not intend to evict people from their homes, but anxiety spread.[26]

"The sins of Albany's political forebears are being visited on 20,000 property owners in upstate New York," wrote the editors of the *New York Times*. Now was not the time, they urged the governor, to back away "from giving the Oneidas their due." The Oneidas said the state was stonewalling regarding the claimed land, which had an assessed value of more than $1 billion. "No governor wants to pay this bill on his watch," said Ray Halbritter. "We regret that we have to litigate." From this point on, New York State, which had more Indian land claims than any other state in the country, would present itself as the protector of the innocent landowner. "We are going to make sure that no one loses their homes," said Governor George Pataki.[27]

"You hit yourself on the head and you ask where do my tax dollars go? Against me?" said a local landowner. She was amazed that the federal government had, as she put it, "basically sided with a foreign nation against us." Some locals criticized the Oneidas for violating their pledge not to target homeowners, while others blamed Albany. "The state screwed up a long time ago, they've dragged their feet on this, and now we the landowners could become the sacrificial lamb," said the president of the Great Swamp Conservancy.[28]

A landowners' group, Upstate Citizens for Equality (UCE), grew to over three thousand members. Founded in 1997 to challenge the Oneidas' "tax-free" status, the group condemned the role of "our own" Department of Justice in seeking the eviction of innocent landowners from their homes, while the actual wrongdoer, the State of New York, stayed out of court. It advocated congressional legislation that ratified the state treaties and provided some financial compensation to the Oneida Indians for their lost land. When the UCE used the term "equality," it meant assimilation. The Oneidas, it believed, should become taxpaying citizens like everyone else.[29]

Bombarded with calls from constituents, local officials held informational meetings at packed high school auditoriums. They tried to reassure residents that no court in the nation had ruled on the eviction of any landowner from his or her property. Their lawyers had the unenviable task of explaining the legal convolutions of years of land claims cases involving Oneidas from New York, Wisconsin, and Canada as well as federal, state, county, city, and town governments. Charged by a UCE member that he and other local leaders were not aggressive enough, Madison County supervisor Rocco DiVeronica pushed back, "We don't need to be going helter skelter on this, Bernie." Officials worried about violence. The following Thanksgiving, a public threat was made to bomb the Turning Stone Casino and to murder a Native person every three days.[30]

The origin of the United States was on people's minds. The UCE accused the Oneidas of exaggerating the importance of their commendable but minor contribution to the US victory in the Revolutionary War. A few people attended the public meeting in Verona dressed up as rebel colonists with a sign that read, "What about Our Rights?" Some dismissed the relevance of treaties signed two hundred years earlier, while others grappled with the complexity of the problem. "Our country as a people first came into existence over the issue of taxation without representation and to end the tyranny of a government that saw us only as a means to personal wealth," reflected a discouraged landowner. "What was done to the Oneidas and all native Americans," he said, is a "moral dilemma that has stuck in the American conscience since the beginning."[31]

In its regular "Cheers and Jeers" editorial, the *Dispatch* extended jeers to the Oneidas for expanding their lawsuit to include homeowners, the state and federal government for doing next to nothing to resolve the long-standing case, and the hotheads who spread hate. The paper's "Sound Off" column printed messages from incensed callers identified as "Paid for my land" and "White property owner," as well as a few pleas for moderation. A local businessman condemned the viciousness directed at Indians. What's next, he asked: "white sheets and burning crosses"?[32]

The UCE advocated a boycott of Oneida Indian enterprises and organized weekend pickets. My niece Holly remembers riding by Oneida-owned gas stations and seeing demonstrators holding signs saying, "Honk if you support us." Everyone seemed to be hitting their horns, so she thought the Oneida Indians must be bad people. In January 1999, protesters formed a long motorcade that drove past the Turning Stone resort. A Wampsville man taped an upside-down US flag, a symbol of distress, with the slogan "Betrayed," to his car window.

While Haudenosaunee chiefs displayed the wampum belt symbolizing the guarantee of their land by George Washington, local landowner groups handed out articles titled, "Who Were the First Americans? Who Cares?" A twelve-year-old Turtle Clan boy stopped wearing his favorite "Oneida Indian Nation" T-shirt to school because he was afraid of what people would say to him.[33]

Dick Lynch learned a history he had never been taught in school, so he could talk about the land claims to audiences in Oneida, Canastota, and Vernon. In addition to doing his job as chief operating officer of the Oneida Indian Nation and carrying out his responsibilities as a member of the Men's Council, he had to get up to speed on the legal complexities of the cases. Dick had acquired a background in media working through college at the local radio station WMCR, which broadcast the farm news and school sports. As someone who had hated doing oral reports in front of the class, he was grateful that the nation hired consultants to help Oneida spokesmen frame their position. They did not want to come off as threatening or condescending while insisting on their rights. Dick had to keep his cool when property owners raged against the notion that their land did not belong to them. Been there, Dick might have said on behalf of his ancestors.[34]

Dick, a descendant of Skenandoah and Shagoyontha, explained that as Revolutionary War allies, the Oneidas had been guaranteed their lands by the federal government. He would talk about how the same men who signed the Declaration of Independence and wrote the Constitution signed the treaties that were the law of the land. There were people who believed him and others who did not. "No matter how much history you cited or how many documents you bring forward, their argument would be—all these years have passed, that history doesn't matter anymore," he recalled. It troubled him to see people he always had respected, including some of our social studies teachers, reject the evidence. Even worse were the nasty rants directed at his family. The whole thing, said Dick, "caused a lot of heartache for a lot of people."[35]

Over the following months, the land claims negotiations between the Oneidas and the state deadlocked over sales taxes, regulation, and the state's demand for 25 percent of the revenue from the Turning Stone Casino. The specter of mass eviction so overshadowed the case that the Justice Department asked permission to remove landowners from its complaint. Federal Judge Neal P. McCurn ruled that the Oneida Indian Nation could sue only the state and local governments. For the first time in the history of the Oneida land claims, New York

State was a defendant. "The real task at hand," wrote McCurn, is to determine "how, in the 21st century, to reconcile the Indians' interest in their homelands, with those of current landowners who, understandably, also view the claim area as their 'homeland.'"[36]

Losing Ground

The Oneida Nation, meanwhile, bought the Curtin farm on West Road. At 2,300 acres, the farm was three times the amount of land the Oneidas had claimed in the still-pending case launched in 1974 against West Road property owners. With this purchase, the Oneidas regained land once owned by my ancestors who, a century and a half earlier, had crowded in on the Doxtator, Cornelius, and Skenandoah families. The nation acquired William and Lizzie Clement's old place on Stockbridge West Hill. Now owner of the largest farm in Madison County, it grew a thousand acres of corn and raised an impressive herd of Black Angus cattle. The nation farm was going strong, said Tom, who stopped by a few times to help repair machinery.[37]

The Curtin Dairy bought Brewer Farm from Herb, Mary Lou, and Tom in 2000. It was "the best farm in Madison County," according to Jack Curtin, because it had big, flat fields of fertile soil with no stones. Over the years, Frank and Jennie, DeVerne and Mabelle, and Herb and Mary Lou had added to the original property bought from Angel and Polly Deferrier's grandchildren by acquiring a total of fifteen parcels from farmers selling out as we now were doing. There were rights-of-way for homeowners, the railroad, and the power and telephone companies as well as the section appropriated by the Erie Canal State Park project. The lawyer Robert McDermott informed Herb that the sale of Brewer Farm "involved tedious legal services because of the history and complexity of title well beyond anything I have experienced in fifty-two years of practice."[38]

Herb replied that it was sad to sell, but it was time to move on. That was easier said than done. From us there was mostly silence, because no one wanted to add to the grief by voicing it. Tom moved his family to Oneida County, where he became the shop foreman for the Curtins' new dairy operation. "We were leaving everything we ever knew," said Tom's son Nate. His sister Casey, who was eleven, remembered begging her dad to take down the Brewer Farm sign on the barn. "We have to take it with us," she pleaded. "It's too old," Tom told her. If he tried to pull it off, it would fall to pieces.[39]

Herb and Mary Lou relocated to Florida and fulfilled their dream of travel around the world. Russ moved back to Oneida because he and his wife wanted to raise their family in a place where people took care of each other. When he became a vice president at the Oneida Savings Bank, the bank announced that the Brewer family had been active in the community for generations. Russ noticed the pressure to take sides on the land claims. He heard it from his neighbor who led Upstate Citizens for Equality and from a friend who was moving up the executive ladder at Turning Stone.[40]

In September 2001, the Oneida Fire Department was too small to spare anyone to help find survivors in the rubble of the World Trade Center in New York City. Instead, firefighters stationed themselves on Genesee Street in front of Walmart and held out their rubber boots to collect donations for the families of the victims of the terrorist attack. The Oneida Indian Nation announced it was organizing a blood drive with disaster relief agencies. Months later, Governor Pataki, joined by Ray Halbritter and county officials, proclaimed a "historic breakthrough" on the land claims, involving a $500 million settlement. Rejected by the administration of President George W. Bush as well as the Wisconsin Oneidas, however, the "historic breakthrough" soon fell apart. Meanwhile, the city of Oneida, which since 1950 had proclaimed itself "A Bit of America at Its Best," celebrated its centennial.[41]

The town of Verona, where nearly one-fifth of all property was now nontaxable Oneida Indian land, made its peace with Turning Stone. It accepted $13 million from the Oneidas for a badly needed water system. "The fight is over, and all of the victories have gone to the nation," said the town supervisor, who years earlier had helped found Upstate Citizens for Equality. "It's time to stop the hatred and start working as a community." At an Earth Day celebration in the town of Lenox, attendees listened to the story of the Peacemaker, planted a white pine as a symbol of peace and healing, and received a gift of a pine seedling handed out by Dick Lynch on behalf of the nation.[42]

A front page of the *Dispatch* in 2004 told of shifting fortunes. Ray Halbritter of the Oneida Indian Nation had breakfast at the White House and met President Bush, who signed an order directing federal agencies to respect Indian sovereignty. Oneida Limited, once the world's largest manufacturer of flatware, was going under. The ban on metal knives and forks on planes after 9/11 had been the final blow following years of a losing struggle against global competition. "City Wants to Ready Site for Manufacturer," declared the headline above a photo of the best land. To boost the tax base, the city planned to make the Cowaselon Creek property into an industrial park with "rare access" to the railroad and the thruway. "Who might buy it?" I asked, distressed by the thought that our old place no longer would be a farm. "The Indians" was one answer, delivered with some bitterness. That prospect made me feel better.[43]

The small city of Sherrill, home to hundreds of former Oneida Limited employees, insisted that the nation owed it property taxes. The property in question was two city blocks that back in 1805 had belonged to the Pagan Party leader Cornelius Doxtator. In addition to the tax issue, local officials complained that on nation land they could not enforce health and safety regulations, consumer and environmental protection laws, or building codes. The Oneidas might be in compliance, or they might not. Officials couldn't tell, but they knew their constituents resented having to obey regulations when the Oneida Nation did not.

City wants to ready site for manufacturer

ROBERT H. BEER
Dispatch Staff Writer

ONEIDA – City officials have announced their involvement with C&S Companies to ready land on Elm Street for serious industrial growth.

C&S is an engineering company out of Syracuse that has worked with the city to devise a feasibility study to make the privately owned property "shovel-ready" and marketable to possible buyers. C & S Companies performed the study free of charge for the city.

"Shovel-ready means a company can come in and already have water, sewer, zoning and trucking routes developed," said Cassie Rose, director of planning and development in Oneida. "They would have to get a building permit."

The land is privately owned, but on the market for sale right now.

Rose said the city will not improve the land for the benefit of a private property owner, but to improve the city's chances to bring in a several hundred jobs.

See SITE, Page 10

Courtesy ONEIDA CITY PLANNING DEPARTMENT

C&S companies put together this graphic superimposed on an aerial photo showing the site of the proposed shovel-ready site on Elm Street near Wampsville.

President signs order to respect Indian sovereignty

By WILLIAM KATES
Associated Press Writer
With Dispatch Staff Reports

SYRACUSE – President Bush on Thursday affirmed the United States' recognition of Indian sovereignty, a significant declaration that could have an impact on the Nov. 2 election, said Oneida Indian Nation Representative Ray Halbritter.

[...] Washington, D.C., this week for the opening of the Smithsonian Institution's National Museum of the American Indian.

During his brief address to tribal leaders, Bush announced he had signed an executive memorandum to all federal agencies directing them to respect tribal sovereignty and self-determination.

"Native American cultures survive and flourish when tribes retain control over [...] yours, alone. Indians on this continent had their own languages and customs, just as you have today. They had jurisdiction over their lands and territories, just as you have today. And these sovereign tribal nations had their own systems of self-governance, just as you have today," Bush said.

Halbritter said Bush did not delve into any of the specific issues that confront Indians, especially those issues that are [...] relationship with Indian nations. Although it has been a long-standing agreement between our cultures, we had not heard that before from this president," Halbritter said in a telephone interview.

Bush's executive memorandum states: "The head of each executive department and agency shall continue to ensure to the greatest extent practicable and as permitted by United States law that the agency's [...]

FIGURE 43. The *Oneida Daily Dispatch* reports on presidential recognition of Indigenous sovereignty and the city's plans for the best land. Visible in the accompanying photograph are the railroad, the Erie Canal, and the New York State Thruway. In the center at the bottom is the Madison County Courthouse on North Court Street in Wampsville. *Oneida Daily Dispatch*, 25 September 2004. Brewer Collection.

The Oneidas claimed the Sherrill properties were on their reservation land protected by the Treaty of Canandaigua and therefore under their sovereign jurisdiction.[44]

When Sherrill started eviction proceedings, the Oneidas sued and won. Following appeals, *City of Sherrill, New York v. Oneida Indian Nation of New York* made its way to the US Supreme Court. Based on Oneida victories in Oneida I and II, many Native and non-Native people assumed the Oneidas would prevail. But the Oneidas lost the *Sherrill* case in an 8–1 decision. The Supreme Court in 2005 ruled that the Oneidas were subject to federal, state, and local taxation and regulation on nation-owned land that was not on its reservation of thirty-two acres.[45]

In her majority opinion, Justice Ruth Bader Ginsburg wrote that allowing the tribe government authority over repurchased land would have "disruptive practical consequences." The checkerboard of alternating state and tribal jurisdiction, she asserted, would seriously burden the administration of state and local governments and would adversely affect landowners. Justice Ginsburg did not deny that New York State had purchased the land in violation of the Trade and Intercourse Acts, but she pointed out that the Oneidas had waited nearly two hundred years to enforce their claim, and that was too long to seek judicial relief for the "grave, but ancient, wrong" of their dispossession. The Oneidas, she wrote, could not rekindle "embers of sovereignty that long ago grew cold."[46]

Local officials rejoiced. "The bottom line is that property held by the Oneidas is the same as property held by any other citizen," said the Madison County attorney John Campanie. "The Court has reaffirmed the right of our cities to govern themselves." He gave voice to a proud American tradition of linking property to equality, citizenship, and self-government. I understood the difficulties regarding jurisdiction, but it seemed to me that this ruling meant the Oneidas not only had to buy back land that rightfully belonged to them but now had to pay property taxes on it.[47]

Known as Oneida III of the Oneida trilogy, the *Sherrill* case is regarded as the seminal case regarding Native land claims and a devastating setback for Indigenous peoples. The ruling said the Oneidas could not buy property on the open market and declare it reservation land. Justice John Paul Stevens, as the lone dissenter on the *Sherrill* decision, noted that "the Court had ventured into legal territory that belongs to Congress." Only Congress, he said, has the power to disestablish a tribe's reservation and revoke a tribe's immunity from state and local taxation.

I noticed that local people who used to argue that the land claims cases did not belong in the courts no longer did.[48]

Two years later, the Oneidas of New York, Wisconsin, and Canada lost the land claims case for their ancestral reservation of three hundred thousand acres that included the best land. Echoing the *Sherrill* decision, Judge Lawrence Kahn ruled that it would be too disruptive to return the land to the Oneidas. But he agreed with the Oneidas that the state knowingly had paid the tribe just a fraction of what the land was worth and resold it at an enormous profit. The judge said the Oneidas had the right to seek redress for "long-suffered wrongs" by suing the state for damages and compensation.[49]

When the Oneidas sued for compensation, they lost. In *Madison County and Oneida County, New York v. Oneida Indian Nation of New York*, the US Court of Appeals for the Second Circuit ruled that the suit for monetary damages over the loss of the three-hundred-thousand-acre reservation would cause too much disruption. The Oneidas tried to appeal to the US Supreme Court, but only Justices Sonia Sotomayor and Ruth Bader Ginsburg wanted the court to hear the case. By letting the lower ruling stand, the Supreme Court reaffirmed Ginsburg's opinion in the *Sherrill* case. It would cause excessive upheaval to address a crime committed long ago. Ginsburg later admitted that more than any other case, she regretted her decision in *City of Sherrill v. Oneida Indian Nation*.[50]

These cases rested on a history that was familiar because we had grown up with it. The brief submitted by Madison and Oneida Counties explained how New York State had purchased Oneida land in treaties that were approved of by the federal government or acquiesced to by its inaction. Citing local nineteenth-century historians, it described how settlers had converted wilderness into cities. It said Oneidas had agreed to the Treaty of Buffalo Creek in 1838 and relocated as part of the federal removal policy described by President Martin Van Buren as humane and beneficial. It quoted from *United States v. Elm*, saying that the few Oneidas who remained had blended in with the population "in everything but the color of their skins." To show that the Oneida Reservation was a "disruptive legal fiction," it cited maps with no reservation on them as well as letters from the BIA denying its existence. The policies and practices that had served to erase the Oneidas in the past had been marshaled to deny the land claims in the present.[51]

In their brief, the counties called for "a fair reading of the historical record," which it was, as kept by the white man, once named "the custodian of history" by state legislators. It did not include the objection of Good Peter to the Treaty of 1788, which the Oneidas had believed was an agreement to lease, not sell, millions of acres. It did not detail how, at treaty councils, the Oneidas secured promise after promise from the state and federal governments to protect their land. It did not mention the churches, schools, mills, and professional societies, presented as evidence of "civilization" when created by white people, that had been established by the Oneidas. It did not cite the opposition of Oneidas to removal, or their objection to the transformation of their reservation by state-imposed severalty into a checkerboard of vulnerable lots.[52]

"A great day in Madison County," said the chairman of the Board of Supervisors about the dismissal of the land claim. Speaking for the Oneidas, Ray Halbritter observed that the court's decision sent the message that the government could act illegally without being held accountable. The *Post-Standard* editors pronounced the ruling "ironic." How, they asked, could it be too late to sue in the 2000s, when it wasn't too late to sue in the 1970s? "After all the twists and turns of these cases," their editorial advised, "don't be too sure the story is over."[53]

I felt like we continued to live in a swirl of contradictions. Back in the 1970s, people on all sides of the land claims issue acknowledged that wrong had been done and recognized that something should be done about it. By 2010, the courts admitted that wrong had been done, but they concluded nothing should be done about it. The ruling echoed the long-held assumption that Indigenous people belonged to another time and place. It was the old "Indian problem" of the continued presence of Oneidas in Oneida. About that, said Dick Lynch, Oneida had always been his home. "I don't see that changing," he added.[54]

In the *Sherrill* decision, the Supreme Court said the proper way for the Oneida Indian Nation to assert its sovereignty was to ask the secretary of the interior to convert reacquired land into trust status and make it "Indian country," the term for land set aside for Indians under federal supervision. But land in trust meant that the United States, not the Oneidas, owned the land, objected Native traditionalists and scholars, who pointed out that such a ruling returned Indians to a state of dependence on the BIA. Putting land in trust was at least a remedy, thought Dick Lynch, who still served on the Men's Council but was no longer involved in day-to-day operations at the nation. It was "as good a solution as could be," he said.[55]

The Oneida Nation applied to the federal government to place land in trust. Three years of lawsuits launched by property owners, the counties, and the state followed. In the meantime, Oneida and Madison Counties started foreclosure proceedings on Oneida-owned properties. The proceedings were halted by a federal judge who ruled that the counties could not seize land from a sovereign nation. Under the Trade and Intercourse Acts, the judge reminded everyone, land owned by an Indian nation is inalienable without the approval of the US government. At public hearings held by the BIA, residents who opposed placing Oneida land in trust were outnumbered by those in favor. Supporters noted how the economic benefits created by Oneida Indian enterprises had spread throughout the region. "You could give all of New York to the Oneida Indian Nation," said an Oneida County businesswoman, "and they would do a beautiful job with it." In 2008, the BIA announced its decision to take 13,004 acres of nation-owned land into federal trust.[56]

Living History

Of the population of central and western New York, 75 percent still lived within twenty-five miles of the Erie Canal as it approached its two hundredth year. The renovated towpath now was traveled by hikers and cyclists. Occasionally commercial shippers used the canal to transport large items like wind turbines and beer fermentation tanks that did not fit on highways or trains. The proliferation of microbreweries coincided with a revival of hop growing in upstate New York. The Madison County Historical Society held an annual Hop Fest, and Oneida County marketed itself as "the Getaway Region," home of the historic Fort Stanwix and the incomparable Turning Stone Casino.[57]

"State Grants Oneida Indians Exclusive Territory for Casino," reported the Associated Press in 2013. In a compact widely viewed as a good deal for the Oneida Indian Nation, the state guaranteed that Turning Stone would have no Las Vegas–style competition within a ten-county region. The state and the counties dropped all litigation on Oneida Nation land and tax issues. In return, the Oneida Indian Nation of New York gave up its land claims and agreed to pay 25 percent of its slot machine revenues, or about $50 million a year, to the state, which would share that money with the counties. In Madison County, disputes over jurisdiction remained unresolved, pointed out critics. Oneida dissenters and Six Nations traditionalists objected to the sacrifice of land for money.[58]

"Exit 33: The Party Starts Here," proclaimed banners promoting the new $33 million entertainment complex at Turning Stone. With gaming profits estimated to be between $200 and $400 million a year, the Oneida Indian Nation expanded its gaming operations into Madison County when it opened the Yellow Brick Road Casino in Chittenango, named in recognition of hometown author L. Frank Baum. County residents felt that the state did not pass on a fair share of the revenue received from the nation. Recalling the Silver Covenant Grants that the Oneidas no longer distributed after the *Sherrill* decision, the local people, noted Russ, "trusted the nation more to give us the money than they can the state."[59]

Have the gaming profits remedied centuries of "unfair treatment by the federal and state government," as Governor Mario Cuomo hoped they would? That is not a question I can answer. I see the casinos as both strange and familiar. It is not the first time the Oneidas have offered hospitality on the main road in the middle of the state. The nation's prosperity spreads around, but the contrast between the glittery resort and the run-down farms and businesses is hard to miss. Russ, Becki, and Dick Lynch talk about the need to revive downtown Oneida, with its vacant storefronts. In Sherrill, two men "who have just repeatedly failed to give up" tried to resuscitate flatware manufacturing. "We're all proud of Oneida," said a local woman. She may have been talking about silverware or the city or the Oneida Indian Nation. "We'd love for it to come back."[60]

On the best land, Tom, Nate, and Josh did field work for Curtin Dairy. Josh learned his way around the creek, the canal, and the railroad while he took out old hedgerows. "You just see progress every day," said Josh about farming. "You take care of something that is bigger than you." Some of the best corn every year grew on our old farm, observed Nate. Instead of plowing certain fields, he used the no-till method, where the seed was drilled directly into the ground. The United Nations warned that soil degradation caused by years of plowing and fertilizing would be one of the central threats to human health in the coming decades. Experts at Cornell University recommended a change in soil practice that echoed the wisdom of Haudenosaunee clan mothers: don't disrupt the soil, plant cover crops, and diversify what grows.[61]

While some farms experienced a surge in productivity with drones, robot milkers, genetically engineered seeds, and reliance on migrant workers, others failed as net farm income across the United States plummeted by half after 2013. The Oneidas shut down their farm on West Road. "It's going back to nature," said Jack Curtin as he recalled how much work went into clearing some of that land. Farmers, once honored as the backbone of the country, felt endangered. Many suffered depression, turned to alcohol and drugs, or committed suicide, which by 2017 was higher among Americans working in agriculture than in any other occupation. Loss of land led to a global suicide crisis among farmers from France to Australia to India, while Indigenous people suffered the greatest suicide risk worldwide. Among young Native men in the United States, it was the second-leading cause of death. One explanation, according to a UN specialist on the rights of Indigenous people, was the loss of "grounding about who they are."[62]

To promote their history and improve popular perceptions of Native people, the Oneida Indian Nation in the early twenty-first century set up Four Directions Media, which included a recording studio called Standing Stone Records and the newspaper *Indian Country Today*. It was the first Indian nation to sponsor a float, called "The True Spirit of Thanksgiving," at the annual Macy's Thanksgiving Day Parade. It produced an award-winning animated film, "Raccoon and Crawfish: An Oneida Legend," the first effort of its kind by an American Indian nation. The media industry had long controlled the message about Indigenous people, explained Jacqueline Johnson, executive director of the National Congress of American Indians. "It's better that a tribe tells the stories rather than Walt Disney."[63]

The nation also funded a reenactment program called Living History. Nate George, a former marine and an Oneida, shaved his head and wore a scalp lock while leading a scouting mission at the Saratoga National Historical Park. The Oneidas chose "the lesser of two evils" when they fought alongside the colonists, he told visitors. "They knew that while the Europeans would come and go, the tribe would always remain rooted on its land." The Oneida Indian Nation was a founding donor of the Museum of the American Revolution in Philadelphia. It pledged $10 million to the Smithsonian's National Museum of the American Indian and commissioned a nineteen-and-a-half-foot-tall statue of Chief Skenandoah towering over George Washington and Polly Cooper.[64]

At public events and in interviews, Ray Halbritter regularly mentioned the alliance between the Oneidas and the American rebels. The other story he often told was about the fire on the West Road territory in 1976, which he recalled as a personal tragedy and the moment when the rebirth of the Oneida Indian Nation began. He spoke about it when the Oneidas lost their land claims case and when criticizing the name of the Washington Redskins football team. "I learned what 'redskin' means through my family—and specifically, through the experience of seeing them left to die by a local fire department that didn't think it was their responsibility to help us because we are Native Americans," he said. "They saw us not as individual human beings or fellow Americans but as people that didn't deserve to be treated as equals. They saw us as redskins."[65]

When asked in a 2010 interview for the *Dispatch* why the Oneida Fire Department did not respond, Ray Halbritter cited jurisdictional issues, the land claims dispute, politics, misunderstanding, racial animosity, and a total breakdown in relations. Former local officials agreed that it was a bad time. One pointed out that certain Oneidas interfered with the police when it suited their agenda and then complained when law enforcement did not respond. "My position was that the Indians couldn't have it both ways," he said, calling it "hypocritical." Online comments reflected divergent recollections of the recent and distant past. A few expressed gratitude to the Oneida Indians for their help during the American Revolution and denounced the mistreatment of Native peoples long ago. Some then urged the Oneidas to "get over it already!"[66]

Who would the Oneidas be if they "got over it"? Dick Lynch points out that as kids in school we were taught about Christopher Columbus and George Washington. We did not learn about how Washington guaranteed Oneida land while also claiming it as a new empire, or how Dick's great-great-great-aunt Mary Honyost Skenandoah resisted eviction from her home. We did not learn about the Covenant Chain relationship negotiated by the Six Nations with European colonizers who nevertheless discounted Native equality and independence. The colonizers and their descendants were masters at having it both ways. If the Oneidas did not live like white people, they were considered uncivilized and therefore unworthy of their land, and if they did, they were no longer real Indians and therefore not entitled to their land.[67]

What if Herb had been aware of his family's history? Near the end of his life, he looked at what happened to the best land in a way that acknowledged the intertwining of our lives with the Oneidas'. When the Oneidas did well with bingo, he said, they bought up the property they claimed on West Road, including the Curtin farm, and then the Curtins bought our place. "It's interesting how the Indian money came around," Herb reflected. "Made a lot of things possible."[68]

What if he had been aware of how many times the Oneidas "made a lot of things possible"? What if he had known that the Oneidas once said to his forefather Harmen, "You must not lie," or that Oneida men and women saved his family during the American Revolution, or that afterward, his squatter and settler ancestors had crowded out the Oneidas on land obtained by illegal treaties? As mayor, I imagine, he still would have insisted that the Oneidas pay their water bill, but he might have understood what the epic effort to regain sovereignty was all about. The history he knew left him at a loss.

I have learned that the home I loved was built on betrayal. The swirl of contradictions persists. I feel grateful to my forefathers and foremothers who struggled to acquire a place here, while I regret the sufferings of so many of Polly's family who lost theirs. I have learned enough about the people of the best land to see them not as heroes and villains but as human beings who could be despicable, brave, greedy, and loving. I discovered that the tale of progress we learned in school retains its potency, while all along Natives and non-Natives have called out injustice and advocated doing something about it.

I understand why people today may claim they are innocent of wrongdoing from long ago, but I don't understand why they deny that wrong was done or ignore how much they have benefited from it. Anyone whose family headed west on the Genesee Road or the Erie Canal or the New York Central Railroad passed through the best land thanks to the dispossession of the Oneidas. Anyone whose family settled in Oneida built on land enriched by those who were here first. As for my family, I now know they made a four-hundred-year career of moving ever closer to the People of the Standing Stone.

In 2018, the original section of the best land was sold by the Curtin family to a company called Green Empire Farms, which planned to grow tomatoes, cucumbers, and strawberries and sought easy access to markets in New York, Philadelphia, and Boston. It wanted a large stretch of flat land on which to build sixty-four acres of greenhouses for its controlled-environment agriculture operation. Our former house became the site office. Russ said it was sad to see the change, but he hoped they succeeded. A lot of the old farms were just growing up hayfields, he said. The Brewers took some comfort in seeing the place still produce food, but I can't help feeling somehow that we have let down those who took care of the land before us.[69]

Before it began construction, Green Empire Farms complied with regulations that required a search for Indigenous bones and relics. "At least they were checking," said Becki. It was an improvement on times past, when builders of the railroad dug up a burial ground of warriors

FIGURE 44. "Stolen Land." Madison County, NY, 2022. Brewer Collection.

and took home the bones to display to their friends. After the search uncovered no bones or relics, the new owners bulldozed huge piles of topsoil out of the way and brought in truckloads of gravel. The sight made Josh feel sick to his stomach. "They ruined a perfectly good working thing," he said. "It's kind of crazy to think that out of all the property in the world they picked that spot." Josh felt a farmer's reverence for the soil venerated by the Haudenosaunee, who believed it was composed of the decayed flesh and bones of their ancestors that replenished Turtle Island.[70]

When Herb died in 2016, we buried his ashes in Glenwood Cemetery north of the thirty-two acres that was the Oneida Indian Territory for much of his lifetime. At the foot of Stockbridge West Hill, the cemetery had been dedicated in 1870 with prayers and brass bands. At the time, the *Dispatch* made the rare observation that the site had belonged to the aboriginal owners Paul Powless and Anthony Big Knife. The connection to the Oneidas, the article suggested, enhanced the hallowed nature of the burial ground. Generations of Brewers and Clements rest in peace there, along with Polly and Angel Deferrier's grandchildren, the Civil War veteran and Native rights activist Abraham Elm, and the storytellers Dolly John Antone and Lydia Doxtator. "In death, all the Native people become one," said the Haudenosaunee educator Richard Hill Sr. "We are connected to the ancient ones who walked and are buried in the same lands from which future generations spring forth."[71]

The bright lights of the Walmart parking lot now penetrate the overgrowth around the graves of Angel and Polly. When my family gathers, we talk about our old farm, which made so much possible. Our emotional connection to the place probably will pass away with us. We have no elders insisting that the land belongs to the children to come through the seventh generation. We have only a glimmer of understanding about that sort of heritage, yet we can feel its power. At a Father's Day celebration, Tom startled me with an echo of a voice heard long ago. "It's still the best land around," he said. The night before her wedding, his daughter Holly gave her sister Casey a necklace engraved with the GPS coordinates that would take them back to their old home. "That's the heart of the family," said Casey. "That's Oneida."[72]

Acknowledgments

This book was inspired by questions about the best land that I have wondered about for much of my life. I thank the many kind people who listened to me go on about these questions and then asked more. The questions began to turn into a written project over twenty years ago, during a residency at the Blue Mountain Center in Blue Mountain, New York, where I thought I might write an article about the family farm and Oneida land claims. My fellow writers and artists helped me to see that there was much more to this story than I had realized, and for that I owe them enormous thanks. As the project grew into something bigger, I set it aside because of other obligations, but when I could return to it, I was fortunate to be granted an immensely rewarding and inspiring fellowship at the Institute for Research in the Humanities at the University of Wisconsin–Madison. I am grateful to the wonderful students, colleagues, and friends from my twenty-five years of teaching at the University of Wisconsin–Stevens Point, where the University Personnel Development Committee awarded me research support, the gallant staff of the library and archives provided resources, and the IT Department rescued me from technical difficulties. Thank you to Marcia Parker for her translations of French histories.

I am indebted to the archivists, librarians, staff, and volunteers at the Albany Institute of History and Art; the Chenango County Clerk's Office; the Christ Episcopal Church of Duanesburg; the Columbia County Historical Society; the Fort Klock Restoration Project; the Hamilton College Library Special Collections; the Herkimer County Historical Society; the Montgomery County Department of History and Archives; the New York Historical Society; the Brooke Russell Astor Reading Room of Rare Books and Manuscripts at the New York Public Library; the New York State Archives; the New York State Library; the Oneida County Clerk's Office; the Oneida County History Center; the Oneida Public Library; the Schoharie County Historical Society; the Schenectady County Historical Society; the University of Rochester's Department of Rare Books and Special Collections; and the

Utica Public Library. I am grateful to Laurent Delenne of the Archives Départementale de Deux-Sevres in Niort, France, for his gracious assistance to a researcher in search of Angel Deferrier. I thank Anne Greer for interpretation. The documents available on the website of the Oneida Nation of Wisconsin, https://www.exploreoneida.com, proved invaluable, especially during the pandemic when archives were closed. I extend a special thank you to director Sydney Loftus and the volunteers at the Mary King Research Library at the Madison County Historical Society, who feared I would never leave, and Madison County historian Matthew Urtz and everyone at the Madison County Clerk's Office who photocopied dusty deeds for me.

From elaborate cartography to family snapshots, maps and images have been an essential part of this project. For maps and illustrations, I thank the Albany Institute of History and Art; the Bibliothèque Nationale de France; the Collection of the Public Design Commission of the City of New York; the Frank J. Basloe Library in Herkimer; the John Carter Brown Library; the Library of Congress Geography and Map Division; the Madison County Historical Society; the Margaret Reaney Memorial Library in St. Johnsville; the Museum of the City of New York; the National Museum of the American Indian; the NASA Jet Propulsion Laboratory Galleries (https://www.jpl.nasa.gov); the New York Historical Society; the New York Public Library; the New York State Archives; the New York State Library Manuscripts and Special Collections; the Norman B. Leventhal Map & Education Center at the Boston Public Library; the Oneida Nation of Wisconsin; the Onondaga Historical Association; the Wisconsin Historical Society; the University of Massachusetts Press; the Yale University Art Gallery; Chris Leonard and the Efner History Center, Schenectady, NY; Gordie Thompson; Richard and Pamela Lynch; Rebecca "Becki" John Karst; and my family.

I am grateful to everyone who, over the years, recommended sources, offered guidance, shared research, wrote in support, or gave me things to read, including Scott Anderson, Carl Benn, Jesse Bergevin, John Campanie, Sherri Cash, Sharon Cooney, Edward Countryman, Corinne Dempsey, Reginald Doxtater, Donna White Draeger, Jack Ericson, Jim Folts, Michael Foret, Robert Foster, Dan Geller, Dayna Goldfine, Brian Hale, Rob Harper, Laurence Hauptman, Ann Hunter, Erin Kramer, Terry McMaster, Richard Niemi, Jon Parmenter, Christine Patrick, Neil Prendergast, Jack Reed, Tom Reich, Denise Roe, Jane Robens, Axel Schmetzke, William Skelton, Barbara Skenandore, Andrea Lynn Smith, Karim Tiro, Matt Urtz, Dawn Vollmer, Jack Wallace, Lee Willis, Michael

Wilson, Anthony Wonderley, and David Wrone. I am grateful to my distant cousin Jody Pettit and her family for allowing me to use the memoir of Edith Ratnour Hammond. I thank my former student Nicolas Reynolds of the Oneida Nation of Wisconsin for his enthusiastic support throughout this project.

I am thankful to all who generously shared their views and memories in conversations and interviews, including John Bortle, Casey Brewer, Elizabeth Brewer, Herbert Brewer, Joanne Brewer, Joshua Brewer, Mary Lou Brewer, Nathan Brewer, Richard Brewer, Robert Brewer, Russell Brewer, Thomas Brewer, Virginia Brewer, Jack Curtin, Becki Karst, Richard Myers, Rex Niles, Holly Brewer Rogers, David Schraver, Robert Witmer, and Anthony Wonderley. I am beholden to Richard "Dick" Lynch for talking to me about his family, his career, and his deep commitment to Oneida. He and his wife, Pam, have been exceedingly gracious with their time, photographs, and family history. Thank you also to the people who invited me to talk on this topic, asked questions, and provided comments, including those at the Applewood Retirement Community in Amherst, MA; the Oneida Indian Nation Battle of Oriskany Symposium, Verona, NY; the Center for Culture, History, and the Environment, University of Wisconsin-Madison; Erie Canal@200: A Symposium Commemorating the Bicentennial of America's Waterway, at Utica College; the Highlands of Pittsford, NY; the History Department at the University of Wisconsin-Madison; the Iroquois Genealogy Society, Salamanca, NY; the Oneida Rotary Club in Oneida, NY; and the Unitarian Church in Barneveld, NY. I am especially grateful to the Conference on Iroquois Research for years of critical insights and welcome suggestions.

I have been most fortunate to have had thoughtful readers of this book at its various stages. I thank the proposal and manuscript reviewers for Cornell University Press, including the amazingly generous Joe Stahlman and Karim Tiro. Carl Benn, Debbie Eveland, Dan Geller, Dayna Goldfine, Theresa Kaminski, Becki Karst, Linda Nemec, Dan Rogers, Beth Brewer, Ginny Brewer, Holly Brewer Rogers, Mary Lou Brewer, Russ Brewer, and Tom Brewer brought a range of expertise and personal experience to their comments. Anne Greer and Bob Erickson made their way through several drafts. These readers have made the book better, while I remain responsible for any mistakes it contains.

At Cornell University Press, I wish to thank Karen M. Laun, Jonathan L. Hall, India Miraglia, and Alfredo Gutierrez Rios. I am deeply grateful to copyeditor Eric Levy for his careful attention to the manuscript. I thank editorial director Mahinder S. Kingra, who inherited the manuscript in its late stages and made excellent suggestions for its improvement. I am greatly indebted to Michael McGandy, now director of the University of South Carolina Press, who believed in this project from its earliest days, always understood its challenges, saw it through years of evolution, and provided critical guidance and patience.

One person I cannot thank enough is Becki Karst. Since our first meeting over a decade ago, Becki has shared her astonishing collection of Oneida genealogies, stories, documents, and photographs, showed me important sites on road trips, and spent hours talking about our discoveries. For a long time, we were focused on sorting out Oneida family histories and did not notice our own. Eventually, as I placed her family and mine on the land, I realized that they had been neighbors for at least three centuries. The relationships of our ancestors became the core of the story of the best land, which has been home to both of us. From the beginning, she claimed me as her kindred spirit, and so it is my honor to be.

It is hard to know where to begin when it comes to thanking my family. I did not know where this project would take me, and they certainly didn't either, but, wary and bemused, they came with me. Some of the journey took us through tangled reminiscences; some of it took us around the countryside as we tried to follow nineteenth-century maps or locate old properties. I still owe my brother Russ a car wash. On my tours of Madison County, multiple generations regaled me with tales of what they remembered about the land and relations. My uncle Dick, my brothers, and my nephews answered numerous questions about farming. My cousins Susan Donaldson Werner, John Donaldson, and Bob Donaldson provided me with photographs and our great-grandfather Frank Brewer's diaries. My aunt Ginny delivered a crate of family mementos. My brother Tom presented me with a file of farm documents. My parents, Herb and Mary Lou, turned over boxes of papers, photographs, and newspaper clippings. My father, my mother, Russ, and I, with assistance from my nieces Holly and Casey, spent years tracing our family. The participation of Herb and Russ in the Brewer DNA Project helped to identify our forebears. To my grandparents DeVerne and Mabelle Brewer, I am indebted for the gift of understanding that love of place, family, and stories of the past were intertwined. I am profoundly grateful for the love and memories, heartfelt and rueful, shared by my relatives who died before the book was completed. I am especially thankful for the generosity of my father, whose recollections were critical to the book and precious to me even though we did not always see eye to eye. I thank my husband, Bob Erickson, for his marvelous companionship, encouragement, and willingness to explore one more "seasonal" road or old graveyard. To my parents, siblings, nieces, nephews, aunts, uncles, and cousins, who opened their hearts to share their memories of the best land, my gratitude and love.

After many years of living elsewhere, I have returned to dwell in the land of the Haudenosaunee. I now often pass by Schenectady, Johnson Hall, Fort Stanwix, the Turning Stone Casino, and Oneida Castle. These places are familiar and strange, rich with the history I have learned and mysterious with questions that remain unanswered. To the Mohawks and Oneidas, I am deeply grateful for many, many things, including the heartsease I feel in their homeland.

Abbreviations

DP	*Daily Press*, Utica, NY
MCCO	Madison County Clerk's Office, Wampsville, NY
MCHS	Madison County Historical Society, Oneida, NY
NA	National Archives, Washington, DC
NYCD	John Romeyn Brodhead, Berthold Fernow, and E. B. O'Callaghan, eds., *Documents Relative to the Colonial History of the State of New York*, 15 vols. (Albany, NY: Weed, Parsons, 1858).
NYSA	New York State Archives, Albany, NY
NYT	*New York Times*, New York, NY
OD	*Oneida Dispatch/Oneida Daily Dispatch*, Oneida, NY
ODU	*Oneida Democratic Union*, Oneida, NY
PS	*Post-Standard*, Syracuse, NY
SHA	*Syracuse Herald American*, Syracuse, NY
SHJ	*Syracuse Herald Journal*, Syracuse, NY
WJP	William Johnson, *The Papers of Sir William Johnson*, 14 vols. (Albany: University of the State of New York, 1925).

Notes

Preface and Note to Readers

1. Raymond Williams, *The Country and the City* (New York: Oxford University Press, 1973), 38, 45, 197, 204; Anne Raver, "Loving and Leaving the Family Farm," *NYT*, 2 December 2004.

2. David L. Preston, *The Texture of Contact: European and Indian Settler Communities on the Frontiers of Iroquoia, 1667–1783* (Lincoln: University of Nebraska Press, 2009); Nancy Shoemaker, *A Strange Likeness: Becoming Red and White in Eighteenth-Century North America* (New York: Oxford University Press, 2006); Alan Taylor, *The Divided Ground: Indians, Settlers, and the Northern Borderland of the American Revolution* (New York: Vintage Books, 2006).

3. The Stockbridge Valley runs north and south between Stockbridge East Hill and Stockbridge West Hill. North of Peterboro Road, this valley also was known as the Oneida Valley. To avoid confusing it with the Oneida Valley located to the north between the city of Oneida and Oneida Lake, I refer to the whole valley south of the city of Oneida as the Stockbridge Valley.

4. Colin Calloway, "My Grandfather's Axe: Living with a Native American Past," in *Reflections on American Indian History: Honoring the Past, Building a Future*, ed. Albert L. Hurtado (Norman: University of Oklahoma Press, 2008), 3–31; Christine DeLucia, "The Memory Frontier: Uncommon Pursuits of Past and Place in the Northeast after King Philip's War," *Journal of American History* 98, no. 4 (March 2012): 975–97.

5. Roxanne Dunbar-Ortiz, *An Indigenous Peoples' History of the United States* (Boston: Beacon, 2014), 1.

6. Jean M. O'Brien, *Dispossession by Degrees: Indian Land and Identity in Natick, Massachusetts, 1650–1790* (New York: Cambridge University Press, 1997), 3–12.

7. "AHR Exchange: Historians and Native American and Indigenous Studies," *American Historical Review* 125 (April 2020): 517–51; Laurence M. Hauptman, "Three Stories of War: History and Memory in an American Indian Community," in Hurtado, *Reflections on American Indian History*, 60–61.

8. Carol Kammen, *On Doing Local History*, 2nd ed. (Walnut Creek, CA: AltaMira, 2003), 26, 61; John C. Mohawk, "Indians and Democracy: No One Ever Told Us," in *Exiled in the Land of the Free: Democracy, Indian Nations, and the U.S. Constitution*, ed. Oren Lyons and John C. Mohawk (Santa Fe: Clear Light, 1992), 44.

9. Jean M. O'Brien, *Firsting and Lasting: Writing Indians Out of Existence in New England* (Minneapolis: University of Minnesota Press, 2010); Susan Sleeper-Smith, Juliana Barr, Jean M. O'Brien, Nancy Shoemaker, and Scott Manning

Stevens, eds., *Why You Can't Teach United States History without American Indians* (Chapel Hill: University of North Carolina Press, 2015).

10. Cornelius Doxtator (great-grandson of Honyery), interview by Lyman C. Draper, 30–31 October 1877, Oneida Reservation, Wisconsin, Series U, Frontier Wars Papers, 1754–1885, 11 U:200, Draper Manuscripts, Wisconsin Historical Society, Madison, WI; Janny Venema, *Beverwijck: A Dutch Village on the American Frontier, 1652–1664* (Albany: State University of New York Press, 2003), 271, 275, 405; Henry Z. Jones Jr., *The Palatine Families of New York: A Study of the German Immigrants Who Arrived in Colonial New York in 1710* (Universal City, CA: Picton, 1985).

1. The People of the Standing Stone and the Axe Makers

1. Charles T. Gehring and William A. Starna, eds., *A Journey into Mohawk and Oneida Country, 1634–1635: The Journal of Harmen Meyndertsz van den Bogaert* (Syracuse, NY: Syracuse University Press, 2013), 14.

2. Joop de Jong, "The Dutch Golden Age and Globalization: History and Heritage, Legacies and Contestations," *Macalester International* 27, art. 7 (December 2011), https://digitalcommons.macalester.edu/macintl/vol27/iss1/7(FDIS2011The Hague); Russell Shorto, *The Island at the Center of the World: The Epic Story of Dutch Manhattan and the Forgotten Colony That Shaped America* (New York: Vintage Books, 2005), 22–23.

3. Shorto, *Island at the Center*, 31–33; Jaap Jacobs, *The Colony of New Netherland: A Dutch Settlement in Seventeenth-Century America* (Ithaca, NY: Cornell University Press, 2009), 21–22.

4. Jon Parmenter, *The Edge of the Woods: Iroquoia, 1534–1701* (East Lansing: Michigan State University Press, 2010), 28, 37.

5. Venema, *Beverwijck*, 128–29; Gehring and Starna, *Journey into Mohawk and Oneida Country*, xxvi–xxvii, xxxi, 1.

6. Gehring and Starna, *Journey into Mohawk and Oneida Country*, xvi, 22.

7. Parmenter, *Edge of the Woods*, xlv; Daniel K. Richter, *The Ordeal of the Longhouse: The Peoples of the Iroquois League in the Era of European Colonization* (Chapel Hill: University of North Carolina Press, 1992), 47.

8. Gehring and Starna, *Journey into Mohawk and Oneida Country*, 1–2, 6, 10–11, 24–25, 56–67.

9. Carol Cornelius, *Iroquois Corn in a Culture-Based Curriculum: A Framework for Respectfully Teaching about Cultures* (Albany: State University of New York Press, 1999), 104–10; William Engelbrecht, *Iroquoia: The Development of a Native World* (Syracuse, NY: Syracuse University Press, 2003), 32–33; Gehring and Starna, *Journey into Mohawk and Oneida Country*, 12–14.

10. The Oneida territory covered all or portions of present-day Madison, Oneida, Chenango, Broome, Lewis, St. Lawrence, and Jefferson Counties. William A. Starna, "The Oneida Homeland in the Seventeenth Century," in *The Oneida Indian Experience: Two Perspectives*, ed. Jack Campisi and Laurence M. Hauptman (Syracuse, NY: Syracuse University Press, 1988), 9–12; Parmenter, *Edge of the Woods*, 44; Engelbrecht, *Iroquoia*, 90–104; Matthew Dennis, *Cultivating a Landscape of Peace: Iroquois-European Encounters in Seventeenth-Century America* (Ithaca, NY: Cornell University Press, 1993), 63–65; Karim Tiro, *The People of*

the Standing Stone: The Oneida Nation from the Revolution through the Era of Removal (Amherst: University of Massachusetts Press, 2011), 1.

11. Harmen and his companions are thought to have carried wheel-lock holster pistols. Gehring and Starna, *Journey into Mohawk and Oneida Country*, 14–15; Carl Benn, *The Iroquois in the War of 1812* (Toronto: University of Toronto Press, 1998), 53.

12. Gehring and Starna, *Journey into Mohawk and Oneida Country*, 15; Richter, *Ordeal of the Longhouse*, 47.

13. Gehring and Starna, *Journey into Mohawk and Oneida Country*, 15–16.

14. Gehring and Starna, *Journey into Mohawk and Oneida Country*, 16–17; Curtis G. Berkey, "United States–Indian Relations: The Constitutional Basis," in Lyons and Mohawk, *Exiled in the Land of the Free*, 236.

15. Gehring and Starna, *Journey into Mohawk and Oneida Country*, 18–19.

16. Gehring and Starna, *Journey into Mohawk and Oneida Country*, 16–22.

17. Dennis, *Cultivating a Landscape*, 93, 112–13; Jack Campisi, "Ethnic Identity and Boundary Maintenance in Three Oneida Communities" (PhD diss., State University of New York at Albany, 1974), 54–55.

18. Gehring and Starna, *Journey into Mohawk and Oneida Country*, 21–26.

19. Deborah Doxtator, "Inclusive and Exclusive Perceptions of Difference: Native and Euro-Based Concepts of Time, History, and Change," in *Decentring the Renaissance: Canada and Europe in Multidisciplinary Perspective, 1500–1700*, ed. Germaine Warkentin and Carolyn Podruchny (Toronto: University of Toronto Press, 2001), 34; Donna Merwick, *The Shame and the Sorrow: Dutch-Amerindian Encounters in New Netherland* (Philadelphia: University of Pennsylvania Press, 2006), 187.

20. Parmenter, *Edge of the Woods*, 46.

21. Richter, *Ordeal of the Longhouse*, 59.

22. Doug George-Kanentiio, "Iroquois Roots," in *Archeology of the Iroquois: Selected Readings and Research Sources*, ed. Jordan E. Kerber (Syracuse, NY: Syracuse University Press, 2007), 393; Anthony Wonderley, *Oneida Iroquois Folklore, Myth, and History: New York Oral Narratives from the Notes of H. E. Allen and Others* (Syracuse, NY: Syracuse University Press, 2004), 57–73; Richter, *Ordeal of the Longhouse*, 10–11; Engelbrecht, *Iroquoia*, 4; Cornelius, *Iroquois Corn*, 92; Campisi, "Ethnic Identity," 57.

23. "Clan Systems—Oneida Nation," Oneida Nation of Wisconsin, accessed 29 December 2023, https://www.oneida-nsn.gov/our-way; Richter, *Ordeal of the Longhouse*, 39–40; Parmenter, *Edge of the Woods*, xlvi.

24. Parmenter, *Edge of the Woods*, xlviii; Berkey, "United States–Indian Relations," 236; Oren R. Lyons, "The American Indian in the Past," in Lyons and Mohawk, *Exiled in the Land of the Free*, 39.

25. Richter, *Ordeal of the Longhouse*, 32–38, 50–74; Parmenter, *Edge of the Woods*, 45–50.

26. Adriaen Cornelissen Van der Donck, "Description of New Netherlands," in *In Mohawk Country: Early Narratives about a Native People*, ed. Dean R. Snow, Charles T. Gehring, and William Starna (Syracuse, NY: Syracuse University Press, 1996), 106; Jacobs, *Colony of New Netherland*, 210; Dennis, *Cultivating a Landscape*, 213, 236.

27. Paul Gorgen suggests that Otstok's full name was Otsistóhkwa (The Star). Paul Gorgen, "Ladies of the Mohawk Valley: Molly Brant, Clarissa Putman and Other Women with Rona'sharó:nih (European) Partners," *Iroquoia* 3, no. 1 (2017): 12; Jacobs, *Colony of New Netherland*, 209–10; Eirlys M. Barker, "Princesses, Wives, and Wenches: White Perceptions of Southeastern Indian Women to 1770," in *Women and Freedom in Early America*, ed. Larry D. Eldridge (New York: New York University Press, 1997); John J. Vrooman, *Forts and Firesides of the Mohawk Country* (Johnstown, NY: Baronet Litho, 1951), 113; Judith L. Jourdan, "Wampum: Our Historical Record," n.d., Oneida Cultural Heritage Department, No. 20, Oneida, WI.

28. Rensselaerswyck consisted of most of present-day Albany and Rensselaer Counties and parts of Columbia and Greene Counties. "Van Curler's Letter to the Patroon," 1643, in John Sanders, *Early History of Schenectady, New York and Its First Settlers* (1879; reprint, Westminster, MD: Heritage Books, 2012), 310; Daniel K. Richter, "Cultural Brokers and Intercultural Politics: New York-Iroquois Relations, 1664–1701," *Journal of American History* 75, no. 1 (June 1988): 46.

29. Gehring and Starna, *Journey into Mohawk and Oneida Country*, xxxi–xxxii; Jacobs, *Colony of New Netherland*, 183; Shorto, *Island at the Center of the World*, 111; Jonathan Pearson, *A History of the Schenectady Patent in the Dutch and English Times* (Albany, 1883), 125.

30. Harmen was named as co-heir of Swits's property, probably as Jellesje's husband and guardian, along with her brother Cornelis Claesen Swits. "Contract of Sale of the Plantation of the Late Claes Cornelissen Swits from Harmen Meyndertsen van den Bogaert to James Smith and William Brown," 30 May 1642, Secretary of the Province, Register of the Provincial Secretary, 1642–1660, Series A0270-78, vol. 2, doc. 19a-b, side 2, NYSA (the records of the government of New Netherland are available at https://www.digitalcollections.archives.nysed.gov); J. H. Innes, *New Amsterdam and Its People* (Port Washington, NY: Ira J. Friedman, 1969), 1:98–99; Jacobs, *Colony of New Netherland*, 76–80; Shorto, *Island at the Center of the World*, 119–28.

31. Venema, *Beverwijck*, 200–201; "Transfer from Christiaen Pietersen Rams to Harmen Meyndertsen van den Bogaert and Cornelis Antonissen of His Share in the Frigate La Garce," 22 July, [1647], A0270, vol. 2, doc. 159f-g, side 2, NYSA; patent to Harmen Meyndertsz van Bogaert for land on Manhattan Island, 16 March 1647, Dutch Colonial Patents and Deeds, 1630–1664, Series A1880-78, vol. GG, NYSA.

32. Dutch Colonial Council minutes, 25 June 1646, vol. 4, p. 262; Dutch Colonial Council minutes, 15 October 1647–21 February 1648, vol. 4, pp. 344–48; and "Sentence of Jan Quisthout van der Linde and Sentence of Hendrick Harmensen," 17 June 1660, vol. 9, Dutch Colonial Council Minutes, 1638–1665, Dutch Colonial Council Minutes, Series A1809-78, NYSA; Jacobs, *Colony of New Netherland*, 205; Gehring and Starna, *Journey into Mohawk and Oneida Country*, xxxiii.

33. Gehring and Starna, *Journey into Mohawk and Oneida Country*, xxxiii; Joop de Jong, "Dutch Golden Age and Globalization"; Jacobs, *Colony of New Netherland*, 211.

34. Gehring and Starna, *Journey into Mohawk and Oneida Country*, xxxiii; Dutch Colonial Council minutes, 1 February 1648, A1809-78, vol. 4, p. 360, NYSA; "Deed from the Director and Council to Adriaen Keyser of a Lot on Manhattan Island Formerly Belonging to Harmen Meyndertsen van den Bogaert," 8 July 1649, A0270-78, vol. 3, p. 39d, NYSA.

35. "Power of Attorney from Jan Labatie to Adriaen van der Donck to Manage the Affairs of Harmen Bogardus, Deceased, Growing Out of His Interest in the Yacht La Garce," 10 November 1648, A0270-78, vol. 3, doc. 25, NYSA; "Deed of Jan Labatie to Jan Gillissen Verbrugge for a House and Lot in New Amsterdam," 22 September 1652, Dutch Colonial Land Deeds, 1652–1653, Series A1882, vol. HH, NYSA; Innes, *New Amsterdam and Its People*, 1:71; Pearson, *History of the Schenectady Patent*, 125; A. J. F. Van Laer, *Settlers of Rensselaerswyck, 1630–1658* (1908; reprint, Baltimore: Genealogical Publishing, 1998), 13–14, 41; Venema, *Beverwijck*, 44, 459.

36. Du Trieux also was spelled as de Truy, Truyx, or Truax. Shorto, *Island at the Center of the World*, 93–101.

37. Jacobs, *Colony of New Netherland*, 64.

38. Jacobs, *Colony of New Netherland*, 42, 55, 61, 215; Harry Macy Jr., "375th Anniversary of the *Eendracht* and *Nieuw Nederland*," *NYG&B Newsletter*, Winter 1999, http://www.newyorkfamilyhistory.org; David Steven Cohen, "How Dutch Were the Dutch of New Netherland?," *New York History* 62, no. 1 (1981): 43–60; "Patent to Philip de Truy," 22 May 1640, A1880-78, vol. GG, NYSA.

39. Jacobs, *Colony of New Netherland*, 31; Adriana E. Van Zwieten, "'Conversing with Each Other, among Other Things of the Sale of Houses': Buying and Selling Real Property in New Amsterdam," 1–2; New Netherland Institute, accessed 29 December 2023, https://www.newnetherlandinstitute.org/application/files/5716/8413/0918/zweiten.pdf.

40. "Adoption of Pieter Wolphertsen van Couwenhoven of Aeltje Peters as His Child and Heir," 7 January 1642, A0270-78, vol. 2, doc. 4a-b, NYSA; Kathlyne Knickerbacker Viele, *Viele Records, 1613–1913* (New York: Tobias A. Wright, 1913), 14–15.

41. "Appointment of Jan Peecq to Be Broker to the Merchants of New Amsterdam," 25 February 1656, A1809-78, vol, 6, NYSA; William T. Horton, *Jan Peeck, Tavern Keeper, Fur Trader and Land Owner* (Peekskill, NY: Department of the City Historian, 1949); Jacobs, *Colony of New Netherland*, 181, 195–97; Viele, *Viele Records*, 14.

42. Van Zweiten, "'Conversing with Each Other,'" 4–5; Venema, *Beverwijck*, 186–91.

43. Horton, "Jan Peeck," 79–81; Viele, *Viele Records*, 17; Jacobs, *Colony of New Netherland*, 133.

44. "Complaint of Mary de Truy against the Provoost," 17 December 1654, A1809-78, vol. 5, NYSA; Horton, "Jan Peeck," 79–81, 87; Erin Kramer, "'That She Shall Be Forever Banished from This Country': Alcohol, Sovereignty, and Social Segregation in New Netherland," *Early American Studies*, Winter 2022, 36–37.

45. Dutch Colonial Council minutes, 26 April 1646, A1809-78, vol. 4, p. 252, NYSA; Kramer, "'Forever Banished,'" 15–16; Jacobs, *Colony of New Netherland*,

115; Peter C. Mancall, *Deadly Medicine: Indians and Alcohol in Early America* (Ithaca, NY: Cornell University Press, 1995), 43–44, 67–97.

46. Jacobs, *Colony of New Netherland*, 107; Horton, "Jan Peeck," 91; "Prosecution of Maria de Truyx for Selling Brandy to Indians," 30 December 1663; "Complaint of Fiscal against Maria Truix for Selling Liquor to Indians," 3 January 1664; "Sentence of Maria de Truix," 3 January 1664; "Petition of Maria Peeck for a Remission of the Sentence Pronounced against Her," 24 January 1664; "Order That Maria Peeck Be Allowed to Remove to Long Island with Remission of the Fine against Her," 28 January 1664, A1809-78, vol. 10, NYSA.

47. Donna Merwick, *Possessing Albany, 1630–1710: The Dutch and English Experience* (New York: Cambridge University Press, 1990), 74–77; "Complaints against Various Citizens for Going to the Woods or Employing Dutchmen as Brokers to Trade There with Indians," 15 July 1660, Dutch Colonial Ordinances, 1647–1658, Series A1875, vol. 16, NYSA.

48. Dennis, *Cultivating a Landscape*, 168, 175, 178–79; Merwick, *Possessing Albany*, 100; Venema, *Beverwijck*, 275; Parmenter, *Edge of the Woods*, 108.

49. Parmenter, *Edge of the Woods*, 113–14; Jacobs, *Colony of New Netherland*, 116; Thomas E. Burke Jr., *Mohawk Frontier: The Dutch Community of Schenectady, New York, 1661–1710* (Ithaca, NY: Cornell University Press, 1991), 30–31.

50. Dennis, *Cultivating a Landscape*, 152–53; Burke, *Mohawk Frontier*, 30.

51. Burke, *Mohawk Frontier*, 16; Merwick, *Shame and the Sorrow*, 197, 207.

52. Merwick, *Possessing Albany*, 196–208; Jacobs, *Colony of New Netherland*, 99–103; Venema, *Beverwijck*, 112–13; Richter, "Cultural Brokers," 49.

53. Sanders, *Early History of Schenectady*, 84.

54. Mohawk Dutch was thought to have added English, Canadian, French, and Native words to a mix of the Mohawk and Dutch languages. I don't know how long the term was used to describe the language or the people, but in 1955, one of Marie's descendants used it to describe her ancestors from the Mohawk Valley. Edith Ratnour Hammond, "Of Me and Mine," 1955, Hammond Family Collection; Pearson, *History of the Schenectady Patent*, xvi–xvii; Burke, *Mohawk Frontier*, 148–49; Jasper Danckearts, "Journal of a Voyage to New York and a Tour in Several of the American Colonies in 1679–1680," in Snow, Gehring, and Starna, *In Mohawk Country*, 195–98.

55. Parmenter, *Edge of the Woods*, 114–23; Merwick, *Possessing Albany*, 259.

56. Campisi, "Ethnic Identity," 36, 54; Richter, *Ordeal of the Longhouse*, 109–11.

57. "Deposition of Jean Labate," 2 July 1688, in *The Livingston Indian Records, 1666–1723*, ed. Lawrence H. Leder (Stanfordville, NY: Earl M. Coleman, 1979), 145–46; Robert J. Miller, "The Doctrine of Discovery, Manifest Destiny, and American Indians," in Sleeper-Smith et al., *Can't Teach United States History*, 89–91.

58. Parmenter, *Edge of the Woods*, 175–76; Richter, *Ordeal of the Longhouse*, 141.

59. "Proposal Made by 3 Maquase Sachems and 4 Sachems of the Oneida, June 17, 1687 and Answer," in Leder, *Livingston Indian Records*, 118–20; Burke, *Mohawk Frontier*, 84, 96, 100; Merwick, *Possessing Albany*, 211–13.

60. "Examination of Three French Prisoners Taken by Ye Maquase & Brought to Shinnechtady," 3 March 1690, in Leder, *Livingston Indian Records*, 158–59; Burke, *Mohawk Frontier*, 105–6.

61. The house of Adam Vrooman had been the home of Marie du Trieux, who died sometime before 1684. "List of Ye People Kild and Destroyed," in Sanders, *Early History of Schenectady*, 330–31; Pearson, *History of the Schenectady Patent*, 170; Burke, *Mohawk Frontier*, 106.

62. Burke, *Mohawk Frontier*, 198–200; Viele, *Viele Records*, 31.

63. Sanders, *Early History of Schenectady*, 99; Burke, *Mohawk Frontier*, 115, 201–7; Oliver Rink, "Before the English," in *The Empire State: A History of New York*, ed. Milton M. Klein (Ithaca, NY: Cornell University Press, 2001), 108.

64. Burke, *Mohawk Frontier*, 202, 205; Victoria Freeman, *Distant Relations: How My Ancestors Colonized North America* (Toronto: McClelland & Stewart, 2002), 256–59.

65. "Major Peter Schuyler's Journal of His Expedition to Canada, 1691," *NYCD*, 3:101; Burke, *Mohawk Frontier*, 196; Parmenter, *Edge of the Woods*, 221, 247.

66. Ann Hunter, "Tiononderogue: The Struggle for a Mohawk Town, 1686–1797," *Iroquoia* 1, no. 1 (Autumn 2015): 64–65.

67. Dennis, *Cultivating a Landscape*, 268; Parmenter, *Edge of the Woods*, 261–66; Richter, *Ordeal of the Longhouse*, 206–13; Danckearts, "Journal of a Voyage," 210–11.

68. Danckearts, "Journal of a Voyage," 216.

69. "Deed of Gift to Arnold Viele by Mohawk Sachems," 26 September 1683, *NYCD*, 4:802.

70. "Journal of Messrs. Hansen and Van Brugh's Visit to Onondaga," September 1700, *NYCD*, 4:802–7.

71. "Hansen and Van Brugh's Visit"; Parmenter, *Edge of the Woods*, 263–64.

72. "Hansen and Van Brugh's Visit."

2. Of One and Many People in the Mohawk Valley

1. Sanders, *Early History of Schenectady*, 142; Hunter, "Tiononderogue," 62–64; Burke, *Mohawk Frontier*, 210.

2. Mancall, *Deadly Medicine*, 14; "At a Meeting of the President Col. Peter Schuyler Esq and the Commissioners of the Indian Affairs in Albany the 3rd of September 1720," *NYCD*, 5:569.

3. John P. Ferguson, *The Schoharie Mohawks* (Howes Cave, NY: Iroquois Indian Museum, 2009), 47; Edith M. Fox, *Land Speculation in the Mohawk Valley* (Ithaca, NY: Cornell University Press, 1949), 4.

4. The most controversial patents included the Claverack Patent on the Massachusetts border between the Van Rensselaer and Livingston properties (Stockbridge), the Kayaderosseras, Fort Hunter, and Canajoharie Patents (Mohawk), and the Oriskany Patent (Oneida). Sung Bok Kim, *Landlord and Tenant in Colonial New York: Manorial Society, 1664–1775* (Chapel Hill: University of North Carolina Press, 1978), 359; Fox, *Land Speculation*, 7.

5. Preston, *Texture of Contact*, 73; J. H. French, *Historical and Statistical Gazetteer of New York State* (Syracuse, NY: R. P. Smith, 1860), Library of Congress, https://loc.gov; Ferguson, *Schoharie Mohawks*, 46–48, 87.

6. Ferguson, *Schoharie Mohawks*, 48–56, 62.

7. *Register of Baptisms, Marriages, Communicants, and Funerals Begun by Henry Barclay at Fort Hunter*, New York Historical Society, https://www.digitalcollections.nyhistory.org; Adriana E. Van Zwieten, "Glimpses of Childhood in the

Colony of New Netherland," 1–2, New Netherland Institute, 2009, https://www.newnetherlandinstitute.org/application/files/5016/8413/0916/Zweiten_chapter.pdf; Preston, *Texture of Contact*, 205.

8. Although the immigrants were called Palatines, most of them were from other German principalities. Philip Otterness, *Becoming German: The 1709 Palatine Migration to New York* (Ithaca, NY: Cornell University Press, 2004), 2–4.

9. Ulrich Simmendinger, *The Simmendinger Register* (1717; reprint, St. Johnsville, NY, n.p., 1934), iv; Otterness, *Becoming German*, 2, 71–73.

10. Jones, *Palatine Families of New York*, 49; Elisabeth Tooker, "The League of the Iroquois: Its History, Politics, and Ritual," in *Handbook of North American Indians*, vol. 15, *Northeast*, ed. Bruce G. Trigger (Washington, DC: Smithsonian Institution, 1978), 421.

11. Otterness, *Becoming German*, 93, 104, 106, 146.

12. Jeptha R. Simms, *History of Schoharie County and Border Wars of New York* (Albany: Munsell & Tanner, 1845), 69–70; Codman Hislop, *The Mohawk* (1948; reprint, Syracuse, NY: Syracuse University Press, 1989), 111–13; Otterness, *Becoming German*, 126–36; Preston, *Texture of Contact*, 78–79; David Guldenzopf, "The Colonial Transformation of Mohawk Iroquois Society" (PhD diss., State University of New York, 1986), 52, https://core.tdar.org/document/367158/the-colonial-transformation-of-mohawk-iroquois-society.

13. For several decades before the town was named St. Johnsville in the early 1800s, it was known as Timmermans. Members of the family spelled their last name as Timmerman and Zimmerman. David Kendall Martin, *The Eighteenth Century Zimmerman Family of the Mohawk Valley* (Church Hill, MD: Mouse House Books, 1994), 53–54; Otterness, *Becoming German*, 147; Nelson Greene, *The Story of Old Fort Plain and the Middle Mohawk Valley* (Fort Plain, NY: O'Connor Brothers, 1915), 285; "The Francis Harrison Patent," Fort Klock Historic Restoration, St. Johnsville, New York.

14. The site of eighteenth-century Canajoharie should not be confused with present-day Canajoharie downriver. Barbara J. Sivertsen, *Turtles, Wolves, and Bears: A Mohawk Family History* (Westminster, MD: Heritage Books, 2006), 122; "Conference between Governor Burnet and the Indians," 14–15 September 1724, *NYCD*, 5:90–93; Doug George-Kanentiio, "Iroquois Found Peace on Ontario's Shores," 31 May 1998, *SHA*, Jack Wallace Collection, Sherrill, NY; Richter, *Ordeal of the Longhouse*, 249–51, 277–79.

15. US Department of the Interior, National Park Service, "Mohawk Upper Castle Historic District," National Register of Historic Places registration form, n.d., Herkimer County Historical Society; Preston, *Texture of Contact*, 105–7; "David P. Schuyler (1688–1762) and Descendants," Schuyler File, Montgomery County Department of History and Archives, Fonda, NY.

16. *The Lawrence Zimmerman Papers, also Maps and Briefs of Snell-Timmerman Patent* (reprinted from *Enterprise and News* [St. Johnsville, NY], 1937), 22; Martin, *Eighteenth Century Zimmerman Family*, 55–57.

17. Martin, *Eighteenth Century Zimmerman Family*, 58–59; Preston, *Texture of Contact*, 214; Euan Cameron, *Enchanted Europe: Superstition, Reason, & Religion,*

1250–1750 (Oxford: Oxford University Press, 2010), 115–16, 160–61; George W. Walter, *Sinners and Saints: Stories of Upstate New York* (Utica, NY: North Country Books, 1973), 22–24; Barbara Alice Mann, *Iroquoian Women: The Gantowisas* (New York: Peter Lang, 2011), 241–89.

18. The information about Honyery and his family is limited and contradictory. I primarily rely on the oral history collected from his great-granddaughter, Mary Catharine Denny Doxtator (Abraham Denny's daughter, who grew up on Cowaselon Creek), and Polly Mytop Doxtator (the wife of Honyery's grandson George, son of Jacob) by the historian Lyman C. Draper during visits to the Oneida reservation in Wisconsin in the 1870s. Catharine Denny Doxtator and Polly Mytop Doxtator, interviews by Lyman C. Draper, 30 October–2 November 1877, Oneida Reservation, Wisconsin, 11 U:191–92, 195, Draper Manuscripts; Doris Dockstader Rooney, *The Dockstader Family* (Dodge City, KS: High Plains, 1983), 5, 9; Jones, *Palatine Families of New York,* 131–32.

19. The man named Schuyler may have been David or his son Peter. Peter's son Honyost Schuyler, born in 1744, was too young to be Plattcop's father as has been claimed. Or the father of Catharine's children may have been one of David's relatives from Albany. Catharine Denny Doxtator and Polly Mytop Doxtator, interviews, Draper Manuscripts; Cornelius File, Karst Collection, Oneida, NY.

20. Benn, *Iroquois in the War of 1812,* 70–72; Greene, *Story of Old Fort Plain,* 23–25; Preston, *Texture of Contact,* 97–109.

21. William Johnson to Peter Warren, 10 July 1739, and Johnson to Edward Collins, 19 February 1739/1740, *WJP*, 1:4–5, 8–9.

22. "Baptism of Ann, Daughter of Catharine Wysenbergh, 8 June 1740, and Baptism of Joseph, Son of Powel and Elizabeth His Wife," 11 May 1740, *Register of Baptisms, Marriages, Communicants, and Funerals Begun by Henry Barclay at Fort Hunter*; Sivertsen, *Turtles, Wolves, and Bears,* 127.

23. Timothy Shannon, *Indians and Colonists at the Crossroads of Empire: The Albany Congress of 1754* (Ithaca, NY: Cornell University Press, 2000), 31; Preston, *Texture of Contact,* 86, 92–93.

24. Shannon, *Indians and Colonists,* 36–43.

25. Colonel Johnson to Governor Clinton, Mount Johnson, 7 May 1747, *NYCD*, 6:361–62.

26. "Order of George Clinton Forbidding Joseph Clements from Trading in Spirituous Liquors with Indians or Soldiers Near Mount Johnson," 2 July 1747, *WJP*, 1:102–3; Josep Cleement to Colonel Wyllem Jansen, 16 August 1748, *WJP*, 1:180.

27. James J. Ross to William Johnson, 25 September 1749, *WJP*, 1:249.

28. Jacobus and Johannis Clement testified on August 23 and 26, 1749. Note on letter from George Clinton to William Johnson, 7 September 1747, *WJP*, 1:113–14.

29. George Clinton to William Johnson, 7 September 1747, and Clinton to the Board of Trade, 27 September 1747, *NYCD*, 6:671.

30. Johnson to Clinton, 7 May 1747; David L. Preston, "George Klock, the Canajoharie Mohawks, and the Good Ship *Sir William Johnson*: Land,

Legitimacy, and Community in the Eighteenth-Century Mohawk Valley," *New York History* 86, no. 4 (Fall 2005): 480, 489–91.

31. *Lawrence Zimmerman Papers*, 8–12; Martin, *Eighteenth Century Zimmerman Family*, 75–76.

32. Preston, "George Klock," 474–77, 480; Shannon, *Indians and Colonists*, 35.

33. "Conference between Governor Clinton and the Indians, 12-16 June 1753," *NYCD*, 6:783–88; Shannon, *Indians and Colonists*, 47–51.

34. "Conference between Governor Clinton and the Indians."

35. Preston, *Texture of Contact*, 113–14.

36. Shannon, *Indians and Colonists*, 102–5.

37. Benjamin Stoddert to William Johnson, 20 May 1751, *WJP*, 1:336–37; Matthew Ferrall to William Johnson, 28 July 1755, *WJP*, 1:785–86; Henry I. Wendall to William Johnson, 3 May 1756, *WJP*, 9:447–48.

38. William Johnson to Goldsbrow Banyar, 20 May 1755, *WJP*, 1:524; William Johnson, "Instructions to Mr. Jacobus Clement," 8 April 1756, *NYCD*, 7:96; Lenore J. Harris, *Clement Family History: Descendants of Lewis Cobes Clement, U.E.* [United Empire] *(1725–1781) and Catharine Eliza Poutman (1726–1807)* (Toronto: Pro Familia, 2002), 6–14, Clement File, Montgomery County Department of History and Archives.

39. Kanagweas, also spelled Kanaghquiesa and Conoghquisa among other variations, meant "a row of ears of corn standing upright." "Conference between Major-General Johnson and the Indians," Mount Johnson, 21–25 June and 3–4 July 1755, *NYCD*, 6:965, 970, 984; Cornelius, *Iroquois Corn*, 95–96; Campisi, "Ethnic Identity," 43.

40. Richard Berlath, *Bloody Mohawk: The French and Indian War & American Revolution on New York's Frontier* (Delmar, NY: Black Dome, 2009), 51–60; meeting with Oneidas and Tuscaroras, 16 February 1756, *NYCD*, 7:52.

41. Oneida conference with Sir William, German Flatts, 28–29 August 1756, and meeting of the Onondagas, Oneidas and Tuscaroras, German Flatts, 3 September 1756, *NYCD*, 7:189–94; William M. Forbes, "Fort Herkimer's Crucial Career," *Legacy: Annals of Herkimer County* 3 (1987): 3–7.

42. Forbes, "Fort Herkimer's Crucial Career," 3–7; William Johnson to William Shirley, 26 May 1756, *WJP*, 9:461–62; "Complaint of the Canajoharie Indians," Fort Johnson, 27 September 1756, *WJP*, 9:546–47; "An Indian Conference," Conojohere Castle, 7 February 1757, *WJP*, 9:600–601; Sivertsen, *Turtles, Wolves, and Bears*, 177; Ann M. Little, "Gender and Sexuality in the North American Borderlands, 1492–1848," *History Compass* 7, no. 6 (November 2009): 1606–15, http://onlinelibrary.wiley.com; Preston, *Texture of Contact*, 185.

43. Martin, *Eighteenth Century Zimmerman Family*, 107; Preston, *Texture of Conflict*, 185–90; Preston, "George Klock," 484–85; "America: Extract of a Letter from Albany," *British Chronicle*, 3–5 July 1758, http://access.newspaperarchive.com.

44. "List of Indians, October 1760," *WJP*, 13:173–74; Tiro, *People of the Standing Stone*, 51.

45. "Memorandum and Jurnel of Jelles Fonda," *WJP*, 13:171–73; "At a Meeting Held at Burnetsfield July 7th," 7 July 1761, *WJP*, 3:432.

46. Preston, *Texture of Contact*, 208; Ulysses Prentiss Hedrick, *A History of Agriculture in the State of New York* (New York: Hill & Wang, 1933), 80; *Johnson*

Hall and *Slavery at Johnson Hall*, pamphlets, Johnson Hall State Historic Site, Johnstown, NY.

47. I have also seen Molly Brant's name spelled as Konwatsitsiaienni. Lois M. Huey and Bonnie Pulis, *Molly Brant: A Legacy of Her Own* (Youngstown, NY: Fort Niagara Association, 1997), 25–39; Preston, *Texture of Contact*, 101–3; Nelson Greene, *History of the Mohawk Valley: Gateway to the West, 1614–1925* (Chicago: S. J. Clarke, 1925), chap. 52, https://schenectadyhistory.org; *Johnson Hall.*

48. Taylor, *Divided Ground*, 49–52; William Johnson to Henry Barclay, 30 March 1763, *WJP*, 4:72–73.

49. William Johnson to Goldsbrow Banyar, 12 October 1754, *WJP*, 1:421–22; William Johnson to Goldsbrow Banyar, 10 February 1761, *WJP*, 3:326-29; Alexander Colden to William Johnson, 22 June 1761, *WJP*, 3:418–20; Goldsbrow Banyar to William Johnson, 22 June 1761, *WJP*, 3:416–17; Goldsbrow Banyar to William Johnson, 24 June 1761, *WJP* 3:423–27; Isabel Thompson Kelsay, *Joseph Brant, 1743–1807: Man of Two Worlds* (Syracuse, NY: Syracuse University Press, 1984), 123; Preston, "George Klock," 492–94.

50. James O. Schuyler, "David Schuyler of Canajoharie, Mohawk Valley, New York," 2006, Schuyler File; William Johnson to Goldsbrow Banyar, 6 December 1761, *WJP*, 3:583–85; William Johnson to Goldsbrow Banyar, 7 January 1762, *WJP*, 3:602–4; deposition of David Schuyler, 23 January 1762, *WJP*, 3:613; William B. Hart, "Black 'Go-Betweens' and the Mutability of 'Race,' Status, and Identity on New York's Pre-revolutionary Frontier," in *Contact Points: American Frontiers from the Mohawk Valley to the Mississippi, 1750–1830*, ed. Andrew R. L. Cayton and Fredrika J. Teute (Chapel Hill: University of North Carolina Press, 1998), 106–8.

51. "To Deer Brother from the Sachems of Canajoharie," 8 July 1763, *WJP*, 4:164–65.

52. The Royal Grant included most of the present-day Herkimer County towns of Norway, Newport, Russia, Fairfield, Manheim, and Salisbury with parts of what would become the villages of Little Falls and Herkimer. Preston, "George Klock," 494; George L. Johnson, "Pioneer Times on the Royal Grant," *Papers Read before the Herkimer County Historical Society* (Herkimer, NY: Citizen, 1899), 66; William Johnson to Goldsbrow Banyar, 5 June 1761, *WJP*, 3:399–400.

53. *Papers of Lawrence Zimmerman*, 22; baptism of Margaret Bellinger, 14 September 1752, Lutheran Trinity Church of Stone Arabia, Ancestry.com, https://ancestry.com; William Johnson to Henry Moore, 3 June 1766, *WJP*, 5:237.

54. Milo Nellis, "Chapter VII: Sir William Johnson," in *The Mohawk Dutch and the Palatines*, 1951, Three Rivers, http://www.threeriversh ms.com; Ken D. Johnson, "George Klock, Sir William Johnson, & the Canajoharie Patent," Fort Plank, last updated 5 May 2009, https://www.fort-plank.com/Canajoharie_Pat_History.html; Preston, "George Klock," 491.

55. Walter, *Sinners and Saints*, 11–12; Jon Butler, *Becoming America: The Revolution before 1776* (Cambridge, MA: Harvard University Press, 2000), 192.

56. Fox, *Land Speculation*, 32–36; Robert William Venables, "Tryon County, 1775–1783: A Frontier in Revolution" (PhD diss., Vanderbilt University, 1967), 54; Jacob Cornelius, interview by Lyman C. Draper, 1 November 1877, Oneida Reservation, Wisconsin, 11 U:212–15, Draper Manuscripts; John Cornelius,

interview by Lyman C. Draper, 2 November 1877, Oneida Reservation, Wisconsin, 11 U:215–17, Draper Manuscripts; Catharine Denny Doxtator and Polly Mytop Doxtator, interviews, Draper Manuscripts; Preston, *Texture of Contact*, 184; "Full Text, End Notes: Oneida Hanyery vs. Joseph Brant," Oneida Indian Nation, 11 August 2008, https://www.oneidaindiannation.com/culture/shako/exhibits/26839509.html.

57. Tiro, *People of the Standing Stone*, 20; Jack Campisi, "Oneida," in Trigger, *Handbook*, 482–83; Colin G. Campbell, *The American Revolution in Indian Country: Crisis and Diversity in Native American Communities* (Cambridge: Cambridge University Press, 1995), 12; Anthony Wonderley, "1777: The Revolutionary War Comes to Oneida Country," *Mohawk Valley History* 1 (2004): 19–20, 23.

58. Several clues suggest that Louis Denny's wife, Maria, was the daughter or close relation of John of the Bear Clan and Marie of the Turtle Clan, well-known Mohawks of Schoharie. Barbara Sivertsen, however, does not name a Maria as one of the known children of John and Marie. Records of St. Paul's Lutheran Church, Schoharie, Reformed Church of Schoharie, and Schenectady Dutch Reformed Church; Sivertsen, *Turtles, Wolves, and Bears*, 189; Guldenzopf, "Colonial Transformation," 71; Catharine Denny Doxtator, interview; William W. Campbell, *The Life and Writings of DeWitt Clinton* (New York: Baker & Scribner, 1849), 173–74.

59. Simms, *History of Schoharie County*, 162; Ferguson, *Schoharie Mohawks*, 101–2.

60. Stuart Banner, *How the Indians Lost Their Land: Law and Power on the Frontier* (Cambridge, MA: Belknap Press of Harvard University Press, 2007), 91, 100.

61. Taylor, *Divided Ground*, 35–36; Colin G. Calloway, *Pen and Ink Witchcraft: Treaties and Treaty Making in American Indian History* (New York: Oxford University Press, 2013), 19.

62. Calloway, *Pen and Ink Witchcraft*, 49, 66–67.

63. "Proceedings of Sir William Johnson with the Indians at Fort Stanwix to Settle a Boundary Line," 30–31 October 1768, *NYCD* 8:122–26; Tiro, *People of the Standing Stone*, 28–31.

64. "Proceedings of Sir William Johnson"; Tiro, *People of the Standing Stone*, 31–34.

65. Calloway, *Pen and Ink Witchcraft*, 77–85.

66. Preston, *Texture of Contact*, 208–14; Hart, "Black 'Go-Betweens,'" 93; Huey and Pulis, *Molly Brant*, 31–33; Mann, *Iroquoian Women*, 352; Warren Johnson, "Journal of Warren Johnson," in Snow, Gehring, and Starna, *In Mohawk Country*, 259.

67. Tryon County covered what are now Delaware, Otsego, Herkimer, St. Lawrence, Jefferson, Franklin, Hamilton, Fulton, Montgomery, and Schoharie Counties. John C. Guzzardo, "Democracy along the Mohawk: An Election Return, 1773," *New York History* 57 (January 1976): 35–37, https://www.jstor.org/stable/23169705; Berlath, *Bloody Mohawk*, 142–48; Sir William Johnson to the Earl of Dartmouth, 16 December 1773, *NYCD*, 8:405–6; Earl of Dartmouth to Sir William Johnson, 6 April 1774, *NYCD*, 8:416; Preston, "George Klock," 495–96.

68. "Meeting of the Six Nations at Johnson Hall on the 9th of July 1774," 9–11 July 1774, *NYCD*, 8:475–79; *Sir William Johnson: His Final Days, 1774*, pamphlet, n.d., Johnson Hall State Historic Site.

69. "Extracts from Sir William Johnson's Will," in Huey and Pulis, *Molly Brant*, 117–19; Gorgen, "Ladies of the Mohawk Valley," 26–27; *Lawrence Zimmerman Papers*, 22.

70. Preston, "George Klock," 494; Edward P. Alexander, *A Revolutionary Conservative: James Duane of New York* (New York: Columbia University Press, 1938), 52–58.

71. John Myers to James Duane, 9 March 1772, box 2, and 6 January 1774, box 3, Duane Family Papers, 1665–1916, New York Historical Society, New York, NY; Alexander, *Revolutionary Conservative*, 61–67.

72. Kim, *Landlord and Tenant*, 237, 279.

73. John McFarland to James Duane, 21 December 1771, box 2, Duane Family Papers; Alexander, *Revolutionary Conservative*, 63.

74. Philip J. Deloria, *Playing Indian* (New Haven, CT: Yale University Press, 1998), 1–9.

3. For King or Country

1. "Palatine Committee, 19 May 1775," in *Mohawk Valley in the Revolution: Committee of Safety Papers & Genealogical Compendium*, by Maryly B. Penrose (Franklin Park, NJ: Liberty Bell Associates, 1978), 4–5; Martin, *Eighteenth Century Zimmerman Family*, 95; Venables, "Tryon County, 1775–1783," 107.

2. Wonderley, "1777," 32; Joseph T. Glatthaar and James Kirby Martin, *Forgotten Allies: The Oneida Indians and the American Revolution* (New York: Hill & Wang, 2006), 87–88; Tiro, *People of the Standing Stone*, 40–42.

3. Taylor, *Divided Ground*, 80; speech of Captain Brant to Lord George Germain, 14 March 1776, *NYCD*, 8:670–71.

4. Catharine Denny Doxtator, Polly Mytop Doxtator, Jacob Cornelius, interviews, 11 U:191, 196, 214, Draper Manuscripts; Lyman C. Draper, "Notes of Conversation with Elijah Skenando," 29 October 1879, Oneida Reservation, Wisconsin, 11 U:243–44, Draper Manuscripts; Tiro, *People of the Standing Stone*, 47; Anthony Wonderley, "An Oneida Community in 1780: Study of an Inventory of Iroquois Property Losses during the Revolutionary War," *Northeast Anthropology*, no. 56 (1998): 33; Wonderley, "1777," 31.

5. The other two members of the congressional committee on Indian affairs were James Wilson of Pennsylvania and Patrick Henry of Virginia. Taylor, *Divided Ground*, 81–83; Philip O. Geier III, "A Peculiar Status: A History of Oneida Indian Treaties and Claims; Jurisdictional Conflict within American Government, 1775–1920" (PhD diss., Syracuse University, 1980), 56.

6. Taylor, *Divided Ground*, 81–82; John Locke, "Of Property," *Second Treatise*, 1689, Electronic Resources from the University of Chicago Press Books Division, https://press-pubs.uchicago.edu.

7. "Treaty in Albany, 28 August 1775," in *Indian Affairs Papers: American Revolution*, by Maryly B. Penrose (Franklin Park, NJ: Liberty Bell Associates, 1981), 23–24; Calloway, *Pen and Ink Witchcraft*, 36.

8. Created at the direction of the Continental Congress, committees of safety promoted independence, organized the war effort, and functioned as civil governments. The Tryon County Committee of Safety, which consisted of members from each of its districts—Kingsland (which was to the north and west

of Little Falls), German Flatts, Canajoharie, Palatine, and Mohawk—answered to the New York Committee (later Council) of Safety. "Committee Meeting, 28 February 1776," in Penrose, *Mohawk Valley*, 75.

9. "County Committee on the 29th Day of June 1775 at the House of Frederick Bellinger in Germanflatts Distt," in Penrose, *Mohawk Valley*, 19–20.

10. "Of the County Committee, 27 August 1775, at the House of Gose Van Alstyne," in Penrose, *Mohawk Valley*, 37–39.

11. "Of the County Committee, 27 August 1775"; "Of the County Committee on Monday the 6 November 1775 at the House of Gose Van Alstyne," and "By Order of This Committee, 25 November 1775," in Penrose, *Mohawk Valley*, 56, 62–63.

12. "Of the County Committee, 7 November 1775," in Penrose, *Mohawk Valley*, 57.

13. "Examinations & Affidavits agst. Lewis Clement," 26 August 1775, in Penrose, *Mohawk Valley*, 35.

14. "Of the County Committee, 13 September 1775" and "Of the County Committee, 6 November 1775," in Penrose, *Mohawk Valley*, 44–45, 55; Harris, *Clement Family History*.

15. Fort Stanwix was renamed Fort Schuyler in honor of General Schuyler. Fort Schuyler was also the name of the fort at present-day Utica. To avoid confusion, as did the locals who knew the fort at the Carrying Place as Fort Stanwix, I call it Fort Stanwix. Lambert Clement, NY W6695, US Revolutionary War Pension and Bounty-Land Warrant Application Files, 1800–1900 Original Data, Records of the Department of Veterans Affairs. Record Group 15, National Archives, Washington, DC, Ancestry.com, https://www.ancestry.com (hereafter cited with pension application number).

16. Gavin K. Watt, *Rebellion in the Mohawk Valley: The St. Leger Expedition of 1777* (Toronto: Dundurn, 2002), 53–54; Glatthaar and Martin, *Forgotten Allies*, 107–8, 133; Taylor, *Divided Ground*, 92.

17. Karim M. Tiro, "A 'Civil' War? Rethinking Iroquois Participation in the American Revolution," *Explorations in Early American Culture* 4 (2000): 149, https://www.jstor.org/stable/23549298; Glatthaar and Martin, *Forgotten Allies*, 140.

18. John [G.] Timerman, NY R21795; Jacob Zimmerman, NY W20002; Watt, *Rebellion in the Mohawk Valley*, 83–84.

19. Nicholas Herckheimer to Major General Schuyler, 15 July 1777, in Penrose, *Indian Affairs Papers*, 89–91; Glatthaar and Martin, *Forgotten Allies*, 154.

20. Glatthaar and Martin, *Forgotten Allies*, 94–96, 155–57.

21. "A County Committee Meeting Held the 17th July 1777 at Col. Wm. Seeber's," in Penrose, *Mohawk Valley*, 121–24; Theobald Meyer (Daybold Moyer), NY W15789; Glatthaar and Martin, *Forgotten Allies*, 143–47.

22. Watt, *Rebellion in the Mohawk Valley*, 127; "Here's to the Red, White, & Blue!!!," Fort Stanwix National Monument, National Park Service, accessed 21 November 2023, https://www.nps.gov.

23. Catharine Denny Doxtator and Cornelius Doxtator, interviews, 11 U:191–92, 202–4, Draper Manuscripts; Watt, *Rebellion in the Mohawk Valley*, 130–33; Glatthaar and Martin, *Forgotten Allies*, 158–59.

24. The middle initials of the Timmerman nephews designate the names of their fathers: Conrad, Jacob, George, and Lawrence. John Zimmerman, NY W16489; William Zimmerman, NY R11990; Henry L. Zimmerman, S14701.

25. John D. Failing, NY W19242; Jacob Timmerman, NY W20002; John Zimmerman, NY W16489; William Zimmerman, NY R11990; Glatthaar and Martin, *Forgotten Allies*, 163.

26. Louis Atayataghronghta (Cook) has been identified as an adopted son of Skenandoah who married Skenandoah's daughter. Cornelius Wheelock (grandson of the Oriske warrior Hendrick Smith), interview by Lyman C. Draper, 30 October–2 November 1877, Oneida Reservation, Wisconsin, 11 U:210, Draper Manuscripts; Elijah Skenando, John Cornelius, Polly Mytop Doxtator, interviews, 11 U:196, 215–16, 243–44, Draper Manuscripts; Laurence M. Hauptman, *Conspiracy of Interests: Iroquois Dispossession and the Rise of New York State* (Syracuse, NY: Syracuse University Press, 1999), 54; Anthony Wonderley, "'Good Peter's Narrative of Several Transactions respecting Indian Lands': An Oneida View of Dispossession, 1785–1788," *New York History* 84, no. 3 (Summer 2003): 257, https://www.jstor.org/stable/23183368; Darren Bonaparte, "Louis Cook: A 'Colonel' of Truth?," Wampum Chronicles, 23 September 2005, https://www.wampumchronicles.com.

27. Glatthaar and Martin, *Forgotten Allies*, 160–62.

28. Cornelius Wheelock, Elijah Skenando, John Cornelius, Polly Mytop Doxtator, interviews, 11 U:196, 210, 215–16, 243–44, Draper Manuscripts; Glatthaar and Martin, *Forgotten Allies*, 162–63.

29. Watt, *Rebellion in the Mohawk Valley*, 156–57.

30. John Dockstader, NY S31654; Watt, *Rebellion in the Mohawk Valley*, 160–64, 172.

31. Watt, *Rebellion in the Mohawk Valley*, 163–69.

32. Polly Mytop Doxtator, John Cornelius, and Elijah Skenando, interviews, 11 U:196, 215–16, 243, Draper Manuscripts; Darren Bonaparte, "Colonel Louis at Oriskany and Valley Forge," Wampum Chronicles, 30 September 2005, https://www.wampumchronicles.com.

33. Watt, *Rebellion in the Mohawk Valley*, 185, 217; Greene, *Story of Old Fort Plain*, 58–59; James F. Morrison, "Colonel Jacob Klock's Regiment Tryon County Militia," 1992, Montgomery County Department of History and Archives; John Cornelius, interview, 11 U:216, Draper Manuscripts.

34. John [G.] Timerman, NY R21795; Jacob J. Failing, W21092.

35. Philip Schuyler to John Hancock, 8 August 1777, in Penrose, *Indian Affairs Papers*, 92–93; Watt, *Rebellion in the Mohawk Valley*, 205–7, 212; Glatthaar and Martin, *Forgotten Allies*, 171–74.

36. Glatthaar and Martin, *Forgotten Allies*, 174; Watt, *Rebellion in the Mohawk Valley*, 224, 228, 237–45.

37. The mother of Honyost Schuyler's daughter Anna, born in 1774, is believed to have been Oneida. Honyost's father, Peter D. Schuyler, recorded Anna's birth in the family Bible without naming her mother. Schuyler File; "Burnets Field, 23 October 1776," in Penrose, *Mohawk Valley in the Revolution*, 93; Watt, *Rebellion in the Mohawk Valley*, 224, 245.

38. Glatthaar and Martin, *Forgotten Allies*, 175–76; Watt, *Rebellion in the Mohawk Valley*, 243–49.

39. Wonderley, "Oneida Community in 1780"; Glatthaar and Martin, *Forgotten Allies*, 176.

40. Schuyler File; Penrose, *Indian Affairs Papers*, 125–34; Huey and Pulis, *Molly Brant*, 45–47.

41. Watt, *Rebellion in the Mohawk Valley*, 278–79; Glatthaar and Martin, *Forgotten Allies*, 180–84; John Hadcock to L. C. Draper, 6 May 1872, 11 U: 264, Draper Manuscripts. The letter conveying the order of General Gates regarding "the wife of Honyas, a principal warrior of the Oneida Nation" most likely refers to Honyery, but it may also refer to his brother Honyost. Isaac Peirce, A. D. Camp, Head Quarters, Behmis's Heights, to Colonel Peter Gansevoort or Officer Commanding at Fort Schuyler [Stanwix], 26 September 1777, Peter Gansevoort Jr. Military Papers, Manuscripts and Archives Division, New York Public Library.

42. Penrose, *Indian Affairs Papers*, 125–34; Maryly B. Penrose, *Compendium of Early Mohawk Valley Families* (Baltimore: Genealogical Publishing, 1990), 1:xvi; Martin, *Eighteenth Century Zimmerman Family*, 96–97; Philip Schuyler to the Chairman of the General Committee of the County of Tryon, 11 March 1778, Oneida Nation of Wisconsin, https://www.exploreoneida.com; Watt, *Rebellion in the Valley*, 322.

43. Odatshedah means "quiver bearer." "Johnstown Conference," 10 March 1778, in Penrose, *Indian Affairs Papers*, 112–17; Cornelius, *Iroquois Corn*, 95; Glatthaar and Martin, *Forgotten Allies*, 189–90.

44. Back then, "stout" meant strong. Glatthaar and Martin, *Forgotten Allies*, 203–9, 216, 218; Hauptman, "Three Stories of War," 63–66; Tiro, *People of the Standing Stone*, 50.

45. Taylor, *Divided Ground*, 90–91.

46. Colonel Peter Vrooman was the great-grandson of Adam Vrooman. Louis Denny was referred to as "Louis the Frenchman" and "Louis the Indianer" in Schoharie church records. See Records of the Reformed Church, Schoharie, NY, 1731–1894, and Records of St. Paul's Lutheran Church, Schoharie, NY, 1728–1899; baptism of Maria [Polly] Denny, 28 March 1775, St. Paul's Lutheran Church, Schoharie, NY; Peter Vrooman to General Ten Broeck, 17 July 1778, and Abraham Ten Broeck to George Clinton, 19 July 1778, in *Public Papers of George Clinton*, ed. Hugh Hastings (Albany: State of New York, 1900), 3:557–58.

47. John Myers, W20271; Berlath, *Bloody Mohawk*, 254.

48. Jacob J. Failing, NY W21092; Jacob Zimmerman, NY W20002; Glatthaar and Martin, *Forgotten Allies*, 226, 230–31.

49. Glatthaar and Martin, *Forgotten Allies*, 232–33, 236.

50. Jacob J. Failing, NY W21092; Peter Suits, NY W13941; Greene, *Story of Old Fort Plain*, 66.

51. Glatthaar and Martin, *Forgotten Allies*, 240; Alexander, *Revolutionary Conservative*, 131–32.

52. Journals of Maj. James Norris, 236; Lt. Erkuries Beatty, 27; Maj. John Burrowes, 48; Lt. Col. Adam Hubley, 156; Lt. William McKendry, 207; Lt. Charles Nukerck, 217; Sgt. Thomas Roberts, 244, in Frederick Cook, *Journals of*

the Military Expedition of Major General John Sullivan against the Six Nations of Indians, 1779 (Auburn, NY: Knapp, Peck, & Thomson, 1887); Tiro, "'Civil War,'" 159–60.

53. Andrea Lynn Smith, "Remembering Washington's 'Sullivan Expedition' of 1779 in Contemporary Times" (paper presentation, Conference on Iroquois Research, Salamanca, NY, October 2022); Glatthaar and Martin, *Forgotten Allies*, 242–45.

54. "Major General Sullivan's Official Report," 30 September 1779, in Cook, *Journals*, 302; Hauptman, *Conspiracy of Interests*, 62.

55. Col. Jacob Klock to Gov. George Clinton, 5 April 1780, in John B. Koetteritz, "The Town of Manheim," in *Papers Read before the Herkimer County Historical Society*, ed. Arthur T. Smith (Herkimer: Citizens, 1899), 403; Harris, *Clement Family History*; "Clement Family U. E. L. [United Empire Loyalists] Claims for Losses in the Revolutionary War," Ancestry.com, accessed 22 April 2015, https://www.ancestry.com; report of Guy Johnson, 11 August 1780, Niagara, in W. Max Reid, *The Story of Old Fort Johnson* (New York: G. P. Putnam's Sons, 1906), 119–22; Lambert Clement, NY W6695.

56. Benn, *Iroquois in the War of 1812*, 10.

57. Glatthaar and Martin, *Forgotten Allies*, 260–62, 270–71.

58. Karim M. Tiro, "The Dilemmas of Alliance: The Oneida Indian Nation in the American Revolution," in *War & Society in the American Revolution: Mobilization and Home Fronts*, ed. John Resch and Walter Sargent (DeKalb: Northern Illinois University Press, 2007), 225; records of the Schenectady Dutch Reformed Church; Taylor, *Divided Ground*, 101; Glatthaar and Martin, *Forgotten Allies*, 272–76.

59. Honyere Tewahangarahken Doxtator, "Indian (N.Y.)" S23019; Jacob J. Failing, NY W21092; Greene, *Story of Old Fort Plain*, 75; Gavin K. Watt, *A Dirty, Trifling, Piece of Business*, vol. 1, *The Revolutionary War as Waged from Canada in 1781* (Toronto: Dundurn, 2009), 183.

60. Abraham Wolleber, NY R17772; Martin, *Eighteenth Century Zimmerman Family*, 96.

61. Theobald Meyer, NY W15789; John D. Failing, NY W19242; Simms, *History of Schoharie County*, 384.

62. The Middle Fort was the home of Johannes Becker, who had sponsored Louis Denny's seven-year-old son, Johannes/Jonathan, at his baptism. Gavin K. Watt, *The Burning of the Valleys: Daring Raids from Canada against the New York Frontier in the Fall of 1780* (Toronto: Dundurn, 1997), 176, 184; baptism of Johannes [Jonathan] Denny, 24 September 1773, records of the Reformed Church of Schoharie; Simms, *History of Schoharie County*, 409; "Indian Affairs Commissioners Meeting with Three Nations," 21 October 1778, in Penrose, *Indian Affairs Papers*, 161–62; John Myers, NY W20271; Nicholas Rightor, NY S14309.

63. Theobald Meyer, NY W15789; Watt, *Burning of the Valleys*, 176, 207–18.

64. William Van Slike, NY W2461; John Zimmerman, NY W16489; William Zimmerman, NY R11990; Glatthaar and Martin, *Forgotten Allies*, 277.

65. Glatthaar and Martin, *Forgotten Allies*, 278; Watt, *Dirty, Trifling, Piece of Business*, 182–86; Barbara Graymont, *The Iroquois in the American Revolution* (Syracuse, NY: Syracuse University Press, 1972), 240.

66. Taylor, *Divided Ground*, 102; John Zimmerman, NY W16489; Johannes Ecker, NY R3182; John D. Failing, NY W19242; Peter Suits, NY W13941; George House, NY S19340; David A. Schuyler, NY S14423.

67. Jacob Zimmerman, NY W20002; John Zimmerman, NY W16489.

68. David Welch, who in 1855 lived in Stockbridge, New York, was identified in the New York State census as Black. Honyere Tewahangarahken Doxtator, "Indian (N.Y.)" S23019; William Bellinger, NY S28641; Watt, *Dirty, Trifling, Piece of Business*, 259; Town of Stockbridge, Madison County, New York State Census, 1855.

69. Glatthaar and Martin, *Forgotten Allies*, 279–80.

70. Lambert Clement, NY W6695; John [G.] Timerman, NY R21795; Martin, *Eighteenth Century Zimmerman Family*, 165; Watt, *Dirty, Trifling, Piece of Business*, 340, 345, 353–54; Hislop, *Mohawk*, 203–4; Simms, *History of Schoharie County*, 479.

71. Glatthaar and Martin, *Forgotten Allies*, 286; Gavin K. Watt, *I Am Heartily Ashamed*, vol. 2, *The Revolutionary War's Final Campaign as Waged from Canada in 1782* (Toronto: Dundurn Press, 2010), 152, 211–18; Martin, *Eighteenth Century Zimmerman Family*, 95–96.

72. Glatthaar and Martin, *Forgotten Allies*, 284–85; Greene, *History of the Mohawk Valley*, chap. 72.

73. Taylor, *Divided Ground*, 145; Glatthaar and Martin, *Forgotten Allies*, 300; Penrose, *Compendium of Early Mohawk Valley Families*, 1:xix–xx.

74. Glatthaar and Martin, *Forgotten Allies*, 289; William W. Campbell, *Annals of Tryon County, or the Border Warfare of New York during the Revolution* (New York: J. & J. Harper, 1831), 189.

4. As Long as the Grass Shall Grow

1. Eleanor Franz, "Memories of the Revolutionary War: Interviews with the Late Emma Timerman Recapture the Way of Life of Beleaguered Palatines," *Legacy: Annals of Herkimer County* 2 (1987): 3–6; Martin, *Eighteenth Century Zimmerman Family*, 164; F. W. Beers, *History of Herkimer County, New York* (New York: F. W. Beers, 1879), 204.

2. François Marbois, "Journey to the Oneidas," in Snow, Gehring, and Starna, *In Mohawk Country*, 309. Tiro, "Dilemmas of Alliance," 229; "Memorial," February 1788, in *Proceedings of the Commissioners of Indian Affairs, Appointed by Law for the Extinguishment of Indian Titles in the State of New York*, by Franklin B. Hough (Albany: Joel Munsell, 1861), 1:124.

3. According to Samuel Kirkland, Schoharie John and his family were living in Oneida in 1796. The quotation is from Lawrence Lawyer, who served as the sponsor at the baptism of Louis and Maria Denny's son John in 1763 and daughter Elizabeth in 1778. Baptism of "Jan, an Indian" [John Denny], 27 March 1763, St. Paul's Lutheran Church, Schoharie; baptism of Elisabet, 10 May 1778, Reformed Church of Schoharie; Henry R. Schoolcraft, *Notes on the Iroquois* (Albany: Erastus H. Pease, 1847), 440–41; Rachel Parkhurst (great-granddaughter of Skenandoah), interview by Lyman C. Draper, 1 November 1877, Oneida Reservation, Wisconsin, 11 U:205–9, Draper Manuscripts; John Cornelius, interview, 11 U:216–17, Draper Manuscripts; Simms, *History of Schoharie*

County, 530–31; Ferguson, *Schoharie Mohawks*, 112–13; Walter Pilkington, ed., *The Journals of Samuel Kirkland* (Clinton, NY: Hamilton College, 1980), 290.

4. Patrick Campbell, *A Journey through the Genesee Country, Finger Lakes Region and Mohawk Valley from Patrick Campbell's Travels in the Interior Inhabited Parts of North America in the Years 1791 and 1792* (Rochester, NY: University of Rochester Libraries, 1978); Rooney, *Dockstader Family*, 31–32.

5. The information on Honyery's wives is confusing and contradictory. Loretta Metoxen, "Oneida Traditions," in Campisi and Hauptman, *Oneida Indian Experience*, 145–46; Jeremy Belknap and Jedidiah Morse, *Report on the Oneida, Stockbridge and Brotherton Indians, 1796* (New York: Museum of the American Indian, 1955), 11; Rooney, *Dockstader Family*, 31–32; Honyere Tewahangarahken Doxtator, "Indian (N.Y.)" S23019.

6. In the records, the many spellings of Doxtator include Dachstätter, Tachstetter, and Dockstader. Denny was spelled Dennie, De Nie, De Ny, Tenny, Te Ny, and Dana. Pomroy Jones, *Annals and Recollections of Oneida County* (Rome, NY: printed by the author, 1851), 798; "An Early History of Early Days in Oriskany," n.d., Oriskany Historical File, Oneida County History Center, Utica, NY.

7. Peter Sailly, "Diary of Peter Sailly on a Journey in America in the Year 1784," in Snow, Gehring, and Starna, *In Mohawk Country*, 297–98.

8. Stephan L. Pevar, *The Rights of Indians and Tribes*, 4th ed. (New York: Oxford University Press, 2012), 24; Calloway, *Pen and Ink Witchcraft*, 100.

9. Glatthaar and Martin, *Forgotten Allies*, 294; Peter L. Bernstein, *Wedding of the Waters: The Erie Canal and the Making of a Great Nation* (New York: Norton, 2005), 64; Alexander, *Revolutionary Conservative*, 143; Taylor, *Divided Ground*, 154–55.

10. James Duane to Gov. George Clinton, [1784], in Hough, *Proceedings*, 1:21–24; Graymont, *Iroquois in the American Revolution*, 269.

11. Duane to Clinton, in Hough, *Proceedings*, 1:21–24.

12. Duane to Clinton, in Hough, *Proceedings*, 1:21–24.

13. George Clinton to James Dean, 14 August 1784, in Hough, *Proceedings*, 1:25.

14. "Meeting of the Commissioners for Indian Affairs and the Oneida and Tuscarora Nations," 4–10 September 1784, Fort Stanwix, in Hough, *Proceedings*, 1:39–59.

15. "Meeting of the Commissioners for Indian Affairs."

16. "Instructions for Major Peter Schuyler," [1784], in Hough, *Proceedings*, 1:63; Graymont, *Iroquois in the American Revolution*, 278–79; "Journal of Lt. Lawrence Tremper," Fort Plank, 1783, https://www.fort_plank.com/Trempers_Journal.pdf; Christine Sternberg Patrick, "The Life and Times of Samuel Kirkland, 1741–1808: Missionary to the Oneida Indians, American Patriot, and Founder of Hamilton College" (PhD diss., State University of New York at Buffalo, 1993), 378.

17. Marbois, "Journey to the Oneidas," 313; Glatthaar and Martin, *Forgotten Allies*, 192–93; Richard W. Hill Sr., "Linking Arms and Brightening the Chain: Building Relations through Treaties," in *Nation to Nation: Treaties between the United States and American Indian Nations*, ed. Suzan Shown Harjo (Washington, DC: Smithsonian Books, 2014), 44–45.

18. Marbois, "Journey to the Oneidas," 305, 308.

19. Marbois, "Journey to the Oneidas," 307–8.

20. Marbois, "Journey to the Oneidas," 317; Tiro, *People of the Standing Stone*, 64; Taylor, *Divided Ground*, 158–61; Glatthaar and Martin, *Forgotten Allies*, 297–98.

21. Tiro, *People of the Standing Stone*, 63, 84; Geier, "Peculiar Status," 68, 86–87; Arthur Breese to James Madison, 11 April 1794, Founders Online, National Archives, https://founders.archives.gov/documents/Madison/01-15-02-0202.

22. The Brothertowns included Narragansetts, Pequots, Mohegans, Niantics, Tunxis, and Montauketts. David J. Silverman, *Red Brethren: The Brothertown and Stockbridge Indians and the Problem of Race in Early America* (Ithaca, NY: Cornell University Press, 2010), 6, 118–22; Hough, *Proceedings*, 1:47, 92; Anthony Wonderley, "Brothertown, New York, 1785–1796," *New York History* 81, no. 4 (October 2000): 465–66.

23. "Early History of Early Days"; Hough, *Proceedings*, 1:222; Rooney, *Dockstader Family*, 32.

24. Greene, *Story of Old Fort Plain*, 163; Peter Schuyler to Governor Clinton, 20 May 1785, in Hough, *Proceedings*, 1:75.

25. Arthur Breese to Sidney Breese, 28 July 1792, box 1, folder 5, Breese Stevens Roby Family Papers, AB83, Rare Books, Special Collections, and Preservation, River Campus Libraries, University of Rochester, Rochester, NY; Kelsay, *Joseph Brant*, 360–61, 474; Joseph Brant to Governor Clinton, 18 June 1789, in Hough, *Proceedings*, 2:330.

26. Alexander, *Revolutionary Conservative*, 166; E. Wilder Spaulding, *New York in the Critical Period, 1783–1789* (Port Washington, NY: Ira J. Freedman, 1963), 15, 20–26; Edward Countryman, "Indians, the Colonial Order, and the Social Significance of the American Revolution," *William and Mary Quarterly* 53, no. 2 (April 1996): 357–58, https://www.jstor.org/stable/2947405; John L. Brooke, *Columbia Rising: Civil Life on the Upper Hudson from the Revolution to the Age of Jackson* (Chapel Hill: University of North Carolina Press, 2010), 182–83.

27. Michael Hetzel to James Duane, 2 May 1784, box 5; George Hetzel to James Duane, 3 May 1784, box 5; John Myers to James Duane, 18 January 1786, box 6; John Myers to James Duane, 14 April 1790, box 7, Duane Family Papers; marriage of John Meyers and Mary Hedzel, 9 March 1791, Records of Schenectady Dutch Reformed Church.

28. John Myers to James Duane, 9 March 1772, box 2; 24 January 1784, box 5; 7 October 1785, 12 July 1786, 9 October 1786, box 6, Duane Family Papers.

29. Winslow C. Watson, *Men and Times of the Revolution; or, Memoirs of Elkanah Watson* (New York: Dana, 1956), 39, 339; Oriskany, NY, petition, n.d. [after 1783], AHMC-Oriskany, New York Historical Society; "Meeting at Fort Herkimer, 23–29 June 1785," in Hough, *Proceedings*, 1:84–108.

30. "Meeting at Fort Herkimer, 23–29 June 1785," in Hough, *Proceedings*, 1:86, 91–97.

31. Hough, *Proceedings*, 1:102; Wonderley, "Good Peter's Narrative," 250; Treaty of 1785, Fort Herkimer, 28 June 1785, in New York State, *Report of the Special Committee to Investigate the Indian Problem of the State of New York, 1888* (Albany: Troy Press, 1889), vol. 1, part 1, pp. 234–36 (hereafter cited as the Whipple Report, as it is commonly known), available online at the New York

State Library, Native American Digital Collections; Tiro, *People of the Standing Stone*, 71; Taylor, *Divided Ground*, 165.

32. Brooke, *Columbia Rising*, 186–93.

33. Tiro, *People of the Standing Stone*, 76–78.

34. Taylor, *Divided Ground*, 214–19.

35. Hough, *Proceedings*, 1:154–56; Jones, *Annals and Recollections*, 721.

36. Watson, *Men and Times*, 311–15; Hough, *Proceedings*, 1:179, 232.

37. Hough, *Proceedings*, 1:227, 232.

38. Clarence Webster, "A Touch of Gray," 1974, Oriskany Historical File, Oneida County History Center; Hough, *Proceedings*, 1:236–40.

39. Hough, *Proceedings*, 1:282–83; Tiro, *People of the Standing Stone*, 79–80.

40. Hough, *Proceedings*, 1:235; Whipple Report, vol. 1, part 1, p. 237; Jack Campisi, "The Oneida Treaty Period, 1783–1838," in Campisi and Hauptman, *Oneida Indian Experience*, 52–54; Taylor, *Divided Ground*, 185–86; Wonderley, "Good Peter's Narrative," 271–72.

41. Hough, *Proceedings*, 1:241, 245–46; 2:279, 300.

42. Hough, *Proceedings*, 1:248.

43. Tiro, *People of the Standing Stone*, 65, 69, 82, 93; Pilkington, *Journals of Samuel Kirkland*, 174–75; Hough, *Proceedings*, 2:320–21, 346–54.

44. Pilkington, *Journals of Samuel Kirkland*, 201, 204, 207; Hough, *Proceedings*, 2:354.

45. Spaulding, *New York in the Critical Period*, 152–59.

46. Little is known about Peter Brewer (Brouwer, Bruer) and his wife Catrina Crisler (probably a member of the Palatine Greisler/Krysler/Chrysler family). Peter, whose family lived in Somerset County, New Jersey, was descended from Jan Brouwer, a blacksmith who was born in Amsterdam in 1632 and arrived in New Amsterdam in the 1650s. My guess is that the Brewers came to Schenectady County when Vought recruited tenants in the early 1770s. John Myers to James Duane, 1 May 1786, box 6, and 8 November 1787, box 7, Duane Family Papers; Alexander, *Revolutionary Conservative*, 230; Spaulding, *New York in the Critical Period*, 60; records of the Schenectady Dutch Reformed Church and Schoharie Reformed Church; Brouwer Genealogy Database, https://www.rootsweb.com; William Gordon Ver Planck, "The Vought Family," 1907, Vought House, http://1759voughthouse.org/uploads/3/4/3/9/3439533/verplanckvought.pdf.

47. John Myers to James Duane, 3 April and 13 June 1788, box 7, Duane Family Papers; Alexander, *Revolutionary Conservative*, 232; Spaulding, *New York in the Critical Period*, 267.

48. John Myers to James Duane, 5 May 1789, box 7; 14 April 1790, 16 January 1792, 24 February 1792, 17 January 1793, box 8, Duane Family Papers; Alexander, *Revolutionary Conservative*, 216, 225.

49. Hough, *Proceedings*, 2:319, 358–67.

50. Hough, *Proceedings*, 2:358–66.

51. Hough, *Proceedings*, 2:365.

52. The military tracts included the counties of Onondaga, Cayuga, Seneca, and Cortland, and parts of the counties of Wayne, Steuben, and Oswego. Watson, *Men and Times*, 316, 335–58; John E. Smith, ed., *Our County and Its People:*

A Descriptive and Biographical Record of Madison County, New York (Boston: Boston History Company, 1899), 3.

53. Taylor, *Divided Ground*, 239; Hill, "Linking Arms," 49.

54. Taylor, *Divided Ground*, 270–72; Tiro, *People of the Standing Stone*, 79, 92.

55. Jo Margaret Mano, "Unmapping the Iroquois: New York State Cartography, 1792–1845," in *The Oneida Indian Journey: From New York to Wisconsin, 1784–1860*, ed. Laurence M. Hauptman and L. Gordon McLester III (Madison: University of Wisconsin Press, 1999), 172–84.

56. Taylor, *Divided Ground*, 232.

57. Taylor, *Divided Ground*, 233–34.

58. Smith, *Our County and Its People*, 629; Campbell, *Journey through the Genesee Country*; Pilkington, *Journals of Samuel Kirkland*, 149, 175; John Maude, *Visit to the Falls of Niagara in 1800* (London: Longman, Rees, Orme, Brown & Green, 1826), 285.

59. John Lincklaen, *Travels in the Years 1791 and 1792 in Pennsylvania, New York and Vermont* (New York: G. P. Putnam's Sons, 1897), 112; Schuyler File; "Pickard Family" (Heritage and Genealogical Society of Montgomery County, Fonda, NY, 1979), Pickard File, Montgomery County Department of History and Archives.

60. Taylor, *Divided Ground*, 224–25; James D. Folts, "Before the Dispersal: Records of New York's Official Relations with the Oneidas and Other Indian Nations," in Hauptman and McLester, *Oneida Indian Journey*, 158; Tiro, *People of the Standing Stone*, 83; Polly Mytop Doxtator, interview, 11 U:198, Draper Manuscripts.

61. James H. Smith, *The History of Chenango and Madison Counties, New York* (Syracuse: D. Mason, 1880); L. M. Hammond, *History of Madison County* (Syracuse, NY: Truair, Smith, 1872), 654–60; "Pickard Family"; "Jacob Seeber Occupant on Onida Reservation, 1795," "Jacob Schuyler Occupant on Onida Reservation, 1795," "Jacob Schuyler & Joseph Mabee Several Occupants on Onida Reservation, 1795," "Testimony of Peter Marsh and Gerrit Van Slyck," 7 December 1795, and "Testimony of Conrad Klock," 9 December 1795, in "Abstract of Claims to Preemption on Onida Reservation, 1798," Field Book No. 27, A4052 MU1, Reel 7, NYSA.

62. Taylor, *Divided Ground*, 148–49; John Zimmerman, NY W16489.

63. Maude, *Visit to the Falls*, 38; Lincklaen, *Travels*, 112; Patrick, "Life and Times," 396; Pilkington, *Journals of Samuel Kirkland*, 265–66, 314.

64. Norman K. Dann, *Peter Smith of Peterboro: Furs, Land and Anguish* (Hamilton, NY: Log Cabin Books, 2018), 3–8, 21–24.

65. William H. Tuttle, "Early History of the Town of Lincoln," *ODU*, 15 January 1931; Anthony Wonderley, "Chief Warriors, Pagan Priests, and Witch Killers: The Division of the Oneida Iroquois, 1789–1805," *New York History* 93, no. 2 (Spring 2012): 133–35, https://www.jstor.org/stable/23645397; John Hadcock to L. C. Draper, 6 February 1878, 11 U:265, Draper Manuscripts; William S. Fenton, ed., "The Journal of James Emlen Kept on a Trip to Canandaigua, New York, 1794," *Ethnohistory* 12, no. 4 (Fall 1965): 327.

66. Robert W. Venables, "Some Observations on the Treaty of Canandaigua," in *Treaty of Canandaigua 1794: 200 Years of Treaty Relations between the Iroquois*

Confederacy and the United States, ed. G. Peter Jemison and Anna M. Schein (Santa Fe: Clear Light, 2000), 84–92, 107–9; Jourdan, "Wampum."

67. For their wartime service, Oneida commissioned officers were awarded land in the military tracts they did not want. Patrick, "Life and Times," 523; Hauptman, *Conspiracy of Interests*, 230n2; Anthony Wonderley, "The Burning of Oneida Castle (1780) and the Oneida Veterans Treaty (1795)," *Mohawk Valley History* 2, no. 1 (2005): 20; Wonderley, "Oneida Community in 1780," 33–41; Taylor, *Divided Ground*, 299–300; Tiro, *People of the Standing Stone*, 94–95; Fenton, "Journal of James Emlen," 300.

68. Taylor, *Divided Ground*, 302–4.

69. Laurence M. Hauptman, "Command Performance: Philip Schuyler and the New York State-Oneida 'Treaty' of 1795," in Hauptman and McLester, *Oneida Indian Journey*, 48; Pilkington, *Journals of Samuel Kirkland*, 228; Taylor, *Divided Ground*, 302–4; Tiro, *People of the Standing Stone*, 96–102.

70. Treaty of 1795, 1 September 1795, Whipple Report, vol. 1, part 1, pp. 244–49; Taylor, *Divided Ground*, 303–6; Tiro, *People of the Standing Stone*, 70, 99.

71. Taylor, *Divided Ground*, 305–6; Tiro, *People of the Standing Stone*, 100–102; Geier, "Peculiar Status," 131–32; François Furstenberg, *When the United States Spoke French: Five Refugees Who Shaped a Nation* (New York: Penguin Books, 2014), 59.

72. Taylor, *Divided Ground*, 306–7; Jones, *Annals and Recollections*, 655.

73. Jeremy Belknap, *Journal of a Tour from Boston to Oneida, June 1796* (Cambridge, MA: John Wilson & Son, 1882), 10–15.

74. Belknap, *Journal of a Tour*, 15–30; Alexander, *Revolutionary Conservative*, 229.

75. Paolo Andreani, "Travels of a Gentleman from Milan, 1799," in Snow, Gehring, and Starna, *In Mohawk Country*, 319, 322; Belknap, "Journal of a Tour," 21; Belknap and Morse, *Report on the Oneida*, 9–10, 13–17; Jones, *Annals and Recollections*, 660–61.

76. Belknap and Morse, *Report on the Oneida*, 22, 30, 37.

77. "New York Tax Assessment Rolls of Real and Personal Estates, 1799-1804," Ancestry.com, https://www.ancestry.com; "Conrad Ingalls," in *Biographical Review: The Leading Citizens of Madison County* (Boston: Biographical Review, 1894), 589-90; William H. Tuttle, "The Purchase of 1802," *ODU*, 15 January 1931, and "Harps and Moots Early Lincoln Settlers," *ODU*, 9 April 1931; Hammond, *History of Madison County*, 487.

78. John Taylor, "On a Mission through the Mohawk and Black River County in the Year 1802," in Snow, Gehring, and Starna, *In Mohawk Country*, 368; Thomas J. Humphrey, *Land and Liberty: Hudson Valley Riots in the Age of Revolution* (DeKalb: Northern Illinois University Press, 2004), 123–24, 134–35; Deloria, *Playing Indian*, 39–41.

79. Tuttle, "Early History"; William H. Tuttle, "Lexington Argonne Lincoln Soldiers," *ODU*, 28 May 1931; Rob Harper, "Settlers, States, and Violence in the Revolutionary Ohio Valley" (paper presentation, annual conference of the Society of Historians of the Early American Republic, "Roundtable: Squatters, Surveyors & States in the Old Northwest," Philadelphia, 4 July 2011); Silverman, *Red Brethren*, 134–35.

80. Colin G. Calloway, "My Grandfather's Axe," in Hurtado, *Reflections on American Indian History*, 10.

81. Frank Clement to "Dear Folks," 6 December 1938, Clement File; Martin, *Eighteenth Century Zimmerman Family*, 97–98; Harris, *Clement Family History*, 35.

82. Martin, *Eighteenth Century Zimmerman Family*, 99, 166.

5. "We Shall All Be Americans"

1. Gary B. Nash, "The Hidden History of Mestizo America," in *Sex, Love, Race: Crossing Boundaries in North American History*, ed. Martha Hodes (New York: New York University Press, 1999), 11.

2. Mrs. Hammond, as the author of the much-cited *The History of Madison County* is known, was born Luna Chase in 1835 and lived in the town of Eaton. Clara M. Houck, "Mrs. Luna M. Hammond," *Madison County Heritage*, no. 8 (July 1980): 9–12; L. M. Hammond, *History of Madison County*, 769; George Russell, "Wampsville, New York: An Historical Sketch," 1909, 2001.A112.01, MCHS.

3. Lester Grosvenor Wells, "Breese Family History," Jack Wallace Collection (a copy of Wells's "Breese Family History," which appears to be an unfinished paper based on Breese family records, including an autobiographical account by Helen Burrows Breese written in 1860, has been donated by Jack Wallace to the Madison County Historical Society and can be found in the Breese Family Collection, MCHS); George W. Walter, "Johann M. Wemple: The Father of Wampsville," n.d., MCHS.

4. Michael A. Blaakman, "The Marketplace of American Federalism: Land Speculation across State Lines in the Early Republic," *Journal of American History* 107, no. 3 (December 2020): 602; Russell A. Grills, "Land Speculations in Southern Madison County during the Late 18th Century," *Madison County Heritage*, August 1977, 2–7.

5. Helen traveled to Cazenovia with her uncle General Jonathan Forman and her cousin Mary, whose son Horatio Seymour would become governor of New York. Her father, Major John Burrows (or Burroughs), went to Georgia after the war and died there. Helen's uncle General Benjamin Ledyard worked in Lincklaen's land office in Aurora. Her cousin Helen Ledyard married John Lincklaen. Her uncle Samuel Forman (1765–1862) arrived in Cazenovia as an employee of the Holland Land Company in 1793. Journal of Major John Burrowes, in Cook, *Journals*, 44–45; Samuel S. Forman, *Narrative of a Journey down the Ohio and Mississippi in 1789–90* (Cincinnati: Robert Clarke, 1888); Wells, "Breese Family History."

6. Wells, "Breese Family History"; Helen Burrows to Lucy Phelps, 21 February 1800, box 2, folder 1, Breese Stevens Roby Family Papers; William Wyckoff, *The Developer's Frontier: The Making of the Western New York Landscape* (New Haven, CT: Yale University Press, 1988), 43–44.

7. "Reminiscences," by J. W. S., one of the few contemporary accounts of Angel and Polly Deferrier, was published in 1858 in the *Waterville Times*, the *Cazenovia Republican*, and the *Oneida Democratic Union*. A fragment of this article is in the Deferrier Family Collection, MCHS. J. W. S., "Reminiscences," *Cazenovia*

Republican, 25 August 1858, https://nyshistoricnewspapers.com; "Court Order," 28 December 1802, Jack Wallace Collection.

8. *Archives historique du Poitou* 22 (Poitiers, 1892), 176; *Histoire de Niort des origins à nos jours* (Poitiers: Projets Editions, 1987), 182–85, 202.

9. "La gazette de St. Mandé-sur Brédoire," no. 10, 2010/2011, Village Site Saint Léger, Municipality of St. Mandé-sur Brédoire, Charente-Maritime, http://www.stleger.fr; J. F. Bosher, "Jacques-Michel Bréard," in *Dictionary of Canadian Biography*, vol. 4 (Université Laval/University of Toronto, 2003), http://www.biographi.ca/en/bio/breard_jacques_michel_4E.html; Niort—St. André (Paroisse de), Baptémes, Mariages, Sépultures, 1769, Archives Départementale de Deux-Sevres, Niort, France.

10. Angel had an older brother who lived only a few months, an older sister, a younger sister, and two younger brothers. Niort—St. André (Paroisse de), Baptémes, Mariages, Sépultures 1767, 1770; Parish Records of St. Mandé-sur Brédoire, Collection Communale, Paroissial-Baptémes, Mariages, Sépultures 1728–, Archives Départementale de la Charente Maritime, http://www.archinoe.fr; William Beik, *A Social and Cultural History of Early Modern France* (New York: Cambridge University Press, 2009), 41; "La gazette sur St. Mandé-sur Brédoire," no. 9, 2009/2010, Village Site Saint Léger, http://www.stleger.fr, and no. 10; "Titre nouvel par les habitants de Gâtebourse à Madame Veuve Gallard-Latouche [Michelle Radegonde Desiree d'Aulede de Ferriere] et autres," 16 February 1836, à Saint-Mandé-sur-Brédoire, Ma Généalogie, http://Christian.audouin.pagesperso-orang.fr/fiches/fiche1511.htm.

11. Registration of Theophile Cesar Ange Daulede DeFerriere in the "Compagnie française des Gardes du Corps du Roi," 1 April 1787, Deferrier Family Collection; J. W. S., "Reminiscences"; Hammond, *History of Madison County*, 768; *Histoire de Niort*, 245; "La gazette sur St. Mandé-sur Brédoire," no. 9.

12. Caroline Moorehead, *Dancing to the Precipice: The Life of Lucie de la Tour du Pin, Eyewitness to an Era* (New York: HarperCollins, 2009), 107–12.

13. Moorehead, *Dancing to the Precipice*, 113–23; Timothy Tackett, *When the King Took Flight* (Cambridge, MA: Harvard University Press, 2003), 130.

14. Furstenburg, *United States Spoke French*, 2, 10, 80, 91; Campbell, *Life and Writings*, 190–91; George B. Russell, "The Angel De Ferriere Family," address before the Madison County Historical Society, 17 February 1909, Deferrier Family Collection; Sharon Cooney, email to the author, 26 July 2012, Lincklaen House, Cazenovia, NY.

15. T. Wood Clarke, *Émigrés in the Wilderness* (Port Washington, NY: Ira J. Friedman, 1967), 57–64, 71, 82–83.

16. Moorehead, *Dancing to the Precipice*, 218–19; Clarke, *Émigrés in the Wilderness*, 82–83; Angel La Farniaux, Town of Franklin, Delaware County, NY, US Federal Census, 1800; Samuel F. Scott, *The Response of the Royal Army to the French Revolution: The Role and Development of the Line Army, 1878–1793* (Oxford: Clarendon, an imprint of Oxford University Press, 1978), 23; Pilkington, *Journals of Samuel Kirkland*, 72, 84; Taylor, *Divided Ground*, 382.

17. Tiro, *People of the Standing Stone*, 108–10; Treaty of 1798, 1 June 1798, in Whipple Report, vol. 1, part 1, pp. 251–52.

18. The Treaty of 1798 appears to have anticipated the removal of the Doxtators from Canaseraga by setting aside lots in the Two-Mile Strip for Sarah, Jacob, Cornelius, and two others, but not for John and Louis Denny, as ordered by the Oneida council. "Oneida Cession, June 1798," Surveyor General Field Books, Series A4016-77:24:151, NYSA; Treaty of 1798; Jacob Cornelius, interview, 11 U:213, Draper Manuscripts.

19. Petition to the legislature of the state of New York from Cornelius Doxtator, Abraham Doxtator, Peter Doxtator, Louis Denny, Louis Denny Jr., John Denny, Abraham Denny, Martin Denny, Jonathan Denny, Abraham Brandt, Henry Walsh, Aaron Steven, Isaac Webster, and John, Peter, and Moses Scanando, n.d., [about 1801], Petitions, Correspondence, and Reports Relating to Indians, Series A1823, MU1, reel 2, NYSA; indenture between Simeon DeWitt, Surveyor General of the State of New York, and John Denney of the County of Chenango, 7 May 1800, D:68–69, Chenango County Courthouse, Norwich, NY; deed, John Danny to Benjamin Drake, 14 November 1805, A:21–22, MCCO; "Oneida Cession, June 1798."

20. "Account of the Expenses of a Treaty with the Oneida in 1802," entry documentation submitted by the Indian Commissioners and Indians for annuities paid to Indians and for other expenditures, Series A0832-77, box 4, folder 5, NYSA; Tiro, *People of the Standing Stone*, 112; Treaty of 1802, 4 June 1802, in Whipple Report, vol. 1, part 1, pp. 256–59; State of New York, "Concurrent Resolution for Treating with the Oneida Indians," 24 February 1802, A4016-77-24:159, NYSA; Taylor, *Divided Ground*, 308, 479n33.

21. Treaty of 1802; Simeon DeWitt re. Petition of Hartman and Conrad Pickard, 7 February 1803, Surveyor General's Reports on Petitions to the State Legislatures, Series A1820-76, MU1, reel 1, NYSA; Charles M. Brodhead, *A Survey of Part of the Late Oneida Reservation, North of the Turnpike Road, and South of the Turnpike Road*, 1803, A4019, vol. 15, MU1, reel 16, Land Survey Field Guide, NYSA; Joseph Annin, "Field Book of the Purchase Made of the Oneida Nation of Indians in the Year of Eighteen Hundred & Two," Surveyor General Land Survey Field Books, Series A4019-77, MU1, reel 6, 13:246, NYSA.

22. "Extract from an Act Entitled 'An Act Relative to the Unappropriated Lands of This State, to Prevent Intrusions and for Other Purposes,'" 5 April 1802, A4016-77:24:154, NYSA; Tiro, *People of the Standing Stone*, 112; indenture, 22 April 1804, F:269–71, Chenango County Courthouse; Hammond, *History of Madison County*, 769.

23. Dann, *Peter Smith of Peterboro*, 82; Smith, *Our County and Its People*, 29–30, 168–69.

24. Tiro, *People of the Standing Stone*, 113; Pilkington, *Journals of Samuel Kirkland*, 390–91.

25. Indian Commissioner Records, A0832-77, box 4, folder 6, NYSA; Tiro, *People of the Standing Stone*, 113.

26. To follow the line of division between the Pagan and Christian Parties by road today, start at Sunset Lake in Kenwood, go west on Union Street, turn north on Route 46, go west on Mount Hope Avenue, turn north on Creek Road, and go west on Clockville Road about halfway to Clockville. This route runs a bit north of the division line. Indenture of 1805, in Whipple Report, vol. 1, part 1, pp. 259–63; Tiro, *People of the Standing Stone*, 113–14.

27. Pilkington, *Journals of Samuel Kirkland*, 169–71, 351; Samuel Kirkland to Alexander Miller, 24 May 1800, Oneida Nation of Wisconsin, https://www.exploreoneida.com.

28. Pilkington, *Journals of Samuel Kirkland*, 418; O'Brien, *Dispossession by Degrees*, 3; Jedediah Morse, *American Gazetteer*, Boston, 1804, Jack Wallace Collection.

29. Hammond, *History of Madison County*, 662.

30. Robert Sutcliff, *Travels in Some Parts of North America, in the Years 1804, 1805, & 1806* (London: n.p., 1815), Karst Collection; W. J. Rorabaugh, *The Alcoholic Republic* (New York: Oxford University Press, 1979), 140–44, 149–50, 166; "Surveyor General's Office Notice," *Albany Register*, 31 May 1803.

31. Hammond, *History of Madison County*, 662; Dolly Denny to Lazarus Tucker, 17 August 1808, C:193–95; Dolly Denny to Samuel Mowers and Clark Stanton, 20 June 1809, C:391–93; Dolly Denny to Elisha Clark, 10 September 1812, G:5; Amos S. Ausdew to Dolly Denny, 10 September 1812, G:6; Dolly Denny to John Dana, August 18, 1813, G:470, MCCO; Peter Smith to Sidney Breese, 18 September 1806, box 2, folder 5; David Dearborn to Sidney Breese, 17 October 1808, box 2, folder 8; and Angel Deferrier to Sidney Breese, 5 June 1809, box 2, folder 9, Breese Stevens Roby Family Papers.

32. Norman K. Dann, "Peter Smith," *Madison County Heritage* 28 (2019): 54–59; Russell, "Wampsville, New York," 18.

33. Christian Party Treaty of 1807 and Christian Party Treaty of 1809, in Whipple Report, vol. 1, part 1, pp. 263–69; Angel DeFerrier receipt, n.d., A0832, box 4, folder 8, NYSA; Tiro, *People of the Standing Stone*, 118; Thomas Dexter's bill, 3 March 1814, A0832, box 2, folder 2, NYSA; Taylor, *Divided Ground*, 390.

34. State of New York to Angel Deferrier, 1809, 1810, and 1811, Letters Patent 12943–78, MU1, reel 10, vols. 24–25, 1802–1842, NYSA; letters patent to Angel De Ferriere, 20 [no month listed] 1810, Deferrier Family Collection; survey of land for Angel Deferrier, A4019-77, vol. 13, reel 6, NYSA; Angel Deferrier to Mindert Wemple, Adam Gray, and Angel Deferrier, 15 May 1811, AQ: 219–20, MCCO.

35. Angel De Ferrier, "To Let," *Columbian Gazette* (Utica, NY), 15 May 1810; Sutcliff, "Travels in Some Parts"; Campbell, *Life and Writings*, 186; Hammond, *History of Madison County*, 493.

36. The canal commissioners were DeWitt Clinton; Simeon DeWitt; Gouverneur Morris, the aristocratic statesman who wrote the "We the People" preamble to the Constitution; the patroon Stephen Van Rensselaer; General William North, the son-in-law of James Duane; the New York City merchant Thomas Eddy; and Congressman Peter Porter, who operated a portage business at Niagara. Peter L. Bernstein, *Wedding of the Waters*, 132–36.

37. Campbell, *Life and Writings*, 190–91.

38. Campbell, *Life and Writings*, 174, 185, 191.

39. Campbell, *Life and Writings*, 186–89, 191; Banner, *Indians Lost Their Land*, 154; Tiro, *People of the Standing Stone*, 120.

40. Tiro, *People of the Standing Stone*, 120–21.

41. Oneida Christian Party Treaties of 1810 and 1811, in Whipple Report, vol. 1, part 1, pp. 272–78; Tiro, *People of the Standing Stone*, 120.

42. Deed, Dolly Denny of Sullivan to Mynart Whemple of Lenox, 21 February 1811, 22:62, Oneida County Clerk's Office, Utica, NY; Wells, "Breese Family History"; Sidney Breese to Elizabeth Breese, 16 October 1813, box 3, folder 3, Breese Stevens Roby Family Papers; Charles Brodhead, "A Map of 200 Acres Ceded to Dolly Denny," Breese Stevens Roby Family Papers; David Maldwyn Ellis, *Landlords and Farmers in the Hudson-Mohawk Region, 1790–1850* (New York: Octagon Books, 1967), 128–29; Jones, *Annals and Recollections*, 830–31.

43. Deed between "Cornelius Dockstader of the Oneida tribe of Indians and Jane his wife" and Peter Smith, 10 October 1807, 16:111, Oneida County Clerk's Office; petition of the Chiefs of the South Party of the Oneida Nation of Indians to Governor Daniel Tompkins, 30 January 1810, Oneida Nation of Wisconsin, https://www.exploreoneida.com; Treaty of 1802; deed between Cornelius Dockstader and Peter Smith, 9 December 1807, B:317, MCCO; Annin, "Field Book."

44. Tiro, *People of the Standing Stone*, 122–23; William H. Tuttle, "Tragedies Marked Early Days of 'Purchase of 1802,'" *ODU*, 22 January 1931.

45. Tuttle, "Tragedies Marked Early Days"; William H. Tuttle, "Mohawk Valley Families Settled in Lincoln," *ODU*, 26 March 1931; William H. Tuttle, "Lincoln Stone in Erie Canal Walls," *ODU*, 20 August 1931; Metchie J. E. Budka, "Journey to Niagara, 1805: From the Diary of Julian Ursyn Niemcewicz," *New York Historical Society Quarterly* 44 (January 1960): 91; Ellis, *Landlords and Farmers*, 73–75, 116–17; Wyckoff, *Developer's Frontier*, 157–58.

46. Friedrich Rohde, "Journal of a Trip from New Jersey to Oneida Lake," 1802, in Snow, Gehring, and Starna, *In Mohawk Country*, 376–77.

47. Robert Earl, "Herkimer and Its People during the First Years of the Country," 1896, in Smith, *Herkimer County Historical Society*, 46–48; David Stradling, *The Nature of New York: An Environmental History of the Empire State* (Ithaca, NY: Cornell University Press, 2010), 27–28; Hammond, *History of Madison County*, 490–91; William H. Tuttle, "Lincoln Settlers Were of Valiant Breed," *ODU*, 21 May 1931; Brooks, *Columbia Rising*, 133, 232.

48. Lincklaen had built a mansion called Lorenzo that is now a state historic site in Cazenovia. Brook, *Columbia Rising*, 132–33, 340; Samuel Forman to Sidney Breese, n.d., box 2, folder 9, Breese Stevens Roby Family Papers.

49. Gerard Koeppel, *Bond of Union: Building the Erie Canal and the American Empire* (Cambridge, MA: Da Capo, 2009), 102–3.

50. David M. Ellis, James A. Frost, Harold C. Syrett, and Harry F. Carman, *A History of New York State*, revised ed. (Ithaca, NY: Cornell University Press, 1978), 139; Tiro, *People of the Standing Stone*, 123–24.

51. John Conrad Moot resigned as captain in 1814. William H. Tuttle, *Names and Sketches of the Pioneer Settlers of Madison County New York*, ed. Isabel Bracy (Interlaken, NY: Heart of the Lakes, 1984), 169; "From the Society's Archives," *Madison County Heritage*, no. 37 (2012): 31–34; Hauptman, "Three Stories of War," 66–68.

52. This Louis Denny was most likely Polly's brother or nephew, although her father, when in his seventies, told DeWitt Clinton that he was eager to go to war. Hauptman, "Three Stories of War," 65; "Madison County Participants in the War of 1812," Madison County, NY (website), accessed 5 January 2024,

https://www.madisoncounty.ny.gov; Tiro, *People of the Standing Stone*, 125–26; Campbell, *Life and Writings*, 174; Benn, *Iroquois in the War of 1812*, 160–65, 171.

53. Cornelius Doxtator, interview, 11 U:200, Draper Manuscripts; Benn, *Iroquois in the War of 1812*, 171–73.

54. Bernstein, *Wedding of the Waters*, 177–79.

55. Petition of the chiefs and warriors of the Christian Party of the Oneida Nation to the legislature of the State of New York, 21 February 1814, CB 503, box 1, William Leland Thompson Collection, Albany Institute of History and Art, Albany.

56. Treaty of 1815, 3 March 1815, in Whipple Report, vol. 1, part 1, pp. 280–83.

57. Treaty of 1815; Charles Brodhead to I. Denniston, 18 June 1815, Selected Audited Accounts of State, Civil, and Military Officers, Series A0802-78, vol. 15, 129–30, NYSA; Oneida Nation of Indians Receipt, 31 May 1815, A0832-77, box 4, folder 6, NYSA.

58. Pete Nelson, "Lost Brook Dispatches: The Incredible Story of Charles Brodhead, Surveyor," *Adirondack Almanack*, 16 March 2013, https://adirondackalmanack.com; Koeppel, *Bond of Union*, 139, 150, 288–90.

59. Marcus Terran Gallo, "Imaginary Lines, Real Power: Surveyors and Land Speculation in the Mid-Atlantic Borderlands, 1681–1800" (PhD diss., University of California, Davis, 2012), 1–48; John Randel Jr., "A Map of Land Granted to John Sagueonta," A4019-77, vol. 13:191, MU1, reel 6, NYSA; John Randel Jr. to Simeon DeWitt, 2 February 1816, A4016:1:101, NYSA; T. Raymond Rathbone, *Brief History of Oneida Castle, N.Y. and the Oneida Indians* (Oneida Castle Fire Department, 1930), Oneida Public Library, Oneida, NY.

60. Sidney Breese to Elizabeth Breese, 7 May 1816 and 17 April 1817, box 3, folder 5, Breese Stevens Roby Family Papers; "Map of Samuel Sidney Breese Homestead," 2001.A042, Breese Family Collection.

61. "A Survey of the Lands Purchased of the Christian Party of Oneida Indians, the 3rd of March 1815," A4019-77, vol. 14, MU1, reel 16, NYSA; DeWitt Clinton to Angel De Ferriere, 7 October 1826, Letters Patent 12943, Book 29: 408–9, NYSA.

62. "Speech of John Scanado," 12 October 1816, *Niles Register*, 11 U:159, Draper Manuscripts.

63. "Funeral of Skenandoh, the Oneida Chief, with a Sketch of His Life," *Washington (PA) Reporter*, 6 May 1816; "Skenandon, The Oneida Chief," *The Intelligencer* (Portsmouth, NH), 18 April 1816; Taylor, *Divided Ground*, 387.

64. Carolyn Eastman, "The Indian Censures the White Man: Indian Eloquence and Early American Reading Responses in the Early Republic," *William & Mary Quarterly* 65, no. 3 (July 2008): 535–64; Dewitt Clinton, "The Iroquois," in Campbell, *Life and Writings*, 251–56.

65. Simeon DeWitt to Isaac Denniston, 12 September 1816, A0832-77, box 4, folder 7, NYSA; Tuttle, *Names and Sketches*, 221; O'Brien, *Firsting and Lasting*, xi–xxvi.

66. Sternberg's deal appears to have fallen through because he never filed a deed on the property. Angel Deferrier to Simeon DeWitt, 5 December 1817, A0832-77, box 4, folder 7, NYSA.

67. DeWitt to Denniston, 12 September 1816.

68. John Denny to Timothy Brown, 1 January 1813, Q:435; Abraham Dana and Kata, his wife, to Timothy Brown, 5 January 1813, I:88; John Dana to Arnold Ballou, 6 January 1813, G:105; John and Susan Dana to Otheniel Powers, 8 December 1813, I:271–72; Abraham Dana and Caty his wife to Timothy Brown, 25 October 1814, K:275; Abraham Dana and Caty to Timothy Brown, 27 May 1815, R:387–88, MCCO.

69. A. G. Ellis to L. C. Draper, 22 August 1882, 11 U:238–39, Draper Manuscripts.

70. Hammond, *History of Madison County*, 521, 665; Jedediah Morse, *A Report to the Secretary of War of the United States on Indian Affairs* (New Haven, CT: n.p., 1822), 24; Tiro, *People of the Standing Stone*, 36–37; Smith, *Chenango and Madison Counties*, 709; Silverman, *Red Brethren*, 101–5.

71. On the 1820 census, Indians not taxed were not to be included under the category of "colored," which may indicate that Polly was included in that category because she and Angel paid taxes. It is possible that Jin, age twenty, an enslaved female bought by James Dean in 1812 for $200, was the same person as Gin. Town of Lenox, Madison County, NY, US Federal Census, 1810, 1820, and 1830; Karim M. Tiro, "James Dean in Iroquoia," *New York History* 80, no. 4 (October 1999): 416–17; Russell, "Wampsville, New York," 13; Russell Thornton, "Who Counts? Indians and the U.S. Census," in *The Great Vanishing Act: Blood Quantum and the Future of Native Nations*, ed. Kathleen Ratteree and Norbert Hill (Golden, CO: Fulcrum, 2017), 144.

72. Smith, *Our County and Its People*, 137–38; Russell, "Wampsville, New York," 17; Hammond, *History of Madison County*, 488.

6. Making Way for the Erie Canal

1. "A Map of the First Tract," A4019, 14:3; patent from the State of New York to Angel DeFerriere, 29 July 1817, and patent from the State of New York to Martines Denny, 12 April 1822, Letters Patent 12943, vol. 27–28, reel 12; petition of Martin Dinney to the State of New York, 21 January 1822, A1823; Simeon DeWitt, 1 February 1822, A1820-78, MU1, reel 1, NYSA.

2. "Indian News," *Albany Gazette*, 23 June 1818; Morse, *Report to the Secretary of War*, 77–78; Banner, *Indians Lost Their Land*, 154.

3. Koeppel, *Bond of Union*, 193–95; Bernstein, *Wedding of the Waters*, 208.

4. John Anthony and Moses Sconnoto to Eleazer Williams, 9 December 1814, box 1, folder 4, Eleazer Williams Papers, Wisconsin Historical Society; Tiro, *People of the Standing Stone*, 138–39; "From the Albany Daily Advertiser," *New York Gazette*, 13 February 1817; "Oneida Indians," *Patriot* (Utica, NY), 29 September 1818.

5. John Kanyegonia, Martinus Denny, Peter John, Jacob Dockstader et al. to the Chiefs of the Second Christian Party, journal, 13 March 1817, box 2, folder 1, Williams Papers; Simeon DeWitt, "To All Whom It May Concern," 5 February 1818, box 1, folder 4, Williams Papers; Tiro, *People of the Standing Stone*, 138; Treaty of 1817, in Whipple Report, vol. 1, part 1, pp. 284–86; John Randel Jr.,

"Field Book of the Cowasselon Tract in the County of Madison," May 1817, A4019-77, vol 13, MU1, reel 6, NYSA.

6. Folts, "Before the Dispersal," 167n53.

7. Treaty of 1817; Gov. Dewitt Clinton to Dolly Denney, Abraham Denney, John Denney, Sally Denney (Carlough/Garlock), 15 July 1817, Letters Patent 12943, vol. 27–28, roll 12, NYSA; John Randel Jr., "A Map of the Cowasselon Tract," Map No. 150, Surveyor General Maps and Field Books, A0273, NYSA.

8. "Certificate of Incorporation of the Lenox Iron Company," founded 22 March 1811, 2001.A112.01, MCHS; Eleazer Williams to the Lenox Iron Company, 18 October 1817, O:449–50; Eleazer Williams to John Nellis, 23 July 1822, T:31; Abraham Dana and his wife to Lenox Iron Company, 8 September 1818, O:446–47; Dolly Dana to the Lenox Iron Company, 9 February 1819, P:164–66; deeds between Dolly and John Denny, N:272–73, 494 and O:445–46; Angel Deferrier to the Lenox Iron Company, January 1827, Y:178, MCCO; Hammond, *History of Madison County*, 504–5; Smith, *Our County and Its People*, 184.

9. Koeppel, *Bond of Union*, 213–14, 247–48, Bernstein, *Wedding of the Waters*, 208–11.

10. Commissioners Report, 31 January 1818 and 25 January 1819, *Laws of the State of New York in Relation to the Erie and Champlain Canals: Together with the Annual Reports of the Canal Commissioners, and Other Documents Requisite for a Complete Official History of These Works* (hereafter cited as Canal Laws) (Albany: E. & E. Hosford, 1825), 1:366–82, 398–417; Koeppel, *Bond of Union*, 237–45, 253; Bernstein, *Wedding of the Waters*, 259; Carl Moon, "Pioneer Names in Lenox Area," Town of Lincoln File, MCHS; Herbert "Herb" Brewer, interview by the author, 19 November 2014, Palm Coast, FL.

11. Commissioners Report, 31 January 1818, Canal Laws, map between pages 168 and 169; Gurdon Evans Town of Lenox Map, 1853, and Beers Town of Lenox Map, 1875, Madison County, NY (website), https://www.madisoncounty.ny.gov.

12. Watson, *Men and Times*, 476; Koeppel, *Bond of Union*, 268.

13. Shagoyontha was joined by his son John Cornelius; John's son, also called John Cornelius, and wife Catherine; Aaron Jacob; Baptist Canada; Peggy Bread; and Jenny Denny, Polly's niece, identified as the granddaughter of a Frenchman adopted by the Oneidas. J. W. S., "Reminiscences"; "War Dance," *Columbian Register* (New Haven, CT), 12 October 1816; "From Niles Register," *Washington (PA) Review and Examiner*, 18 May 1818; advertisement for the Royal Circus and Surrey Theatre, *The Times* (London), 22 January–12 February 1819, Oneida Nation of Wisconsin, https://www.exploreoneida.com; "Notice," *Patriot*, 27 July 1819.

14. "London, May 24," *Scioto Gazette* (Chillicothe, OH), 6 August 1819.

15. Statement of Angel Deferrier, 27 October 1819, and Albert Gallatin to Angel Deferrier, 11 September 1819, Albert Gallatin Papers, 1794–1952, New York Historical Society.

16. Albert Gallatin to Isaac Cox Barnet, US Consul in Paris, 11 September 1819; Albert Gallatin to Secretary of State John Quincy Adams, 27 October 1819, Gallatin Papers.

17. Gallatin to Marquis Dessolle, 11 September 1819; Gallatin to Adams, 27 October 1819, Gallatin Papers.

18. Albert Gallatin to Captain Williams, 29 October 1819; statement of Angel Deferrier; receipt signed by Isaac Cox Barnet, 28 October 1819; Albert Gallatin to Reuben G. Beasley, 28 October 1819; Thomas Taylor for R. G. Beasley to Albert Gallatin, 1 November 1819, Gallatin Papers; "Ship News," *Franklin Gazette* (Philadelphia), 30 November 1819; "From France—Latest," *Weekly Visitor* (Kennebunk, ME), 4 December 1819; Tiro, *People of the Standing Stone*, 131–33; J. W. S., "Reminiscences"; "Titre nouvel par les habitants de Gâtebourse."

19. General A. G. Ellis, "Recollections of Rev. Eleazer Williams," 351, Wisconsin Historical Collections, 1855–1915, Wisconsin Historical Society.

20. Michael Leroy Oberg, *Professional Indian: The American Odyssey of Eleazer Williams* (Philadelphia: University of Pennsylvania Press, 2015), 84–85; Darren Bonaparte, "Eleazer Williams: The Lost Mohawk," Wampum Chronicles, 29 April 2005, https://www.wampumchronicles.com.

21. Hauptman, *Conspiracy of Interests*, 19; Sidney Breese to Elizabeth Breese, 15 August 1820, box 3, folder 7, Breese Stevens Roby Papers; Morse, *Report to the Secretary of War*, 63.

22. Morse, *Report to the Secretary of War*, app. M.

23. Eleazer Williams to Right Rev. Father, 16 May 1820, box 1, folder 4, Williams Papers; Oberg, *Professional Indian*, 93; "Albany, Aug. 13," *Repertory* (Boston), 18 August 1821.

24. Tiro, *People of the Standing Stone*, 143–44.

25. The Holland Land Company sold its preemption rights to western New York to the Ogden Land Company in 1810. Tiro, *People of the Standing Stone*, 142–43; Silverman, *Red Brethren*, 164; Hauptman, *Conspiracy of Interests*, 115; Geier, "Peculiar Status," 146.

26. Pevar, *Rights of Indians*, 24–25; Vine Deloria Jr., "The Application of the Constitution to American Indians," in Lyons and Mohawk, *Exiled in the Land of the Free*, 298–301; David E. Wilkins and K. Tsianina Lomawaima, *Uneven Ground: American Indian Sovereignty and Federal Law* (Norman: University of Oklahoma Press, 2002), 52–63; *Johnson and Graham's Lessee v. William M'Intosh*, 21 US 543 (1823).

27. *Johnson and Graham's Lessee.*

28. Ellis, "Recollections of Eleazer Williams," 332; Tiro, *People of the Standing Stone*, 146–47.

29. Treaty of 1824, 26 August 1824, in Whipple Report, vol. 1, part 1, pp. 287–90; "Field Book of the Oneida Purchase of 1824," A0452-79, vol. 48, MU1, reel 11, NYSA; Geier, "Peculiar Status," 172.

30. Treaty of 1824, in Whipple Report, vol. 1, part 1, pp. 287–90; "Field Book of the Oneida Purchase of 1824"; Land Grant from New York to Martin Denny and to Abraham Denny, 15 February 1827, Letters Patent 12943, book 29, reel 13, NYSA.

31. A. Levasseur, *Lafayette in America in 1824 and 1825* (Philadelphia: Carey & Lea, 1829), 2:195–96, 198.

32. Bernstein, *Wedding of the Waters*, 309–21.

33. Stradling, *Nature of New York*, 82; Koeppel, *Bond of Union*, 308–9; Nathaniel Hawthorne, "The Canal Boat," *New England Magazine*, December 1835, 398–409.

34. Hawthorne, "Canal Boat"; "The Great Water Highway through New York State, 1829," Erie Canal, last accessed 4 February 2024, https://www.eriecanal.org.

35. Hawthorne, "Canal Boat"; William H. Tuttle, "Fighting Farmers of Lincoln were Boatmen," *ODU*, 12 February 1931; Oberg, *Professional Indian*, 117.

36. Letters Patent 12943, Book 26:1; Book 27:109, 252; Book 29:408–9; Book 30:94, 232, NYSA.

37. Sidney Breese to Catharine Breese, 27 October 1829, box 4, folder 5; Helen and Sidney Breese to Elizabeth Breese Stevens, 21 March 1832, box 5, folder 1, Breese Stevens Roby Papers; Wells, "Breese Family History"; "Historic Homestead Story Uncovered by Attorney," undated news clipping, Deferrier Family Collection.

38. Thurlow Weed, "Staging Forty Years Ago," *OD*, 29 April 1870.

39. Angel and Polly Deferrier had another son, who must have died young, and another daughter named Lucy (1812–14), who is buried in the family cemetery. Town of Franklin, Delaware County, NY, US Federal Census, 1800; "Charles J. DeFerrier: A Brief Sketch of an Interesting Character," undated news clipping (around 1877), Deferrier Family Collection; Sidney, Helen, and Margaret Breese to Elizabeth Breese, 10 August 1826, box 4, folder 2; Helen Platt Breese to Catharine Breese, 28 October 1835, box 5, folder 5, Breese Stevens Roby Papers.

40. Thomas Taylor Loomis does not appear to be connected to the infamous Loomis Gang that operated out of the town of Georgetown. "I Anthony Otsequette hereby authorize . . . ," 26 June 1826, and "Received from the people of the state of New York," 1 June 1827, A0832-77, box 4, folder 6, NYSA.

41. Oneidas in Wisconsin in 1869 referred to John Hadcock as having "a full power to act as our Agent." Daniel Bread, Jacob Cornelius, Baptist Doxtator, Elijah Scanondo et al. to John Hadcock, 15 February 1869, 2001.A110, MCHS; Hadcock Family Tree, Hadcock File, Herkimer County Historical Society, Herkimer, NY; John Hadcock to Mr. Draper, 6 February 1878, 11U:266, Draper Manuscripts; Hammond, *History of Madison County*, 740–41.

42. Statement of John Hadcock, 23 March 1874, in *Documents of the Senate of the State of New York*, No. 79, 16–17, Oneida Nation of Wisconsin, https://www.exploreoneida.com.

43. Martinus White was referring to the language in the Treaty of 1788 that reserved for the Oneidas half a square mile every six miles on the north shore of Oneida Lake. Statements of John Hadcock, Jacob L. W. Doxstader, Jacob Cornelius, Cornelius Hill, and Elija Skenado, in *Documents of the Senate of the State of New York*, No. 79, 16–18, Oneida Nation of Wisconsin, https://www.exploreoneida.com.

44. "Field Book of the Lots in the Tract Ceded to the People of the State of New York by the Second Christian Party of the Oneida Indians, Feb. 1826," A4019-77, 34:1, 6, MU1, reel 12, NYSA; Tiro, *People of the Standing Stone*, 148–50; Treaty of 1826 and Treaty of 1827, in Whipple Report, vol. 1, part 1, pp. 298–303.

45. Hammond, *History of Madison County*, 742–43; "The History of Siloam, New York," n.d., MCHS.

46. Tiro, *People of the Standing Stone*, 131.

47. Weed, "Staging Forty Years Ago"; John Fowler, *Journal of a Tour in the State of New York in the Year 1830* (London: Whittaker, Treacher, & Arnot, 1831), 83–84, Oneida Nation of Wisconsin, https://www.exploreoneida.com.

48. Lafayette Theater advertisement, *National Advocate* (New York), 28 February 1827; "Extraordinary Novelty," Boston Theatre advertisement, *Boston Traveler* (published as *American Traveler*), 30 October 1827; "The Great Indian War Dance," *Newburyport (MA) Herald*, 16 November 1827; Eastman, "Indian Censures the White Man," 561; George Wilson Pierson, *Tocqueville in America* (1938; Baltimore: Johns Hopkins University Press, 1996), 194–95.

49. Rathbone, *Brief History of Oneida Castle*, 15; Tiro, *People of the Standing Stone*, 193.

50. Ten acres of the October 1829 cession were set aside for John Denny. Treaties of 1829, in Whipple Report, vol. 1, part 1, pp. 291–97; Field Book of Oneida Purchase of 1829, A4019-77, 34:113–14, MU1, reel 12, NYSA; First Christian Party Petition to Committee on Indian Affairs, In Senate, No. 46, 27 February 1849, Oneida Nation of Wisconsin, https://www.exploreoneida.com; Tiro, *People of the Standing Stone*, 151.

51. Deed, Martin Denny of Vernon to Cornelius Van Brocklin and Garet Van Brocklin, 26 February 1829, AB:13–14, MCCO; Martin and Abraham Denny to the Honorable Legislature of the State of New York, 5 January 1831, NY Legislative Assembly Papers, vol. 41:449–51; "Remonstrance of the Heirs of Abram Denny against His Petition," 6 January 1831, NY Legislative Assembly Papers, vol. 41:457–60, Denny File, Karst Collection; Carl Moon, "Pioneer Names in Lenox Area."

52. Deed, Abraham and Katharine Dana to Erastus Willard, 6 May 1831, AD:72; deed, Erastus and Sally Willard to Thomas B. Hart, 2 February 1833, AG:115–16; Thomas B. and Nancy Hart to William Cobb and Charles Deferrier, 2 May 1836, AN:391; deed, Martin and Hannah Denny to Angel Deferrier, 15 October 1827, AC:227, MCCO; Russell, "Wampsville, New York."

53. Helen B. Breese to Catharine Breese, 2 August 1832, and Sidney Breese to Catharine Breese, 9 August 1832, box 5, folder 3, Breese Stevens Roby Papers; Jones, *Annals and Recollections*, 551; Smith, *Our County and Its People*, 185.

54. Helen P. Breese to Catharine Breese, 28 October 1835, box 5, folder 5, Breese Stevens Roby Papers; S. B. Wilsey, "DeFerriere Cemetery," 2008, Deferrier Family Collection.

55. Catharine Denny Doxtator and Polly Mytop Doxtator, interviews, 11 U:191–94, 195–98, Draper Manuscripts; Denny File, Karst Collection.

56. William Bellinger, NY S28641; Jacob Lawyer, NY R6209; Nicholas Righter, NY S14309; John Dockstader, NY S29121.

57. Declaration of Henry Wakarantharaus (Powlis) on behalf of his father, Captain James Wakarantharaus, R11007, in Penrose, *Indian Affairs Papers*, 360–62; Jacob J. Failing, NY W21092; Peter Suits, NY W13941; Franz, "Memories of the Revolutionary War."

58. Honyery's pension application includes some valuable first-person accounts by John Cornelius, Peggy Johnson (Margaret Beechtree), Henry Powless, and David Welch, but it also contains suspect testimonies that repeat, sometimes word for word, the same information, some of which is incorrect or contradicted or not confirmed by other sources. Honyere Tewahangarahken Doxtator, S23019; Cornelius Sauquayunk, R9222; James Wakarantharaus, R1107.

59. The section of Route 46 south of the turnpike within the city of Oneida is also known as Glenwood Ave. David Alvord, "The Beginning of a Community," City of Oneida Centennial, *OD*, May 2001; Smith, *Our County and Its People*, 289–90; "Report of a Majority of the Committee on Indian Affairs, on the Petition of Henry Jourdan, in Behalf of the Orchard Party of the Oneida Indians," In Assembly, 22 March 1838, No. 287, Oneida Nation of Wisconsin, https://www.exploreoneida.com; Wells, "Breese Family History."

60. Contract between the Syracuse and Utica Railroad and Polly Deferrier, 23 December 1853, AQ:406, MCCO.

61. Russell, "Wampsville, New York"; Hammond, *History of Madison County*, 524; Rachael Protzman, "Owner Restoring Wampsville Home to Its 1839 Glory," *OD*, 1 January 2005, https://www.oneidadispatch.com.

62. Baptist Powlus, Henry Ninham, Antony Big Knife, Jacob Powlis, and Jacob L. W. Doxtator to A. C. Flagg, Comptroller, 29 June 1837, A0832, box 4, folder 8, NYSA; Tiro, *People of the Standing Stone*, 159–60; Geier, "Peculiar Status," 175, 179; Thomas Gordon, *Gazetteer of the State of New York* (Philadelphia: printed by the author, 1836), 518.

63. "Report of the Committee on Indian Affairs, on the Petition of John Denny," 12 February 1834, doc. 51, in *Documents of the Senate of the State of New York*, 1834, 2:1–3.

64. Two New York Oneidas, Baptist Powless and Jonathan Jordan, signed the Treaty of Buffalo Creek. Each received a $500 bonus from the Ogden Land Company, but they did not claim to represent all New York Oneidas. Tiro, *People of the Standing Stone*, 162–63; Arlinda Locklear, "The Buffalo Creek Treaty of 1838 and Its Legal Implications for Oneida Indian Land Claims," in Hauptman and McLester, *Oneida Indian Journey*, 85–89.

65. Testimonies of Lewis Denny and Moses Denny, 1859, Denny File, Karst Collection.

66. Tiro, *People of the Standing Stone*, 167–68; Morse, *Report to the Secretary of War*, app. A, 4.

67. Campisi, "Ethnic Identity," 263–64.

68. Treaties of 1840, 1841, and 1842, in Whipple Report, vol. 1, part 1, pp. 309–63; Tiro, *People of the Standing Stone*, 163–65.

69. Treaties of 1840, 1841, 1842; Nathan Burchard, "Field Book of the Survey and Allottment [*sic*] of the Oneida Purchase of 1840," A4019, 46:118–95, MU1, reel 16, NYSA; Tiro, *People of the Standing Stone*, 166.

70. Campisi, "Ethnic Identity," 265–66; Tiro, *People of the Standing Stone*, 166–67.

71. Treaties of 1841, in Whipple Report, vol. 1, part 1, pp. 329–55; Tiro, *People of the Standing Stone*, 168–69.

72. Campisi, "Ethnic Identity," 413; Tiro, *People of the Standing Stone*, 168–70.

73. Nelson Cobb was born around 1817 in Onondaga to parents from Massachusetts. I do not think he was related to William Cobb, who bought out Charles Deferrier's half of Lot 2 of the 1824 Purchase, because William Cobb's family was from Connecticut. It is more likely that Nelson was related to Captain Harvey Cobb of Massachusetts, the Seneca Turnpike agent who lived in Onondaga in 1800 and next door to the Deferriers by the late 1820s. Deed, Charles Deferrier to William Cobb, AN:392, MCCO; Town of Lenox, Madison County, NY, US Federal Census, 1850; Town of Lenox, Madison County, New York State Census, 1855; Denny File, Karst Collection.

74. William H. Tuttle, "Timmerman Farm in Family since 1855," *ODU*, 11 June 1831; Russell, "Wampsville, New York."

75. "Report of the Commissioners of the Land-Office, on the Bill Entitled 'An Act Directing the Sale to John Gregg of 250 Acres of Land, in the New Stockbridge or Oneida Reservation,'" 18 January 1831, No. 10, in *Documents of the Senate of the State of New York*, Oneida Nation of Wisconsin, https://www.exploreoneida.com; Geier, "Peculiar Status," 196–97; Hammond, *History of Madison County*, 743, 747.

76. At the time the Clements arrived, their farm was in the town of Lenox. In 1836, the town of Stockbridge was created out of parts of Vernon and Augusta in Oneida County and Smithfield and Lenox in Madison County. From then on, their farm was on the northern border of the town of Stockbridge. "Two Hundred Acres Very Fine Land," *Albany Argus*, 18 January 1828; Smith, *Our County and Its People*, 50; Hammond, "Of Me and Mine."

7. Squatters, Tenants, Owners

1. Frederick Spencer of Wampsville studied at and later became the director of the American Academy of Fine Arts in New York. Polly's daughter Nancy Hadcock died in 1852. Lucy Deferrier, who married George Pine, died three years later in childbirth. "Last Will and Testament of Polly Defferiere," 2 January 1852, MCCO and Madison County Surrogate Court, Wampsville, NY.

2. J. W. S., "Reminiscences."

3. "Is Eleazer Williams Louis XVII?," *Plattsburgh Republican*, 12 February 1853.

4. Oberg, *Professional Indian*, 166–92; J. W. S., "Reminiscences"; Bonaparte, "Eleazer Williams"; Darren Bonaparte, "The Unquiet Rest of Eleazer Williams," Wampum Chronicles, 6 May 2005, https://www.wampumchronicles.com.

5. Ellis, "Recollections of Rev. Eleazer Williams," 351–52.

6. "Intercepted Correspondence," *Southern Literary Messenger*, September 1840, 11 U, Draper Manuscripts.

7. Schoolcraft, *Notes on the Iroquois*, 440–41; "The Oneida Stone," *Green Bay Advocate*, 6 December 1849, Oneida Nation of Wisconsin, https://www.exploreoneida.com; Rathbone, *Brief History of Oneida Castle*, 6–7; Wonderley, *Oneida Iroquois Folklore*, 1–4.

8. Tiro, *People of the Standing Stone*, 173–79; Franklin B. Hough, *Census of the State of New York for 1855* (Albany, 1857), 501, 506; "Indian School," *Oneida Sachem*, 9 April 1859.

9. Caroline Harp married Charles Green, the son of Jeduthan Green and Sally Gregg. Tiro, *People of the Standing Stone*, 173–79; census of Oneida Reservation, 1845, New York State Archives Digital Collection, https://www.digitalcollections.archives.nysed.gov; Hough, *Census of the State of New York*; Brewer Collection.

10. Sophia was the daughter of Polly's nephew Louis Denny and Jenny Skenandoah. Tiro, *People of the Standing Stone*, 178, 184; Hammond, *History of Madison County*, 117.

11. W. H. Farnham, "Old Dr. Sundown," *ODU*, 28 August 1924, Denny File, Karst Collection.

12. "Death of William Doxtator," *ODU*, 21 March 1894, Doxtator File, Karst Collection; Susan Fenimore Cooper, *Rural Hours* (reprint; Syracuse, NY: Syracuse University Press, 1968), Oneida Nation of Wisconsin, https://www.exploreoneida.com; Tiro, *People of the Standing Stone*, 179–84.

13. "Seneca: Janice Sundown Hallett and Her Children," in *Wisdom's Daughters: Conversations with Women Elders of Native America*, by Steve Wall (New York: HarperCollins, 1993), 146; John File, Karst Collection; Campisi, "Ethnic Identity," 418.

14. Tuttle, *Names and Sketches*, 168–69; William H. Tuttle, "Lincoln Farms Passed through Many Hands," *ODU*, 5 February 1931.

15. Daniel Crouse and his brother John became millionaires and later relocated to Utica and Syracuse. Hammond, *History of Madison County*, 512–13; "Oneida Valley National Bank Elected Directors," *OD*, 14 January 1870; Daniel Crouse to John Moot, 24 September 1839, AU:349; John Moot to Daniel Crouse, 6 January 1841, AW:106; John Moot to William Henry Moot, 26 August 1892, 180:395 and 181:274; New York State to John Moot, 12 January 1851, CN:356–57, MCCO.

16. Two of Catharine's ten children had died very young. Duanesburg 1803, New York Tax Assessment Rolls of Real and Personal Estates, 1799–1804, Ancestry.com, https://www.ancestry.com; Charles Tulloch Papers, Schenectady County Historical Society, Schenectady, NY; Records of Christ Episcopal Church, Duanesburg, NY.

17. Ellis, *Landlords and Farmers*, 227–28, 235–49.

18. Ellis, *Landlords and Farmers*, 242–52; Reeve Huston, *Land and Freedom: Rural Society, Popular Protest, and Party Politics in Antebellum New York* (New York: Oxford University Press, 2000), 117–23.

19. Ellis, *Landlords and Farmers*, 287–98.

20. Ellis, *Landlords and Farmers*, 301–12; Brook, *Columbia Rising*, 467; Huston, *Land and Freedom*, 199–205.

21. Catharine Brewer's eldest daughter, Mary Ann, married and lived in Lenox Furnace, and her second son, John, married and lived southwest of Clockville. The Lenox Iron Company trustees sold the company to Abraham Van Eps, James Ingalls, Jacob Van Slik (Slyck), and Gardner, Jared, and Calvin Avery. "Certificate of Incorporation of the Lenox Furnace Company Founded March 22, 1811," 1835, 2001.A112.01, MCHS; deed, James and Maria Brewer to Levi Miller, April 1853, BW:318, MCCO; Town of Lenox, Madison County, NY, US Federal Census 1850, 1860, 1870; James and Maria Avery Brewer Bible, Brewer Collection.

22. Helen Breese to Catharine Breese, 4 January 1826, box 4, folder 2, Breese Stevens Roby Papers; Whitney R. Cross, *The Burned-Over District: The Social and Intellectual History of Enthusiastic Religion in Western New York, 1800–1850* (New York: Harper Torchbook, 1965), 15–51.

23. Elias Andrews, "Rev. Thomas Cornelius," Scrapbook, MCHS, accessed 8 January 2024, Oneida Nation of Wisconsin, https://www.exploreoneida.com; Hammond, *History of Madison County*, 112–16; David B. Danbom, *Born in the Country: A History of Rural America*, 3rd ed. (Baltimore: Johns Hopkins University Press, 2017), 90; William J. Szlemko, James W. Wood, and Pamela Jumper Thurman, "Native Americans and Alcohol: Past, Present, and Future," *Journal of General Psychology* 133, no. 4 (October 2006): 435–51.

24. Anthony Wonderley, *Oneida Utopia: A Community Searching for Human Happiness & Prosperity* (Ithaca, NY: Cornell University Press, 2017), 48–63; Hammond, *History of Madison County*, 538.

25. G. W. Noyes, "The Oneida Indians and the Oneida Community," *Oneida Telegraph*, 10 July 1852; Wonderley, *Oneida Utopia*, 49, 88.

26. Tuttle, *Names and Sketches*, 56; "Conrad Ingalls," 589.

27. "Town Meeting in Lenox," *Oneida Sachem*, 10 March 1855; "How the Thing Was Done: A Brief Review of the Manner in Which the Hindoos Carried Town Meeting in Lenox," *Oneida Sachem*, 31 March 1855.

28. Hammond, *History of Madison County*, 722–23; Cross, *Burned-Over District*, 327.

29. Dann, *Peter Smith of Peterboro*, 86, 150.

30. Norman K. Dann, "Attitudes and Networks at an Underground Railroad Station: The Example of Gerrit Smith in Madison County, New York," *Madison County Heritage*, no. 31 (2005): 15–19; Michael Kammen, *In the Past Lane: Historical Perspective on American Culture* (New York: Oxford University Press, 1997), 223.

31. Wonderley, *Oneida Utopia*, 62; Tiro, *People of the Standing Stone*, 181.

32. "Gerrit Smith's Meeting at Oneida," *Oneida Sachem*, 23 October 1858.

33. Cross, *Burned-Over District*, 276; "Charles J. Deferrier"; W. Robert Mayer, "The Oneida Independent Company of Cavalry Formation and Training," *Madison County Heritage*, no. 37 (2012): 26.

34. New York, Civil War Muster Roll Abstracts, Ancestry.com, accessed 14 April 2020, https://www.ancestry.com; Town of Lenox, Madison County, New York State Census,1865; Liz Obomsawin, "Those Who Remained: The New York Oneidas," in Hauptman and McLester, *Oneida Indian Journey*, 140–41.

35. William Tuttle, Miscellaneous Records, MCCO; "Town of Lenox, Madison County, New York State Census, 1865; Muster Rolls of 2nd Artillery, 86th Infantry, 114th Infantry, 157th Infantry, Rosters of the New York Regiments during the US Civil War, 1864, New York State Military Museum and Veterans Research Center, Saratoga Springs, NY, https://www.museum.dmna.ny.gov.

36. "157th Infantry Regiment," US Civil War, 1861–1865, Infantry 107-194 (NY Volunteers and State Militia/National Guard), New York State Military Museum and Veterans Research Center, accessed 8 January 2024, https://www.museum.dmna.ny.gov; Obomsawin, "Those Who Remained," 141.

37. Stradling, *Nature of New York*, 58–75; "Indigenous Dispossession and the Founding of Cornell: Part 1 with Jon Parmenter," Humanities Pod,

2020–21, Society for the Humanities, Cornell University, accessed 5 February 2024, https://societyhumanities.as.cornell.edu/-humanities-pod.

38. "Production of Agriculture in the Town of Lenox in the County of Madison, New York," Agricultural Schedule of 1860, Ancestry.com, accessed 13 June 2012, https://www.ancestry.com; diary of Edmund Adams, 1885, 2001.A008, Adams Family Collection, MCHS; diaries of William Clement, 1873, 1874, 2001.A059, Brewer Family Collection, MCHS; diaries of James Holt, 1876, 1878, 1880, courtesy of Jack Wallace, Brewer Collection.

39. Mark H. Howard, "Curds and Whey," *Madison County Heritage*, no. 5 (June 1979): 24–25; Ellis et al., *History of New York State*, 274; Hammond, "Of Me and Mine."

40. Diary of William Clement; deed, Lewis and Doratha Clement to William and Lewis H. Clement, 19 February 1861, CU:485–86, MCCO; Town of Lenox, Madison County, NY, US Federal Census, 1870.

41. Diaries of William Clement, Edmund Adams, and James Holt; Hammond, "Of Me and Mine."

42. Diaries of William Clement, Edmund Adams, and James Holt; Russell G. Hubbard, "A Brief History of the Hop Industry in Madison County," *Madison County Heritage*, no. 15 (July 1984): 21–22; Dick Case, "Ray Elm Is Weary of Issues, but He Can Tell You How His Land Was Lost," *SHA*, 14 April 1985, Karst Collection; Hammond, "Of Me and Mine."

43. Diary of James Holt; Hammond, "Of Me and Mine"; Thomas J. Kernan, "When the Hop Was King," *Madison County Heritage*, no. 21 (1996): 6–7.

44. The federal government suppressed the Ku Klux Klan in the early 1870s, but it was not until 11 June 1875 that the *Oneida Democratic Union* reported that there was no Ku Klux baseball organization in Oneida that year. Coverage of the baseball tournament was reported in the *Oneida Dispatch* on 21 August, 28 August, 4 September, and 11 September 1874.

45. Hope Allen notes, 5 March 1918 (from HEA Notebook, Special Collections, Hamilton College Library, Clinton, NY), John File, Karst Collection; Hubbard, "Brief History"; Hammond, "Of Me and Mine."

46. Hubbard, "Brief History"; diaries of Edmund Adams and James Holt; The People v. John J. Moot, 20 October 1879, "Hops Related Court Cases & Other Documents," Madison County, New York, Document Center, accessed 20 November 2023, https://www.madisoncounty.ny.gov/DocumentCenter/View/554/Hops-1826---1898-PDF; "Inventory of William Clement Estate," 17 April 1875, Madison County Surrogate Court; "From the *Oneida Democratic Union* of March 21, 1872," *Madison County Heritage*, no. 10 (July 1981): 26.

47. Cornelius Doxtator's father, Peter Doxtator, may have been the son of Honyost Thaosagwat. Doxtator File, Karst Collection; "Lenox Town Fair," *Oneida Sachem*, 9 October 1858; "Fair," *Oneida Sachem*, 3 October 1861; "Lenox Fair," *OD*, 16 November 1867.

48. Elm was the last name taken by Captain or Pagan Peter, the son of Good Peter. Amelia Cornelius, "Tribal Discord and the Road to Green Bay," in Hauptman and McLester, *Oneida Indian Journey*, 127; "Illegal Voting," *OD*, 13 April 1877; "The Indian as Voter" and "The Test Question," *OD*, 18 May 1877.

49. Whipple Report, vol. 1, part 1, pp. 385–90; Laurence M. Hauptman, *The Iroquois in the Civil War: From Battlefield to Reservation* (Syracuse, NY: Syracuse University Press, 1993), 148–49.

50. Diary of James Holt; Olive S. Boylan, "Prelude to Prohibition: The Early Years," *Madison County Heritage*, no. 8 (July 1980): 4–5, 8.

51. Diary of William Clement; family Bible of Hazel Brewer Taylor, Brewer Collection.

52. Fred Clement, the grandson of Lewis, eventually sold the Clement homestead and moved to a West Road property that had belonged to Oneida Indians and was acquired through foreclosure by Philander Spaulding. "Inventory of William Clement Estate"; John Moot to John J. Moot, 8 May 1889, 173:216; John Moot to Franklin P. Moot, 10 February 1892, 181:209; John Moot to William Henry Moot, 26 August 1892, 180:395 and 181:274, MCCO. "Estate of Lewis Clement," 30 September 1878, Madison County Surrogate Court; Hammond, "Of Me and Mine."

53. Contract between Elizabeth Clement and Charles Snyder, 1880, Brewer Family Collection; autograph album of Jennie Clement, 1881, Brewer Collection.

54. Frank Brewer no longer worked at the mill by the time his cousin Adelia Brewer, the daughter of James, married George Beecher Cady. "Lenox Furnace: Once a Busy Place," n.d., 2001.A112.02, MCHS; Moon, "Pioneer Names in Lenox Area"; Ellis, *Landlords and Farmers*, 129.

55. My father thought that Abraham's acre on Lot 8 of the Oneida Purchase of 1826 may have been his retirement package after working for the Ingalls family. Luther Ingles to Abram Brewer, 15 January 1881, 149:226, MCCO.

56. Wonderley, *Oneida Utopia*, 149–61; Smith, *Chenango and Madison Counties*, 734.

57. Hope Allen notes, 10 March 1918, John File, Karst Collection; Whipple Report, vol. 1, part 2, p. 507.

58. William Doxtator also was known as Chief Billy Beechtree. Xylon, "Kenwood," *OD*, 27 August 1909; George W. Walter, "Chief Beech Tree," *Mid-York Weekly*, 24 August 1967, Doxtator File, Karst Collection.

59. *Memorial of the Centennial Celebration of the Battle of Oriskany, 6 August 1877* (Utica, NY: Oneida Historical Society, 1878); "The Battle of Oriskany, Proceedings of the Celebration, 6 August 1877," in *The Centennial Celebrations of the State of New York*, by Allen Beach (Albany: Weed, Parsons, 1879), 55–149; "Our Chief Magistrate," *Daily Inter Ocean* (Chicago), 14 July 1887.

60. B. F. Burleson to L. C. Draper, 8 October 1877, 11 U, Draper Manuscripts; Denny File, Karst Collection; "Denny Family," Oneida Indian Ancestry, accessed 16 January 2024, https://www.angelfire.com.

61. "Memorial of the Chiefs and Head-Men of the Oneida Nation of Indians," 6 March 1874, 43rd Cong., 1st Sess., No. 85, Oneida Nation of Wisconsin, https://www.exploreoneida.com; Journal of the NY Assembly, 52nd Assembly, 1829, 100, Oneida Nation of Wisconsin, https://www.exploreoneida.com; "Report of the Committee of Indian Affairs Relative to the Petition of Daniel Bread and Others," In Assembly, 12 March 1865, No. 198, in *Documents of the Assembly of New York* (Albany: C. Wendall, 1865), 9:2.

62. "Report of the Commissioners of the Land Office," 9 March 1866, No. 50, in *Documents of the Senate of the State of New York* (Albany: C. Wendell, 1866), 2:3–5.

63. "Claim of the Oneida Indians," *ODU*, 25 April 1872; "Report of the Committee Appointed by the Legislature of 1877 to Investigate the Financial Relations of the Oneida and Stockbridge Indians with This State," 24 May 1878, No. 142, in *Documents of the Assembly of the State of New York* (Albany: Van Benthuysen, 1878), 7:3–4.

64. Whipple Report, vol. 1, part 1, p. 1.

65. Whipple Report, vol. 1, part 2, pp. 506–8.

66. Whipple Report, vol. 1, part 1, pp. 45–46, 69; part 2, pp. 508–10.

67. Mann, *Iroquoian Women*, 202; Whipple Report, vol. 1, part 1, pp. 45–46, 68–69, 79; Chris Anderson, "Global Indigeneity, Global Imperialism, and Its Relationship to Twentieth-Century U.S. History," in Sleeper-Smith et al., *Can't Teach United States History*, 298.

68. David Treuer, *The Heartbeat of Wounded Knee: Native America from 1890 to the Present* (New York: Riverhead Books, 2019), 8.

69. Whipple Report, vol. 1, part 2, pp. 507, 528–29; N. L. Tilden to A. B. Weaver, Superintendent of Public Instruction, "Oneida and Madison Reservation," December 1871, *Eighteenth Annual Report of the Superintendent of Public Instruction*, 104–5, Oneida Nation of Wisconsin, https://www.exploreoneida.com.

70. The Doxtator sisters were sent to boarding school after the death of their father, Louis Doxtator, at age thirty-eight of tuberculosis, a common cause of early death among the Oneidas that was especially virulent in the 1890s. Dunbar-Ortiz, *Indigenous Peoples' History*, 211–14; Laura Cornelius Kellogg, *Our Democracy and the American Indian, and Other Works*, ed. Kristina Ackley and Cristina Stancia (Syracuse, NY: Syracuse University Press, 2015), 96; Irma Altman, telephone interview by Helen Schwartz, 12 January 1999, Doxtator File, Karst Collection.

71. Campisi, "Ethnic Identity," 215–16; Hammond, "Of Me and Mine"; Allison M. Dussias, "The Reports of Our Death Are Greatly Exaggerated—Reflections on the Resilience of the Oneida Indian Nation of New York," *BYU Law Review* 2018, no. 6 (2019): 1253, https://digitalcommons.law.byu.edu/lawreview/vol2018/iss6/5.

72. City of Oneida, NY, US Federal Census, 1900; Oneida, New York State Census, 1905; "In His Narrow Bed: Thomas Taylor Loomis, an Old Settler, Laid to Rest," n.d., Deferrier Family Collection; Dewitt C. Hadcock, "Early Days in Wampsville at DeFerrier Home," ca. 1900, "An Interesting Frenchman," 1899, and "More or Less True," n.d., Deferrier Family Collection.

73. Mary Hartwell Catherwood, "Lazarre," *San Francisco Call*, 24 August 1902; Mark Twain, *The Adventures of Huckleberry Finn* (1885; New York: Bantam Books, 1965), 120.

74. L. C. Draper note on A. G. Ellis, "Recollections of Rev. Eleazer Williams," 352; Hammond, *History of Madison County*, 662; undated newspaper clipping, Deferrier Family Collection.

75. Charles's daughter Theresa Deferrier, who lived in New York, inherited his personal property worth $50,000. Charles left $500 each to his nieces Mary and Irene. "Charles J. Deferrier"; will, Charles J. Deferrier to Charles Cobb et al., 24 January 1891, 177:494–97, MCCO.

76. Articles of agreement between Nelson Cobb and Charles E. Brophy, 10 February 1894, 187:264; deed, Charles S. Cobb et al. to Frank Brewer, 3 March 1904, 203:396–97, MCCO; Danbom, *Born in the Country*, 123.

8. Realms of Orchards

1. Frank Brewer Diaries, 1901–33, Brewer Collection.

2. Frank Brewer's diaries from 1901 to 1909 contain entries of his and Jennie's daily activities. From 1910 on, he mostly used the diaries, which also contained receipts, to keep track of farm business.

3. Stradling, *Nature of New York*, 73; William F. Helmer, "The Old West Shore," *Madison County Heritage*, no. 14 (2008): 31–33.

4. George W. Walter, "The County Seat Fight," n.d., MCHS; Kammen, *In the Past Lane*, 103–8.

5. David Alvord, "A City Is Formed," in "City of Oneida: A Centennial Celebration," special section, *OD*, May 2001; Hammond, "Of Me and Mine"; "Madison County Centennial Celebration a Grand Success," *OD*, 29 June 1906; "Magnificent Parade in Oneida," *Syracuse Herald*, 28 June 1906; "Two Thousand Men Seen in Madison County Parade," *PS*, 29 June 1906, in William L. Leete, *Madison County Centennial Scrapbook, 1906*, 1911, MCHS.

6. The Cherry Street School later became known as the Washington Avenue School. "Two Thousand Men Seen"; "One Hundred Years Old," *Oneida Post*, 30 June 1906; "Salute Opens Madison Centennial," *Syracuse Herald*, 27 June 1906, in Leete, *Madison County Centennial Scrapbook.*

7. Richard W. Hill Sr., "Regenerating Identity: Repatriation and the Indian Frame of Mind," in Kerber, *Archeology of the Iroquois*, 410–21; Wonderley, *Oneida Iroquois Folklore*, 133–37.

8. "Address of Ex-Gov. Hoard," *Oneida Union*, 12 July 1906, in Leete, *Madison County Centennial Scrapbook.*

9. "Address of Ex-Gov. Hoard."

10. "Miss Laura M. Cornelius," *Oneida Union*, n.d., and "One Hundred Years Old," *Oneida Post*, 30 June 1906, in Leete, *Madison County Centennial Scrapbook.*

11. "Nick Honyost's Children: Indians played Hiawatha for the Historical Society Last Night," *Evening Courant* (Canastota), 28 February 1908, and "West Avenue," *ODU*, 15 February 1908, Honyost File, Karst Collection.

12. Xylon, "Kenwood"; City of Oneida, NY, US Federal Census, 1910, 1920.

13. Hon. Robert J. Fish, "The Lands of the Oneida Indians," *OD*, 5 and 12 January 1912, 2001.A110, MCHS; Solomon John obituary, *ODU*, 27 August 1925, and "History Bits," unidentified newspaper, 21 October 1954, John File, Karst Collection.

14. Alexander Burning, Marshall John, Simeon Elm, Baptist Day, Joseph J. Johnson, and W. H. Rockwell, "Memorial of a Band of Indians," State of New York, No. 70, In Assembly, 18 May 1910, Oneida Nation of Wisconsin,

https://www.exploreoneida.com; "Indians Residing on the Oneida Indian Reservation in the County of Madison and Oneida," Alexander Burning, Enumerator, New York State Census, 1905; Indian Population, Oneida City, US Federal Census, 1910; "Obituary of Mrs. Abraham Skenandoah, Gar-gea-junt-tar," unidentified newspaper, 5 January 1922, Honyost File, Karst Collection; Campisi, "Ethnic Identity," 413; Laurence M. Hauptman, *An Oneida Indian in Foreign Waters: The Life of Chief Chapman Scanandoah, 1879–1953* (Syracuse, NY: Syracuse University Press, 2016), 21, 68.

15. Philander Spaulding was constable, deputy sheriff, assistant revenue collector, founder of the Central Bank of Oneida, and a landowner who acquired several Oneida Indian properties, including that of Phoebe Cornelius, the widow of Thomas Cornelius, who claimed she was defrauded out of half her land. "Non-suit in the Case of Phoebe Cornelius against John Morris and Philander Spaulding," *ODU*, 14 July 1886; "Chronology of Thomas Cornelius," courtesy of Barb Skenandore, Oneida, WI; Case, "Ray Elm Is Weary"; *United States v. Julia Boylan and Anna Siver Moyer*, 1915–19, Karst Collection; Wonderley, *Oneida Iroquois Folklore*, 196–99; Hammond, "Of Me and Mine"; "Philander Spaulding," in *Biographical Review*, 112–14.

16. Chapman Skenandoah typically spelled his last name Scanandoah. Hauptman, *Oneida Indian*, 36–62.

17. Chapman Schanandoah, *U.S.S. Atlanta*, Montevideo, Uruguay, to Mrs. Julia Boylan, 1 May 1902, Exhibits, *Julia Boylan and Anna Siver Moyer*, 133–34; Barnum, Spicer, & Wells (law firm) to Hon. E. A. Hitchcock, Secretary of the Interior, 26 December 1905, Karst Collection; Campisi, "Ethnic Identity," 432–36.

18. "William Honyost and Sister Dispossessed," *PS*, 1 December 1909, Honyost File, Karst Collection; Hauptman, *Oneida Indian*, 70–72; Wonderley, *Oneida Iroquois Folklore*, 50, 200–203.

19. "Aged Indian Squaw in White Brother's Court," *Syracuse Herald*, 26 July 1916, Karst Collection; Wonderley, *Oneida Iroquois Folklore*, 205–6.

20. "Had Undertakers," undated news clipping, Honyost File, Karst Collection; Wonderley, *Oneida Iroquois Folklore*, 206.

21. Wonderley, *Oneida Iroquois Folklore*, 206–8; Campisi, "Ethnic Identity," 438–39.

22. "Court Gives Land Back to Indians," *OD*, 12 March 1920, and "New Light on the Indian Land Case," *OD*, 19 March 1920, Karst Collection.

23. At this time, the Bureau of Indian Affairs was known as the Commission of Indian Affairs, but for the sake of consistency I refer to it as the BIA. B. B. Weber, Special Agent for New York Indians, to Hon. Commissioner of Indian Affairs, 24 May 1909; F. H. Abbott, Acting Commissioner, to Wilson Cornelius, 18 August 1909, Bureau of Indian Affairs, Record Group 75 (hereafter RG 75), NA, Oneida Nation of Wisconsin, https://www.exploreoneida.com; Kristina Ackley, "Haudenosaunee Genealogies: Conflict and Community in the Oneida Land Claims," *American Indian Quarterly* 33, no. 4 (September 2009): 462–78, https://www.jstor.org/stable/40388482; Obomsawin, "Those Who Remained," 139–40.

24. C. F. Hauke, Second Assistant Commissioner, to Wilson Cornelius, 19 July 1911; William Zimmerman Jr., Assistant Commissioner, to Wilson

Cornelius, 17 October 1933; E. B. Meritt to Peter Cole, 23 February 1923; E. B. Meritt to Walter Funk, 17 April 1923, RG 75, NA, Oneida Nation of Wisconsin, https://www.exploreoneida.com.

25. "Madison County, New York, World War I Soldiers," Madison County, NY (website), 10 August 2017, https://www.madisoncounty.ny.gov.

26. The heirs of William Cobb sold Myron Peebles (pronounced Pebbles) Lot 2 and Lot 5 (Abraham Denny's lot) of the Oneida Purchase of 1824 (91.65 acres) and the 2-acre mill lot on the creek that was part of Angel Deferrier's Lot 6 of the 1815 purchase. Indenture, C. Augusta Cobb et al. to Myron G. Peebles, 22 April 1914, 244:418; Myron G. Peebles to Frank Brewer, 10 January 1916, 246:276, MCCO.

27. Patent to Frank Brewer, 9 July 1918, Letters Patent 12943, vol. 46–59, Roll No. 22, NYSA; Coville & Santry to Frank Brewer, 25 July 1918, Brewer Collection; Danbom, *Born in the Country*, 151.

28. Wonderley, *Oneida Utopia*, 181–89.

29. Arthur Austin Boccaccio, "Constant and Chiffonette: Personal Names in 19th Century Madison County," *Madison County Heritage*, no. 5 (June 1979): 18–23.

30. Mabelle Brewer, "God's Green Acre," 1984, Brewer Collection; "Mabelle A. Greene Marries D. F. Brewer," undated news clipping, Brewer Collection.

31. Helen M. Upton, *The Everett Report in Historical Perspective* (Albany: New York State American Revolution Bicentennial Commission, 1980), 80–83.

32. Conference of New York State and National Indian Commissions, 27 July 1920, Saratoga, NY, in *Report of the New York State Indian Commission 1922* (hereafter Everett Report), 34, 41–42, New York State Library, Native American Digital Collections.

33. Everett Report, 15–50.

34. "Onondaga Reservation, Onondaga Tribe, 16 August 1920," in Everett Report, 58–61, 88–90.

35. "Onondaga Reservation, Oneida Tribe, 17 August 1920," in Everett Report, 95–98.

36. "Onondaga Reservation, Onondaga Tribe," and "Onondaga Reservation, Oneida Tribe," in Everett Report, 67–70, 99–101.

37. "Onondaga Reservation, Oneida Tribe," in Everett Report, 88–111.

38. Geier, "Peculiar Status," 265–66; Upton, *Everett Report in Historical Perspective*, 112–13.

39. A copy of the Everett Report sent to the US Justice Department was mislaid, and a copy sent to the Department of the Interior was discovered uncatalogued on a shelf by a researcher in 1975. The remaining copy, as well as the underlying documentation, was preserved by Mrs. Lulu Stillman, the secretary of the commission, who is spoken of with reverence at the New York State Archives. Upton, *Everett Report in Historical Perspective*, 102–10.

40. Geier, "Peculiar Status," 259–60.

41. Hauptman, *Oneida Indian*, 78; Geier, "Peculiar Status," 274; "Obituary of Mrs. Abraham Skanandoah" and "Weird Ceremonials Mark Burial of Indian Woman," *ODU*, 7 January 1922, Karst Collection.

42. "Onondaga Reservation, Oneida Tribe," in Everett Report, 93–94; Wonderley, *Oneida Iroquois Folklore*, 208–9; "Seventy-Five Years Ago," *OD*, 24 July 2020, Brewer Collection; Ivah Greene diary, Brewer Collection; Ellen Faulkner Gregg, "Lines to the Elm Tree," West Avenue, 1912, 2001.A110, MCHS; City of Oneida, NY, US Federal Census, 1920.

43. Nash, "Hidden History," 22–23; François Weil, *Family Trees: A History of Genealogy in America* (Cambridge, MA: Harvard University Press, 2013), 131–34.

44. Nash, "Hidden History," 22–23; George C. Shattuck, *The Oneida Land Claims: A Legal History* (Syracuse, NY: Syracuse University Press, 1991), 24–25.

45. David H. Alvord, "The Ku Klux Klan in Madison County in the 1920s," *Madison County Heritage*, no. 21 (1996): 11–19; Dorris Lawson, "Italians of Canastota," *Madison County Heritage*, [no. 1]: (August 1977): 8–14.

46. Hauptman, *Oneida Indian*, 101; K. Tsianina Lomawaima, "Federalism: Native, Federal, and State Sovereignty," in Sleeper-Smith et al., *Can't Teach United States History*, 284n8; Kellogg, *Our Democracy*, 88, 243; Upton, *Everett Report in Historical Perspective*, 121–24; Pevar, *Rights of Indians*, 19.

47. Laurence M. Hauptman, "Designing Woman: Minnie Kellogg, Iroquois Leader," in *Indian Lives: Essays on Nineteenth- and Twentieth-Century Native American Leaders*, ed. L. G. Moses and Raymond Wilson (Albuquerque: University of New Mexico Press, 1985), 159–86; Thelma Cornelius McLester, "Oneida Women Leaders," in Campisi and Hauptman, *Oneida Indian Experience*, 109–11; Kellogg, *Our Democracy*, 1–62; Katie Honyost John to Emma Meade, 28 May 1923, John File, Karst Collection.

48. Irma Altman, telephone interview; William Rockwell to Hon. Franklin D. Roosevelt, 29 March [no year], Doxtator File, Karst Collection.

49. "Indians Claim Land Cannot Be Sold," *ODU*, 3 November 1927; "Thurston Gets Verdict in Miller Ouster Proceedings," *OD*, 6 May 1931; "Seek Aid in Indian Case," *OD*, 21 May 1931; "Who Now Owns the Lydia Doxtator Place?," *ODU*, 14 May 1931, Karst Collection; Irma Altman, telephone interview; W. H. Rockwell to Hubert Work, Secretary of the Interior, 22 November 1926; C. J. Rhoads, "Memorandum for Secretary Work," 6 December 1926; Hubert Work to Mr. Rockwell, 9 December 1926; C. J. Rhoads to Mr. Davenport, 4 June 1931, RG 75, NA, Oneida Nation of Wisconsin, https://www.exploreoneida.com; Rockwell to Hon. Franklin D. Roosevelt. Irma Miller Altman was Stella's niece and adopted daughter. Doxtator File, Karst Collection.

50. Irma Altman, telephone interview; Hauptman, *Oneida Indian*, 90; R. Patrick Corbett, "A Land Claim Could Shape the Future," *Observer Dispatch* (Utica, NY), 28 July 1991, Karst Collection.

51. Hope Allen notes, 5 March 1918; "To the Editor" from "A Friend," unidentified newspaper, n.d., John File, Karst Collection; Susan Hébert George, "Researching the Past with Becky Karst," *Oneida Indian Nation News*, May 2000, John File, Karst Collection; Wonderley, *Oneida Iroquois Folklore*, 51; Rebecca "Becki" John Karst, telephone interview by the author, 2 June 2020.

52. By the 1970s, blood quantum rules applied to the official roll kept by the Oneidas. The Oneidas of New York based enrollment on quarter-degree blood descendancy through the mother. Wisconsin Oneidas enrolled through either

the mother or the father. Canadian Oneidas enrolled though the father. Keshia Clukey, "Oneidas Fight to Save Culture," *Observer Dispatch*, 29 July 2012; Doug Kiel, "Bleeding Out: Histories and Legacies of 'Indian Blood,'" in Ratteree and Hill, *Great Vanishing Act*, 89–90.

53. Robert "Bob" Brewer, interview by the author, 16 August 2013, Chestertown, NY; Herb Brewer, interview; Virginia "Ginny" Brewer, interview by the author, 31 March 2019, Amherst, MA.

54. Jacques Tourneur, dir., *The King without a Crown* (MGM, 1937); Bob Brewer, Ginny Brewer, interviews; Ivah Greene and Mabelle Brewer, 1936 diary; Ella Taylor Greene, *Five Year Diary*, 1947–1951, Brewer Collection.

55. Last will and testament of Frank Brewer, dated 15 May 1926 and probated 17 May 1940; agreement between Frank Brewer and Stephen Willis Putman, 3 April 1939, Brewer Collection.

56. Bob Brewer, Herb Brewer, and Ginny Brewer, interviews.

57. Bob Brewer, Herb Brewer, and Ginny Brewer, interviews.

58. Bob Brewer, Herb Brewer, and Ginny Brewer, interviews; George M. Walter, "Madison Youth Uses Poultry Profits for College Expenses," *OD*, 4 October 1949; Herb Brewer, "Chickens and College," 3 April 1952, Brewer Collection.

59. *O.J.H.S. Gazette*, 17 December 1943 and 17 February 1944, Brewer Collection.

60. "Madison County, New York World War II Casualties," Madison County, NY (website), 10 August 2017, https://www.madisoncounty.ny.gov; Martin John File, Karst Collection.

61. Dunbar-Ortiz, *Indigenous Peoples' History*, 221; "Military Record and Report of Separation of Service," 18 December 1945; "Headquarters Special Troups 12th Army Group, SO 142, 24 May 1945"; "Johns on Terminal Leave," *OD*, 31 October 1945, Martin John File, Karst Collection; Wonderley, *Oneida Utopia*, 196.

62. John File, Karst Collection; "Champion for Indian Rights," n.d., Karst Collection; William Rockwell Exhibit, Shako:wi Cultural Center, Oneida Indian Nation, Oneida, NY; Michael T. Smith to Director, Office of Indian Services, "Report on the History of the New York Oneida Indians," 24 February 1982, BIA, US Department of the Interior, Oneida Nation of Wisconsin, https://www.exploreoneida.com; G. W. W., "Chief Rockwell," 26 January 1956, 2001.A110, MCHS.

63. Smith to Director; Mary Cornelius Winders to Charles Berry, Superintendent, 15 April 1943, Records of the New York Agency, 1938–1949, RG 75, NA, Karst Collection; Commissioner to Charles H. Berry, 11 May 1943, RG 75, NA, Oneida Nation of Wisconsin, https://www.exploreoneida.com; Susan Hébert George, "Mary Winder: A Full Life with Land Claim at Its Center," *Oneida Onyota a Ka: Oneida Indian Nation News*, n.d., Oneida Public Library; Susan Hébert George, "90 Years Well Spent: William Honyost Rockwell," *Oneida Onyota a Ka: Oneida Indian Nation News*, July 2009, 2001.A100, MCHS; Campisi, "Ethnic Identity," 413, 466.

64. "Indian Adoption at Fair Postponed, Guest Late," *PS*, 11 September 1954; "40,840 at Fair, Attendance Is Ahead of 1954: Gov. Williams Made Brother

of Iroquois Indians," *PS*, 10 September 1955; "Today at the Fair," *PS*, 12 September 1959; Hauptman, *Oneida Indian*, 88–89.

65. Dunbar-Ortiz, *Indigenous Peoples' History*, 173–74; Charles Wilkinson, *Blood Struggle: The Rise of Modern Indian Nations* (New York: W.W. Norton, 2005), 66–69.

66. Hauptman, *Oneida Indian*, 108–9; Upton, *Everett Report in Historical Perspective*, 139–61.

67. An estimated 90 percent of the forty-eight states had been acquired through treaties with Indian nations. Dunbar-Ortiz, *Indigenous Peoples' History*, 173; William T. Hagan, "'To Correct Certain Evils': The Indian Land Claims Commission," in *Iroquois Land Claims*, ed. Christopher Vecsey and William A. Starna (Syracuse, NY: Syracuse University Press, 1988), 17, 21.

68. Hauptman, *Oneida Indian*, 110–11; George, "Mary Winder."

69. Walter, "Madison Youth"; "Summary of Record," July 1950, NY State College of Agriculture at Cornell University, Brewer Collection; Herb Brewer, interview.

70. Herb Brewer, interview; Richard "Dick" Brewer, interview by the author, 20 October 2018, Piseco, NY; "Thrilling Scenes at Thruway Opening Ceremonies Here," *PS*, 25 June 1954.

71. DeVerne Brewer and Son, "Farm Inventory for Five Years," 1953–1957, Brewer Collection; Bob Brewer, Herb Brewer, Ginny Brewer, and Dick Brewer, interviews.

72. George W. Walter, "Brewers Are Successful Dairymen," *OD*, 27 August 1958, Brewer Collection.

73. Herb Brewer and Dick Brewer, interviews.

74. Laura Ingalls Wilder, *Little House on the Prairie* (New York: HarperCollins, 1971), 236–37; Wendy McClure, *The Wilder Life: My Adventures in the Lost World of "Little House on the Prairie"* (New York: Penguin, 2011); Frances W. Kaye, "Little Squatter on the Osage Diminished Reserve: Reading Laura Ingalls Wilder's Kansas Indians," *Great Plains Quarterly* 20, no. 2 (2000), https://digitalcommons.unl.edu/greatplainsquarterly/23.

75. Campisi, "Ethnic Identity," 450.

76. Lyman Johns, Ray Halbritter, and Richard Chrisjohn to James G. Watt, Secretary of the Interior, 4 September 1981, Oneida Nation of Wisconsin, https://www.exploreoneida.com; "Iroquois Likely to Accept White House Invitation," *PS*, 18 July 1954; Campisi, "Ethnic Identity," 443–44, 450; Smith to Director, "Report on the History"; R. Patrick Corbett, "Treaty Cloth Still a Living Symbol for Oneidas," *Observer Dispatch*, 28 July 1991; George, "Mary Winder."

77. Cowaselon is thought to mean branches hanging over water. Mrs. Hammond says it was pronounced "Kwos-a-lone" or "Squash-a-lone." Richard "Dick" Lynch, interview by the author, 3 November 2019, Oneida, NY; Hammond, *History of Madison County*, 489.

78. Becki Karst, conversations with the author, n.d.; "New Oneida Indian Chief Was Chosen by Women," *OD*, 13 October 1960, 2002.A110, MCHS.

79. This is my short version of the corn husk doll story as told by Mary Winder's daughter, Maisie Shenandoah. Maisie Shenandoah, "The No-Face

Doll," *Eidos* 3, no. 2 (Winter 1981): 34–35, Wisconsin Historical Society; Becki Karst, conversations.

80. "Frenchman: A Tale of Colonial Love," *PS*, 12 February 1961.

9. Fire and Water

1. James R. Borcherding, "Low-Cost Setup Geared for an Expanding Partnership," *Successful Farming*, February 1974, 6–7, Brewer Collection.

2. Herb Brewer, interview.

3. Russell "Russ" Brewer, interview by the author, 3 November 2019, Oneida, NY; Thomas "Tom" Brewer, interview by the author, 23 February 2020, Cassville, NY; Elizabeth "Beth" Brewer, interview by the author, 6 August 2019, Piseco, NY.

4. Judy Gerbig, "Williams, Brewer Discuss Concerns of City," *OD*, 31 October 1975, Brewer Collection; Herb Brewer, interview; Rex Niles, interview by the author, 2 July 2020, via Zoom.

5. Herb Brewer, interview; Jeff Coplon, "Tale of Two Nations Unfolds in Court Battle," *Rome (NY) Daily Sentinel*, 26 August 1974; "Trailer Sale: FBI Probe," *SHJ*, 27 April 1977.

6. Herb Brewer, interview.

7. Shattuck, *Oneida Land Claims*, 11; Campisi, "Ethnic Identity," 445.

8. Shattuck, *Oneida Land Claims*, 7–12.

9. "Oneida Nation Petition to the Constitutional Convention of New York State," 12 June 1967, in Shattuck, *Oneida Land Claims*, 85–86; "Louis J. Lefkowitz, Attorney General, to the Constitutional Convention Committee on Indian Affairs, 3 August 1967," in Shattuck, *Oneida Land Claims*, 92–93; Shattuck, *Oneida Land Claims*, 15–19.

10. Shattuck, *Oneida Land Claims*, 20–32.

11. Shattuck, *Oneida Land Claims*, 20–37.

12. Shattuck, *Oneida Land Claims*, 37–38, 77–81, 159.

13. Throughout the decades of land claims cases regarding the Oneida reservation, the size of the reservation would be cited as ranging from 250,000 to 300,000 acres. I refer to it as 300,000 acres to be consistent. The Native American Rights Fund (NARF) was a nonprofit organization that represented Indians in hunting, fishing, water, and land rights claims throughout the country. Created in 1969, it was funded by the Ford Foundation and the US Office of Economic Opportunity. While the test case went through the process of discovery, trial, and appeal, *Oneida v. Oneida County*, Civ. No. 74-CV-187 and *Oneida Tribe of New York v. Abraham Williams* Civ. No. 74-CV-167 were held in abeyance because the three cases involved many of the same legal issues. Arlinda Locklear, "Oneida—Status Report of Land Claims," 20 October 1978, NARF, Oneida Nation of Wisconsin, https://www.exploreoneida.com; Shattuck, *Oneida Land Claims*, 78. Wilkinson, *Blood Struggle*, 171, 242.

14. Jack Curtin, interview by the author, 9 July 2020, Cassville, NY; Michael Conner, "Brewer Speaks in County Tour," *PS*, 6 April 1978.

15. I am indebted to Becki Karst for sharing her collection of newspaper articles clipped by her and by Mrs. Abraham (Pearl) Williams during the land

claims dispute. Other articles are from the Brewer Collection and online and archival sources. Boby Conley, "Land Value Eyed," *PS*, 4 April 1974; "Oneida May Aid Defense," *Rome Daily Sentinel*, 26 August 1974; Judy Gerbig, "West Rd. Residents to Withhold Tax Payments," *OD*, 5 June 1974.

16. Some Oneidas said that Jacob Thompson, whose mother was Mohawk, was not an Oneida Indian, while others identified him as an adopted Oneida. Judy Gerbig, "Chief Ray Elm Vows to Aid West Rd. Residents," *OD*, 23 April 1974; Douglas Carroll, "Indian Claims Hobble Landowners," *Observer Dispatch*, 18 May 1980; "Relic Returning to Indian Lands," *PS*, 24 May 1974; "Sacred Stone of Oneidas to be Returned Saturday," *OD*, 23 May 1974; Case, "Ray Elm Is Weary."

17. Coplon, "Tale of Two Nations"; Jay Reiner, "Indian Land Issue Complex," *DP*, 6 June 1974; Gerbig, "West Rd. Residents"; Jay Reiner, "Citizens Want Stay of Taxes," *DP*, 5 June 1974; Robert W. Curley, "Indians Will Seek U.S. Aid," *SHA*, 25 August 1974.

18. Shattuck, *Oneida Land Claims*, 43–57.

19. Dunbar-Ortiz, *Indigenous Peoples' History*, 191; Sherry L. Smith, *Hippies, Indians & the Fight for Red Power* (New York: Oxford University Press, 2012), 184.

20. Wilma Luebbe, "Oneidas' Existence Just 1 of Many Questions," *OD*, 15 July 1974; Judy Gerbig, "Oneida Will Intervene in Indian Dispute," *OD*, 1 May 1975; Shattuck, *Oneida Land Claims*, 79–81.

21. Becki Karst, telephone interview; Shattuck, *Oneida Land Claims*, 40–42, 47–48; "Indian Unit Claims Ban from Talks," *PS*, 18 October 1976; "Fight Fire at Indian Territory," *OD*, 16 December 1975; Judy Gerbig, "2 Indians Killed in Trailer Fire: City Denies Aid to Callers," *OD*, 25 June 1976.

22. Fred Ferretti, "'Cold War' Pits Indian vs. Indian and Both against City of Oneida," *NYT*, 2 August 1976; Herb Brewer, interview.

23. Herb Brewer, interview.

24. "City's Services Being Withdrawn," *OD*, 17 December 1975; Herb Brewer, interview; Richard Myers, interview by the author, 25 March 2019, Fayetteville, NY.

25. Beth Brewer, conversation with the author, n.d.; Richard Myers, interview; Herb Brewer, interview; Dick Lynch, interview; Ferretti, "'Cold War.'"

26. Gerbig, "2 Indians Killed"; "A Tragic Day," editorial, *OD*, 25 June 1976; Garry L. Sherman, "Appalled by Refusal," letter to the editor, *OD*, 25 June 1976; Anthony J. Melisr, "Ashamed of Decision," letter to the editor, *OD*, 25 June 1976; Douglas P. Bailey, "The Other Side," letter to the editor, *OD*, 15 July 1976; Associated Press, "Indians, City Split over Fire Protection," *Daily Star* (Oneonta, NY), 1 July 1976; Herb Brewer, interview.

27. Associated Press, "Indians, City Split"; "Oneida Stand Same," *PS*, 2 July 1976; Bob Curley, "Rambling Round Madison County," *SHJ*, 26 August 1976; "Board Contemplating Legal Action against Warrior Society," *OD*, 18 October 1976.

28. "Board Contemplating Legal Action"; "Indian Unit Claims Ban."

29. Mike Connor, "FBI Investigating Deaths of Indians," *PS*, 8 December 1976; Doug Carroll, "City under Investigation by FBI," *OD*, 7 December 1976; Herb Brewer, interview.

30. Kim Landon, "Oneidas' Water Still Flowing," *DP*, 12 March 1977; Roxanne Gromelski, "City Delays Water Cutoff," *OD*, 11 March 1977; Robert W. Curley, "Indians Get Extension on Oneida Water Bill," *PS*, 12 March 1977.

31. Curley, "Indians Get Extension"; Herb Brewer, interview.

32. Chet Mullin, "Indians' Claim to Territory in Oneida Defended," *DP*, 6 January 1977; Landon, "Oneidas' Water Still Flowing,"; Doug Carroll, "Indians May Lose Water on Territory," *OD*, 3 March 1977; Bruce Entelisano, "1976 Deaths Still Haunt Halbritter," *Rome (NY) Observer*, 25 June 2010; Treuer, *Heartbeat of Wounded Knee*, 302–7; Wilkinson, *Blood Struggle*, 142–43; Smith, *Hippies, Indians*, 171–82; Dunbar-Ortiz, *Indigenous Peoples' History*, 185.

33. Winnie Jacobs, "Halbritter's Status," letter to the editor, *DP*, 16 May 1977; "City-Territory Relations Better," *OD*, 23 December 1977; Steve Galante, "Expelled Indians Sue," *PS*, 20 July 1977; Mike Connors, "Halbritter Answers Charges," *PS*, 29 July 1977.

34. Doug Carroll, "Oneida Nation Wins Case," *OD*, 13 July 1977; "Feds on Their Side—Indian Attacks Are Succeeding," editorial, *DP*, 20 July 1977; Hart Seely, "Indians Could Collect $400,000 in Rent from Counties," *SHJ*, 15 September 1981; Louis H. Roper, "Old Wine in New Bottles: New York, the Federal Government and the Oneida Land Claims Cases," *New York History* 72, no. 2 (April 1991): 144, https://www.jstor.org/stable/23178782.

35. David E. Williams, "Tryon Militiamen Leave Fort Dayton, Head West," *Observer Dispatch*, 4 August 1977; Kim Landon, "Bloody Oriskany Battle Re-enacted as 15,000 Watch," *Observer Dispatch*, 7 August 1977; Oriskany Historical File, Oneida County History Center; Robert W. Curley, "Tribe Wins in Courts," SHA, 7 August 1977; "Indians Want Justice, Not Evictions," *SHA*, 7 August 1977.

36. Robert W. Merry, "Don't Say 'Indian Giver' Here," *National Observer* (Washington, DC), 8 January 1977; Robert W. Curley, "Farmers May Lose All," *SHA*, 13 March 1977; Jack Curtin, interview; Herb Brewer, interview.

37. "City Offer," *OD*, 13 September 1977; Doug Carroll, "Mayor Reveals Details of Indian Negotiations," *OD*, 13 September 1977; "Oneida, Justice Dept. Agree on Indian Action," *OD*, 27 September 1977; "Council Oks Justice Pact," *OD*, 20 October 1977; Mike Connor, "Mayor Yields to Pressure," *PS*, 15 September 1977; "Oneida-Indians Case: See End of Lawsuit," *PS*, 27 September 1977; "Indian Issue Rebuttal Filed," *PS*, 30 September 1977; "Federal Court Oks City-Indian Pact," *PS*, 18 October 1977.

38. Mike Connor, "Oneidas Get Protection," *PS*, 3 September 1977; Kim Landon, "Officials Try to Clear Way for Negotiations," *DP*, 12 October 1977; Robert W. Curley, "City, Indians on Precipice of Peace," *SHJ*, 11 September 1977; Ferretti, "'Cold War.'"

39. Connor, "Oneidas Get Protection"; Curley, "City, Indians on Precipice"; Dick Lynch, interview.

40. Mike Connor, "Mayor List Steps Taken in Indian Claim," *PS*, 23 September 1977; "Indian Claims Aid Asked by Mayor," *OD*, 23 September 1977.

41. Robert W. Curley, "Fear Oneida to be Sued," *PS*, 29 October 1977; Mike Connor, "Meeting Upcoming on Indian Claims," *PS*, 20 October 1977;

Jay Reiner, "Former Mayor Challenges Incumbent," unidentified newspaper, n.d. [1975]; Doug Carroll, "Brewer, Williams Trade Charges," *OD*, 3 November 1977; Judy Gerbig, "Brewer Wins with Surprising Ease," *OD*, 7 November 1973; "Oneida Mayoral Race Could Be Close," *OD*, n.d. [1975]; "We Endorse Brewer," n.d. [probably 1977]; "We Endorse," editorial, *OD*, 29 October 1979, Brewer Collection.

42. Manuel L. and Arabella G. Peebles and Roland F. and Cora F. Peebles to Herbert D. and Mary Louise Brewer, 10 October 1977, Brewer Collection; Mary Lou Brewer, interview by the author, 1 July 2020, Pittsford, NY.

43. Becki Karst, telephone interview.

44. Doug Carroll, "Suits Mark Milestone for Indians," *OD*, 4 March 1978; Mike Connor, "Oneida Indians Sue N.Y. State," [probably *PS*], 4 March 1978; "Indian Policy by U.S. Needed," editorial, *DP*, 7 March 1978.

45. The test case, it turned out, did not include the courthouse and jail, which were on land acquired in the Treaty of 1815. "Indian Claims Response Eyed," *PS*, 12 February 1978; John L. Simson, "Burke Hits Hanley on Indian Claims," unidentified newspaper, 28 February 1978; Marj Patrick, "Land Area, Value in Indians' Claim 'Shrink,'" *DP*, 15 March 1978; Robert W. Curley, "Land Claim Hinders Plan for New Jail," unidentified newspaper, 22 November 1978, Karst Collection.

46. "City-Territory Relations Better," *OD*, 23 December 1977; Doug Carroll, "Past Shaped Oneida Indians' Land Claims," *OD*, 27 February 1978; Doug Carroll, "Brewer Feels Congress Should Help," *OD*, 10 March 1978; Doug Carroll, "Oneida Indians May Claim 5 Million Acres," *OD*, 30 November 1979; Herb Brewer, interview.

47. The Oneidas decided to pursue their land claims cases in court and withdrew their Indian Claims Commission complaint in 1982. Karim M. Tiro, "Claims Arising: The Oneida Nation of Wisconsin and the Indian Claims Commission, 1951–1982," *American Indian Law Review* 32, no. 2 (2008): 509–24, LexisNexis, https://www.lexisnexis.com; Doug Carroll, "Court Ruling Favors Indians," *OD*, 18 May 1978; "Court Views Law Suit Filed by Oneida Indians," *OD*, 14 July 1978; Doug Carroll, "Oneida Indians Win Claims Battle," *OD*, 3 October 1978; Robert W. Curley, "Oneida Leader Cites ICC Decision," *PS*, 4 October 1978.

48. Doug Carroll, "RAIN President's Comments Criticized," *OD*, 25 July 1978; Landon, "Officials Try to Clear Way."

49. The fire department reported that the water shutoff would not have any real effect on firefighting. Doug Carroll, "City Shuts Off Water to Indians," *OD*, 1 November 1978; Robert W. Curley, "Mayor Denies 'Secret Fund,'" unidentified newspaper (probably *PS*), 1 May 1978; Robert W. Curley, "Oneida Threatens to Cut Water Main," *PS*, 2 November 1978; Rex Niles, interview.

50. Dave Hollis, "Indians Threaten to Stop Water Flow," *OD*, 2 November 1978; Curley, "Oneida Threatens to Cut Water Main"; Doug Carroll, "Déjà Vu on Territory," *OD*, 3 November 1978; Doug Carroll, "Water Line on Agenda," *OD*, 6 November 1978; Richard G. Case, "'This Has Always Been Ours . . .,'" *SHA*, 17 June 1979; Rex Niles, interview.

51. Carroll, "Water Line on Agenda"; Doug Carroll, "Water Plan Suggested," *OD*, 9 November 1978; Robert W. Curley, "Indians Withdraw Water Line Threat," *PS*, 10 November 1978; Robert W. Curley, "City to Bypass Oneidas with Second Line," *PS*, 11 November 1978; Robert W. Curley, "City Water to Flow through Bypass," *PS*, 23 November 1978.

52. Doug Carroll, "City Water Flowing to Territory Again," *OD*, 5 September 1979; "Mayor, Indians Mum on Parley," *PS*, 29 November 1978; "Oneidas, City Stage Talks on Water Bill," *PS*, 15 September 1979.

53. Robert W. Curley, "Oneida Faction Disclaims Water Debt," *PS*, 6 December 1978; Roger Van Der Horst, "City, Indians Agree on Water Service," *PS*, 7 December 1979; Rex Niles, interview.

54. Kim Landon, "Oneida Indians Claim Action Would Violate Their Tradition," *DP*, 3 March 1977; "Tribe Meets Today on Land Settlement," *DP*, 12 March 1977; Mike Connor, "Halbritter Plans to Question Vote," *PS*, 14 March 1977; Robert W. Curley, "BIA Poll Begins despite Boycott," *PS*, 3 April 1979; "Let's Settle the Land Claims!," editorial, *OD*, 23 May 1979; "BIA's Hopes for Oneidas Poll 'Dead,'" *PS*, 24 May 1979; Robert W. Curley, "Challenges BIA to Admit Error," *PS*, 26 June 1979; James Ehmann, "Elected Oneidas Lost BIA Action," *PS*, 21 November 1979; Smith to Director, "Report on the History," 9.

55. Republican Donald Mitchell, whose Thirty-First District included Oneida County, joined Hanley in sponsoring this legislation. Doug Carroll, "Hanley Preparing Indian Claims' Bill," *OD*, 10 May 1977; Doug Carroll, "Hanley Reverses Thinking on Indian Claims," *OD*, 21 July 1979; Mike Connor, "Hanley Issues Challenge," *PS*, 27 February 1978; Mike Connor, "Oneidas' Lawsuit Opposed," *PS*, 10 May 1977.

56. Robert W. Curley, "Oneida Leader Raps Proposed Bill," *PS*, 22 August 1979; Peter Kovler, "Native American Land Rights," *Inquiry* 15 (May 1978): 21, Oneida Nation of Wisconsin, https://www.exploreoneida.com.

57. "Wampum Yes, Land No: Hanley Fights Indians Claims," *SHJ*, 10 May 1977; Douglas Carroll, "Indian Claims Cloud Some Property Titles," 10 August 1980, *Observer Dispatch*; Connor, "Meeting Upcoming"; Mike Connor and Louis A. Rappaport, "Interior Dept. Urges Suit on Behalf of Indians," *PS*, 21 April 1977.

58. Case, "'This Has Always Been Ours . . .'"; Roger Van Der Horst, "Indians, Officials Initiate Fire Policy," *PS*, 2 July 1980; Rex Niles, interview.

59. "Oneida, City Mum," *PS*, 9 July 1980; Roger Van Der Horst, "Honyost Descendant Weighs Oneida Territory Eviction," *PS*, 10 July 1980; Richard Myers, interview.

60. Herb was somewhat out of step with the national Republican Party in 1980 because he supported the Equal Rights Amendment, opposed a constitutional amendment prohibiting abortion, and did not support tax cuts but advocated instead for a balanced budget. Kenn Peters, "Six Candidates Vie for Hanley's Seat," unidentified newspaper, n.d.; "We Endorse . . .," editorial, *OD*, n.d. [1980]; Brian Held, "Brewer Returns to the Farm," unidentified newspaper [probably *Evening Sun* (Norwich, NY)], n.d. [September 1980], Brewer Collection.

61. Dick Brewer, interview; Joanne Brewer, interview by the author, 28 December 2018, Piseco, NY.

62. Robert W. Curley, "Rich Heritage Shared by Last Descendant," news clipping in Donna White to the author, November 1978; Mary Lou Brewer to the author, 5 December 1982, Brewer Collection.

63. Wilma Luebbe, "Oneida Linked to French Family's Tradition," *OD*, 31 October 1975.

64. Journal of the author, 30 March 1983, Brewer Collection.

65. Herb Brewer to the author, 6 May 1983, Brewer Collection; Herbert D. Brewer to Countess d'Andigné, 25 May 1983, Brewer Collection; Susan Clark, "Oneida, from France, Visits City for First Time," *OD*, 17 October 1989, Brewer Collection.

66. Clark, "Oneida, from France."

67. Joe Mecca, "Brewer: No 7th Term," *OD*, 31 March 1983, Brewer Collection; Herb Brewer, interview; Herb Brewer, conversation with the author, n.d.

68. Mary Lou Brewer, interview; David W. Hollis, "Ex-mayor Finds That He Enjoys His New Career," *SHA*, 6 November 1988, Brewer Collection.

69. Debbie Weingarten, "Why Are America's Farmers Killing Themselves?," *The Guardian*, 6 December 2017, https://www.theguardian.com/us-news/2017/dec/06/why-are-americas-farmers-killing-themselves-in-record-numbers; Danbom, *Born in the Country*, 234–39; Russ Brewer, interview.

70. The case known as Oneida II was argued before the Supreme Court by Arlinda Locklear, a Lumbee Indian and attorney for the Native American Rights Fund. George Shattuck and his firm withdrew from representing the Oneidas in 1977 because of potential conflict-of-interest problems over suing landowners in a mass-ejectment strategy. Associate Justice Lewis F. Powell Jr. wrote the majority opinion and was joined by Thurgood Marshall, Sandra Day O'Connor, Harry Blackmun, and William Brennan. Laurence M. Hauptman, "A Historical Introduction," in Shattuck, *Oneida Land Claims*, xix–xx; *Oneida & Madison Counties v. Oneida Indian Nation*, US Supreme Court decision, 4 March 1985, in Shattuck, *Oneida Land Claims*, 75–76; Terence J. Kivlan, "Oneidas' Land Claim Upheld," *PS*, 5 March 1985; "Supreme Court Upholds Claim by Oneida Indians," *NYT*, 5 March 1985.

71. Chief Justice Warren Burger and Associate Justices William Rehnquist and Byron White signed Stevens's dissenting opinion. Shattuck, *Oneida Land Claims*, 227, 236.

72. Kivlan, "Oneidas' Land Claim Upheld"; "Indian Claim Could Cost Millions," *SHJ*, 5 March 1985; Erik Kriss, "Landowners: 'Not Our Mistake,'" *SHJ*, 5 March 1985; "Land Claims: Governor Is on Target," editorial, *SHA*, 8 March 1985; "Indian Land," *SHA*, 10 March 1985.

73. Steve Carlic, "Oneida Nation Bitterly Split but Encouraged," *PS*, 5 March 1985; Beth Baker and Stacy Books, "New Beginnings for Native Americans," *Eidos* 3, no. 2 (Winter 1981): 33, Wisconsin Historical Society.

10. Ancestral Claims

1. The other soils on the farm included Howard fine sandy loam and Palmyra gravelly loam. Russ Brewer, Soil Map and Survey Research, Brewer Collection; *Oneida Lake: State of the Lake and Watershed Report* (Central New York Regional

Planning & Development Board, April 2003), https://www.cnyrpdb.org; Dick Brewer, interview.

2. Herb Brewer to the author, 10 April 1988, Brewer Collection; Beth Brewer to the author, [1988], Brewer Collection; Russ Brewer, interview.

3. Holly Brewer Rogers, telephone interview by the author, 22 June 2020; Casey Brewer, telephone interview by the author, 17 June 2020; Nathan Brewer, telephone interview by the author, 21 June 2020; Joshua Brewer, telephone interview by the author, 20 June 2020.

4. Tom Brewer, interview by the author, 23 February 2020, Cassville, NY; "Blaze Destroys Former Mayor's Barn," *OD*, 12 August 1989, Brewer Collection.

5. Robert W. Curley, "Dispute with Indians Smolders from the Past," *PS*, 13 January 1979; Robert W. Curley, "Clubs Circulating Petitions on Gambling," *PS*, 19 January 1979; Robert W. Curley, "Jurisdiction Key Issue on 'Indian Bingo,'" *PS*, 10 May 1979; Robert W. Curley, "Trial Date Set for Oneidas, but Indians May Not Appear," *PS*, 28 June 1979; Roger Van Der Horst, "Indians Fined in Gambling Counts: Oneidas Send Telegram to President Carter Claiming 'Selective Prosecution,'" *PS*, 6 June 1980.

6. Paul DeMain, "Our Grandchildren Want a Place of Their Own: Called Home," in *Kalihwisaks: Land Claims Special*, Oneida Tribe of Indians of Wisconsin, September 1988, Oneida Nation of Wisconsin, https://www.exploreoneida.com; Clifford D. May, "Divided Oneida Tribe Seeks End to Feud," *NYT*, 29 December 1986; Dale Seth, "Family Claims They Own Indian Territory," *OD*, [illegible], 1992; Johnathan Croyle, "From the Archives: When the Oneida Bingo Hall Burst into flames," Syracuse.com, 22 March 2019, https://www.syracuse.com; Jack Curtin, interview.

7. Dale Seth, "Mayor Critical, Oneidas Say System Failed Them," *OD*, 22 February 1988; Dale Seth, "Nation Residents Fear Further Violence," *OD*, 23 February 1988; Andy Marino, "Halbritter Won't Invest in Oneida Because of Police Chief," *OD*, 20 January 1994; Croyle, "From the Archives"; "Memorandum of Understanding between the United States Department of Justice and the City of Oneida," 8 February 1989, Oneida Nation of Wisconsin, https://www.exploreoneida.com.

8. "Oneida Indian Nation Historical Timeline," Oneida Indian Nation, 2018, https://www.oneidaindiannation.com.

9. Associated Press, "Court Refuses Oneidas' Claim for Treaty Land: 1780s Actions Upheld by U.S. Appeals Panel," *NYT*, 2 November 1988.

10. "Chief Oren Lyons December 1992 Address to the United Nations," Southern Methodist University, https://s2.smu.edu/twalker/orenlyon.htm; Wilkinson, *Blood Struggle*, 250.

11. "Lyons December 1992 Address."

12. Management Assistance Agreement, 1993, Brewer Collection; Tom Brewer, interview; Holly Brewer Rogers, interview.

13. Under the compact between New York and the Oneidas, the Turning Stone Casino was run by an outside management company, which under law must give 70 percent of the net gambling profits to the tribe. In exchange for state approval, the Oneidas agreed that state gambling regulators and the state police would oversee the casino. James Dao, "Accord Signed for a Casino in New

York State," *NYT*, 11 March 1993; James Dao, "Cuomo Signs Pact with Indians for Casino in Upstate New York," *NYT*, 17 April 1993; Theresa Vargas and Annys Shin, "A CNY Powerhouse," *PS*, 24 November 2013.

14. Francis X. Clines, "Where Profit and Tradition Mingle," *NYT*, 2 August 1994.

15. James Dao, "Gambling in the Middle of Nowhere: Oneidas' Casino Wins without Slots or Eastern Seaboard," *NYT*, 10 November 1997; Michelle York, "Saving Oneidas' Language, One Long Word at a Time," *NYT*, 18 July 2005.

16. Keisha Clukey, "Nation Reviving Traditions" and "Oneidas Fight to Save Culture," *Observer Dispatch*, 29 July 2012; Becki Karst, telephone interview; Dick Lynch, interview, Wonderley, *Oneida Iroquois Folklore*, 137.

17. According to the historian Robert W. Venables, in many of the more than three hundred federally recognized Indian nations, there are deep rifts between rival groups that all claim they are the true custodians of their nation's traditions. The US government, he notes, often is aligned with Native governments that the traditionalists say are illegitimate. William Glaberson, "Struggle for Oneidas' Leadership Grows Bitter as Casino Succeeds," *NYT*, 17 June 1996; Becki Karst, telephone interview; Associated Press, "Oneida Indian Leadership in Flux after U.S. Flip-Flop," *NYT*, 19 September 1993; Associated Press, "Indian Affairs Head Reverses Recognition of Oneida Leader," *NYT*, 26 September 1993; Andy Marino, "BIA Unconditionally Recognized Halbritter as Oneidas' Leader," *OD*, 5 February 1994; Paul Lipkowitz, "Dissidents Might Sue over Surveillance," *PS*, 10 March 1998; Paul Lipkowitz, "County Denies Role in Alleged Spying," *PS*, 11 March 1998; Vargas and Shin, "CNY Powerhouse."

18. Dao, "Gambling in the Middle of Nowhere"; David W. Chen, "Suit by Oneidas over Land Stirs Up Resentments," *NYT*, 22 January 1999; David W. Chen and Charlie LeDuff, "Bad Blood in Battle over Casinos," *NYT*, 28 October 2001; "'Turning Stone' a Turning Point for Oneidas, Region," *A Nation of Progress*, Oneida Indian Nation, Fall/Winter 1994–95, 2001.A110, MCHS.

19. James Dao, "Tribe's No-Arm Bandits Called a Dodge," *NYT*, 11 March 1995; Erika Rosenberg, "Casino Deal Bet Heavily on Slots," *Observer Dispatch*, 18 August 2001; Clines, "Where Profit and Tradition Mingle"; "Repost: Morning Edition Profile of Charlie Hill," *Turtle Talk* (blog), 30 December 2013, https://turtletalk.blog.

20. "Nation Gives $50,000 to Stockbridge," *Bee Journal*, 4 March 1998; BIA, "Oneida Nation of New York Conveyance of Indian Land into Trust," draft environmental impact statement, 2006, 328; Wilkinson, *Blood Struggle*, 239.

21. "Peterboro Man Sues State over Oneidas' Land," *OD*, 5 May 1995; Aaron Gifford, "Peterboro Man Vows to Continue Lawsuit against State on Tax Issue," *OD*, 10 May 1995; Richard Petrillo, "Oneidas Buy Canastota Property for Casino," *Bee Journal*, 16 October 1996; Richard Petrillo, "Oneidas Take Title to Village Property," *Bee Journal*, 4 February 1997; Eleanor Randolph, "New York's Native American Casino Contributes, but Not to Tax Rolls," *NYT*, 18 October 2003.

22. Jack Curtin, interview.

23. Tom Brewer, interview; Elizabeth Becker, "As House Prepares Farm Bill, Questions of Who Needs Help, and How Much," *NYT*, 9 September 2001;

Timothy Egan, "The Seeds of Decline," *NYT*, 8 December 2002; Stradling, *Nature of New York*, 233.

24. Becki Karst, telephone interview.

25. "Notes for Reunion Program," 28 August 1998, Brewer Collection; Ginny Brewer, phone conversation with the author, 24 February 2021; Kristen Buske, "Oneidas' Cultural Festival Celebrates Tradition," *OD*, 10 August 1988.

26. The federal government's plan to submit this suit on behalf of the Oneidas had been announced back in 1977. "Suit for Area Land Planned," *OD*, 2 July 1977; James Dao, "Anxiety Growing over Indian Claim in New York State," *NYT*, 13 January 1999; David W. Chen, "Battle over Iroquois Land Claims Escalates," *NYT*, 16 May 2000.

27. "The Oneidas' Claim on New York," *NYT*, 30 January 1999; Dao, "Anxiety Growing"; Associated Press, "Pataki Says State Will Hire Law Firm to Defend Local Property Owners," *OD*, 11 December 1998.

28. Dao, "Anxiety Growing"; Kristen Buske, "Local Leaders Concerned over Indian Court Action," *OD*, 9 December 1998; Michael Ackerman, "Local Landowners Nervously Waiting," *OD*, 10 December 1998.

29. Upstate Citizens for Equality, "Federal Indian Policy and the Oneida Land Claim," 9 December 2001, Brewer Collection; Jack Rossen, "Research and Dialogue: New Vision Archeology in the Cayuga Heartland of Central New York," in *Cross-Cultural Collaboration: Native Peoples and Archeology in the Northeastern United States*, ed. Jordan E. Kerber (Lincoln: University of Nebraska Press, 2006), 252–53.

30. Michael Ackerman, "Madison County Officials Try to Calm Fears of Landowners about Land Claims," *OD*, 21 January 1999; "Residents Learn Little from Officials on Land Claim," *OD*, 1 January 1999; Associated Press, "Landowners Get Backing of State in Indian Claims," *NYT*, 11 December 1998; Rossen, "Research and Dialogue," 254.

31. Upstate Citizens for Equality, "Federal Indian Policy"; Lenny Snyder, "Landowner Discouraged by Meeting," letter to the editor, *OD*, 4 January 1999; Dao, "Suit by Oneidas."

32. Madison Muskie, "Jeers to Lawsuit, Jeers to State, Jeers to Hotheads," *OD*, 12 December 1998; letters to the editor, *OD*, 15 and 16 December 1998, 8 and 27 January 1999.

33. "Property Owners Protest Land Claims by Indians," *NYT*, 1 February 1999; Alex Bonaface, "Hundreds Protest Land Claim," *OD*, 1 February 1999; Holly Brewer Rogers, interview; Rex Niles, interview; Chen, "Battle over Iroquois Land"; David W. Chen, "U.S. Eases Stance on the Eviction of Landowners in Oneidas' Suit," *NYT*, 30 March 1999; Chen, "Suit by Oneidas."

34. Dick Lynch, interview; Hill, "Regenerating Identity," 413.

35. Dick Lynch, interview.

36. David W. Chen, "Talks to Settle Oneida Indians' Land Claim Fall Apart," *NYT*, 11 March 2000; Associated Press, "Judge Excludes Landowners from Oneida Lawsuit," *NYT*, 27 September 2000; "Oneida Indian Nation Historical Timeline"; Kathryn Fort, "Disruption and Impossibility: The New Laches and the Unfortunate Resolution of the Modern Iroquois Land Claims," *Wyoming Law*

Review 11, no. 2 (January 2011): 384–86, https://scholarship.law.uwyo.edu/wlr/vol11/iss2/4; Brief of Amici Curiae Town of Lenox, New York; Town of Stockbridge, New York; and Town of Southampton, New York in Support of Petitioner City of Sherrill, New York, No. 03-855, Supreme Court of the United States, 3.

37. Jack Curtin, interview; Tom Brewer, interview.

38. Jack Curtin, interview; John M. Curtin and Daniel E. Curtin to Herbert D. Brewer, Mary Lou Brewer, and Thomas J. Brewer, 10 October 2000, Brewer Collection; Robert F. McDermott to Herb and Mary Lou Brewer, 4 January 2001, Brewer Collection.

39. Russ Brewer, interview; Nathan Brewer, interview; Casey Brewer, interview.

40. "Oneida Savings Bank Welcomes New Vice President," *OD*, 6 February 2002, Brewer Collection; Russ Brewer, interview.

41. Mike Bilodeau, "Oneida Firefighters Raise Money for Victims' Families," *OD*, 17 September 2001, https://www.oneidadispatch.com; Cliff Drought, "Oneida Indian Nation Offers Resources in Crisis," *OD*, 17 September 2001, https://www.oneidadispatch.com; James C. McKinley Jr., "Pataki Works Out Deal with Indians for Upstate Land," *NYT*, 17 February 2002; Shaila K. Dewan, "After 5 Days, Oneida Deal Is Unraveling," *NYT*, 22 February 2002; Jay Gallagher, "State Plans to Borrow Money to Pay for Indian Claims," *Press & Sun Bulletin* (Binghamton, NY), n.d. [2002]; Associated Press, "Opposition Grows to Deal Struck by Oneidas, State," unidentified newspaper, n.d., [2002], Brewer Collection; *Oneida—A Bit of America at Its Best: Celebrating 100 Years as a City, 1901–2001* (Oneida, NY: City of Oneida Centennial Committee, 2001).

42. Iver Peterson, "Neighbors See Lesson in Oneida Casino Deal: What Not to Do," *NYT*, 30 July 2003; BIA, "Conveyance of Indian Land"; Michael Ackerman, "Tree Planting Brings Harmony to Area," *OD*, 28 April 2000, https://www.oneidadispatch.com.

43. William Kates, "President Signs Order to Respect Indian Sovereignty," *OD*, 25 September 2004; Associated Press, "Feds Put Lien on Oneida Ltd," *OD*, 25 September 2004; Robert H. Beer, "City Wants to Ready Site for Manufacturer," *OD*, 25 September 2004, Brewer Collection; Aaron Gifford, "Industrial Park Proposed for Oneida," *PS*, 10 November 2000.

44. "Oneida Tax Case in Sherrill Heads to High Court," *Rochester Democrat and Chronicle*, n.d. [October 2005], Brewer Collection; Kent Gardner, Center for Government Research, "Jurisdictional and Economic Impacts of Granting the OIN's Application to Take Lands into Trust in Oneida and Madison Counties," Madison County, NY (website), 2006, https://www.madisoncounty.ny.gov.

45. "Oneida Tax Case"; *Oneida Indian Nation of New York v. City of Sherrill, New York*, 337 F. 3d 139, Court of Appeals for the Second Circuit, 21 July 2003; "Appeals Court Upholds 1794 Oneida Treaty," Indianz.com, 22 July 2003, https://www.indianz.com; Rachael Protzman and Kurt Wanfried, "Sherrill Wins in High Court," *OD*, 30 March 2005, https://www.oneidadispatch.com.

46. *City of Sherrill, New York, Petitioner v. Oneida Indian Nation of New York, et al.*, 544 U.S. (2005); Carole Goldberg, "Finding the Way to Indian Country: Justice Ruth Bader Ginsburg's Decisions to Indian Law Cases," *Ohio State Law Journal* 70, no. 4 (2009): 1027–35; Pevar, *Rights of Indians*, 21–22, 25.

47. *City of Sherrill*; Protzman and Wanfried, "Sherrill Wins."

48. *City of Sherrill*, 544 U.S. (2005) (Stevens, J., dissenting); Dunbar-Ortiz, *Indigenous Peoples' History*, 200, 204, 214; Jim Adams, "Supreme Court Rejects Oneida Taxation Defense," *Indian Country Today*, 6 April 2005; Pevar, *Rights of Indians*, 269–70; Jennifer R. Sunderlin, "One Nation, Indivisible: American 'Indian Country' in the Wake of *City of Sherrill v. Oneida Indian Nation*," *Albany Law Review* 70 (2007): 1563–87, https://www.albanylawreview.org.

49. Ken Belson, "Judge Says Oneida Indians Deserve a Chance for Redress," *NYT*, 22 May 2007; Leeanne Root, "Court: Tribe Can't Claim Land," *OD*, 22 May 2007, https://www.oneidadispatch.com; Samuel Pokross, "'Dramatically Altered the Legal Landscape'? *City of Sherrill v. Oneida Indian Nation* in the Lower Courts," *American Indian Law Review* 43, no. 1 (2018): 243–305.

50. Laura Hand, "Supreme Court Won't Hear Oneida Nation's Land Claim," CNY Central, 17 October 2011, https://www.cnycentral.com/news/story; Caitlin Traynor, "High Court Won't Hear Oneidas' Land Claim," *OD*, 17 October 2011; "Appeals Court Dismisses Land Claim," *OD*, 9 August 2010, https://www.oneidadispatch.com; "Consider This: Land Claim Saga: The End?," editorial, *PS*, 19 October 2011, https://www.blog.syracuse.com/opinion; "Ruth Bader Ginsburg Wants Trump to Appoint a Native American Woman to the Supreme Court," *Buffalo Chronicle*, 5 May 2020, https://www.buffalochronicle.com.

51. Opening Brief for the Petitioners, Madison County and Oneida County, New York v. Oneida Indian Nation of New York, US Supreme Court, No. 10–72, NARF Tribal Supreme Court Project, 2010, https://www.sct.narf.org.

52. Opening Brief for the Petitioners; Michael Leroy Oberg, "On the Notorious RGB and Sherrill," Native America: A History, 29 March 2017, https://michaelleroyoberg.com.

53. Sarah Blazons, "Local Officials React to Oneida Land Claim Decision," Your News Now, 18 October 2011, https://www.centralny.ynn.com; Caitlin Traynor, "Halbritter 'Concerned' over Ruling," *OD*, 10 August 2010, https://www.oneidadispatch.com; "Consider This."

54. Calloway, "My Grandfather's Axe," 6; Dick Lynch, interview.

55. Associated Press, "U.S. Suggests Trust Plan for Oneida Nation Land," *NYT*, 23 February 2008; Pevar, *Rights of Indians*, 20; Sarah Krakoff, "*City of Sherrill v. Oneida Indian Nation of New York*: A Regretful Postscript to the Taxation Chapter in *Cohen's Handbook of Federal Indian Law*," *Tulsa Law Review* 41, no. 1, revised (2013): 18, https://digitalcommonslaw.utulsa.edu/tir/vol41/iss1/2; Dussias, "Reports of Our Death," 1268–69; Doug George-Kanentiio, "Oneida Nation Compact with New York a Bad Deal for All Iroquois," Syracuse.com, 22 May 2013, https://www.blog.syracuse.com/opinion; Dick Lynch, interview.

56. The land to be placed in trust included the casino, the golf courses, four out of the thirteen gas stations and convenience stores, 80 percent of the nation's housing, most of its governmental operations, the Ray Elm Children and Elders Center, and almost ten thousand acres of farmland. Elizabeth Cooper, "County to Delay Foreclosures," *Observer Dispatch*, 10 August 2005, Brewer Collection; Andrew Brown, "The Nation and Sherrill Finally Make Peace," *OD*, 7 October 2005; "Oneida Nation Sues Oneida City," *OD*, 23 November 2005;

"Judge: No Foreclosures Allowed on Nation Land," *OD*, 28 October 2005, https://www.oneidadispatch.com; BIA, "Conveyance of Indian Land"; Gardner, "Jurisdictional and Economic Impacts"; Jody McNichol, "BIA Wants 13,086 Acres Put into Trust," *OD*, 23 February 2008, https://www.oneidadispatch.com; "Oneida Indian Nation Historical Timeline"; Meghan Y. McCune, "'It's a Question of Fairness': Fee-to-Trust and Opposition to Haudenosaunee Land Rights and Economic Development," in *Gambling on Authenticity: Gaming, the Noble Savage, and the Not-So-New Indian*, ed. Becca Gercken and Julie Pelletier (East Lansing: Michigan State University Press, 2017), 126–31.

57. Jesse McKinley, "Shippers Turn to Erie Canal When Size Matters," *Buffalo News*, n.d. [2017], Brewer Collection; Madison County History, https://www.madisoncounty.ny.gov; *The Getaway Region: Official 2010 Oneida County Travel Guide* (Utica, NY: Oneida County Tourism, 2010).

58. The ten-county area included Cayuga, Chenango, Cortland, Herkimer, Lewis, Madison, Oneida, Onondaga, Oswego, and Otsego Counties. The compact was approved by the state legislature and the federal courts. "Governor Cuomo Announces Landmark Agreement between State, Oneida Nation, and Oneida and Madison Counties," Governor Andrew Cuomo (state website), 16 May 2013, https://www.governor.ny.gov/news/governor-cuomo-announces-landmark-agreement-between-state-oneida-nation-and-oneida-and-madison; Associated Press, "State Grants Oneida Indians Exclusive Territory for Casino," *NYT*, 17 May 2013, https://www.nytimes.com/2013/05/17nyregion/new-york-grants-oneida-indians-exclusive-territory-for-casino.html; Glenn Coin, "Madison County Approves Oneida Nation Land, Taxes Agreement," Syracuse.com, 30 May 2013, https://www.syracuse.com/news; George-Kanentiio, "Oneida Nation Compact"; Vargas and Shin, "CNY Powerhouse."

59. The nation noted that in 2016, $62 million went to New York State, which in turn shared $27.6 million with ten central New York counties. "Oneida Fact Sheet: Economic Impact," Oneida Indian Nation, 2016, https://www.oneidaindiannation.com; Elizabeth Cooper, "Madison County Wants Do-Over on Oneidas' Deal," *Observer Dispatch*, 13 June 2015; Vargas and Shin, "CNY Powerhouse"; Russ Brewer, interview; Rex Niles, interview.

60. Vargas and Shin, "CNY Powerhouse"; Kevin Roose, "Seeing a Future in Flatware," *NYT*, 6 January 2012; Stacy Cowley, "Silver Spoons Gone, but One Factory Keeps Churning Out Flatware," *NYT*, 21 October 2015; Rex Niles, interview; Becki Karst, telephone interview; Dick Lynch, interview; Russ Brewer, interview.

61. Tom Brewer, interview; Josh Brewer, interview; Nathan Brewer, interview; Chrystia Freeland, "The Triumph of the Family Farm," *The Atlantic*, July/August 2012, 50–53; Jane Mt. Pleasant, "The Problem with Plows: Examining the Role of Tillage in Iroquois Agriculture" (paper presentation, Conference on Iroquois Research, Cortland, NY, 6 October 2012); Jenny Hopkinson, "Can American Soil Be Brought Back to Life?," *Politico*, 13 September 2017, https://www.politico.com/agenda/story/2017/09/13/soil-health-agriculture-trend-usda-000513.

62. Jack Curtin, interview; Alexandra Chang, "Charting New York's Milky Way," *periodiCALS: The Magazine of Cornell University's College of Agriculture and Life Sciences* 6, no. 2 (2016): 11–16; Weingarten, "America's Farmers Killing Themselves";

Danbom, *Born in the Country*, 240–51; Charles Lyons, "Suicides Spread through a Brazilian Tribe," *NYT*, 4 January 2015.

63. Oneida Indian Nation and Four Directions Productions, *Raccoon and Crawfish: An Oneida Legend* (2009); Shadi Rahimi, "A Tribe Turns to 3-D Animation for Modern Storytelling," *NYT*, 10 February 2007; "Oneida Nation Float in Macy's Thanksgiving Day Parade," *OD*, 27 November 2013, https://www.oneidadispatch.com.

64. Shadi Rahimi, "Including Indians in Colonial History," *NYT*, 24 September 2005; "Oneida Indian Nation Historical Timeline."

65. David W. Hollis, "Oneidas Hope Their Seventh Business Venture Wears Well," *Bee Journal*, 26 April 1995; Michael Cieply, "Starring: The Oneida Nation in the Revolutionary War," *NYT*, 18 July 2011; Vargas and Shin, "CNY Powerhouse"; Fred Kaplan, "Oneida Indian Nation Suing for Return of Land," *Baltimore Sun*, 12 June 1999, https://www.baltimoresun.com; Bruce Entelisano, "1976 Deaths Still Haunt Halbritter," *OD*, 25 June 2010, http://www.oneidadispatch.com/articles/2010/06/25/news/doc4c25738ald3fc893485379.txt.

66. Entelisano, "1976 Deaths."

67. Doxtator, "Inclusive and Exclusive Perceptions," 46–47; Dick Lynch, interview.

68. Herb Brewer, interview.

69. Russ Brewer, interview; Tom Brewer, interview; Jack Curtin, interview.

70. Becki Karst, telephone interview; Jack Curtin, interview; Josh Brewer, interview.

71. "Dedication of Glenwood Cemetery," *OD*, 9 September 1870; Richard W. Hill Sr., "Making a Final Resting Place Final: A History of the Repatriation of the Haudenosaunee," in Kerber, *Cross-Cultural Collaboration*, 11.

72. Tom Brewer, conversation with the author, n.d.; Mary Lou Brewer, Russ Brewer, Nathan Brewer, Holly Brewer Rogers, and Casey Brewer, interviews.

Bibliographic Essay

Any presentation of the sources I consulted while researching and writing *The Best Land* suggests an orderly process without twists and turns, dead ends, and accidental revelations. My exploration of what happened to a homeland lost and revived, gained and lost, was accompanied over the years by a stunning mix of anger, confusion, frustration, grief, love, and pride. "Sometimes you have to laugh or else you cry," said Becki Karst. As encouragement, I wrote "My heart is open" on a Post-it Note and stuck it on my printer. I began with reading histories of the Oneidas and the Six Nations while also conducting genealogical research on my family and Polly Denny Deferrier's. I consulted documents and newspapers of the day as well as studies by experts on a range of historical eras. For more references, consult the endnotes. This essay is written with gratitude to the scholars and storytellers without whom I could not have undertaken this book.

On the Oneidas, see Jack Campisi, "Ethnic Identity and Boundary Maintenance in Three Oneida Communities" (PhD diss., State University of New York at Albany, 1974); Jack Campisi and Laurence M. Hauptman, eds., *The Oneida Indian Experience: Two Perspectives* (Syracuse, NY: Syracuse University Press, 1988); Laurence M. Hauptman and L. Gordon McLester III, eds., *The Oneida Indian Journey from New York to Wisconsin, 1784–1860* (Madison: University of Wisconsin Press, 1999); Daniel Koch, *Land of the Oneidas: Central New York and the Creation of America, from Prehistory to the Present* (Albany: State University of New York Press, 2023); Karim Tiro, *The People of the Standing Stone: The Oneida Nation from the Revolution through the Era of Removal* (Amherst: University of Massachusetts Press, 2011); and Anthony Wonderley, *Oneida Iroquois Folklore, Myth, and History: New York Oral Narratives from the Notes of H. E. Allen and Others* (Syracuse, NY: Syracuse University Press, 2004). On their websites, the Oneida Indian Nation of New York (https://www.oneidaindian.com) and the Oneida Nation of Wisconsin (https://oneida-nsn.gov) post histories, family stories, timelines, and, in the case of the Oneida Cultural

Heritage Department of the Oneida Nation of Wisconsin, a useful series of historical documents on the nation's website, at https://www.exploreoneida.com. In addition, they publish *Oneida Onyota a Ka: Oneida Indian Nation News* and *Kalihwisaks* (She looks for news).

For more on Haudenosaunee and Native history, see Philip J. Deloria, *Playing Indian* (New Haven, CT: Yale University Press, 1998); Roxane Dunbar-Ortiz, *An Indigenous Peoples' History of the United States* (Boston: Beacon, 2014); Suzan Shown Harjo, ed., *Nation to Nation; Treaties between the United States & American Indian Nations* (Washington, DC: Smithsonian Books, 2014); G. Peter Jemison and Anna M. Schein, eds., *Treaty of Canandaigua 1794: 200 Years of Treaty Relations between the Iroquois Confederacy and the United States* (Santa Fe, NM: Clear Light, 2000); Jordan E. Kerber, ed., *Archeology of the Iroquois: Selected Readings and Research Sources* (Syracuse, NY: Syracuse University Press, 2007); Jordan E. Kerber, ed., *Cross-Cultural Collaboration: Native Peoples and Archeology in the Northeastern United States* (Lincoln: University of Nebraska Press, 2006); Kathleen Ratteree and Norbert Hill, *The Great Vanishing Act: Blood Quantum and the Future of Native Nations* (Golden, CO: Fulcrum, 2017); David Truer, *The Heartbeat of Wounded Knee: Native America from 1890 to the Present* (New York: Riverhead Books, 2019); Christopher Vecsey and Robert W. Venables, eds., *American Indian Environments: Ecological Issues in Native American History* (Syracuse, NY: Syracuse University Press, 1980); Steve Wall, *Wisdom's Daughters: Conversations with Women Elders of Native America* (New York: HarperCollins, 1993); David E. Wilkins and K. Tsianina Lomawaima, *Uneven Ground: American Indian Sovereignty and Federal Law* (Norman: University of Oklahoma Press, 2002); Charles Wilkinson, *Blood Struggle: The Rise of Modern Indian Nations* (New York: W. W. Norton, 2005).

On the challenges of writing histories of Native and non-Native relations, see Carol Cornelius, *Iroquois Corn in a Culture-Based Curriculum: A Framework for Respectfully Teaching about Cultures* (Albany: State University of New York Press, 1999); Deborah Doxtator, "Inclusive and Exclusive Perceptions of Difference: Native and Euro-Based Concepts of Time, History, and Change," in *Decentring the Renaissance: Canada and Europe in Multidisciplinary Perspective, 1500–1700*, ed. Germaine Warkentin and Carolyn Podruchny (Toronto: University of Toronto Press, 2001), 33–47; Victoria Freeman, *Distant Relations: How My Ancestors Colonized North America* (Toronto: McClelland & Stewart, 2002); Albert L. Hurtado, ed., *Reflections on American Indian History: Honoring the Past, Building the Future* (Norman: University of Oklahoma Press, 2008); Oren Lyons and John C. Mohawk, eds., *Democracy, Indian Nations, and the U.S.*

Constitution (Santa Fe: Clear Light, 1992); Gary Nash, "The Hidden History of Mestizo America," in *Sex, Love, Race: Crossing Boundaries in North American History*, ed. Martha Hodes (New York: New York University Press, 1999), 10–32; Jean M. O'Brien, *Dispossession by Degrees: Indian Land and Identity in Natick, Massachusetts, 1650–1790* (New York: Cambridge University Press, 1997); Nancy Shoemaker, *A Strange Likeness: Becoming Red and White in Eighteenth-Century North America* (New York: Oxford University Press, 2006); Susan Sleeper-Smith, Juliana Barr, Jean M. O'Brien, Nancy Shoemaker, and Scott Manning Stevens, eds., *Why You Can't Teach United States History without American Indians* (Chapel Hill: University of North Carolina Press, 2015). See also "AHR Exchange: Historians and Native American and Indigenous Studies," *American Historical Review* 125 (April 2020): 517–51.

For state and local histories, see David M. Ellis, James A. Frost, Harold C. Syrett, and Harry F. Carman, *A History of New York State*, rev. ed. (Ithaca, NY: Cornell University Press, 1978); Ulysses Prentiss Hedrick, *A History of Agriculture in the State of New York* (New York: Hill & Wang, 1933); Milton M. Klein, ed., *The Empire State: A History of New York* (Ithaca, NY: Cornell University Press, 2001); David Stradling, *The Nature of New York: An Environmental History of the Empire State* (Ithaca, NY: Cornell University Press, 2010); L. M. Hammond, *History of Madison County* (Syracuse, NY: Truair, Smith, 1872); Pomroy Jones, *Annals and Recollections of Oneida County* (Rome, NY: printed by the author, 1851); Raymond Rathbone, *Brief History of Oneida Castle, N. Y. and the Oneida Indians* (Oneida Castle Fire Department, 1930), Oneida Public Library, Oneida, NY; James H. Smith, *The History of Chenango and Madison Counties, New York* (Syracuse, NY: D. Mason, 1880); John E. Smith, ed., *Our County and Its People: A Descriptive and Biographical Record of Madison County New York*, (Boston: Boston History, 1899); and Mollie Smith, "Sketches of the Old Town of Lenox and Madison County," Oneida Public Library. William H. Tuttle, the author of *Names and Sketches of the Pioneer Settlers of Madison County New York*, ed. Isabel Bracy (Interlaken, NY: Heart of the Lakes, 1984), wrote a detailed series about early settlers on the "Purchase of 1802" for the *Oneida Democratic Union* in 1931. Local historians have published in *Legacy: Annals of Herkimer County*; *Papers Read before the Herkimer County Historical Society*, 1899; and *Madison County Heritage*. About local history, see Carol Kammen, *On Doing Local History*, 2nd ed. (Walnut Creek, CA: AltaMira, 2003), and Jean M. O'Brien, *Firsting and Lasting: Writing Indians Out of Existence in New England* (Minneapolis: University of Minnesota Press, 2010).

To trace my family and Polly Denny Deferrier's, I consulted the Brouwer Genealogy Database at https://www.rootsweb.com (about this Brouwer Genealogy Project, see https://www.brouwergenealogy.blogspot.com); Lenore J. Harris, *Clement Family History: Descendants of Lewis Cobes Clement, U. E. (1725–1781) and Catherine Eliza Poutman (1726–1807)*, (Toronto: Pro Familia, 2002); William T. Horton, "Jan Peeck: Tavern Keeper, Fur Trader and Land Owner," (Peekskill, NY: Department of the City Historian, 1949); Henry Z. Jones Jr., *The Palatine Families of New York: A Study of German Immigrants Who Arrived in Colonial New York in 1710*, 2 vols. (Universal City, CA: Henry Z. Jones, 1985); David Kendall Martin, *The Eighteenth Century Zimmerman Family of the Mohawk Valley* (Church Hill, MD: Mouse House Books, 1994); Jonathan Pearson, *A History of the Schenectady Patent in the Dutch and English Times* (Albany, NY: Joel Munsell's Sons, 1883); Maryly B. Penrose, *Compendium of Early Mohawk Valley Families*, 2 vols. (Baltimore: Genealogical Publishing, 1990); Doris Dockstader Rooney, *The Dockstader Family* (Dodge City, KS: High Plains, 1983); John Sanders, *Early History of Schenectady, New York and Its First Settlers* (1879; reprint, Westminster, MD: Heritage Books, 2012); Ulrich Simmendinger, *The Simmendinger Register* (1717; reprint, St. Johnsville, NY: n.p., 1934); Barbara Sivertsen, *Turtles, Wolves, and Bears: A Mohawk Family History* (Westminster, MD: Heritage Books, 2006); Edwin Henry Vedder, *The Vedder Family in America, 1657–1973* (Amherst, NY: Vedder, 1974); and Kathlyne Knickerbacker Viele, *Viele Records, 1613–1913* (New York: Tobias A. Wright, 1913). For background on Angel Deferrier, I consulted *Archives historique du Poitou* 22 (Poitiers, 1892), and "La gazette de St. Mandé-sur Brédoire," http://www.stleger.fr.

I relied on church records available at county historical societies, libraries, and archives, as well as online, including the Records of the Episcopal Church of Duanesburg; *Register of Baptisms, Marriages, Communicants, and Funerals Begun by Henry Barclay at Fort Hunter*, New York Historical Society Museum and Library, https://www.digitalcollections.nyhistory.org; Schenectady Dutch Reformed Church; Reformed Church, Schoharie; St. Paul's Lutheran Church, Schoharie; Lutheran Trinity Church of Stone Arabia; the Parish Records of Niort—St. Andre, Archives Départementale de Deux-Sevres, in Niort, France; and Parish Records of St. Mandé-sur Brédoire, Archives Départementale de la Charente Maritime, http://www.archinoe.fr. The US Dutch Reformed Church Records in Selected States, 1639–1989, on Ancestry.

com (https://www.ancestry.com), were useful, as were the New York Tax Assessment Rolls of Real and Personal Estates, 1799–1804, and Civil War Muster Roll Abstracts, New York, 1861–1900.

The county historical societies contain a trove of information. I consulted family records at the Columbia County Historical Society, Kinderhook, NY; the Herkimer County Historical Society, Herkimer, NY; the Montgomery County Department of History and Archives, Fonda, NY; the Oneida County History Center, Utica, NY; the Schoharie County Historical Society, Schoharie, NY; and the Schenectady County Historical Society in Schenectady, NY. The Schenectady County Public Library has an excellent digital genealogy and history archive at https://www.schenectadyhistory.org. The Madison County Historical Society, located in the former Higinbotham home in Oneida, NY, holds invaluable materials, including the Adams Family Collection, the Breese Family Collection, the Brewer Family Collection, the Deferrier Family Collection, and the Oneida Indian Collection. I learned about my Duanesburg ancestors in the Duane Family Papers at the New York Historical Society, New York, NY. The Wisconsin Historical Society in Madison, Wisconsin, holds the indispensable Lyman C. Draper Manuscripts, containing interviews, conducted in the nineteenth century, of members of the Doxtator and Denny families as well as other Oneidas.

Some sources on Polly's family and mine are in private hands. The beautiful memoir "Of Me and Mine," written in 1955 by Edith Ratnour Hammond, a daughter of Jennie Clement's cousin, is part of the Hammond Family Collection. The "Breese Family History," written by Lester Grosvenor Wells, is from the Jack Wallace Collection. Over the years, my relatives have deposited with me Bibles, baby books, letters, photographs, autograph albums, school papers, wills, farm records, maps, news clippings, diaries, and memoirs that I refer to as the Brewer Collection to distinguish it from the Brewer Family Collection at the Madison County Historical Society. From the extraordinary and irreplaceable Rebecca John Karst Collection, I have relied on years of Becki's research contained in the Cornelius File, Denny File, Doxtator File, Elm File, Honyost File, John File, Martin John File, Johnson File, Skenandoah File, and Land Claims Newspaper File, among others.

By locating the best-land families on the land, I came to understand more about these people and their place. I scoured deeds at the Chenango County Clerk's Office, Norwich, NY; the Madison County Clerk's Office, Wampsville, NY; and the Oneida County Clerk's Office,

Utica, NY. Essential maps include the maps of the Oneida Reservation in the New York State Archives Digital Collection (https://www.digitalcollections.archives.nysed.gov); the New York State Library Manuscripts and Special Collections; *The Lawrence Zimmerman Papers, also Maps and Briefs of Snell-Timmerman Patent* (reprinted from *Enterprise and News*, St. Johnsville, NY, 1937); and the maps of the town of Lenox from the 1853 Gurdon Evans map; the 1859 Gillette Map, and the 1875 Beers Map, available at the excellent website of the Madison County historian (https://www.madisoncounty.ny.gov); and the Library of Congress Geography and Map Division. About maps, see Juliana Barr and Edward Countryman, "Maps and Spaces, Paths to Connect, and Lines to Divide," in *Contested Spaces of Early America*, ed. Juliana Barr and Edward Countryman (Philadelphia: University of Pennsylvania Press, 2014), 1–28. The indispensable US Indian Census Rolls (1885–1940), the New York State Census (1855–1925), and the US Federal Census (1790–1940) are available at Ancestry.com. The 1845 census of the Oneida Reservation can be found at https://digitalcollections.archives.nysed.gov. I visited the Canastota Canal Town Museum, Canastota, NY; the Fort Herkimer Church, Mohawk, NY; the Fort Klock Historic Restoration, St. Johnsville, NY; the Fort Plain Museum and Historical Park, Fort Plain, NY; the Gerrit Smith Estate National Historic Landmark, Peterboro, NY; the Nicholas Herkimer Home and Indian Castle Church, Little Falls, NY; the Johnson Hall State Historic Site, Johnstown, NY; Old Fort Johnson, Fort Johnson, NY; the Mabee Farm Historic Site, Rotterdam Junction, NY; the Old Stone Fort Museum, Schoharie, NY; the Oneida Nation Museum, De Pere, WI; and the Shako:wi Cultural Center, Oneida, NY.

The fascinating records of the Dutch colony of New Netherland are available from the New York State Archives, with translations by the New Netherland Institute, at https://www.digitalcollections.archives.nysed.gov. I used the Dutch Colonial Council Minutes, 1638–1665, Series A1809; Dutch Colonial Land Deeds, 1652–1653, Series A1882; Dutch Colonial Ordinances, 1647–1658, Series A1875; Dutch Colonial Patents and Deeds, Series A1880; and Secretary of the Province of New York, Register of the Provincial Secretary, 1642–1660, Series A020. The fifteen volumes of *Documents Relative to the Colonial History of the State of New York*, edited by E. B. O'Callaghan (Albany, NY: Weed, Parsons, 1858), are essential. Also informative is Lawrence H. Leder, ed., *The Livingston Indian Records, 1666–1723* (Stanfordville, NY: Earl M. Coleman, 1979). Firsthand accounts include Charles T. Gehring and William A. Starna, eds., *A Journey into Mohawk and Oneida Country, 1634–1635: The Journal of Harmen Meyndertsz van den Bogaert* (Syracuse, NY: Syracuse University Press, 2013), and Dean R. Snow, Charles T. Gehring, and William Starna, eds., *In Mohawk Country: Early Narratives about a Native People* (Syracuse, NY: Syracuse University Press, 1996).

For histories of Iroquoia, New Netherland, and colonial New York, see Thomas E. Burke Jr., *Mohawk Frontier: The Dutch Community of Schenectady, New York, 1661–1710* (Ithaca, NY: Cornell University Press, 1991); David Steven Cohen, "How Dutch were the Dutch of New Netherland?," *New York History* 62, no. 1 (1981): 43–60; Matthew Dennis, *Cultivating a Landscape of Peace: Iroquois-European Encounters in Seventeenth-Century America* (Ithaca, NY: Cornell University Press, 1993); William Engelbrecht, *Iroquoia: The Development of a Native World* (Syracuse, NY: Syracuse University Press), 2003; Jaap Jacobs, *The Colony of New Netherland: A Dutch Settlement in Seventeenth-Century America* (Ithaca, NY: Cornell University Press, 2009); Joop de Jong, "The Dutch Golden Age and Globalization: History and Heritage, Legacies and Contestations," *Macalester International* 27, art. 7 (December 2011), http:digitalcommons.macalester.edu/macintl/vol27/iss17(FDIS2011TheHague); Erin Kramer, "'That She Shall Be Forever Banished from This Country': Alcohol, Sovereignty, and Social Segregation in New Netherland," *Early American Studies*. Winter 2022, 3–42; Peter C. Mancall, *Deadly Medicine: Indians and Alcohol in Early America* (Ithaca, NY: Cornell University Press, 1995); Donna Merwick, *Possessing Albany, 1630–1710: The Dutch and English Experience* (New York: Cambridge University Press, 1990); Donna Merwick, *The Shame and the Sorrow: Dutch-Amerindian Encounters in New Netherland* (Philadelphia: University of Pennsylvania Press, 2006); Jon Parmenter, *The Edge of the Woods: Iroquoia, 1534–1701* (East Lansing: Michigan State University Press, 2010); Daniel K. Richter, "Cultural Brokers and Intercultural Politics: New York–Iroquois Relations, 1664–1701," *Journal of American History* 75, no. 1 (June 1988): 40–67; Daniel K. Richter, *The Ordeal of the Longhouse: The Peoples of the Iroquois League in the Era of European Colonization* (Chapel Hill: University of North Carolina Press, 1992); Russell Shorto, *The Island at the Center of the World: The Epic Story of Dutch Manhattan and the Forgotten Colony That Shaped America* (New York: Vintage Books, 2005); Adriana E. van Zwieten, "Conversing with Each Other, among Other Things of the Sale of Houses': Buying and Selling Real Property in New Amsterdam," n.d., and "Glimpses of Childhood in the Colony of New Netherland," 2009, New Netherland Institute, https://www.newnetherlandinstitute.org; Janny Venema,

Beverwijck: A Dutch Village on the American Frontier, 1652–1664 (Albany: State University of New York Press, 2003).

For documentary records of eighteenth-century colonial New York, see the indispensable William Johnson, *The Papers of Sir William Johnson*, 14 vols. (Albany: University of the State of New York), 1925, widely available online, as well as *Documents Relative to the Colonial History of the State of New York*. Local histories include Nelson Greene, ed., *History of the Mohawk Valley: Gateway to the West, 1614–1925* (Chicago: S. J. Clarke, 1925), https://schenectadyhistory.org; Nelson Greene, *The Story of Old Fort Plain and the Middle Mohawk Valley* (Fort Plain, NY: O'Connor Brothers, 1915); Ken D. Johnson, "George Klock, Sir William Johnson, & the Canajoharie Patent," 2009, https://www.fort-plank.com/Canajoharie_Pat_History.html; Milo Nellis, *The Mohawk Dutch and the Palatines*, 1951, Three Rivers, http://www.threerivershms.com; George W. Walter, *Sinners and Saints: Stories of Upstate New York* (Utica, NY: North Country Books, 1973).

For histories of the land and the people of the Mohawk and Schoharie Valleys before the American Revolution, see Stuart Banner, *How the Indians Lost Their Land: Law and Power on the Frontier* (Cambridge, MA: Belknap Press of Harvard University Press, 2007); Richard Berlath, *Bloody Mohawk: The French and Indian War & American Revolution on New York's Frontier* (Delmar, NY: Black Dome, 2009); Colin G. Calloway, *Pen and Ink Witchcraft: Treaties and Treaty Making in American Indian History* (New York: Oxford University Press, 2013); John P. Ferguson, *The Schoharie Mohawks* (Howes Cave, NY: Iroquois Indian Museum, 2009); Edith M. Fox, *Land Speculation in the Mohawk Valley* (Ithaca, NY: Cornell University Press, 1949); David Guldenzopf, "The Colonial Transformation of Mohawk Iroquois Society" (PhD diss., State University of New York, 1986), https://core.tdar.org/document/367158/the-colonial-transformation-of-mohawk-iroquois-society; John C. Guzzardo, "Democracy along the Mohawk: An Election Return, 1773," *New York History* 57 (January 1976): 30–52, https://www.jstor.org/stable/23169705; William B. Hart, "Black 'Go-Betweens' and the Mutability of 'Race,' Status, and Identity on New York's Pre-revolutionary Frontier," in *Contact Points: American Frontiers from the Mohawk Valley to the Mississippi, 1750–1830*, ed. Andrew R. L. Cayton and Fredrika J. Teute (Chapel Hill: University of North Carolina Press, 1998), 88–113; Codman Hislop, *The Mohawk* (1948; reprint, Syracuse, NY: Syracuse University Press, 1989); Lois M. Huey and Bonnie Pulis, *Molly Brant: A Legacy of Her Own* (Youngstown, NY: Fort Niagara Association, 1997); Ann Hunter, "Tiononderogue: The Struggle for a Mohawk

Town, 1686–1797," *Iroquoia* 1, no. 1 (Autumn 2015): 61–79; Paul Gorgen, "Ladies of the Mohawk Valley: Molly Brant, Clarissa Putman and Other Women with Rona'sharó:nih (European) Partners," *Iroquoia* 3, no. 1 (2017): 7–40; Isabel Thompson Kelsay, *Joseph Brant, 1743–1807: Man of Two Worlds* (Syracuse, NY: Syracuse University Press, 1984); Sung Bok Kim, *Landlord and Tenant in Colonial New York: Manorial Society, 1664–1775* (Chapel Hill: University of North Carolina Press, 1978); Barbara Alice Mann, *Iroquoian Women: The Gantowisas* (New York: Peter Lang, 2011); Philip Otterness, *Becoming German: The 1709 Palatine Migration to New York* (Ithaca, NY: Cornell University Press, 2004); David L. Preston, "George Klock, the Canajoharie Mohawks, and the Good Ship *Sir William Johnson*: Land, Legitimacy, and Community in the Eighteenth-Century Mohawk Valley," *New York History* 86, no. 4 (Fall 2005): 472–99, http://www.jstor.org/stable/42677837; David L. Preston, *The Texture of Contact: European and Indian Settler Communities on the Frontiers of Iroquoia, 1667–1783* (Lincoln: University of Nebraska Press, 2009); Timothy Shannon, *Indians and Colonists of Empire: The Albany Congress of 1754* (Ithaca, NY: Cornell University Press, 2000).

The most amazing source about the best-land families during the American Revolution is the US Revolutionary War Pension and Bounty-Land Warrant Application Files, 1800–1900, Records of the Department of Veteran Affairs, Record Group 15, National Archives, Washington DC, accessed at Ancestry.com. Also helpful are the *Documents Relative to the Colonial History of the State of New York*; the *Public Papers of George Clinton*, 10 vols. (Albany: State of New York, 1900); Maryly B. Penrose, *Indian Affairs Papers: American Revolution* (Franklin Park, NJ: Liberty Bell Associates, 1981), and *Mohawk Valley in the Revolution: Committee of Safety Papers & Genealogical Compendium* (Franklin Park, NJ: Liberty Bell Associates, 1978); the Peter Gansevoort Jr. Military Papers, Manuscripts and Archives Division, the New York Public Library, Astor, Lenox, and Tilden Foundations; and Frederick Cook, *Journals of the Military Expedition of Major General John Sullivan against the Six Nations of Indians, 1779* (Auburn, NY: Knapp, Peck & Thomson, 1887). Old local histories include William W. Campbell, *Annals of Tryon County, or the Border Warfare of New York during the Revolution* (New York: J. & J. Harper, 1831); W. Max Reid, *The Story of Old Fort Johnson* (New York: G. P. Putnam's Sons, 1906); and Jeptha R. Sims, *History of Schoharie County and Border Wars of New York* (Albany, NY: Munsell & Tanner, 1845).

For histories of the Oneidas, the Six Nations, and New Yorkers during the American Revolution, see Edward P. Alexander, *A Revolutionary*

Conservative: James Duane of New York (New York: Columbia University Press, 1938); Darren Bonaparte's series on Colonel Louis Atiatonharonkwen (Atayataghronghta), or Cook, Wampum Chronicles, http://www.wampumchronicles.com; Colin G. Campbell, *The American Revolution in Indian Country: Crisis and Diversity in Native American Communities* (Cambridge: Cambridge University Press, 1995); Joseph Glatthaar and James Kirby Martin, *Forgotten Allies: The Oneida Indians and the American Revolution* (New York: Hill & Wang, 2006); Barbara Graymont, *The Iroquois in the American Revolution* (Syracuse, NY: Syracuse University Press, 1972); Andrea Lynn Smith, "Remembering Washington's 'Sullivan Expedition' of 1779 in Contemporary Times" (paper presentation, Conference on Iroquois Research, Salamanca, NY, October 2022); Alan Taylor, *The Divided Ground: Indians, Settlers, and the Northern Borderland of the American Revolution* (New York: Vintage Books, 2006); Karim M. Tiro, "A 'Civil' War? Rethinking Iroquois Participation in the American Revolution," *Explorations in Early American Culture* 4 (2000): 148–65, https://www.jstor.org/stable/23549298; Karim M. Tiro, "The Dilemmas of Alliance: The Oneida Indian Nation in the American Revolution," in *War & Society in the American Revolution: Mobilization and Home Fronts*, ed. John Resch and Walter Sargent (DeKalb: Northern Illinois University Press, 2007): 215–34; Robert William Venables, "Tyron County, 1775–1783: A Frontier in Revolution" (PhD diss., Vanderbilt University, 1967); Gavin K. Watt's military histories, including *Rebellion in the Mohawk Valley: The St. Leger Expedition of 1777* (Toronto: Dundurn, 2002), *The Burning of the Valleys: Daring Raids from Canada against the New York Frontier in the Fall of 1780* (Toronto: Dundurn, 1997), *A Dirty, Trifling, Piece of business*, vol. 1, *The Revolutionary War as Waged from Canada in 1781* (Toronto: Dundurn, 2009); and *I Am Heartily Ashamed*, vol. 2, *The Revolutionary War's Final Campaign as Waged from Canada in 1782* (Toronto: Dundern, 2010); Anthony Wonderley, "1777: The Revolutionary War Comes to Oneida Country," *Mohawk Valley History* 1 (2004): 15–48; Anthony Wonderley, "An Oneida Community in 1780: A Study of an Inventory of Iroquois Property Losses during the Revolutionary War," *Northeast Anthropology*, no. 56 (1998): 19–41; and Anthony Wonderley, "'Good Peter's Narrative of Several Transactions respecting Indian Lands': An Oneida View of Dispossession, 1785–1788," *New York History* 84, no. 3 (Summer 2003): 237–73, https://www.jstor.org/stable/23183368.

On the early republic and the dispossession of the Oneidas, covered in chapters 4 and 5, see Franklin B. Hough, *Proceedings of the Commissioners of Indian Affairs, Appointed by Law for the Extinguishment of Indian Titles in the State of New York*, 2 vols. (Albany, NY: Joel Munsell, 1861); and New York State, *Report of the Special Committee to Investigate the Indian Problem of the State of New York, 1888* (Albany, NY: Troy Press, 1889), commonly known as the Whipple Report (available online at the New York State Library Native American Digital Collections). At the New York State Archives, the history of the best land is found in Field Books, Series A4052; Surveyor General Field Books, Series A4016; Surveyor General Land Survey Field Books, Series A4019; Petitions, Correspondence and Reports Relating to Indians, Series A1823; Selected Audited Accounts of State Civil and Military Officers, Series A0802; Entry Documentation Submitted by the Indian Commissioners and Indians for Annuities Paid to Indians and for Other Expenditures, Series A0832; Survey Maps of Lands in New York State, Series A2073; Surveyor General's Reports on Petitions to the State Legislature, Series A1820-76; and Letters Patent 12943. The petition from the Oneidas of Oriske written in the late 1780s is at the New York Historical Society, and the petition from Christian Party men and women in 1814 is from the William Leland Thompson Collection, Albany Institute of History and Art, Albany, NY. The Breese Stevens Roby Family Papers, AB83, Rare Books, Special Collections, and Preservation, River Campus Libraries, University of Rochester, Rochester, NY, and the Duane Family Papers at the New York Historical Society, contain information about the best-land families and the early development of central New York State.

Eyewitness accounts include Jeremy Belknap, *Journal of a Tour from Boston to Oneida, June 1796* (Cambridge, MA: John Wilson & Son, 1882); Jeremy Belknap and Jedediah Morse, *Report on the Oneida, Stockbridge and Brotherton Indians, 1796* (New York: Museum of the American Indian, 1955); William W. Campbell, *The Life and Writings of DeWitt Clinton* (New York: Baker & Scribner, 1849); Walter Pilkington, ed., *The Journals of Samuel Kirkland* (Clinton, NY: Hamilton College, 1980); and Winslow C. Watson, *Men and Times of the Revolution, or Memoirs of Elkanah Watson* (New York: Dana, 1956). Travel narratives include Metchie J. E. Budka, "Journey to Niagara, 1805: From the Diary of Julian Ursyn Niemcewicz," *New York Historical Society Quarterly* 44 (January 1960): 73–113; Patrick Campbell, *A Journey through the Genesee County, Finger Lakes Region and Mohawk Valley from Patrick Campbell's Travels in the Interior Inhabited Parts of North America in the Years 1791 and 1792* (Rochester, NY: University of Rochester Libraries, 1978); William S. Fenton, ed., "The Journal of James Emlen Kept on a Trip to Canandaigua, New York, 1794," *Ethnohistory* 12, no. 4 (Fall 1965): 279–342; John Lincklaen, *Travels in the*

Years 1791 and 1792 in Pennsylvania, New York, and Vermont (New York: G. P. Putnam's Sons, 1897); John Maude, *Visit to the Falls of Niagara in 1800* (London: Longman, Rees, Orme, Brown & Green, 1826); Robert Sutcliff, *Travels in Some Parts of North America, in the Years 1804, 1805 & 1806* (London: n.p., 1815), Karst Collection. See also Snow, Gehring, and Starna, *In Mohawk Country*.

For studies of the land, see Michael A. Blaakman, "The Marketplace of American Federalism: Land Speculation across State Lines in the Early Republic," *Journal of American History* 107, no. 3 (December 2020): 583–608; Rob Harper, "Settlers, States, and Violence in the Revolutionary Ohio Valley" (paper presentation, annual conference of the Society of Historians of the Early American Republic, "Roundtable: Squatters, Surveyors & States in the Old Northwest," Philadelphia, 4 July 2011); David Maldwyn Ellis, *Landlords and Farmers in the Hudson-Mohawk Region, 1790–1850* (New York: Octagon Books, 1967); Marcus Terran Gallo, "Imaginary Lines, Real Power: Surveyors and Land Speculation in the Mid-Atlantic Borderlands, 1681–1800" (PhD diss., University of California, Davis, 2012); Philip O. Geier III, "A Peculiar Status: A History of Oneida Indian Treaties and Claims; Jurisdictional Conflict within American Government, 1775–1920" (PhD diss., Syracuse University, 1980); Laurence M. Hauptman, *Conspiracy of Interests: Iroquois Dispossession and the Rise of New York State* (Syracuse, NY: Syracuse University Press, 1999); Thomas J. Humphrey, *Land and Liberty: Hudson Valley Riots in the Age of Revolution* (DeKalb: Northern Illinois University Press, 2004); William Wyckoff, *The Developer's Frontier: The Making of the Western New York Landscape* (New Haven, CT: Yale University Press, 1988).

On the peoples of the era, see Carl Benn, *The Iroquois in the War of 1812* (Toronto: University of Toronto Press, 1998); John L. Brooke, *Columbia Rising: Civil Life on the Upper Hudson from the Revolution to the Age of Jackson* (Chapel Hill: University of North Carolina Press, 2010); T. Wood Clarke, *Émigrés in the Wilderness* (Port Washington, NY: Ira J. Friedman, 1967); Edward Countryman, "Indians, the Colonial Order, and the Social Significance of the American Revolution," *William and Mary Quarterly* 53, no. 2 (April 1996): 342–62, http://www.jstor.org/stable/2947405; Norman K. Dann, *Peter Smith of Peterboro: Furs, Land and Anguish* (Hamilton, NY: Log Cabin Books, 2018); Carolyn Eastman, "The Indian Censures the White Man: Indian Eloquence and Early American Reading Responses in the Early Republic," *William and Mary Quarterly* 65, no. 3 (July 2008): 535–64; François Furstenberg, *When the United States Spoke French: Five*

Refugees Who Shaped a Nation (New York: Penguin, 2014); Caroline Moorehead, *Dancing to the Precipice: The Life of Lucie de la Tour du Pin, Eyewitness to an Era* (New York: HarperCollins, 2009); Christine Sternberg Patrick, "The Life and Times of Samuel Kirkland, 1741–1808: Missionary to the Oneida Indians, American Patriot, and Founder of Hamilton College" (PhD diss., State University of New York at Buffalo, 1993); W. J. Rorabaugh, *The Alcoholic Republic* (New York: Oxford University Press, 1979); Henry R. Schoolcraft, *Notes on the Iroquois* (Albany, NY: Erastus H. Pease, 1847); David J. Silverman, *Red Brethren: The Brothertown and Stockbridge Indians and the Problem of Race in Early America* (Ithaca, NY: Cornell University Press, 2010); E. Wilder Spaulding, *New York in the Critical Period, 1783–1789* (Port Washington, NY: Ira J. Freedman, 1963); Karim M. Tiro, "James Dean in Iroquoia," *New York History* 80, no. 4 (October 1999): 391–422; Anthony Wonderley, "Brothertown, New York, 1785–1796," *New York History* 81, no. 4 (October 2000): 457–92; Anthony Wonderley, "Chief Warriors, Pagan Priests, and Witch Killers: The Division of the Oneida Iroquois, 1789–1805," *New York History* 93, no. 2 (Spring 2012): 121–45, https://www.jstor.org/stable/23645397; and Anthony Wonderley, "The Burning of Oneida Castle (1780) and the Oneida Veterans Treaty (1795)," *Mohawk Valley History* 2, no. 1 (2005): 7–23.

For the era of the Erie Canal, removal, and farming in nineteenth-century central New York, discussed in chapters 6 and 7, I used the Papers of Albert Gallatin, New York History Society; the Eleazer Williams Papers and General A. G. Ellis, "Recollections of Rev. Eleazer Williams," Wisconsin Historical Collections, 1855–1915, Wisconsin Historical Society; Jedediah Morse, *A Report to the Secretary of War of the United States on Indian Affairs* (New Haven, CT: n.p., 1822); *Laws of the State of New York in Relation to the Erie and Champlain Canals: Together with the Annual Reports of the Canal Commissioners, and Other Documents Requisite for a Complete Official History of These Works* (Albany, NY: E. & E. Hosford, 1825); *Documents of the Assembly of New York* and *Documents of the Senate of the State of New York*, available at https://babel.hathitrust.org; and Rosters of the New York Regiments during the Civil War, New York State Military Museum and Veterans Research Center, Saratoga Springs, NY, https://www.museum.dmna.ny.gov.

See Peter L. Bernstein, *Wedding of the Waters: The Erie Canal and the Making of a Great Nation* (New York: Norton, 2005); Darren Bonaparte, "Eleazer Williams: The Lost Mohawk," 29 April 2005, and "The Unquiet Rest of Eleazer Williams," 6 May 2005, Wampum Chronicles, https://www.wampumchronicles; Whitney R. Cross, *The Burned-Over District: The*

Social and Intellectual History of Enthusiastic Religion in Western New York, 1800–1850 (New York: Harper Torchbook, 1965); David B. Danbom, *Born in the Country: A History of Rural America*, 3rd ed. (Baltimore: Johns Hopkins University Press, 2017); Laurence M. Hauptman, *The Iroquois in the Civil War: From Battlefield to Reservation* (Syracuse, NY: Syracuse University Press, 1993); L. Gordon McLester III and Laurence Hauptman, eds., *The Oneida Indians in the Age of Allotment, 1860–1920* (Norman: University of Oklahoma Press, 2006); Reeve Huston, *Land and Freedom: Rural Society, Popular Protest, and Party Politics in Antebellum New York* (New York: Oxford University Press, 2000); Michael Kammen, *In the Past Lane: Historical Perspectives on American Culture* (New York: Oxford University Press, 1997); Gerald Koeppel, *Bond of Union: Building the Erie Canal and the American Empire* (Cambridge, MA: Da Capo, 2009); Michael Leroy Oberg, *Professional Indian: The American Odyssey of Eleazer Williams* (Philadelphia: University of Pennsylvania Press, 2015); Anthony Wonderley, *Oneida Utopia: A Community Searching for Human Happiness and Prosperity* (Ithaca, NY: Cornell University Press, 2017).

Literary contributions and travel accounts include Mary Hartwood Catherwood, "Lazarre," *San Francisco Call* 87, no. 85, 24 August 1902; Susan Fenimore Cooper, *Rural Hours* (1850; reprint, Syracuse, NY: Syracuse University Press, 1968); Nathaniel Hawthorne, "The Canal Boat," *New England Magazine*, December 1835, 398–409; Mark Twain, *The Adventures of Huckleberry Finn* (1885; New York: Bantam Books, 1965); A. Levasseur, *Lafayette in America in 1824 and 1825*, vol. 2 (Philadelphia: Carey & Lea, 1829); George Wilson Pierson, *Tocqueville in America* (1938; Baltimore: Johns Hopkins University Press, 1996).

For chapters 8, 9, and 10, on the best land in twentieth- and twenty-first-century Oneida, I relied on interviews conducted with Casey Brewer, Elizabeth Brewer, Herbert Brewer, Joanne Brewer, Joshua Brewer, Mary Lou Brewer, Nathan Brewer, Richard Brewer, Robert Brewer, Russell Brewer, Thomas Brewer, Virginia Brewer, Jack Curtin, Rebecca John Karst, Richard Lynch, Richard Myers, Rex Niles, and Holly Brewer Rogers. I drew on several newspapers, especially the *Bee Journal* (Canastota, NY), *Daily Press* (Utica, NY), *Indian Country Today*, *New York Times* (New York, NY), *Observer Dispatch* (Utica, NY), *Oneida Democratic Union*, *Patriot* (Utica), *Oneida Dispatch/Oneida Daily Dispatch* (formerly *Oneida Sachem*), *Rome Daily Sentinel*, *Rome Observer*, *Post-Standard* (Syracuse, NY), *Syracuse Herald American*, and *Syracuse Herald Journal*. Other newspapers are cited in the notes. Most helpful were documents from the Bureau of Indian Affairs, Record Group 75, National Archives, available at Oneida Nation of Wisconsin, https://www.exploreoneida.com, and the *Report of the New York State Indian Commission 1922* (the Everett Report), New York State Library, Native American Digital Collections.

See also Chrystia Freeland, "The Triumph of the Family Farm," *The Atlantic*, July/August 2012; Laurence M. Hauptman, *An Oneida Indian in Foreign Waters: The Life of Chief Chapman Scanandoah, 1879–1953* (Syracuse, NY: Syracuse University Press, 2016); Laurence M. Hauptman, "Designing Woman: Minnie Kellogg, Iroquois Leader," in *Indian Lives: Essays on Nineteenth and Twentieth-Century Native American Leaders*, ed. L. G. Moses and Raymond Wilson (Albuquerque: University of New Mexico Press, 1985); Laura Cornelius Kellogg, *Our Democracy and the American Indian, and Other Works*, ed. Kristina Ackley and Christina Stancia (Syracuse, NY: Syracuse University Press, 2015); Frances W. Kaye, "Little Squatter on the Osage Diminished Reserve: Reading Laura Ingalls Wilder's Kansas Indians," *Great Plains Quarterly* 20, no. 2 (May 2000): 123–40, https://digitalcommons.unl.edu/greatplainsquarterly/23; Wendy McClure, *The Wilder Life: My Adventures in the Lost World of "Little House on the Prairie"* (New York: Penguin, 2011); Jane Mt. Pleasant, "The Problem with Plows: Examining the Role of Tillage in Iroquois Agriculture," (paper presentation, Conference on Iroquois Research, Cortland, NY, 6 October 2012); Sherry L. Smith, *Hippies, Indians & the Fight for Red Power* (New York: Oxford University Press, 2012); Helen M. Upton, *The Everett Report in Historical Perspective* (Albany: New York State Revolution Bicentennial Commission, 1980); Laura Ingalls Wilder, *Little House on the Prairie* (New York: HarperCollins, 1971).

For the land claims cases, see *Oneida Indian Nation of New York v. City of Sherrill, New York*, 337 F. 3d 139 (2003); Brief of Amici Curiae Town of Lenox, New York; Town of Stockbridge, New York; and Town of Southampton, New York in Support of Petitioner City of Sherrill, New York, No. 03-855, Supreme Court of the United States; *City of Sherrill v. Oneida Indian Nation of New York*, 544 US (2005); *City of Sherrill*, 544 US (Stevens, J., dissenting); Opening Brief for the Petitioners, Madison County and Oneida County, New York v. Oneida Indian Nation of New York, US Supreme Court, No. 10-72, 2010, NARF Tribal Supreme Court Project, https://www.sct.narf.org; Kristina Ackley, "Haudenosaunee Genealogies: Conflict and Community in the Oneida Land Claim," *American Indian Quarterly* 33, no. 4 (September 2009): 462–78, https://www.jstor.org/stable/40388482; Allison M. Dussias, "The Reports of Our Death Are Greatly Exaggerated—Reflections on the Resilience of the Oneida Indian Nation of New York," *BYU Law Review* 2018, no. 6 (2019): 1231–74, https://digitalcommons.law.byu.edu/lawreview/vol2018/iss6/5; Kathryn Fort, "Disruption and Impossibility: The New Laches and the Unfortunate Resolution of the Modern Iroquois Land Claims," *Wyoming Law Review* 11, no. 2 (January 2011): 376–405, https://scholarship.law.uwyo.edu/wlr/vol11/iss2/4; Carole Goldberg, "Finding the Way to Indian Country: Justice Ruth Bader Ginsburg's Decisions in Indian Law Cases," *Ohio State Law Journal* 70, no. 4 (2009): 1003–35; Peter Kovler, "Native American Land Rights," *Inquiry* 15 (May 1978): 17–22, https://www.exploreoneida.com; Sarah Krakoff, "*City of Sherrill v. Oneida Indian Nation of New York*: A Regretful Postscript to the Taxation Chapter in *Cohen's Handbook of Federal Indian Law*," *Tulsa Law Review* 41, no, 1, revised (2013): 5–19, https://scholar.law.colorado.edu/faculty-article/418; Meghan Y. McCune, "'It's a Question of Fairness': Fee-to-Trust and Opposition to Haudenosaunee Land Rights and Economic Development," in *Gambling on Authenticity: Gaming, the Noble Savage, and the Not-So-New Indian*, eds. Becca Gercken and Julie Pelletier (East Lansing: Michigan State University Press, 2017), 111–34; Stephan L. Pevar, *The Rights of Indians and Tribes*, 4th ed. (New York: Oxford University Press, 2012); Samuel Pokross, "'Dramatically Altered the Legal Landscape'? *City of Sherrill v. Oneida Indian Nation* in the Lower Courts," *American Indian Law Review* 43, no. 1 (2018): 243–305; Louis H. Roper, "Old Wine in New Bottles: New York, the Federal Government and the Oneida Land Claims Cases," *New York History* 72, no. 2 (April 1991): 133–54, https://www. jstor.org/stable/23178782; George C. Shattuck, *The Oneida Land Claims: A Legal History* (Syracuse, NY: Syracuse University Press, 1991); Jennifer R. Sunderlin, "One Nation, Indivisible: American 'Indian Country' in the Wake of *City of Sherrill v. Oneida Indian Nation*," *Albany Law Review* 70 (2007): 1563–87, https://www.albanylawreview.org; Karim M. Tiro, "Claims Arising: The Oneida Nation of Wisconsin and the Indians Claim Commission, 1951–1982," *American Indian Law Review* 32, no. 2 (2008): 509–24, LexisNexis, https://www.lexisnexis.com; Christopher Vecsey and William A. Starna, eds., *Iroquois Land Claims* (Syracuse, NY: Syracuse University Press, 1988).

The fundamental source, of course, is the home of the Oneidas, with its lakes, creeks, waterfalls, hills, valleys, swamps, and level open country, including the best land. Everything is about the land.

INDEX

Page numbers for figures are in italics

Abourezk, James, 212
Adams, Edmund, 161
Adams, John, 102
Adams, John Quincy, 128
Albany, 2, 11; during American Revolution, 50, 53, 58, 60, 67, 70; in colonial New York, 17, 19–22, 27–28, 31, 33–35; as state capital, 86, 93, 97, 110, 123–24, 132, 215–16, 235; as treaty site, 92, 103, 106, 115, 118, 136
Albany Congress of 1754, 34–35
Albany County Militia, 62, 67, 84, 94
alcohol, 6, 18, 20, 33, 90, 92, 106, 159, 165, 246; cause of disturbance, 14–15, 25, 31, 40, 75, 81, 129; and diplomacy, 20, 31, 36, 45, 53, 60, 77; and dispossession, 39, 105, 118, 138, 156, 233
Allen, Ethan, 73
Algonquin people, 8, 77
American Museum of Natural History, 178, 232
American Revolution, xiii, 79; history and memory of, ix, xvi, 48, 72, 118, 136, 181, 189, 195, 236–37, 246–48; pension applications, 52–53, 140–41; and Oneidas, 48–51, 53–65, 67–70, 91, 102, 114, 139. *See also* Oriskany, battle of; Saratoga, battle of; Sullivan Expedition; Tryon County Militia; Valley Forge
Amherst, Jeffrey, 37
Anne, Queen, 24, 26–27
Annin, Joseph, 90, 103
Anti-Rent War, 154–55
Antone, Aaron, 160
Antone, Dolly John, xxiv, 153, 160, 172, 250
Antone, Jake, 153
Antone, Polly, xxiv, 152
Arnold, Benedict, 58–59
Articles of Confederation, 74, 230
Atayataghronghta, Louis (Cook), 77, 80, 82, 84, 104, 273n26; during American Revolution, 56, 58, 63, 67, 69
August, Peter, 110, 116, 118–19, 135, 139
Avery, Calvin, 156, 295n21

baseball, 162–63
Baum, L. Frank, 171, 245
Baxter, Thomas, 51
Beauchamp, William M., 179
Beecher, Sylvester, 111, 113–14, 139, 147, 154, 167
Beechtree, Christian, xxiv, 152, 178
Belknap, Jeremy, 93–94
Bellinger, Johan Friederich, xix, 27
Bellinger, Peter, 57
Bellinger, William, 141
Beverwyck, 11, 15–17, 202
Big Knife, Anthony, 250
Blâcons, Marquis de, 101, 224
Blâcons, Oneida de, 101, 223–24
blood quantum, 192, 303n52
Boston Tea Party, 44, 47, 94
bounty land, 69, 78
Boylan, Julia, 181–82, 184
Boylan case, 181–84, 186, 188, 190, 199, 207
Branigan, John, 209–10
Brant, Joseph, 39–41, 44, 74–75, 78; and Revolutionary War, 49–50, 53, 55–58, 61–62, 64–65, 67, 69
Brant, Molly, 38–39, 42, 44–45, 56, 60, 77, 89, 95
Bread, Daniel, 131, 139
Bread, Peter. *See* Kanadolock

Breard, Jacques-Michel, 99, 101
Breard, Marie Angelique, xxiv, 99, 109
Breese, Helen Burrows, 97–99, 117, *133*, 140, 156, 163, 282n5
Breese, Helen Platt, 135–36, 140
Breese, Margaret, 135
Breese, Samuel, 154, 163
Breese, Samuel Sidney, 99, 104, 113, 129, *133*, 135, 163; and Oneida land, 106, 110–11, 117, 120, 131, 142, 147
Brewer, Abraham (the elder), xx, xxi, 154
Brewer, Abraham (the younger), xxi, 156, 161, 167, 175
Brewer, Casey, xxi, 228, 238, 250
Brewer, Catharine Myers, xx, xxi, 78, 154–55
Brewer, DeVerne, ix, xiii, xxi, 108, *174*, 175, 184–86, *185*, 189, 220, 223, 225; and Brewer Farm, 192–94, 198–99, 202–4, 216, 238
Brewer, Elizabeth "Beth," xxi, 198, 204, *205*, 209, 211, 227–28
Brewer, Frank, xi, xxi, 120, 167; and Orchard Place Dairy, ix, 174–77, 184, 192, 216, 238
Brewer, Harry, *174*, 184
Brewer, Hazel (Taylor), xxi, *174*, 184, 198, 234
Brewer, Herbert, x, xxi, 108, 192–93, *205*, 209, 223–24, 234, 239, 250; and Brewer Farm, 197–98, 203, 216–17, 227, 238, 247; and Oneidas, 204–5, 208, 210–16, 218–22
Brewer, Holly (Rogers), xxi, 228, 236, 250
Brewer, James, xxi, 155–56
Brewer, Jennie (Burgess), 167, 184
Brewer, Jennie Clement, xi, *xii*, *166*, 166–67, 173; and Orchard Place Dairy, ix, 120, 175–77, 184, 192, 238
Brewer, Joanne Fedder, xxi, 203, 223
Brewer, Joshua, xxi, 228, 245, 249
Brewer, Leo, 175, 192
Brewer, Lucy Clement, xxi, *166*, 166–67, 175
Brewer, Mabelle Greene, xiii, xxi, 184–86, *185*, 189, 192–94, 198–99, 203, 220, 238
Brewer, Mae (Newcomb), 175, 184, 192
Brewer, Mary, 167
Brewer, Mary Adelia (Guy), 167
Brewer, Mary Lou Sipperley, xxi, 198, *205*, 209, 216–17, 223, 225, 238–39
Brewer, Nathan, xxi, 228, 238, 245
Brewer, Peter, xx, 84–85, 154, 279n46
Brewer, Reta, xxi, 184, 192, 198, 234
Brewer, Richard "Dick," xxi, 194, 197, 203, 216, 227
Brewer, Robert "Bob," xxi, 192–94, 197
Brewer, Russell, xxi, 198, 203–4, *205*, 209, 225, 227, 239, 245, 248
Brewer, Susan, ix–xiv, 198, 202–4, *205*, 209–11, 222–25, 227, 229–30, 243, 248, 250
Brewer, Thomas, xxi, 198, 203–4, *205*, 209, 225, 227–31, 234, 238, 245, 250
Brewer, Virginia "Ginny," xxi, 192–93, 197
Brewer, Willie, 167, 184
Brodhead, Charles C., 116–18
Brothertown Indians, 77, 128, 278n22
Brown, Edwin J., 177, 181, 183, 186
Burchard, Nathan, 144
Bureau of Indian Affairs, 183, 190, 196, 206, 208–9, 213, 221, 242–44
Burgoyne, John, 53–54, 58–60
Burke, William L., 218
Burleson, B. F., 168–69
Burning, Catherine Skenandoah, 152–53
Burr, Aaron, 98–99
Burr, Robert, 212–13, 220–21, 226
Burrows, John, 98, 282n5
Bush, George W., 239
Butler, John, 57–58
Butler, Walter, 58–59, 62, 69

Cady, Asa, 125
Cady, George Beecher, 167, 298n54
Calhoun, John C., 129–30
Canada, ix, 17, 45, 77–78, 85, 95, 99, 123, 230; and American Revolution, 48, 52–53, 55, 60, 67; and POWs, 20, 71, 85, 89; War of 1812, 114–15. *See also* French and Indian Wars; Oneidas of Canada
Canajoharie, 16, 28–30, 32, 36, 39–45, 78, 89, 95, 266n14; and American Revolution, 51, 53, 56, 62, 64–65, 67, 69
Canajoharie Patent, 28, 33–34, 39–40, 45, 49–50
Canaseraga, 88–90, 92, 95, 98, 101–3, 106, 109, 120, 149, 169
Canastota, 89, 102–3, 154, 163, 177, 180, 190, 197, 228, 233, 237
Captain John, 88, 91–92, 95
Captain John (Ha Yank), 153

Captain Peter, 88, 90, 104, 109, 114, 297n48
Carinci, Army, 229
Carroll, Doug, 218
Carter, Jimmy, 216
Catharine, Oneida Wolf Clan, xxiii, 29, 202
Catherwood, Mary Hartwell, 173
Cayuga people, ix, xvii, 3, 73, 76–77, 86, 91, 161, 196; and American Revolution, 53, 55, 62–64
Cazenove, Theophile, 98, 101
Cazenovia, 98–99, 101, 104, 106, 113, 177, 180; Town of, 90, 158
Chancellorsville, battle of, 160
Chapin, Israel, Jr., 92, 103
Chapman, Stephen, 113, 125, 178
Charles II, 16, 18
Chenango County, 80, 99, 106
Cherry Valley, 62, 65, 70, 104
Chippawa, battle of, 114–15
Chittenango, 171, 245
Chrisjohn, Mary, xxv, 168
Chrisjohn, Richard, 231
Civil War, xvi, 159–61, 163, 165
Clement, Anna Peake, xix, 22, 24, 26, 30, 32, 52, 95
Clement, Dorothy Vedder, xx, xxi, 148, 161, 165
Clement, Elizabeth "Lizzie" Moot, xxi, 161–63, 166–67, 175–76, 184, 238
Clement, Elizabeth (Powell), xx, 30, 32, 38
Clement, Ellen, 165, *166*
Clement, Jacobus, xx, 32, 36
Clement, Jennie. *See* Brewer, Jennie Clement
Clement, Johannes, xx, 32, 35
Clement, Joseph, xix, 24–26, 30–32, 52, 95, 148, 157
Clement, Joseph (lieutenant), xx, 52, 64–65, 67
Clement, Lambert, xx, 52–53, 64, 69, 95, 148
Clement, Lewis, xx, xxi, 148, 157, 161–62, 165–66
Clement, Lewis Cobes, xx, 35–36, 52, 95
Clement, Lewis H., 161
Clement, Lucy. *See* Brewer, Lucy Clement
Clement, William, xxi, 148, 161–63, 165–66, 175, 238
Clement family, 35, 45, 52, 162–63, 250
Clinton, DeWitt, 108–10, 115, 119, 126, 129, 132, 135
Clinton, George (colonial governor), 31–33
Clinton, George (governor of New York State), 74, 77–78, 84, 108; and American Revolution, 62–64, 67–68, 70; and the Oneidas, 75, 79–83, 85–86, 89, 92, 103, 218
Clinton, James, 63, 108
Clinton, NY, 168
Clock, Conrad, 89–90, 136
Clock family, 90, 94, 103, 113. *See also* Klock family
Clockville, 90, 111, 125, 147, 154
Cobb, Charles, xxv, 164, 174–77
Cobb, F. Dewitt, xxv, 193, 223
Cobb, Irene, xxv, 176
Cobb, Mary Deferrier, xxiv, xxv, 135, 145, 149, 159–60, 173–75, 228
Cobb, Nelson, xxiv, xxv, 145, 159, 163–64, 174–75, 228, 294n73
Cobb, William, 139, 142, 184, 294n73, 302n26
Cobleskill, 62, 162
Cobus, Dolly, xxiii, 69, 72
Colbraith, William, 75, 80, 89–90
Colden, Cadwallader, 33, 46
Collins, Edward, 32
Columbus, Christopher, 172, 230, 247
Comte, Louis, 127
condolence ceremony, 8, 20, 36, 37, 45, 61, 92, 144
Continental Army, 53–54, 58, 61–64, 69, 88
Continental Congress, 44, 48, 50–51, 54, 58, 63–65, 68–69
Cooper, James Fenimore, 138, 153
Cooper, Margaret, 153
Cooper, Polly (American Revolution), 61, 196, 246
Cooper, Polly (War of 1812), 114, 180
Cooper, Susan Fenimore, 153
corn, 28, 32, 60, 64, 98, 113; and the Brewers, ix, 161, 176–77, 193, 198, 203, 229, 245; cornhusk doll, 201–2; and Oneidas, 4–5, 7, 59, 61, 81, 109, 120, 122, 195–96, 201, 212, 231, 238
Cornelius, Henry. *See* Shagoyontha
Cornelius, Jacob (grandson of Shagoyontha), 137
Cornelius, Jacob (son of Thomas), 160
Cornelius, John, 117, *127*

Cornelius, Laura. *See* Kellogg, Laura
Cornelius, Thomas, 152–53, 156, 160, 163, 169, 178
Cornelius, Wilson, 183, 190, 195
Cornell University, xi, 161, 195, 197–98, 225, 227, 245
Covenant Chain, 15, 18, 28, 34, 36, 50, 91, 247
Cowaselon, 102, 106, 110, 120, 140, 150, 234. *See also* Wampsville
Cowaselon Creek, 102, 116, 120–23, 125, 131, 137, 161, 200, 240; and the Brewers, ix, 175–76, 193, 216–17, 227–28, 230, 245
Cox, Ebenezer, 41, 53, 56–57
Crouse, Daniel, 154, 295n15
Cuomo, Mario, 226, 231–32, 245
Curtin, Jack, 207–8, 215, 231, 233–34, 238, 245; Curtin Dairy, 247–48

Danbom, David B., 175
Danckearts, Jasper, 21
d'Andigné, Countess, 223–24
d'Andigné, Oneida, 224
Davis, Oscar H., 218
Dawes, Henry, 171
Day, William, 137, 143
Dean, James, 50, 63, 75, 80, 91–93, 97, 110, 120, 288n71
Deferrier, Angel, xi, xxiv, 96, 99–102, 135, 140, 149–51, 250; descendants of, 175–76, 193, 223, 238, 250; and Oneidas, 104, 106, 108–10, 115–16, 119–20, 126–28, 136, 147; property of, ix, 103, 108, 118, 121–22, 135–36, 140, 176, 198; as remembered, 173–74, 177–78, 202
Deferrier, Charles, xxiv, 135–36, 140, 145, *146*, 149, 159–60, 174, 223, 300n75; property of, 139, 142, 184
Deferrier, Lucy (Pine), xxiv, 135–36, 145, 294n1
Deferrier, Mary. *See* Cobb, Mary
Deferrier, Nancy. *See* Hadcock, Nancy
Deferrier, Polly. *See* Denny, Polly
Deferrier, Sophia. *See* Loomis, Sophia
Deferrier, Theresa Bedlow, xxiv, 145
de Ferrierre, Charles César d'Algret d'Olède, xxiv, 99–100
Deferrier family, 120–21, 135–36, 142, 150–51, 176, 216
de la Croix, Jeronimus, 3, 5
Democratic Party, 143, 157, 159, 204; Democratic-Republican Party, 113
Denny, Abraham, xxiv, 105–6, 121, 143, 145, 152; land of, 120, 124–25, 131, 139, 142, 154, 184, 216, 234
Denny, Catharine Nellis, xxiv, 121, 139, 145
Denny, Dolly Doxtator, xxiii, xxiv, 72, 102, 104–6, 109–10, 120, 124–25, 140, 153
Denny, John, xxiii, xxiv, 72–73, 79, 89, 92, 98, 102, 105–6, 109, 153
Denny, John "Dr. Sundown," xxiv, xxv, 105, 120, 124, 142–43, 165, 173, 180, 200; as medicine man, 153, 168–69
Denny, John (son of Dr. Sundown), xxv, 180, 184, 192
Denny, Jonathan, 103
Denny, Lewis S., xxiv, 143
Denny, Louis, xxiii, 41–42, 76, 102–4, 106–9, 116, 121, 284n18, 287n52; in Revolutionary War, 62, 65, 67, 70, 91
Denny, Louis, Jr., xxiii, 73, 103, 145, 287n52
Denny, Louis (son of Dolly), xxiii, xxiv, 287n52
Denny, Maria, xxiii, 41–42, 62, 65, 70, 97, 109, 121, 270n58
Denny, Martin, xxiv, 130–32, 139
Denny, Martinus, xxiii, 73, 116, 120, 122, 140, 145, 173; as interpreter, 103, 130, 136, 151
Denny, Polly, ix–xiii, *xii*, xvi, xxiii–xxv, 97–98, 177, 202, 248; ancestors of, 1, 7, 22, 24–25, 27; and best land, 106, 108–10, 120–23, 126, 135, 140, 142, 149–51, 248, 250, 288n71; descendants of, 145, 153, 169, 173–76, 193, 223, 238, 250; marriage to Angel, 96, 101–4, 120–21, 149, 151; in Schoharie, 41–42, 48, 62, 72
Denny, Sarah "Sally" (Garlock), xxiv, 72, 105, 124
Denny, Sophia (Jordan), xxiv, 153, 163
Denny family, 8, 45, 72–73, 76, 88, 95–96, 101–5, 120, 123, 134, 142
Dessolle, Marquis, 127–28
Dewey, Thomas, 197
DeWitt, Simeon, 88, 116, 119–20, 122, 136–37, 139, 169, 285n36
disease, 8, 17, 21, 26, 28, 37, 90, 140, 299n70; smallpox, 4, 7, 20, 65, 85
DiVeronica, Rocco, 236
Doctrine of Discovery, xiv, 6–7, 18, 130
Douglass, Frederick, 158–59

Doxtator, Anna (Johnson Skenandoah), xxv, *172*, 201
Doxtator, Cornelius, xxiii, 56, 58, 89, 102, 104, 110–11, 114–15, 240, 284n18
Doxtator, Cornelius (son of Peter), 163
Doxtator, Electa (John), xxv, *172*, 191, 194
Doxtator, Emily (Johnson), xxv, *172*, 200, 202
Doxtator, Jacob, xxiii–xxv, 89–90, 92, 102, 104, 106, 114, 132, 136, 139–40, 284n18; and the best land, 116, 119–20, 135; descendants of, 137, 152
Doxtator, Jacob L. W., xxiv, 137
Doxtator, Louis, xxiv, xxv, 153, 164, *164*, 299n70
Doxtator, Lucretia, 163
Doxtator, Lydia, xxv, 172, 180, 190–91, 250
Doxtator, Mary Catharine "Catharine" Denny, xxiv, 267n18
Doxtator, Peter (son of Honyery), xxiii, 72, 141
Doxtator, Peter, 153, 163, 297n47
Doxtator, Sarah Martin Tyonajanegan, xxiii, 41, 72, 121, 140; during American Revolution, 55–58, 60, 65, 70; land of, 102, 111, 139, 154, 158
Doxtator, Stella, xxv, 172, *172*, 190–91
Doxtator, William, xxiv, xxv, 152–53, 158, 168, 170–73, 180, 298n58
Doxtator family, 29, 73, 88, 95, 102–5, 120, 148, 238
Draper, Lyman C., 168, 173, 267n18
Drums Along the Mohawk, 214
Duane, James, 46, 50, 62, 68, 78, 80, 84–85, 93; and Indian policy, 61, 63, 73–75, 106
Duanesburg, 46, 62–63, 78, 84–85, 93, 154–55, 197
Duke of York (James II), 16, 18
Dunbar-Ortiz, Roxane, xiv
Duncan, William A., 170
Dutch Republic, 2, 10–12
Dygert, Peter, 59–60

Ellis, A. G., 128, 151
Elm, Abraham, 160, 164–65, 179, 250, 297n48; *United States v. Elm*, 165, 243
Elm, Ray, 179, *179*, 208
Elm, Simeon, 179, *179*
Elm, Sylvia Honyost, 179, *179*, 208
Erie Canal, 132, 140–42, 173; and best land, ix, 115, 118, 125–26, 131, 134, 175, 177, 193, 197, 199, 238, 245; economic and social impact, 126, 129, 132–35, 145, 156–57, 244, 248; planning and construction, 108–9, 113–14, 123, 125, 285n36
Everett, Edward A., 186–88; Everett Report, 188, 302n39

Fairfield Academy, 135–36
farming, 160–67, 175, 184, 225–26, 234, 245–46, 248; Brewers and, xiii, 176–77, 184, 192–93, 197–99, 203–4, 216, 225, 227–31, 245, 248–49; non-native women and, xi, xiii, 27, 29, 159, 161–63, 166–67, 176–77; settlers and, 16, 26–27, 29, 66, 111–13, 145–47. *See also* Oneida people and agriculture; tenant farmers
Federal Bureau of Investigation, 212
Federalist Party, 84, 92, 113, 157
Fish Creek, 103, 113, 137, 162
Five Chimneys, 137, 234
Five Nations. *See* Haudenosaunee
Fonda, Henry, 214
Fonda, Jelles, 37–38, 52, 60
Forman, Samuel, 98–99, 101, 113, 282n5
Fort Herkimer, 37; Church, 72
Fort Hunter, 24, 30, 57, 67
Fort Johnson, 32, 38
Fort Niagara, 64–65, 76
Fort Orange, 2–3, 5–6, 10–11, 206
Fort Stanwix, 42, 74–77, 81–83, 89, 110, 123, 244; during Revolutionary War, 51, 53, 55–59, 64, 67–68, 272n15
Fort Timmerman, 66–69, 71–72
4-H, 197–98, 211, 225
Fowler, John, 138
France, 76, 80, 194, 223–24, 246; and American Revolution, 60–61, 69, 184; during colonial period, 2, 5–6, 15, 17–21, 24, 26–27, 31–38, 45; Deferriers and, 99–101, 126–28, 136, 151, 177, 202; French Revolution and émigrés, 99–101, 121, 174, 185, 223; and Oneidas, 5, 18, 37, 61, 73, 76, 80–81, 101, 126–28, 195
Franklin, Benjamin, 35, 42, 44
Free Soil Party, 157–59
French and Indian Wars, 19–21, 26–27, 31, 35–38, 44, 56, 123
fur trade, 2, 5, 8, 10, 13, 15–17, 28, 31, 33, 88, 90

Gallatin, Albert, 127–28, 147
Gansevoort, Peter, 55–56, 58

Garlock, John, xxiv, 105
Gates, Horatio, 60
Genesee Company of Adventurers, 80
Genesee Road, ix, 88–89, 91, 97, 102–4, 248; as Genesee Street, 234, 239. *See also* Seneca Turnpike
George, Nate, 246
George II, 28, 31
George III, 40, 45, 48–49, 55, 84
German Flatts, 29, 37, 40, 50–51, 56–57, 62, 65, 70, 72. *See also* Herkimer
Gettysburg, battle of, 159–60
Ginsburg, Ruth Bader, 241–42
Glen, Anna Peake, 17, 19
Glenwood Cemetery, 250
Good Peter, 77, *87*, 88, 95, 103, 164, 170, 235, 243; as POW, 65, 72; at treaty council, 79, 81–82, 87, 126, 235, 243
Grant, Madison, 189
Grasshopper, 61, 69, 75–77, 95
Great Britain: and American Revolution, 48, 50–51, 53, 55, 57–61, 63–65, 68–69; during the colonial period, 6, 13, 16–18, 21, 24, 26, 28, 30, 32, 34–38, 41–47; and the early republic, 73, 87, 110, 114–15
Great Law of Peace, 3, 8, 230
Great War (World War I), 184, 186
Green, Caroline Harp, xx, xxi, 152
Green Bay, 131, 136, 140, 143–44, 151, 157, 170
Green Empire Farms, 248
Green family, 137, 148, 189
Gregg, Absalom, 154
Gregg, John, xx, 137, 147

Hadcock, Daniel, 60, 136
Hadcock, Dewitt C., xxv, 173
Hadcock, John, xxiv, xxv, 136–37, 154, 291n41
Hadcock, Nancy Deferrier, xxiv, xxv, 135–37, 145
Halbritter, Gloria Winder, 213, 234
Halbritter, Ray, 213–15, *214*, 219, 221–22, 226; as Oneida Nation representative, 231–33, 235, 239, 243, 246–47
Haldimand, Frederick, 65, 68–69
Hamilton, Alexander, 78, 84, 93, 98
Hamilton College, 93, 158, 168
Hammond, L. M., 97, 105, 142, 156, 173, 282n2
Hancock, John, 58
Hanley, James M., 221–22
Haring, Alexander, 137–38
Harjo, Suzan, 221–22
Harp, Barney, 160
Harp, Christian, xx, xvii, 139, 147, 152, 158, 160
Harp, George, xx, 111, 139
Harrison, William Henry, 115
Haudenosaunee, ix, xiii, xvii, 3–9, 76, 88, 96, 130, 144, 172, 244–45, 249–50; and the American Revolution, 49–51, 53–54, 57, 60–61, 63–65, 69–70; during the colonial period, 10–11, 15–22, 24, 28–30, 32, 34–38, 41–42, 44–46; as remembered, 72, 119, 178, 187, 203, 247; and US, 73, 76, 87, 91, 114, 143, 181, 199, 247; twentieth century, 186, 188, 190, 195–97, 232, 237. *See also* New York State and Haudenosaunee land
Hawthorne, Nathaniel, 132, 134
Haywentha (Hiawatha), 3, 8; "Song of Hiawatha," 180, 182
Heemstraat, Barbara, 20
Hendrick Theyanoguin, 28, 33–34, *34*, 36
Herkimer, 21, 29, 135. *See also* German Flatts
Herkimer, Honyost, 37
Herkimer, Nicholas, 37–38, 44, 51–58, 60, 141
Hetzel, George, 78
Hetzel, Mary. *See* Myers, Mary Hetzel
Hetzel, Michael, xx, 78
Higinbotham, Abby, 136
Higinbotham, Niles, 154
Higinbotham, Sands, 136, 141–42, 144, 147
Hill, Charlie, 233
Hill, Richard, Sr., 250
Hoard, William D., 178
Holland Land Company, 98–99, 101, 110, 130, 290n25
Ho-Chunk people, 130
Holt, James, 161–62, 165
Honyery's sister, xxiii, 29, 56, 59, 73, 156
Honyery Tehawenkaragwen, xxiii, xvi, 29, 32, 37, 39–40, 88–91, 95, 103; descendants of, 102, 121, 126, 141, 148, 168, 194, 217; at Oriske, 41, 43, 45, 50, 56, 71–74, 77, 79, 81–86; during the Revolutionary War, 49–50, 55–57, 59–61, 63, 65, 68–70
Honyost, David, 210–11
Honyost, Isaac, 180–81
Honyost, Nick, 160, 162, 165, 180, *182*

Honyost, William, 181–82, *182*
Honyost family, 173, 180–82
Honyost Thaosagwat, xxiii, 29, 37, 61, 63–64
hops, 162–63, 165, 175, 244
House, Christian, 51–52, 55; Captain House's company, 55, 62–63, 67
Hudson, Henry, 2, 187
Hunter, Robert, 24–25, 27

immigrants, xiii, xv, 73, 156, 158, 189–90; Irish, 125–26, 156; Italian, 190–91; Walloons, 11–12. *See also* Palatines
indentured servitude, 12, 22, 26, 30, 38, 46, 62, 78, 94
Indian Claims Commission, 196–97, 199, 206, 218, 221, 309n47
Indian Commissioners: colonial New York, 21–22, 25, 31, 33, 46; New York State, 61, 77, 80–81, 85, 88, 91–92, 144; US, 75–77, 87, 91–92, 102, 104, 186
Indian Gaming Regulatory Act, 231
Indian Reorganization Act of 1934, 192
Ingalls, James, 157
Ingalls, Lucius, 163
Ingalls, Luther, 167
Ingalls, Nancy Moot, 157
Iroquois. *See* Haudenosaunee

Jay, John, 64, 92, 94, 102
Jefferson, Thomas, 42, 96, 100–101, 103, 121, 128
John, Electa. *See* Doxtator, Electa
John, Ella Mae Staudt, xxv, 191, 194, 201
John, Katie Honyost, 190
John, Lyman, xxv, *171*, 191, 195
John, Lyman K. "Jake," xxv, 201, 214, *214*, 231
John, Marshall, 187–90
John, Martin, xxv, 191, *194*, 194–95, *201*, 201, 210, 234
John, Melinda Skenandoah, 168, 187
John, Solomon, 180
Johnson, David, 153
Johnson, Jacqueline, 246
Johnson, John, 30, 45, 48, 52–53, 55, 57–58, 67–68
Johnson, Joseph, 187
Johnson, Rose Honyost, 200, *201*
Johnson, William, 46, 52, 59; and Canajoharie, 32–33, 39–41; and Clement family, 30–33, 35–36; and guarantee of Oneida land, 35–36, 38, 79, 85–86; as Superintendent of Indian Affairs, 34, 36–39, 41–45. *See also* Royal Grant
Johnson Hall, *38*, 38–39, 44
Johnson v. McIntosh, 130–31
Johnstown, 38, 44, 52, 57, 61, 63; battle of, 69
Jordan, Henry, xxiv, 153
Jordan, Nicholas, 76–77, 80, 93

Kahn, Lawrence, 242
Kahnawake, 56, 123, 153
Kammen, Michael, 159
Kanadolock (Peter Bread), 56, 92, 104, 131, 136
Kanagweas, 36–37, 41–42, 45, 82, 170
Kanonwalohale, 41, 55, 64–65, 69–70, 88, 90, 93, 97. *See also* Oneida Castle
Kansas, 143, 153, 169, 199; Kansas Claims, 181, 234
Karst, Rebecca "Becki" John, xxv, *201*, 201–2, 210, 217, 232, 234, 245, 248
Karst, Terry, xxv, 217
Kellogg, Laura Cornelius, 172, 178–79, 190; Kellogg Party, 190, 206
Kieft, William, 10
Kirkland, Samuel, 41, 50, 91, 93, 104, 118, 135, 200; and Oneida land, 75, 80, 88; and Oriskes, 84–86, 90, 105
Klock, George, 32–33, 39–41, 44–46, 49, 53, 68, 78, 89
Klock, Jacob, 39–40, 52, 55–57, 60, 64, 68, 89
Klock family, 27–28, 40, 60, 89. *See also* Clock family
Klock's Field, battle of, 67–68
Know-Nothing Party, 157–59
Ku Klux Klan, 163, 190

Labatie, Jean, 9, 11, 18
lacrosse, 29, 93, 162, 230
Lafayette, Marquis de, 100–101, *133*, 173, 184; and Oneidas, 61, 69, 76, 81, 132, 141
Lakota people, 171
land speculators, 25, 27–28, 33, 41–42, 73, 77, 80, 86, 94, 129, 147
Lee, Robert E., 160
Lenape people, 13, 25, 77
Lenox Furnace, 125, 142, 155–56, 176
Lenox Iron Company, 125, 139, 155–56, 167, 295n21
Lenox, Town of, 106, 114, 128, 139, 155, 158–61, 163–64; and Erie Canal, 125, 134, 145; land of, 140, 148, 239, 294n76

Liberty Party, 157–58
Lincklaen, John, 98–99, 101, 104, 106, 113, 177, 282n5
Line of Property (1768), 43–44, 49, 53, 73
Little Abraham, 52, 61, 65
Little Falls, 28, 40, 132
Livingston, John, 80
Livingston, Philip, 28, 34, 50
Livingston, Robert (1st lord), 25, 27
Livingston, Robert (3rd lord), 46
Livingston family, 25, 39, 44, 94, 155
Livingston Manor, 27–28, 80, 94
Locke, John, 50
Locklear, Arlinda, 230, 311n70
Loomis, Angel Deferrier, xxv, 159, 164, 173
Loomis, Sophia Deferrier, xxiv, xxv, 135–36, 145, 174
Loomis, Thomas T., xxiv, xxv, 136, 142
"Lost Dauphin," 150–51, 173, 192
Louis, Prince (the Dauphin), 100–101, 150
Louis XIV, 18–19
Louis XV, 99
Louis XVI, 80–81, 100–101, 150
Loyalists, 48–49, 51–53, 95; and attacks in Mohawk Valley, 55–58, 61–64, 68–69, 141; property of, 78, 81, 84–85, 95
Lynch, Richard "Dick," 200, *201*, 202, 211, 216, 232, 237, 239, 243, 245, 247
Lyons, Oren, 230

Madison, James, 76–77, 84, 106, 230
Madison County: nineteenth century, 106, 128, 154, 156–61, 165, 173, 185; and Oneidas, 82, 181, 188, 205–6, 209–10, 214, 218, 221, 225–26, 229, 232–33, 235–36, 238, 241–45; twentieth century, ix, 177–79, 189–90, 194, 197, 208, 227, 234
Madison County Historical Society, 173, 177, 180, 183, 223, 234, 244
Mahican people, 16, 20
Manhattan, 1, 9–11, 13, 15, 46, 116, 230
Mano, Jo Margaret, 88
Marbois, François de Barbé, 76
Margaret, Mohawk Turtle Clan, 28–29
Marie Antoinette, 100–101, 151
Marshall, Ann, 193
Marshall, John, 130–31
Massachusetts, 11, 48, 73, 77, 93, 123, 126, 132, 136–37, 171
Matthews, William, 215
McCurn, Neal P., 237–38
McDermott, Robert, 238
Menominee people, 130
Meritt, Edgar B., 183–84, 190
Methodists, 156, 168, 199
Miles, Marion John, xxv, *200*, 232
military tracts, 86, 89, 279n52
militia, 35, 48, 50, 78, 100, 140–41; of colonial New York, 19–21, 26–27, 31, 35–37, 40; of New York State, 94, 106, 114–15, 155; *See also* Albany County Militia; Tryon County Militia
Miller, Elizabeth Smith, 159
Miller, Gerrit Smith, 161
Miller, Irma, xxv, 191
missionaries, 8, 18, 50, 94, 118. *See also* Kirkland, Samuel; Williams, Eleazer
Mohawk Dutch, 17, 22, 24, 28, 30, 35, 37–38, 46, 50, 192, 264n54; in Canaseraga, 89, 103, 105–6
Mohawk people, ix, xiii, xv–xvii, 18, 73, 76, 95, 150, 188, 196; during the American Revolution, 48–49, 52–53, 55, 59–62, 64–65, 67; Canajoharie Mohawks, 28–30, 32–33, 35, 38–41, 44–45, 52, 56, 59–60, 78; and colonial New York, 19–22, 24–39, 44–47; and the Dutch, 1–4, 7–11, 15–17; Schoharie Mohawks, 25–27, 42, 62, 72
Mohawk River, xiii, 3, 16–17, 21–22, 24, 27–30, 33, 56, 69, 77, 97, 125
Mohawk Valley, xiii, 44, 47, 71, 202; during Revolutionary War, 48, 53–54, 61–64, 67–71, 86, 94, 141; settlers in, 24, 26–28, 30, 40, 78–79, 95, 111, 148
Mohican people, 25, 77, 138. *See also* Stockbridge Indians
Monroe, James, 74, 77, 130
Monroe, Michael, 212
Montauk people (Montaukett), 189, 278n22
Moot, Conrad, xx, 94, 103, 125, 154
Moot, Elizabeth "Lizzie." *See* Clement, Elizabeth Moot
Moot, Franklin Pierce, 157
Moot, John (Johannes Moet), xx, 94
Moot, John, xx, xxi, 154, 157, 160–61, 165
Moot, John Conrad, xx, 114–15, 154, 286n51
Moot, John J., 163
Moot, Lucy Bc:tle, xx, xxi, 161
Moot, William, xx, 160, 162

Moot, William Harrison, 115
Morrisville, 161, 177; Morrisville College/SUNY, 185–86, 227
Morse, Jedidiah, 93–94, 105, 129
mourning wars, 8, 18
Myer, Dillon S., 196
Myers, John, xx, 46, 52, 62, 67, 78, 84–85, 154
Myers, Mary Hetzel, xx, 78, 154
Myers, Richard B., 210, 212

Nash, Gary, 189
National Congress of American Indians, 246
National Museum of the American Indian, 246
Native American Party, 157–59
Native American Rights Fund, 207, 221, 306n13
Nemec, Linda, 223–24
New Amsterdam, 9–15, 17, 203. *See also* New York City
New England, 1, 15, 36, 53, 178, 189; New Englanders, 2, 36, 50, 78–79, 113
New Netherland, 2, 9–10, 13, 15–16
New York Central Railroad, ix, 142, 153–54, 157, 175, 177, 197–99, 248
New York, colony of, xiii, 17–19, 25–26, 31, 33, 37–38, 42, 46
New York City, 78, 101, 135, 145, 157, 178, 230, 239; during the colonial period, 2, 17, 31, 33, 53; Oneidas in, 85, 138, 153; trade and transportation, 90, 108, 123, 132, 197, 248
New York Council of Safety, 54, 272n8
New York Historical Society, 118–19
New York State, ix, xvii, 73, 84–85, 95, 101, 114–15, 156, 231, 244; and Haudenosaunee land, 64, 69, 71–75, 78, 88, 98, 123, 129–30, 180, 188; economic development, 108, 145, 160, 162, 216; policies of removal and severalty, 129, 143–45, 153, 170–72, 178, 183, 196, 199. *See also* Erie Canal; Oneida land claims; treaties
New York State Archives, 234
New York State Fair, 195–96, 198
New York State Thruway, 197, 231, 233, 240
Niagara Falls, 41, 89, 132, 177, 232
Niles, Rex, 219–20
Niort, France, 99–100, 128
Noyes, John Humphrey, 157, 167

O'Brien, William F., 210
Odatshedah, 61, 77, 82
Odawa people, 8
Ogden Land Company, 130, 143, 290n25, 293n64
Old Fort Schuyler, 56, 90, 97, 106. *See also* Utica
Old Oneida, 41, 64, 92
Oneida Carrying Place, xiii, 2, 50, 53, 55, 70, 231; during colonial period, 22–23, 28, 35–37, 41–45; in the early republic, 73, 77, 81, 86, 91, 93, 123, 125–26
Oneida, city of, ix–xiv, 239, 245, 250; fire and police departments, 204, 208, 210–13, 215–16, 222, 228–29, 239, 247; in nineteenth century, 139, 142, 159, 162–63, 165; and Oneidas, 180, 183, 191, 201, 208–12, 215, 237; in twentieth century, 176–77, 184, 190, 192–93; 198, 204, 223–25
Oneida Castle, 98, 106, 109–10, 116, 131, 135–36, 139–41, 162, 168, 228. *See also* Kanonwalohale
Oneida Community, 157, 159, 163–64, 167, 180
Oneida Community Ltd, 184, 191, 195, 208, 215, 224, 239–40
Oneida County, 82, 113, 116, 152, 162, 229, 232–33, 238, 244; and land claims, 205–7, 209, 214, 225–26, 235–36, 242–44
Oneida Creek, xiii, 4, 41, 77, 109, 122, 125, 137, 141, 144, 158–59, 180, 204
Oneida Lake, xiii, xvii, 1, 22, 70, 86, 106, 110, 125, 162, 177, 227, 232; and reserved Oneida land, 82, 137, 169, 180
Oneida land claims, ix, xiii, 169–70, 183–84, 190, 197, 211, 218–23, 225, 229, 236–39, 244, 246–47; *City of Sherrill v. Oneida Indian Nation*, 241–43, 245; *Oneida v. Oneida County* (300,000 acres), 207, 218, 233–36; *Oneida Tribe of New York v. Abraham Williams et. al.* (West Road), 207–9, 215, 218, 238; *Oneida Indian Nation of New York v. State of New York* (six million acres), 217–18, 230; *Madison County and Oneida County v. Oneida Indian Nation of New York*, 242–43; test case/ Oneida I and II (100,000 acres), 205–9, 213–14, 218, 221, 225–26. *See also* Indian Claims Commission

Oneida people, ix–xvii; and agriculture, 4, 41, 90, 93–94, 103, 109–10, 122, 129, 138–39, 152, 162, 170, 180, 195, 238, 245; bingo and gaming, 229, 231–33, 244–45, 247; Christian Party, 104–10, 115, 130–31, 139, 142; and citizenship, 127, 145, 164–65, 172, 186–87, 190; clan mothers, 8, 49, 77, 82, 92, 137, 168, 195, 208, 226, 229; the Home Party, 144–45, 147–48, 151–52, 156, 165, 172, 207, 232; hunting and fishing, 21, 29, 41, 82, 93, 109, 113, 136–38, 152, 169, 182; and language, 172, 191, 200, 231–32; and leasing, 79–83, 89–92, 102, 113, 137, 152, 229; Oneidas of Canada, 143, 183, 188, 218, 230, 235–36, 242; Oneidas at Onondaga, 188, 191, 195, 197, 200, 212–13, 218–21, 226; Oneidas of Wisconsin, 139, 144, 157, 172, 178, 188, 218, 230, 235–36, 239, 242; Pagan Party, xvii, 90, 104–6, 109–11, 123; as performers, 126–27, 138, 153, 195–96; and schooling, 129, 139, 152, 171–72, 188, 191, 201, 231; Second Christian Party, 123–24, 129–31, 137; and settlers, 20, 27–28, 30, 32, 37, 44–46, 84, 89, 94–95, 101, 113, 120, 122, 138; Warrior Society, 210–13, 219, 229; women, xiii, xv, 4, 58–59, 68–69, 93, 109, 114–15, 145, 148, 153, 159, 162, 168, 170, 180, 191, 220. *See also* American Revolution and Oneidas; Oriskes
Oneida Savings Bank, 239
Oneida standing stone, 4, 93, 152, 208
Oneida Valley National Bank, 154
O'Neill, Thomas P. "Tip," 216
"one people," 8–9, 16, 22, 36, 96, 120
Onondaga people, ix, xvii, 3, 6, 8, 22, 73, 76–77, 134, 152, 162–63, 188, 196; and Revolutionary War, 53, 55, 64; territory and reservation, 18, 28, 86, 91, 144, 153, 187
Oquaga, 62, 65, 70, 102
Orchard/Marble Hill, 93, 152, 156, 179, 190–91, 195, 200, 206
Oriskany, battle of, 56–60, 86, 144, 168, 214
Oriskany Patent, 41, 43, 45, 75, 81, 155
Oriske, 29, 41–43, 45; during the American Revolution, 48, 50, 53, 55–59, 61, 69, 70; rebuilding and dispossession, 71–73, 75, 77, 79, 81, 85–86, 93, 95, 149
Oriskes, 64, 84; as dispossessed, 88–90, 93, 102, 105, 140, 169, 132, 153
Osage people, 199
Oswego, 22, 28, 36–37, 52–53, 76, 114
Otsequette, Anthony, 132, 136
Otsequette, Peter, 81–82, 88, 132
Otstok, 9, 16–18, 22, 45

Palatines, 26–30, 33, 35, 37–38, 40, 45
Parrish, Jasper, 122, 130
Pataki, George, 235, 239
patents, 25, 39, 84, 113, 265n4; to Angel Deferrier, 109, 122, 135; to author's family, 33, 147, 154, 184. *See also* Canajoharie Patent; Oriskany Patent
Peacemaker, 3, 8, 239
Peake, Jacobus, xix, 19, 22
Peake, Jan, xix, 13–15
Peebles, Myron, 184; Peebles farm, 216–17
Penet, Peter, 80–81, 83, 89
Pennsylvania, ix, 35, 42, 62, 101, 160, 217
People v. Van Rensselaer, 155
Peterboro, 90, 140, 147, 158–60, 233
Philadelphia, 44, 61, 63, 69, 87–88, 108, 246, 248
Pickering, Timothy, 87–88, 91–92
Platt, Jonas, 92–93, 110, 113
Plattcop Tonyentagoyon, xxiii, xxiv, 29, 32, 73, 79, 82, 104, 130, 132, 144, 267n19; during Revolutionary War, 56, 58–59, 61, 63, 68
Port, Edmund, 209, 213, 215, 221
Powless, Baptist, 184
Powless, Henry, 141
Powless, John, 184
Powless, Martin, 160
Powless, Paul, 55, 82, 136, 250
property: American beliefs about, 50, 75, 78, 84–85, 94, 154–58, 169, 241; European beliefs about, 13, 16, 21–22, 28, 46–47, 50; strategy of Denny and Doxtator families, 102–3, 106, 110–11, 119–20, 122–24, 139–40; titles, 113, 130, 183, 207, 222, 230, 238

Quackenbush, Abram, 57

Randel, John, Jr., 116–17
Ray, George W., 183

Raymond, Penny, *200*, 232
Reed, Jacob, 80, 89–90, 92
Rights of American Indians Now (RAIN), 212
Rensselaerswyck, 9, 19, 262n28
Republican Party, 159, 164, 204, 310n60
Rockwell, William Honyost, *182*, 182–83, 188–91, 195–97, 199, *200*, 208
Rome, NY, xiii, 123, 134, 136, 156, 177
Romer, Wolfgang, 22–23
Roosevelt, Franklin D., 191
Royal Grant, 40, 45, 77–78, 95, 269n52
Russell, George, 96

Sacket's Harbor, 114
Salisbury, Edward Elbridge, 135
Saratoga, 70, 132, 168; battle of, 60, 62, 86, 136; National Historical Park, 246
scalping, 4, 31, 37, 58, 64–65, 68, 118, 138
Schenectady, 73, 84–85, 98, 181; during American Revolution, 65, 68, 70; during colonial period, 16–17, 19–22, 24–25, 37, 46
Schoharie John, 62, 67, 72, 276n3
Schoharie Valley, xiii, 72, 85, 95, 109; during American Revolution, 48, 61–62, 67; during colonial period, 24–27, 41–42, 45–46
Schoolcraft, Henry Rowe, 152
Schuyler, David, 28, 33, 37, 39, 60, 267n19
Schuyler, David, Jr., 60, 89
Schuyler, Elizabeth Herkimer, 37, 59
Schuyler, Henry. *See* Plattcop
Schuyler, Honyost, 59–60, 89, 119, 267n19, 273n37
Schuyler, Moses, xxiv, 130–31, 136, 142–44
Schuyler, Peter, 20–21
Schuyler, Peter D., 37, 59, 267n19
Schuyler, Peter P., 75, 77, 80
Schuyler, Philip, 44, 73, 75, 78, 86, 91–94, 98; during American Revolution, 50, 53–55, 58, 60, 63, 65, 70
Sconondoa, 110, 131, 135, 228
Seneca people, ix, xvii, 3, 8, 18, 73, 91, 132, 143, 172, 196; during the American Revolution, 53, 55, 57–58, 62, 64–65; and Oneidas, 76, 144, 152, 169, 188
Seneca Turnpike, 103–4, 106, 108, 111, 116, 131, 135, 138–39, 142, 169, 197, 234. *See also* Genesee Road
Seven Years War, 35–38
Seward, William, 143, 145, 155
Shagoyontha, xxiii, 73, 79, 82, 104, 114, 132, 140–41; during American Revolution, 56–57, 59, 61; descendants of, 117, 137, 148, 156, 237; in France, 126–28, *127*
Shattuck, George, 206–7, 209, 311n70
Shawnee people, 8, 41
Shenandoah, Maisie Winder, 226, 229
Sherrill, 41, 102, 111, 184, 240–41, 245; *Sherrill* case, 241–43, 245
Silver Covenant Chain of Friendship Grants, 233, 245
Sinavis, Thomas, 55, 61
Skenandoah, Chapman, 181, *182*, 187, 190, 195–96
Skenandoah, Chief, 54, 65, 72, 89–90, 93, 109, 131; descendants of, 111, 153, 237; as remembered, 135, 151, 178, 181, 246; and treaties, 82, 92, 104, 108, 118
Skenandoah, Daniel, 152, 163, 168–70
Skenandoah, Jenny (Doxtator Denny), xxiii, xxiv, 111
Skenandoah, Mary Honyost, 180–82, *182*, 188, 247
Skenandoah, Mrs. Daniel, 163
Skenandoah, Nelson, xxv, 195
slavery and enslaved people: during the colonial period, 10, 13, 20, 25, 26, 35, 38, 52, 60; in the US, 115, 119–21, 156, 158–59, 288n71
Smith, Gerrit, 140, 158–59, 161
Smith, James H., 167
Smith, Peter, 88, 90–92, 98, 104, 106, 111, 140, 158
Smithfield, Town of, 90, 106
Snyder, Charles, 166–67
Sotomayor, Sonia, 242
sovereignty, 74, 170, 216, 222, 233; native, 165, 230, 239; and Oneidas, 95, 195, 209–10, 213, 229, 241–44, 248; and US, 114, 130
Spain, 2, 6, 9, 10, 230
Spaulding, Philander, 181, 298n52, 301n15
Spencer, Frederick, 149, 294n1
squatters, 27, 45, 129; author's family as, xiii, 94–96, 98, 103, 111, 139, 152, 175, 199, 248; on Oneida land, 89, 110, 116, 131, 137–38
Stanton, Elizabeth Cady, 158–59
Sternberg, Peggy Schuyler, 119

Sternberg, William, 119
Stevens, John Paul, 226, 241
St. Leger, Barry, 53, 55, 57–60
Stockbridge, 109, 145, 161, 165
Stockbridge, Town of, 90, 158, 294n76
Stockbridge Indians, 77, 128, 137
Stockbridge Valley, xiii, 4, 136, 162, 178, 259n3
Stockton, Benjamin, 108
Strong, Nathaniel T., 152
Stuyvesant, Peter, 11, 13–14, 16, 187
Sullivan, John, 63–64, 106
Sullivan, Town of, 106, 119, 161
Sullivan Expedition, 63–64, 67, 98, 106, 187
surveyors and surveys, 25, 33, 45, 114; and Oneida land, 83–85, 88–90, 103, 111, 116–19, 122, 131–32, 144, 169
Swits, Claes Cornelissen, 9–10
Swits, Jellesje Claesen, xix, 9–11, 16–18, 22
Syracuse, 123, 126, 170, 195, 197, 213, 217, 221
Sylvan Beach, 162, 168

taverns, 89, 103, 105–6, 108, 119, 134, 137–38; during the colonial period, 13–15, 17, 25, 31, 39, 44
Tayler, John, 85
Tecumseh, 114–15
temperance movement, 156–59, 165
tenant farmers, 32, 106; author's family as, 46, 78, 84–85, 111, 152, 154, 156, 161, 167, 174–76, 197; of Oneidas, 80, 89, 102–3, 118; tenant rebellions, 94, 154–55
Thanksgiving, 1, 236, 246
Thomassen, Willem, 3, 5
Thompson, Geralda, 205
Thompson, Jacob "Jake," 205, 208, 210, 213, 307n16
Three Sisters, 4, 113, 201
Tilden, N. L., 171
Timmerman, Adam, 68
Timmerman, Anna Rosina (Vedder), xix, xx, 56, 69
Timmerman, Conrad, 39, 55, 68
Timmerman, Conrad L., 56
Timmerman, Henry, xix, 29, 40, 48, 71, 95, 148, 217; during American Revolution, 51–53, 56, 58, 60, 66, 68–70
Timmerman, Henry L., 56
Timmerman, Jacob, xix, 27
Timmerman, Jacob J., 53, 56, 68
Timmerman, Jacob L., 56, 68
Timmerman, John C., 55–56, 68
Timmerman, John G., 56, 58
Timmerman, Margaret Bellinger, xix, 40, 56, 66, 70–71
Timmerman, Margaret Schütz, xix, 27–29, 33, 37, 39–40, 45, 161
Timmerman, William C., 55
Timmerman family, 28–29, 33, 38–41, 45, 95; during American Revolution, 52, 60, 63, 66, 68
Tiononderogue, 24–25, 32, 39, 43, 95; during American Revolution, 52, 57, 61, 64–65
Tocqueville, Alexis de, 138
Tompkins, Daniel, 116
Trade and Intercourse Acts, 88, 197, 207, 213, 241, 244
"Trail of Broken Treaties," 213
treaties, xv, xvii, 87, 183, 187, 196, 200, 206, 230, 242, 248; with the Dutch (1642), 9; with the English, 18; Grand Settlement (1701), 21; of Fort Stanwix (1768), 42–43; of Paris (1783), 73; of Fort Stanwix (US, 1784), 76–77, 188, 217; of Fort Herkimer (NY, 1785), 80, 218; of Fort Stanwix (NY, 1788), 81–82, 85, 98, 126, 136, 195, 218, 235, 243, 291n43; of Canandaigua (US, 1794), 91, 168, 199, 206, 241; Oneida veterans' (US, 1795), 91; of 1795 (NY), 92, 187, 206–9, 213; of 1798 (NY), 102; of 1802 (NY), 103; partition of 1805 (Christian and Pagan Parties), 104; of 1807 (NY), 106, 108; of 1809 (NY), 106, 108, 137; of 1810 and 1811 (NY), 110; of 1815 (NY), 115–20, 122, 135–36, 175, 198; of 1817 (NY), 124–25; with Ho-Chunks and Menominees (1821–22), 130; of 1824 (NY), 131–32, 135, 139; of 1826 (NY), 137; of 1827 (NY), 137; of 1829 (NY), 139; of Buffalo Creek (US, 1838), 143, 181, 242, 293n64; of 1840–42 (NY), 144, 207; making of, 21, 42–43, 51, 74–76, 106, 124, 137; rights of, 95, 127, 136–37, 142, 169–70, 188, 208–9, 215, 221–22, 235–37
treaty cloth, 91, 168, 199–200, 206, 218, 234
Trieux, Marie du, xix, 11–17, 22, 24–25, 32, 45, 148, 157
Trieux, Philip du, xix, 13
Truman, Harry, 196

Tryon County, 44, 48, 58, 61, 68, 85, 270n67
Tryon County Committee of Safety, 51–52, 55, 59–61, 271n8
Tryon County Militia, 51–53, 55–62, 65, 67–70, 168
Tubman, Harriet, 158
Turning Stone Casino, 231–33, 236–37, 239, 244
Tuscarora people, xvii, 25, 28, 36, 76, 144, 196; during American Revolution, 53, 55, 59–60, 69–70
Tuttle, William H., 90
Twain, Mark, 173

Underground Railroad, 158
Union Army, 147, 160, 169
United Nations, 230, 245
United States: and guarantee of Oneida land, 53, 69–70, 72, 76, 79, 91, 95, 140, 206, 230; and land-grant system, 161, 198; and Oneidas, ix, 48, 60, 87–88, 127, 187–88, 205, 243; policy of assimilation, severalty, and termination, 170–71, 192, 196, 209, 242; and removal, 129–30, 142–43, 242. *See also* Boylan case; Bureau of Indian Affairs; citizenship; Haudenosaunee and US; Indian Claims Commission; US Department of Justice; US Supreme Court; Trade and Intercourse Acts; treaties
United States Colored Troops, 160
United States v. Elm, 165, 242
Upstate Citizens for Equality (UCE), 235–36, 239
US Constitution, 84–85, 87, 124, 237
US Department of the Interior, 183, 186, 191, 216, 218
US Department of Justice, 212, 215–16, 220, 229, 235, 237
US Supreme Court, 130–31, 181, 188, 190, 207, 225–26, 233, 241–43, 311n70
Utica, 56, 106, 123, 132, 135–36, 140, 152, 208

Valley Forge, 61, 86, 92, 196, 212
Van Buren, Martin, 142, 242
Van den Bogaert, Claes, xix, xx, 20
Van den Bogaert, Frans, xix, 19–20
Van den Bogaert, Harmen Myndertsz, xix, 1–7, 9–11, 23, 148, 206, 248
Van Eps, Abraham, 72–73, 92–93, 111, 140, 295n21
Van Gestel, Allan, 226
Van Rensselaer, Killian, 9
Van Rensselaer, Robert, 67, 94
Van Rensselaer, Stephen, 78, 93, 110, 129, 154–55, 285n36
Van Rensselaer family, 16, 25, 44, 155
Van Slyck, Charles, 160
Van Slyck, Cornelis Antonissen (Broer Cornelis), 9–10, 16, 18, 22
Van Slyck, Hilletie, 17–18, 20
Van Slyck, Jacques Cornelissen, 16–17, 20, 26
Van Slyck family, 105
Vermont, 73, 160
Vernon, 92–93, 104, 135, 141, 158, 190, 237
Vernon Center, 41, 156
Verona, 136, 231, 236, 239
Versailles, 99–100, 223
Viele, Arnout, xix, 13, 17–20, 22
Viele, Cornelis, 17
Viele, Cornelis Volkertsen, xix, 13
Virginia, 2, 17, 35, 42, 69, 76–77, 160
Von Steuben, Friedrich, 61
voting rights, 84–85, 155, 159, 164–65, 190
Vought, John Christopher, 84–85
Vrooman, Adam, 19–20, 25–27
Vrooman, Peter, 62, 67, 274n46
Vrooman, Peter C., 72
Vrooman family, 42, 67

Walmart, 234, 239, 250
Walter, George W., 198
Wampsville, 106, 124, 134, 142, 145, 162, 202–3, 211, 228–29, 236; and Deferrier family, 149, 174, 223; as Madison County seat, 177, 184, 218, 221; school, 108, 192, 199. *See also* Cowaselon
wampum, 3, 11, 178, 232; in diplomacy, 21, 36–38, 74–76, 82, 91, 136, 197, 237; in trade, 5, 16; Wampum Law, 178
War of 1812, 114–15, 123, 126, 153
Washington, DC, 130, 181, 213, 225, 234
Washington, George, xiii, 35, 42, 73, 77, 88, 115; during American Revolution, 55–56, 61, 63, 67–70; and the Haudenosaunee, 63, 87, 91, 199, 237; and the Oneidas, 55, 61, 69–70, 75, 136, 141, 246–47
Washington, Martha, 61
Waterman, Delia Cornelius, 195, 197, 204–6

Watson, Elkanah, 79, 81, 86, 93, 126
Webster, Daniel, 178
Webster, Ephraim, 72
Webster, Hannah, 163
Weed, Thurlow, 135, 138
Weisenberg, Catharine, 30, 38–39
Welch, David, 69, 276n68
Wemple, Myndert, 98, 103, 106, 108, 110–11, 116, 118, 120
Western Inland Lock Navigation Company, 86, 92, 93, 98
West India Company, 2, 9, 12–13, 18, 22
Westmoreland, 80, 93, 97
Wheeler, Burton K., 192
Wheelock, Eleazer, 39, 50
Whig Party, 143, 157, 159
Whipple Report, 170–72
White, Byron, 207
White, Martinus, 136–37, 169
Whitestown, 93, 110
Wilder, Laura Ingalls, 199, 209
Willet, Marinus, 55, 68–70
William of Canajoharie, 52
Williams, Abraham, 204, 207–8, 216
Williams, Eleazer, 123–25, *124*, 128–31, 150–51, 156, 192
Williams, Eunice, 123
Williams, Mary Ann, 151
Winder, Janice, 211
Winder, Mary Cornelius, 195, 197, 200, 204, 211, 213
Winder, Samuel, Jr., 211
Windfall, 152, 154, 156, 173, 179–81, 188–90, 195, 200
Wisconsin, xi, 139, 144–45, 147, 178
Wisconsin Historical Society, 168
World War II, 193–95
Wounded Knee, 171, 209, 221
Wyandot people, 8

Yankees, 113, 137
Yates, Joseph C., 136
Yorkers, 113, 204